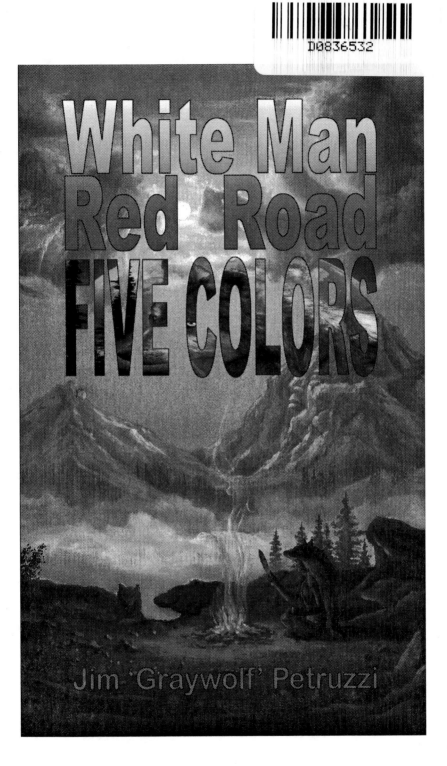

White Man Red Road FIVE COLORS

Jim 'Graywolf' Petruzzi

Table of Contents

Acknowledgments

I WILL WRITE ABOUT THE CIRCLE OF LIFE IN THIS BOOK MANY TIMES, IN various ways with differing interpretations. It is important that I therefore recognize the circle that formed around this book, allowing it to flow to all who read it. I have felt this book in me for over ten years, yet was unable to write it until now. I do not trouble myself with why that is, but I give gratitude to all who helped with this 'birthing'. I am the one who sat and wrote this book: The one given the task to capture the words and ideas in print. But the thanks I extend to any and all who played a role in this is for their aide, support and work, but also for their thoughts and energy, which guided the words that flowed.

First, I thank my partner, Sue. She encouraged, held my hand, suggested and supported in every way. Then my relative, my spiritual brother, Bearcloud. When I saw the best cover would be one of his paintings, he offered the cover and created the computer files needed. And Gerri Ann who stepped up and did a masterful job of editing—and commenting. Jack, my buddy, my Philadelphia brother, who asked to read the book while it was half done and, after doing so, told me it needed to be published. And who has walked with Sue and I through that process. And my other close friend, Jim, who has been brother and guide along the road and who is also working with us to get the book to people. My mother, who has given so much over the years and who wants a printed copy to replace her computer one, needs special thanks. My stepdaughter, Dana, and her husband, Stephen for support and advice on agents. My sister, Donna—my clone—for always being there, through dark and light. And thanks to the handful of others who I gave drafts to read, whether they opted to comment or not. Their energy still flowed to the final version. And any other people who sent energy and support as I worked through this emerging gathering of words.

In addition to those who walk beside me now, I give huge thanks to those who have worked with me in the past and are critical to the end product before you. Those who have passed on—my wife, Bonnie, my father, my friends and casual acquaintances from my life and the pages of the book. Especially my wife Bonnie, who supported my walk and road as I did hers. You will come to know her in these pages, many of which would not exist without her.

I next thank all my spirit and animal guides who eased my fears and guided my work. And I give the most thanks to Great Spirit who has allowed me to play this role in the Universe and has given me the tools to do so.

Finally, I thank all those people, ancestors, guides and Great Spirit for all the help they are about to give me in the future on my walk through life and the books I am to write in the future.

It is with a full heart and sincere gratitude I offer these thoughts.

Foreword

I HAVE KNOWN FOR SOME TIME I WAS TO SHARE THE ROAD I HAVE walked and some of the teachings and understandings that have come my way. Yet I hesitated, as the time did not seem quite right. Maybe I wasn't ready to write or maybe there was more I needed to experience first. Now, however, I am being guided by my inner voice and the heavens above me to begin. As I sit writing this I am unsure where it will go, but I am certain it will follow the 'script' that Great Spirit has given me. I sense it may evolve as part journal, part shared stories and part teachings. We shall see together.

I invite you to take this journey with me. See what I have seen as you experience the pleasure and pain of my walk and all it has put before me. As several of my native teachers always counseled me: "Take with you what you need and leave the rest behind." Maybe there will be nothing for you – maybe just a good story to enjoy – and maybe some pieces will resonate with your spirit and guide part of your walk forward. I can only share what my eyes have seen, my mind has absorbed and my spirit has come to understand. I welcome you along. Be well and enjoy the journey.

"It is all about the journey, not the destination."

◇ ◇ ◇

People ask me what motivated me to seek out indigenous people to learn their ways. Easy answer – I didn't. And they want to know how I found the Red Road and how I have learned to walk it. Again an easy answer – I didn't find it, it found me as I listened and learned from many teachers over time. As a 'white guy' from Philly, raised Catholic, I had never heard of the Red Road – nor did I know much of Native American or other indigenous ways and beliefs. I did, however, know nature first hand and I wanted to know and understand more of its workings. I had always valued nature at a deep, soul-filling way – at conscious and sub-conscious levels. I valued all about Mother Earth and was unhappy with what abuse we humans had heaped upon our planet. I looked for ways to find unspoiled areas of the planet to enjoy, but did not yet understand the new connection we humans needed to establish with our planetary home. What I was looking for, in retrospect, was a better and stronger understanding and connection to 'me'.

I will share all that I can as we walk together here, possibly repeating things at times. I will talk more of how I am capturing my walk in our journey here together soon. For now, I ask you to remember a teaching of an elder I knew, "The more times something is repeated, the more truth it may hold. Pay attention to those things which repeat themselves". I will speak of how I see myself at times because I believe it puts some things I say about what I have seen and learned into better context. For now, as I tell those I work with, I do not call myself a sage or seer, espousing my 'truths' from atop some 'intellectual mountain-top'. I am, however, a man blessed by many opportunities to live and learn from many diverse elders in many parts of the world. And I am a man allowed to understand and use some of the healing and teaching arts gifted to me. Always remembering and accepting that, as I do my work, I am a two-legged human with some knowledge and understanding still with a huge chasm of 'storage space' within me still unfilled. Yet what I have experienced, learned and practiced I am certain will have benefits to others wishing to explore their inner selves as well as ways to think and live. I know my life walk has morphed, evolved and grown with what my teachers and the Earth Mother have given me – changing my life, goals, beliefs and understandings.

Whatever you receive from reading this work, the circle will be complete with us as I will learn more in writing things down I have not thought about in some time and from feedback I will receive from you later. I do not yet know how this will work out, but will patiently wait to see this piece evolve. For now, if my sharing as best I can gives you any insights, smiles, tears, laughs, or thoughtfulness I will feel the effort well spent. As I already know it is – for all of us.

Thank you for joining me here in a good way.

JIM GRAYWOLF PETRUZZI
Hota Sugmanitu tanka (Graywolf)

On the Good Red Road

"'The Good Red Road' is a phrase used by many different Native American tribal communities to represent one who is walking the road of balance, living right and following the rules of the Creator.

One may be of any race or of almost any religion and walk the Red Road. The Good Red Road is a path, a way of living. Its full meaning is the way one acts, the methods one uses, and what directs ones' doing. There is more to the Red Road than spoken word or written words on paper. It is behavior, attitude, a way of living, and a way of "doing" with reverence—of walking strong yet softly, so as not to harm or disturb other life. The Red Road is a pathway to truth, peace and harmony.

Walking in balance is more than just the physical action; it also encompasses the mental, emotional, and spiritual aspects of our being. In experiencing the Good Red Road, one learns the lessons of physical life, or of being human. This road runs South to North in the circle of the medicine wheel. After the graduation experience of death, one enters the Blue or Black Road, that is the world of the grandfathers and grandmothers. In spirit, one will continue to learn by counseling those remaining on the Good Red Road. The Blue Road of the spirit runs East to West.

We must speak in one united voice to awaken the people of the world to the catastrophic consequences we face if we don't change the way we relate to each other and our Mother Earth."

SOURCE UNKNOWN

Black Elk Speaks

"IT WAS EVEN THEN ONLY AFTER THE HEYOKA CEREMONY IN WHICH I performed my dog vision, that I had the power to practice as a medicine man, curing sick people; and many I cured with the power that came through me. Of course it was not I who cured. It was the power from the outer world, and the visions and ceremonies had only made me like a hole through which the power could come to the two-leggeds. If I thought that I was doing it myself, the hole would close up and no power could come through. Then everything I could do would be foolish. There were other parts of my great vision that I still had to perform before I could use the power that was in those parts. If you think about my great vision again, you will remember how the red man turned into a bison and rolled, and that the people found the good red road after that. If you will read again what is written, you will see how it was."

BLACK ELK
From *Black Elk Speaks* by John G. Neihardt

About the Author

JIM GRAYWOLF PETRUZZI IS LIVING just north of Santa Fe, New Mexico, with his half-side, Sue, Onyx the dog and Raven the cat. In this picture they are boarding their RV to begin traveling around Turtle Island - the U.S. - working on the Sanctuaries of the Earth Mother non-profit begun to advance the visions Jim shares in this book. They will all be connecting with nature and the Earth Mother, documenting what they see and feel to share with others. Sue is photographer and videographer: While Jim continues to write.

Although they are unsure how long they may be roaming, knowing they are 'home' anywhere they are as long as they are connected with the Earth and her creatures allows them a sense of place. They intend to meet with many new people, sharing the vision of Sanctuaries. Connect with them at www.SOTEM.org or at the Facebook group 'Sanctuaries of the Earth Mother'.

Jim is working on future books, which he looks forward to sharing soon.

White Man, Red Road . . . Five Colors

1 | Beginning

I HAVE NO INTENTION OF BORING YOU WITH TOO MUCH OF MY background, but I think some understanding of how I lived before beginning the walk I will share in this book may give some perspective of what follows. It will certainly give an understanding that what I 'was' for my first forty years – I am not any more. This is not a positive or negative statement – just a recognition that, like many, as I have learned, accepted and lived I have changed. Maybe I have changed more than many, but we each change. I offer to you that this is the first teaching we must learn to accept – that we will change and this is a good thing. We must learn not to fight it, but welcome it as a friend. We always have the choice of how much we are willing to change, so we need not fear this six-letter word so many people do fear.

First, I am nothing special. I walk on two legs; suffer fear and pain; enjoy pleasure; and deal with ego, love, loss and doubt like all my kindred two-leggeds. Yet we each have gifts and strengths that, hopefully, we contribute to others, no matter who or what they are. And I have been given the opportunity to learn many healing ways and many spiritual lessons from people in different places around the globe. Indigenous people have given much of this knowledge to me; other blocks of knowledge by more westernized teachers. I will share more of this as we journey together. Without holding back – as now is not the time for that. Some things I will write here I have only shared with a few closest to me. Partly in fear of what "people would think". And, as we go along, I will share my successes, advancements as well as my failures and mistakes. Each of these has also been a great teacher to me.

I was born on 11/11 of 1949 in Philadelphia of parents who were more Italian than American and with grandparents who were almost all Italian. I am not sure exactly who 'came over on the boat', but it doesn't matter because the old world influence was still so strong throughout my family. As a boy of Italian heritage, whose family was recently relocated from Italy, born on the East Coast, it was almost preordained that I would be raised Catholic with strong family influence. As the oldest male of my generation I was expected to 'be there' for all the siblings and cousins. To serve them in any way I possibly could. To always put others before myself. And to similarly serve the elders of my extended family as they aged. Something I attempted to do for many years – many decades. And I was expected to be a 'good Catholic boy'. Even as a youngster I knew Catholicism was not for me. Happily I was sent to public school and went to Sunday School to learn about the faith as was mandated for public school kids. I completed the various rituals, but soon was questioning the teachings and behavior of those sharing the Catholic faith. I rebelled when I was chastised by an ancient nun for looking around the room, walked out and never partook of these lessons again. I did continue to attend church, but never felt any connection to what I heard and saw there. Later, when I was about to marry a Lutheran woman, which I was told would send me to Hell; I finally severed all ties with organized religion. This held until I found a spiritual path that I could embrace many years later. But that is for later in this journey.

As a child I always felt different from my peers and an outsider from much around me. I was tall and big yet did not feel the need to prove myself as I saw many other boys doing. I was teased for my size and peaceful spirit. Now I see it was others sensing my difference that caused them to challenge and ridicule me. But then it simply hurt and confused me. Layered on top of that was some unconscious self-recognition that I saw and sensed things others did not. I pushed this down as deep as I could and did not look at it for years. And I was intelligent – another 'curse' to a young boy trying to fit in. I could write well and school was easy for me. This I hid by making intentional mistakes on tests and writing below my abilities. Are you sensing a pattern here? I hid from others, which, actually meant I was hiding from myself.

As I reached my teens I became rebellious. I always asked "why" and if given no answer – or if an answer that made no sense to me – I did what I felt was best. Again, from the perspective of time and distance, I see I wanted to be whom and what I was, but felt trapped by what I was told I should be. Should...a word I believe needs to be eliminated from the vocabulary of anyone seeking spiritual growth. Anyone attempting to grow in mind, body and spirit needs to follow what the inner spirit offers and ignore the imprisoning 'should' commands. That with the caveat that the road one walks does not harm or damage others or the natural world around you.

I married young the first time after trying college on for size for a year. College did not work for me then and it was some years before I better understood what I could get from college. My first wife was a wonderful person but, after seven years, I felt the mismatch of our marriage. I truly wished to grow and experience new places and things. She was very comfortable where we were. I ended that marriage and I am certain I caused her great pain. Pain I am sorry for, as I am for the pain I have caused anyone on my life's path. I have learned to accept, through hard inner work, and to forgive myself for pain caused and forgive others for pain caused me. We do the best with what we know at any given time and sometimes this causes pain to others and ourselves. Being human means being fallible. This sounds simple and basic, but it often takes us a very long time to truly accept all the ramifications of this lesson.

While in my twenties I began talking with my grandmother – my fathers' mother. She spoke of how her mother was a medicine person for her family—clan—community in Italy. And that she, my grand-mother, was learning those ways but, once she arrived in the States, she abandoned this work. She also told me that one day I would acquire teachers and begin to walk a spiritual, healing path. I thought her a bit addled. That was a defense mechanism of my own, as I was not ready to hear talk of this sort yet. At a cousins' wedding she called me aside and we spoke—for what was to be the last time. She said she was sorry she had not had the time to share more with me, but reminded me others would follow to mentor me as the time was not yet right for me to truly hear. I smiled and told her it was fine – wondering how I could make a graceful exit. She then told me it was time for her to "step over" and that she would do so that night. That night she died in her sleep—passing into the spirit world as she had predicted. When she was speaking to me at the wedding I did not even realize she was speaking of dying. I was shaken and scared and I pushed this part of my life deep down, with everything else I had submerged for years. I never shared this with my parents or friends. Until recently, I "deleted" it from my conscious awareness level to protect myself.

I remarried a couple of years later, to a woman, Bonnie, who was to be my partner for thirty-two years. Thirty-two eventful, pleasant, difficult, joyful, sad, and, in hindsight, from mutually challenging, yet growthful, years. I had graduated college by this time, with a degree in education and theater. I worked two jobs and she worked in real estate. We were opposites in so many ways. Bonnie was conservative and mindful of making money, saving, having a job with potential and not at all spiritual. While I was, and am, a liberal, spending for today and wanting jobs that fulfilled me, becoming more of a spiritual being as I moved ahead. Our connection was through nature and the natural world. Bonnie was connected to the rocks of any place we visited or lived and a master with plants. Her 'green thumb' extended to her shoulders. I was connected to wildlife, oceans and wild plants.

After some years of me running a business for someone else we decided it was time for a move. We lived in a home that dated to the 1700's in Chester County, Pennsylvania; about 50 miles west of

Philadelphia. We had restored the home and hated to leave it, yet we sensed we needed to be elsewhere. We moved to Florida – Melbourne, on the east coast. Little did we know this was the first of many moves and shifts to come later. After a year we were ready to move back to Pennsylvania. The heat and humidity of Florida was getting to us. So back we went. I decided to begin my own business and, putting up all we had for security, I landed a bank loan. For the next twelve years I opened and ran many businesses, while Bonnie sold commercial real estate. We bought things. After all...is that not the judge of success? And we began travelling. I believed all the money we were making was due to our exceptional skills. Ego is a hard teacher. A hard habit to break, especially in our society which does measure your worth based on your bank assets. As we travelled around the world, I began learning about the natural world of many areas. And began learning from local and indigenous people about the world they knew. I had always been most connected to the natural world and all its wonders. Later I would grow to better understand this connection to the Earth Mother (a term I did not know then) and how best to serve her, all her creatures and myself. Now I see the money we acquired was to allow us to travel and for me to see and learn about so many places. If this book serves others as a map, guide, teaching tool or an amusing story as I hope, then I will write of all I saw and learned during these travels some day in the future.

Then, at forty-three, Bonnie was diagnosed with breast cancer. Our daughter was in eleventh grade at the time and the doctors told her she would not see her graduate from high school. We were in shock, fear, confusion and panic. After all, the doctors knew these things. They must be right. They are doctors. So, a mastectomy and chemotherapy followed. And, finally, one doctor who pushed aside the others predictions and told us anything was possible when it came to healing. Bonnie and I spoke at length and she told me we had more to do together. She wanted another twenty years. I prayed – something I had not done for years. I committed to going into non-profit work and getting advanced degrees in natural resources to better work with the natural world if she were granted these twenty years. Her cancer went into remission soon after and we decided to move elsewhere so that I could keep my promise to God and the universe. Much of our savings was gone to medical bills. But we still owned a home outright. After a couple of years of getting ready and working the businesses so our daughter could get established in college, we moved to Fort Collins, Colorado. I enrolled in a graduate degree in natural resources at Colorado State University. And so begins the walk I really wish to share with you.

2 | Arrival

And so we arrived in Fort Collins, Colorado, ready to spend whatever time we had left together in new adventures. Why Fort Collins and Colorado State University? I certainly had no answer at that time. I had visited eight colleges around the country, which had respected graduate degrees in Natural Resources. Several offered me a teaching assistantship and a stipend. One especially, Penn State, had offered this, housing compensation and a tuition waiver. And Penn State was a school I had strong emotional ties to. The Department of Natural Resource and Interpretation (as it was called then) in the College of Natural Resources of CSU offered me nothing. I did not yet comprehend how the Universe guides us in where to be and what road is the one we are asked to walk. So I thought I must be crazy coming to Colorado. Fort Collins was a nice enough town then – in 1990 – but it did not have a lot to offer other than the University. Yet, here we were—proud owners of a new house with no income and tuition bills before me.

Bonnie quickly found a job selling real estate with a local firm. We thought we had a cash flow solution, as least temporarily. I went to classes and tried to fit in, at 40, one of the older graduate students in the college. After a few months we both realized Bonnie was no longer able to keep up with the rigors of selling. Nor did she want to spend her time in this old pattern. So she left real estate once again, enrolled in classes in Geology (her life's passion) and we used the little savings we had to pay for necessities. After our encounter with her cancer and the doctors' prognosis, running out of money was a small concern to us. This was my first real 'steeping' in surrendering and trusting the Universe. Even though much was happening to me and us at this time, I had no conscious awareness of this.

We had hauled all of our possessions from Pennsylvania to Colorado, a process we would repeat many times over the next twenty some years. We 'owned' these things. We 'owned' our home and the land it sat on. Or so I thought, following the teachings of the culture I had grown up in. Looking back I marvel at how little I really understood. How many things I accepted as fact – questioning nothing. And I wonder further down this road I am on if I will again look back and marvel at how little I knew and understood as I write this today. This is not just age and experience, although they certainly are quality teachers, but it is understanding and walking a different way – the way of our ancestors – that allows these perspectives into what truths really can stand up to honest scrutiny. I know I was excited and eager to begin fulfilling my promise to the Universe around me. Eager to serve, but not as someone this role has been assigned to and put upon as in my past.

When we left Pennsylvania, three days in front of our possessions, we had to leave another home we had restored and the long faces of parents and siblings. Especially those of my mother and father. My parents were wonderful in providing for me as I grew up and lovingingly caring for myself and my brother and sister. But there was always an implied, but expected, 'return' on their parenting. And here I was, the oldest of my generation, moving 3,000 miles away. Even when we had moved to Florida, my parents lived there – twenty miles from where we settled. Hindsight again shows me I moved there, at least in part, to continue serving them. This was different. My father had been ill for some time and we never knew when he might pass on. This was very subtlely used by my mother (unconsciously on her part I believe) as a 'guilt' tool to keep me near. My own wife's illness had smashed this hold on me. I was finally realizing you must serve yourself in the best way for you before you can truly provide for others. Those who continue to serve others through coercion, guilt, or threat I see continuing to lead unfulfilled, often unhappy lives. As teachers were to share with me later, "Walk your own road in a good way first then, when able, reach back a hand to assist others in their walk." This teaching is one which has taken me many years to fully understand and accept.

After a few months in our new life we sat together one morning, counting our meager remaining funds and trying to devise a plan for the future. You may have heard the Native American teaching of "If you want to make God laugh, make a plan." I use it often with those who come to me for guidance. I hadn't heard it to that point – so we made a plan! How Bonnie would work part-time, as would I. How we would invest one-half of our remaining funds, betting on the stock market. How we would sell one car and car pool together. I assumed God laughed because our plan did not work.

I immersed myself in my studies and began to volunteer for service projects around the campus and the community. I had not been in a class for many years and felt out of place at first. Yet I quickly made friends amongst the graduate students and the faculty. People began asking my thoughts and advice, especially based on my past business and teaching experience. I have always attracted people to me. They seem to either really like me or try to avoid me. Usually more of the first type then the second. I did not understand why this was – and is, until recently. I am friendly, if a bit shy at first, and I tend to move fast with things always happening around me. I have led many things, as I do to this day. I will share my thoughts on this as we proceed along this road together. Mostly, they sense I am different. And to many that is a draw...they want to understand what I am. How and why I function. Why I seem to 'just know things'. Others, especially those closed to themselves and afraid of change, I scare the willies out of. I have learned to accept this and react accordingly, but back then it confused me. I was here to use my gifts to work with others for some worthy cause. Using my skills and gifts while welcoming theirs. Why were some afraid of me? And why did others obviously strongly dislike me?

A small side road here – a lane that will quickly rejoin the main road we walk. Partly because of the expectation for me to serve at all times imprinted on me from an early age, I wanted everyone to like me. Partly ego – I wanted to hear what a fine fellow this Jim is! Wow, look what he has done. Didn't the Catholic Church teach me we were to love everyone? (well, at least if they were Catholic) I would speak about how I had no ego for myself as an individual, but had a lot of ego for the projects I worked on. I shared how I had abated my ego while building my businesses and making a lot of money. In part, this was true. In part, a fantasy built by me for me. I wanted to be as successful in the work I did now as I had been making money in the past. While the measure of that success was purer than the old "more money = more worth", the trap of ego yawned just as wide and deep. Ego is a wicked master, forcing us to miss valuable assets and blinding us to the worth of others. As we reach this critical time in human existence here, today, we must be able to excise ego from our being. Those trapped in thinking theirs is always the best way – or only way – will not be able to move forward effectively any longer. They often try to be the primary leader; carrying the lance as they advance on whatever is before them. I know individuals trying to do their work alone or 'in control' of others involved, will only succeed short term, if at all. I have proved this theory many times on my walk, as you will see. Now is the time of the Circle, functioning as "we", not "I" – as the collective of energy and skills. This new way is the old way, when many cultures worked through guiding councils whose members periodically exchanged roles, as tasks required certain skills. But I am jumping ahead. I knew none of this then. Then, Jim was here offering a hand and a smile and a willing heart – yet wearing his undershirt with the big, red S on it. And, if it were a conscious thought rather than the unconscious feeling it was, I would have been checking constantly to be certain my cape was not peeking out under my jacket.

After all, I knew the best way to make the things happen that were needed to move projects along. And others always asked me to lead. Until they got weary of it, and me, and claps become smacks. I suspect this may strike a chord in some of you. Or you may want to visit it now. I have – it hurts. But it releases so much expectation of yourself when you do shift it.

Okay, back on the main road. The last thing I want to sound is preachy and I sensed I was approaching it above. As I made friends and got out into the community and the campus I was having a great deal of fun. Not second-guessing myself as I had for so long. Could I have done something better? Something more? And loving the attention I was getting. At the same time staying focused on my commitment to serve people and the planet. Bonnie and I began exploring the land around us together and separately. We took long rides and hikes in the mountains, on the plains and the cities of Colorado. Meeting people and studying the animals and plants we encountered. Since no part-time jobs had materialized aka "our plan", we had plenty of time for this. Coincidences? There are none.

We had only been in Colorado about four months and were still waiting for our bodies to acclimate to 5,000 feet. We were two flat-landers now living a mile up. We were beginning to feel a little less tired after hiking and so decided to extend our range. We went up to Rocky Mountain National Park for a hike to an old abandoned ranch where the elk were said to be. And we made a painful mistake. The hike was eight miles in – sixteen miles round trip. We had built up to this; a distance we did often back East. The piece forgotten was that we climbed to 9,000 feet altitude to the trailhead. And only had a quart of water each.

"Why don't we park here, use the restroom, and start hiking in by the old trail. It will only add about a mile and I bet we won't see anyone," I suggested to Bonnie as we approached a pull off I knew from driving by.

"I guess so. Seventeen miles instead of sixteen doesn't really seem to matter. Why don't we get an early dinner afterwards at that café in the little town west of the Park? Might be fun," Bonnie chimed in. And so we parked, peed, got our hats and walking sticks and headed off. It was early in the morning and chilly, so we moved at a good pace to stay warm. There was no one in the lot and no one on the trail as we moved forward.

After about an hour the trail started winding up. Not a steep incline, but a constant one. We were engrossed by the plants and birds around us. As we were used to doing, we sipped our water as we walked and talked. "Boy, I can feel the altitude a bit," I shared.

"Me too. I guess it's this slope we are on. I feel older than I am. I bet we work through it soon. Wow, look at that huge woodpecker!" She pointed him out and he was amazing in his many-colored robes. We rested and watched him a while, then moved on as he flew to his next place to be. "See these rocks, they are volcanics," Bonnie shared as we continued. Rocks and minerals were a realm she was part of. She could speak for hours on any formations we came across. And often did.

"I'm looking more for one big enough I can sit on," I said. She pulled out her Colorado Geology book and checked some facts as we sat on the ground and ate the cheese and bread we had brought.

After another two hours we were approaching the old homestead. "I'm glad we are almost there. I'm almost out of water and really need a break," I called out, as she was ten feet in front of me.

"I am out of water and I'm chilled. It hasn't warmed up much like it usually does. That looks like a cabin and some fence over this rise," she told me coming back so as not to waste her breath yelling back.

We got to the homestead ten minutes later – tired, thirsty and cold. A sign immediately told us the site was currently unstaffed. And, worse, no potable water. "Oh boy. That's not good. I just realized we are at 9 or 10 thousand feet now. Twice as high as Fort Collins. I forgot that," I said as it hit me.

"We can rest or nap, but we need water. We will be in really bad shape if we can even make it back without water," Bonnie worriedly said.

We walked all around the site not really enjoying what it had to offer as we were beginning to feel fear creep in. We had seen no one all day and, on top of everything else, it was clouding up and getting colder.

As we considered what to do next we walked slowly (as we were dehydrating rapidly) around the buildings of this compound. And right into the large herd of elk on the backside of the property. A very large herd – at least 200 of these majestic animals. We had seen this herd before – crossing the road near where we parked. We sat then for a half-hour watching them meander across in front of us. We were up close and personal now, not separated by the glass and metal of our car, as we had been when we watched them on that past ride. We stood and soaked in their energy and presence. They were trooping, in no rush, into the trees beyond the site towards some open fields down below us.

After a while the elk were far below us and we decided to slowly start back. Our throats felt like sandpaper and our heads were beginning to throb. I knew of the frequent line of visitors to the Rockies who ended up in the hospital due to lack of water, altitude sickness or exposure to the rapidly changing temperatures. And had no desire to join this circle. A light snow/rain began to fall and I felt something directing me to try and capture some of this water. We stopped and spread the waxed paper that had carried our bread and waited. The intensity of the snowrain falling increased and I positioned the paper below some large leafs to also gather their runoff. After a while we had enough for a few sips each. Nowhere near what our bodies needed, but it tasted like honey going down.

"We had better try and start back. This is turning to all snow and we could end up out here in worse shape than we are now," I spoke.

"Okay, but I feel miserable," Bonnie said. I felt no fear for some reason that I could not explain then. Foolish and unprepared – but not afraid. And so we began trudging back down the trail.

"Here is a little rivulet of water. What do you think?" I asked as I saw a meager trickle going off to the side of the trail. It must have been caused by the rain and snow, as I had not seen in on the way in.

"I don't know, I would hate to pick up parasites and end up as sick from that as from water loss," Bonnie responded – logically as ever.

"You're right, but if we lose much more water we could be in real trouble." The snow was not stopping, but the cold was increasing. "I think we should drink just what we feel we need," I said unsurely.

"Okay," she responded, also with no real conviction. As I went towards the streamlet, I felt a strong sense of the word 'no'. Much like the 'NO' that was bouncing around in my head. I looked more carefully and saw greenish/brownish particulates in the water.

"Well, maybe not," I said. "It looks like something is in the water and I am getting a strong sense we had better not try it."

We turned and started back towards the car, and the water there. After another ten minutes and our legs began to cramp. "Maybe we need to go back to that water," Bonnie put out. "Let's stop a few minutes and see what happens," I suggested. As we were about to decide between going back to the water or moving on, two hikers appeared. Just as I was about to say we should go drink from the stream. The 'should' word again. There are always things we could do, but never anything we should do.

The two hikers approached – a man and woman probably in their thirties, clad in coats and hats, sipping from water bottles. "Hi," said the woman who was in the lead, "It's a cold day to be out here. Where did you hike in from?"

"Our car is back about 8 miles, down by the highway," I filled them in. "We hoped to see the elk herd we heard were in this area. We left them on the far side of the old ranch property," I continued. "It wasn't too cold when we started in, so we wore our lighter coats. The cold's not as bad as our thirst. We didn't bring near enough water," I added.

"Oh yeah," spoke the man as he neared us, "You need a lot of water anytime you hike at this elevation. I learned that the hard way when I moved here two years ago."

"We carry at least a gallon each for any hike over five miles," the woman added.

"Well," Bonnie chimed in, "we had less than a gallon between us and we ran out as we approached the ranch. Is there anywhere we can get some clean water before we continue back?"

"No, and drinking any surface water here will give you giardia nine times out of ten," the woman told her.

So, I had been correct in listening to the voice (inner voice?), which stopped us from drinking from the streamlet. If only I had realized that this 'voice' was one I needed to listen for always, I could have saved myself a lot of discomfort and pain later on my walk through this life. We humans don't always learn quickly and so lessons need to be repeated. And we need to have our spirits truly awaken to each other, all around us and the universe before we begin to understand the meanings of what we do hear or feel. If you are not yet listening, or listening only on occasion, I offer the advice to begin staying aware at all times. Asking the God above or within for guidance when needed and then being alert to however the answers may come.

I remember a lesson from one of my Lakota teachers as I write this, so I believe I will take another brief side road and share it here. Many of my teachers, especially my indigenous ones, taught me through stories. It is the old way and the way many peoples around the world have passed on the old knowledge. Often I did not understand the full meanings of these stories but, as other things transpired on my road, the meanings of these stories became clear – and useful. As other people began to populate the tale of my journey I will name them. When I can reach those I have learned from and worked with, I will ask permission to use their names. Where I cannot, I will create names. I do this out of respect and integrity – important concepts our Western society seems to have discarded. The words and actions will remain as they were, only the names assigned will change.

And so, the story from Two Bears, a Lakota teacher. Two Bears told me this was a Lakota story. Later, when I heard a very similar version from an Apache elder, he told me it was an Apache story. And later again, from another, a Ute story. It doesn't matter, nor change the teaching. Actually it makes a teaching stronger when many have a very similar story to share. I had asked Two Bears whether it was wise for me to attend a Lakota ceremony I was invited to. He told me it was not Two Bears I should ask, but Jim and Spirit. Then offered to share his story.

"There was a young brave who wanted to know if the way of being a hunter for his tribe was the way he was to go," Two Bears began as we sat by a roaring fire on a cold night in the Colorado mountains. He approached an old medicine man of the tribe with his question. "Grandfather," he asked, "I have been seeking an answer to whether I should become a hunter for the tribe. And I have no answer. What should I do?"

"Relative," the Medicine Man responded, "Who have you asked? Where have you asked the question?"

"I have asked the other hunters and some of the elders. None has been able to answer," the young brave answered.

"You have asked in the wrong places," the Medicine Man responded back, "You must ask Great Spirit and listen carefully for the answer."

"How do I do that Grandfather?"

"Go into the field over by that tree and move seven rocks around you in a circle. Then sit inside that circle and ask your question of Great Spirit. Then sit quietly for two hours and listen with all your senses. You are never sure how your questions of the universe may be answered. Then come back and tell me what you have learned," the Medicine Man counseled the young brave. The young brave went off and did as he was told. Two hours later he returned to the lodge of the Medicine Man.

"Grandfather, I did as you told me. And I heard no answer from Great Spirit. I still do not know what to do."

"Grandson," the Medicine Man calmly answered, "Go back, sit, open a prayer to Spirit and then again ask your question. Remain still and quiet until dusk and alert to any way an answer may come. Then return and tell me what you have learned."

And so the brave went back to the circle, offered a prayer of gratitude to Great Spirit and implored Spirit, "Great Spirit. I have given thanks and ask if I should be a hunter for my tribe. You have not answered me. Please give me a sign if this is what I am to be." He then sat and waited, listening for almost four hours until dusk came. He arose, irritable and tired, and went back to the Medicine Man.

"Grandfather, I have done all you told me and I still have no answer." "Grandson, are you truly connected? Are you part of the Earth Mother as you sit there? Are all your senses engaged?" the Medicine Man asked. "Yes, Grandfather. I gave thanks. I prayed. I stayed alert. And I have no answer still," the brave testily responded.

"Come into my lodge and share some elk stew with me Grandson. And then I shall send you out once more," the Medicine Man invited.

And so they ate and the Medicine Man spoke of surrender and trust and being connected to the world around you. The brave listened but remained anxious to receive an answer so he might return to his lodge.

"Now that you are fed and warm, I want you to go back to the circle, again offer prayers and remain there until dawn. Your answer may come at any time, in any way. Be aware of soft answers," the Medicine Man instructed.

The brave went back to the circle and gathered his robes about him, as the night would get cold. He made a small fire and said his prayer of thanks. Then he sang a song of gratitude. Then he asked his question of Great Spirit once again. And then he sat and waited.

In the morning, as the sun came up, it began to warm quickly. The sky was blue and clear. Insects and birds began awakening. And the brave again spoke to Great Spirit. "Great Spirit, I have sat here three times asking my question and seeking an answer. And still I have none! Please send me a sign. Am I to be a hunter for the tribe?" As he asked his question a large, red butterfly flew against his cheek. He brushed him away. "Great Spirit, please, I ask you for an answer. Am I to be a hunter?" Again the butterfly stroked his face. He roughly brushed him away and waited for his answer. Then, one last time, "Great Spirit, I suppose I am to have no answer. Yet I ask once more. Am I to be a hunter? Please guide me." The large butterfly again returned, flew around his head and bumped into his face three times. The brave pushed him off, got up, gathered his robes and left the circle. He did not go back to the Medicine Man, but began to walk towards his own lodge with no answer to his question. "Crazy old man. His medicine is not strong. I do not know why Great Spirit will not guide me. I still have no answer," he mumbled angrily to himself as he walked.

The Medicine Man had been watching from in front of his lodge. He shook his head. He knew the brave was not yet ready to receive the answer the butterfly had brought him three times from Great Spirit. He had not truly listened to his advice to use all his senses and be tuned in to the Earth Mother.

I HAD NOT HEEDED the message of the map, which showed the elevation we would be hiking at or the level of my water going too low before I reached halfway on the hike. Yet I had listened to the voice that told me not to drink from the surface water. And had spread wax paper to gather snow and rain. None of this was within my conscious awareness then, but later I realized I was beginning to listen to all around me.

Back to the side road of our journey now and the hikers Bonnie and I met. "Can you spare a little water so we can make the trek back?" Bonnie asked.

"Actually we brought more than we needed today, so we can give you a quart," the woman responded.

"You are lifesavers!" Bonnie told them, "My name's Bonnie and this is my husband, Jim."

"Good to meet you. I am Ann and this is Frank, my boyfriend. We are volunteers here in the Park. We were checking to see if the large elk herd was here. How many did you see?" We shook hands as we continued speaking.

"We saw at least 200," I answered, "Bulls, cows and young."

"Great, we won't need to go further then. Shall we hike back together?" Ann asked. We drank as we started back the way we had come.

We got back to the car and said goodbye to our new friends. We were really ill and headed into the town nearby to eat. We drank some more water we had left in the car as we drove. We stayed the night at a local motel, both in great pain. By the morning the stomach pain was somewhat lessened and we drove home to Fort Collins. This was a lesson we happily did not have to repeat and one we could share with visitors and new students – hopefully saving some of them great discomfort.

3 | New Directions

I AM CAPTURING WHAT I WRITE HERE AS IT APPEARS TO MY SPIRIT, SO THE positioning may seem odd. If you can read with your heart you will see how and why elements seem to shift in place and time. A very old Mayan teacher of mine once shared with me that time is also like the sacred hoop – with no beginning and no end. What was, is. What is, will be. Past, present and future are all one. We are simply better able to see, hear and feel the present as our physical body walks there. Only recently have I come to grasp the meaning of this. You can, with practice, be where you were and where you will be at any moment. When this first happened to me it was unintentional and scared me to the core. I thought I had finally lost my mind. I will share some of these episodes and what they taught me further down the road. But I felt you, the reader, needed to have a sense of this to help with the flow of the work.

I had become friendly with many of the faculty in my department, as I shared earlier. One, especially, was my department chair, Ron. Ron was a great guy with an engaging personality. People liked him on sight, as did I. We also shared similar roots – both were from the same area of Pennsylvania and both attended Penn State. We soon began sharing beers at the end of the day and Bonnie and I began socializing with he and his wife, Lora. Ron taught me, over the years

I was with CSU, how to use my theater background with groups and classes. In a way that made the ideas I shared fun and compelling. He was a great mentor in this realm. He also chaired my graduate committee and so our interactions were diverse. Ron was also a master at delegating anything that needed to be done, while rarely doing any of the actual work himself. He loved to play and he played well. Another trait of his – one which caused me anger several times – was his willingness to take full credit for anything done by anyone under his supervision. This was a trait I have carefully avoided mimicking over the years. Yet none of us are perfect, our imperfections just vary. So I accepted his as I hope he accepted mine.

Ron also oversaw a non-profit for the University, the Environmental Learning Center (ELC). This was a tract of two hundred acres where environmental education was supposed to be occurring. It was also a place with trails meandering along the Poudre River where students and townspeople were invited to walk. In reality it was the best-kept secret of CSU. Few used it or even knew about it. Ron has installed another graduate student, Sam, to 'run' it. Sam had a small house on the property and taught a couple of courses in the department. We also became friendly... for a time. Ron asked my opinion, from my background of running businesses, why the Center had so little recognition and use. I offered to look into it. I already knew the answer. Nothing was being done to make it visible. Ron, as I said, would never spend his time trying to build the site and its programs. And Sam was, while a nice fellow, incredibly lazy. He was there to earn his degree and felt his position at the Center was owed to him to reimburse him for his time.

So, here we were. A laissez-faire supervisor, a lazy site manager and a new guy who had learned how to run his businesses in a hard and fast way. A potential train wreck ahead. I could not, really would not, tell this to Ron. So I offered to work with Sam in trying to get some recognition for the Center. And so I began bringing word of the Center and what it had to offer to the groups I was beginning to meet and work with. And I spent time at the site creating ideas for its upgrading.

Shortly after I became involved with the Center I was enrolled in a budget and finance course. The instructor, Hal, was another person I had gotten friendly with. Shortly into the course he asked me if I would teach for three weeks as he had some off campus research to conduct. Since it was an area familiar to me from business, I agreed. I took his lesson plans and got ready. Hal was another very friendly, very outgoing guy who loved nature and outdoor fun. He was also was another who liked to play outdoors more than teach. Hal ran a program in Belize, Central America, which enrolled some twenty-five CSU students each year. Hal took them to Belize to learn about natural resources in places around that beautiful country. A great program – and one that would play a strong role in my acquiring indigenous teachers later.

The teaching was uneventful and Hal returned with thanks and a stipend for the three weeks. Turns out he was in Belize doing his 'research'. At the end of my second semester Ron asked me if I would take a teaching assistantship. Here was some cash flow I had stopped looking for. This waived my tuition and provided medical insurance for my wife and myself. What a coincidence!

Coincidences – again, there are none. I did not know this then, but fully appreciate it now. And, the cash flow I was looking so hard for did not materialize until I quit looking. Surrender and trust – themes I will go to often.

And so I began teaching various courses in the department. And loving it. I included an element of service-learning in each course I taught so that the students had some real life experience using the academic material I gave. Service-learning involves the student in planning, implementing and evaluating a project somewhere in the community. I began having some of my students offering programs or helping with site maintenance at the Environmental Center. Soon I met the director of the Northern Colorado AmeriCorps program. We hit it off well and his groups began working with the CSU students.

Then came the students from the local alternative schools – those labeled at-risk. Which really meant the system had no idea how to program educational opportunities for them. I'm sharing this progression of partnerships because my connections to Native American students, and then elders and mentors, grew out of it. A strong collaboration between diverse teachers, students and organizations – my first immersion into the circle of four colors: although I had never heard these words.

At the end of my first year Ron asked me to take over directing the Environmental Learning Center. Sam stayed in the house, but had to begin maintaining it and the property around it. He was no longer a friend, but hid his animosity well. Attacks came later, but that's a story that may or may not evolve later in this book.

I had been working with the Community Services Department of the University for several months, integrating my classes into what they did in the community. One morning, about a year and a half after I arrived at CSU, their director called me at my office. My 'office' was a small, small room tucked away in the rear of the building that housed our department. But at least it brought some reality and grounding to the work of the Environmental Center.

"Hi Jim, it's Sandy."

"Hi Sandy, up early?"

"Yes, I had an early meeting with the director of the Native American Student Services, Carolyn Fiscus. Do you know her?" Sandy asked.

"I haven't met her. But I've heard good things about the work they do with the Native American students," I said.

"She's looking for other options for the Native students. Options around nature and their tribal customs. Too many of them leave because the adjustment is so severe. I suggested she meet with you. I hope that's okay?"

"Absolutely. I'm not sure how I can help, except maybe to tell them more about the Environmental Center and invite them widow."

"Great. She's going to call later this morning. I guess she had a meeting with the dean first. Thanks, Jim, any help you can give will be a huge plus to her. Students seem to really be drawn to you so I'm sure you'll come up with some ideas."

"I'll give it my best Sandy. Thanks for putting us together."

About an hour later Carolyn called and we agreed to meet early that evening at the Center. I had no idea then what doors were about to begin opening for me, and others, when we met that evening. My initial idea of telling the Native American students about the Center and inviting them out would seem funny to me later. I was thinking tiny. Just a spur of the moment small thought. Carolyn and I would talk bigger and then the roads before many people of different walks would begin intersecting, as this part of the journey would take on a life of its own.

As I had no class to teach that day I called home and Bonnie said her geology class had been cancelled that day also. We decided to take a ride up to Wyoming where Bonnie had wanted to visit an area where numerous dinosaur bones had been uncovered in the past. And so we started up the road toward Laramie shortly after. This is a scenic road we had taken before, winding up out of the northwest side of Fort Collins through treed and rock-strewn landscape for the 50 miles to Laramie. We stopped twice so Bonnie could study rock outcroppings more closely. She explained the thrust and lift that had created these formations so many eons ago. And how the weathering had created their current look, with the harder rock being on top and thus preserving the softer rock below.

I walked off towards the hogbacks, as she wanted some time to take pictures and make notes. A hogback is a large rock edifice sloping up from ground level to a drop at the end opposite where the slope begins. They look like the back of a hog – at least so I am told. I had no real association with hogs to that point. As I walked across the gravelly land towards these hogbacks, four coyotes appeared on top of the one nearest me. "Appeared" is the word for it; it seemed they were not there one moment and all visible the next. I stopped and watched as they did the same. Neither they nor I moved for some minutes. They seemed to have no fear of me and I was fascinated by them. I could feel their energy coming down to me from their higher perch. I almost felt as if I was up next to them and I asked myself how this could be. I tried to 'figure out' this feeling and then simply put it to my love of the outdoors and wildlife. As soon as I did that the feeling vanished, as did the coyotes above me. As quietly and quickly as they had come. I began hiking forward again and released the conscious awareness of this unique event. Many times in the future, as I learned more of spiritual ways and the power of the Earth Mother, I would remember this meeting and wish I had been more in tune with my spiritual side that day. Yet each gift or power we are given comes at the best time for our journey. So I assume this meeting and melding with the coyotes must have opened some part of me to the point I was able to accept at that time. I give gratitude to these coyotes each time I remember that day and our paths crossing.

I reached the bottom of the hogback the coyotes had alit on top of in another ten minutes. I sat and drank some water and realized I could not climb it with the New Balance walking shoes I had worn. So I rested and enjoyed the scene from there. I was disappointed, as I wanted to see if I could spot the coyotes traveling down the other side. As I sat, relaxed with my thirst quenched, some dozen bees appeared around me. They began landing on my arms and legs and I watched them do their circular wiggle-dance on my extremities. Bees have shown themselves to me often, as they did in my home yesterday, here in Sedona, Arizona, as I wrote. Usually it is at a time when I need to stop and go into myself for some message. Other times it is as I prepare to do ceremony. But, once again, at this point in my journey, I was unaware of the number of times and the significance of their appearances. I simply sat and enjoyed their natural dance.

After some fifteen minutes, the bees went their way and I arose and started back to the car. Bonnie was just finishing her communion with the rocks and we headed north once again. We had planned to stop for lunch in Laramie, but decided to risk it and drive into the sparsely inhabited area where the dinosaurs once roamed. And trust we would find a place to eat. Worse case, we had some cheese and fruit – food we always brought along.

Another hour or so brought us into dinosaur land. We passed a little general store or café covered in antelope and buffalo horns. I thought we might stop, but Bonnie wanted to roam the area just a half-mile be-hind this place. So we turned up the dirt road we had been told about and continued—followed by the cloud of dust our Jeep was creating. We bounced and slid up the road and, after about two miles, assumed we had gone too far. We were looking for an old dig that had been de-scribed to us. So we turned around – accompanied by an even bigger cloud of dust – and slowly wended our way back the way we had come. A little over a mile passed and suddenly we saw an opening to the right. This was hidden by a rock outcropping when we were headed in, but was now clear. We pulled in and saw the remains of the old dig.

As we got out we realized how much hotter it had gotten. We drank water and carefully navigated the 'crumbly' rock to the dig. There was shade created by the rocks beside us, which was a wel-comed gift.

"I need some time with these rocks before beginning to explore the dinosaur aspect. Is that okay with you?" Bonnie asked. It was really a rhetorical question – she always needed some time with the rocks first. As I always did with the animals and the land. And it was always fine with both of us.

"Sure, just so I am back to the Center to meet Carolyn at 6:30," I replied.

"How would you feel about going back to that store and seeing if they had some food and some diet colas for us? Or do you need time on the land as I look at the rocks?" she asked. "If you're comfortable out here I can do that." We both were always comfortable outside in nature and never felt threatened or alone.

"I'm fine. Take your time, these rocks have a lot to teach me."

So I drove the half-mile, which was actually a mile and why in part why we missed the site earlier, back to the store/café.

4 | Dinosaurs Remembered

ALTHOUGH I AM FORTUNATE TO BE ABLE TO GO BACK TO ANY TIME OR place and relive events, which allows me to write them as they occurred, I did write about some people and places shortly after they crossed my path. I will include these as I document this journey, and a few others here, shortly after they occurred. The 'voice' you hear as you read this story, which I share now may be a little different because that was 'me' then and this is 'me' now. But I feel I captured these at the time for some reason, so I share them that way. Unchanged and unaltered, unless I feel a note is needed for clarity. When I wrote this piece I melded together four different trips I would make to this region in the course of six months. My thought was to better give a feel for this part of the country and the people who live in it as I was asked to do by a group of international students I was working with at the time. The section about Tom Deering in the café (or general store) was from the trip I have been sharing with you.

◇ ◇ ◇

I had decided in the past to meet some of the people who populate this area. I want to know how they feel about their land. I soon find that for many of these people it seems to be a love-hate relationship between themselves and their world. They curse the weather and the wind, talk about how hard it is to scratch out a living, bemoan the fact they have to travel great distances to get anywhere...and yet all say they wouldn't live anywhere else. They tell me the land has history; a beauty of its own; it won't beat them; their grandparents fought it, and so will they; it destroyed the dinosaurs, but can't destroy them; there are too many rules in other places, the only rule here is to survive. Bits and pieces, snatches, many oft-repeated, providing a collage of reasons why these people chose to be here.

Dinosaurs come up often in conversation with the area's people. They are the land's claim to fame, and local heroes of the people. I am told to hike about four miles past my last stopping point and I will reach an area where two enormous digs took place in the 1920's. These digs provided some of the largest, best preserved, dinosaur skeletons ever found.

In a tiny, dilapidated general store, reached by a rutted pull-off from the highway, about a mile from my past trailhead, I meet an old-timer, Tom Deering. The general store has an inventory you could count on the fingers of two hands. Tom slumps in an old, straight-backed chair, pushed back on its rear legs, with his feet propped up on a cold, blackened pot-bellied stove. Tom tells me he has lived here his whole life, and I ask if he would tell me about the area. "Ain't much to tell, but I'm the one to tell it to you," comes back from Tom so quickly I know I've found a talker. I grab us a couple of pops, pull over another chair next to Tom, straddle it backwards, and prepare to listen.

Tom was a young brushman on one of the dinosaur digs. He spent his days meticulously removing sand and dirt from the skeleton pieces wrested from their grave with a small, fine-bristled brush. He tells me how hard it was to fight the howling winds, the pelting rains, and the blanketing snows, which constantly tried to reclaim the bones the excavators uncovered while the digs were in operation. "It was a bitch," Tom spits out. "Some damn crap weather always hitting us, making us miserable. Diggin' rigs were always throwing up dirt, and the wind would grab it and play hell with it." As the diggers fought with these elements, which seemed to rally against their work, the two outfits running the digs also battled each other. They fought legally in the courts, and illegally with sabotage raids on one another's sites. "Their sons of bitches would sneak over to our site at night and put grit in our equipment's gas tanks so they wouldn't start in the morning, and our sons of bitches would go pull their earth stakes. Piles of dirt would run back over their exposed work. Like little kids playin' war games. Problem was, the two owners hated each other, and had egos bigger than this country, so they encouraged the site bosses to keep the battles goin'. Got nasty though, and real fights broke out between their folks and ours. Some shovels landed on heads, and a few workers were hurt pretty bad, so a truce was kinda called. Some things still happened though."

Tom tells me about the huge craters that were dug to haul the impressive number of skeletons and bones from the earth. These skeletons were then shipped around the globe. Many of these man-made craters still dot the land. Tom says he never thought much about the digging, or the selling off of the bones, in the days of the digs. If he thought about his part in it at all, it was to see himself as an adventurer fighting the hard land to pull out some relics doing no one any good where they were. In retrospect, he sees himself, and the others, as grave robbers and despoilers of the landscape, who then sold a vital piece of their lands' natural history for a short-term gain. It saddens him that only a few bones remain in his homeland, while people in New York, London, and Paris can ogle "his people's heritage."

DOWN THE ROAD from the general store, I pull into a service station for gas. A service station right out of the 1950's. "Service with a smile" decorates the faded wall next to the single pump, as does a sign for Coke showing a bottle type Coke hasn't used in twenty years. "I'll get that for ya," comes from behind me as I reach for the nozzle. A short, heavyset, deeply tanned woman with a big smile is approaching me, hand out for the nozzle. "We still wait on our customers out this way," comes from the woman as she reaches me, "besides, the pump is cranky." I give her the hose and back off as she slams the starter mechanism up twice, then waits a few seconds before trying to pump my gas. "You'll want 'er filled; not too many stations out here. Might take a few minutes, this thing's slow. I'm Rose, and this is Rose's Oasis. Not really, just a joke my husband likes to throw at me every day. You headin' cross state?" All of this shoots out of Rose with no pauses, along with a smile that gets ever wider. I like Rose. I like her for two reasons: she's the type of person anyone would like right off, and she's the first 'Rose' I've met since my favorite Aunt Rose died some years back. "No," I tell her, "I'm going to hike out to the dinosaur digs." "Good! It's a great day for it, and almost nobody goes out there this time of year. Doctor Ketchins brings his students out two or three times in the spring, but nobody is there now." She grabs a soapy cloth and starts lathering up my windshield as we talk. "Go on in, get a pop if you like. I'll be in in two."

The inside of the station shows some real time invested, and care given, by Rose. Some new curtains and fresh paint dress up the walls, as do the pictures of horses hung everywhere. I am thirsty again, so I pull a Pepsi (apologies to the Coke sign) out of the old cooler in the corner and wait for Rose. A few minutes later she bubbles in with, "Good, good, you get parched out here pretty quick. Either the heat or the wind can dry ya right out. So, how do you like our country out here? Cash or charge?"

"Charge," I tell her as I ponder her other question. "It's impressive," I put out.

"Impressive, that's pretty good," she chuckles at me. "Too many people say big. Hell, we know it's big, anybody can see that. Still it's better than empty, barren, or ugly. Get all of those sometimes. Usually from the big Buick people barrel-assing their way through here. Hope you spend a little time out at the digs; I'd like your thoughts on our country after that. Stop for gas again if you find enough to bring you back." Rose loves to string thoughts together, and I find it comfortable. I sign the charge slip, thank her and head out to my car, thinking how most of the people I have met here are friendly and outgoing, not taciturn and uncommunicative as I had been told. If the people are not as hard as depicted, maybe the land isn't either.

I'M STANDING NEAR the point where I was defeated by the weather on my last hike, ready for another try. Maybe this time I'll fare better. The day is bright and sunny, cool enough for a jacket, with only a little wind. No harsh, biting grit is lashing my face, nor is any cumulus rain-bearing enemy in the skies above me. It caught me last time, soaking and freezing me before I was able to retrace my steps. Cold, wet, and stinging from the wind, I made it to my car that time— uncomfortable and chastised for not being prepared for the elements, but not defeated.

I can't see any evidence of the digs I was told about from here, but the trail winds around another group of hills and out of sight up ahead. There are some small sparrow-like birds winging to the sides of me today. I don't know them, and don't want to take the time to look them up in my field guide, so I'll lump them with the LBJ's—little brown jobs.

The vultures are gone, but the evidence of their feast is here, an antelope carcass picked clean. If I hadn't seen this feeding spot last time, I wouldn't know if these bones were a week old or a year old. No guts, no gore, no blood, no disturbance of the land around the skeleton; this land takes quickly and covers its tracks.

I'm a couple of miles from the digs and realize I am thinking about the land's past, its dinosaurs, its weather, enjoying the sunny day; looking for, and finding tracks and scat, thinking about the people I met and smiling at some of their comments, thinking how grand the vista is, and not once wondering what this land has to offer. It would never be my choice of a place to live, but I am beginning to understand its allure, and its challenge. I am even beginning to see its worth, beyond my desire to see all natural areas preserved, as lands to cherish. It has natural history, eons of it, and human history of a much shorter span. It has had history's largest beasts, the dinosaurs, walk it, and expire on it. Rainforests and inland seas have been part of its past, as have cataclysmic upheavals. Finally mountains, now scraped down by the elements, have given way to its present sculpting. It survives, like the life it supports, ready for the next chapter in its existence. Sitting here, trailside, on a cold, hard rock, thinking about how very diverse and complex I finally realize this land is, I know I must savor its offerings slowly. I pull some beef jerky and my cigarettes from my back pocket, put the cigarettes aside, gnaw the meat, and let my mind wander.

A shadow herd of stampeding buffalo crossing the flat terrain before me begins to take shape in my mind's eye, chased by a band of Indians on horseback. The buffalo are charging ahead, wide eyed and ferocious, Indian ponies straining forward, huge clouds of dust rolling out behind them. A scene all energy, power, and motion, at the same time holding their place before me. They fade out as I bite my lip on my last hunk of jerky. I slide down the rock, back to it on the ground, and light up. I think about the hard life the Indians must have had here and try to bring back the images. I can't, they're gone. Break done, I get up, stretch, crack my knuckles, and move on.

THE TRAIL BEGINS to loop north toward a row of hogbacks. I know I am close, since the digs are "in the guts and the shadows of the hills," as Tom had told me. I don't know what I'll see at the digs, and I am expecting to be disappointed, but I don't really care about their physical appearance. Just being in an area where dinosaurs, the largest creatures to ever walk the planet, were plentiful is enough for me.

Suddenly I'm in the middle of it. Large holes and craters are visible ahead, and some old, half-rotted, scaffolding is trying to stay erect off to my right. The bones of the tools of the diggers next to the bones of their prey. This was the first dig, the largest one, in the area. Two old shacks, one without a roof, come into view. Tom told me he stayed in one of these cabins for six months with a Chinese worker, Lin, when he first started working on the dig. It was not a prime location. It was too close to the dig, and dust filled the air most of the night, but he liked laying in his roll at night thinking about the dinosaurs whose remains were only a few feet away.

I scrabble up the backside of the hogback, behind the cabins, where Tom had told me to go and see the faint trail I am to follow. Up about twenty feet I slip and backslide, gashing my knee on a rock. I let out a good, loud curse for the silent landscape, sit back, and put my bandana to the wound. It's not too deep, but doing a good job of bleeding, so I'll need to keep pressure on it for a few minutes. I sit there hurting, pissed at my own clumsiness, as I watch my blood stain the ground. My blood mingling with the blood of all the other creatures that have walked this land. Blood brothers with the dinosaurs, the Indians and the settlers. A truly philosophical justification for my own stupidity. These thoughts may ease my soul a little, but they don't do anything for the pain or bleeding.

After ten minutes the bleeding stops, and I tie the bandana around my knee. It hurts a bit to walk, but not enough to turn me back. I head up the side trail again, slower, and more cautiously, than before. Up another forty feet I come to the dig spot Tom wanted me to see. The contours of the land make it almost invisible from below—so few people ever come up here. I start prodding around on the side of the hole and soon unearth three small pieces of bone. Now comes my dilemma: Do I take my finds, like so many have in the past, justifying it to myself by saying someone else will if I don't—or do I appreciate them and put them back? I unclip my canteen, take a long drink, and sit with my finds. Realizing I hadn't even washed my knee I unwrap it and douse it with the water. It's throbbing and I know the downhill climb from my perch will hurt, so I ease back for a rest.

I can see a lot of old dig scaffolding and a few pieces of rusted equipment, along with several excavation sites from here. As I let my mind wander again, I can begin to see sweating laborers pulling dinosaur ribs from the ground superimposed over mental images of full-fleshed, lumbering dinosaurs. Almost like I'm watching two movies at once. The dinosaurs win the mental cinema battle, and take my full focus. Building-high ferns sprout up around a steaming body of water, giving my dinosaurs something to mush through and devour. Incredibly large, leather winged avians cut the sky, as their earthbound brethren scamper below them. I sit there a long time, wrapped in my thoughts and my images, almost believing I can hear and smell my scene.

When I do come back from my voyage, I feel completely relaxed and energized. I'm ready to start back, already looking forward to my next outing here. I love to let natural areas enfold me, let my mind go, and feel part of them, and here there is a cornucopia of objects for the imagination. I put my dinosaurs to rest for today, laying the three bone shards back in their hole and begin to limp down the hill, thinking about choosing my descriptive words for this country to deliver to Rose on my next visit.

◇ ◇ ◇

On today's trip, after talking with Tom, I left the café with some sandwiches and a six-pack of Diet Cokes and headed back to the dig. As I trundled in, with dust, Bonnie was just coming down from the high rocks. We ate and I shared the tale from the café and she shared what the rocks had told her. This was an eventful day and we still wanted to explore the dig bottom before heading home. After eating we had to walk back into the sun to reach the floor of the dig. It was hot and dusty, with a cloudless sky unable to lessen the impacts of the heat. We donned our western hats after pouring water over our heads and carried on. We puttered around the dig and the adjacent land for about ninety minutes, sensing the presence of the huge 'land whales' of the past. But any bones or bone chards were long gone. Not that we expected to find any, just looking was gratifying enough. I had yet to learn that when you look diligently for something you almost never find it. When you enjoy and just 'be present' often things find you.

Finally we limped back towards the car, dried out and heat weary. But with high spirits after an eventful natural excursion, I wanted enough time for a quick shower – a cold one – before meeting Carolyn at the Environmental Center. After about thirty minutes Bonnie laid her head back for a 'short' nap. That lasted well over an hour, which gave me time to process what I had heard and seen today.

5 | Beginning to Walk the Red Road

WE GOT BACK HOME JUST IN TIME TO WATCH THE RED FOXES FROLICKING in the field behind our house. We sat with tall, sweating glasses of iced tea and watched them until they retired to their den. And I went upstairs to wash off the dust and smell of the day. Bonnie and I chatted about the day and our desire to return to those places – on a cool day – as we ate a light dinner. Then I left for the meeting with Carolyn.

At this time the Environmental Learning Center was, as I said earlier, a little known, little used natural area owned by CSU. It is a couple hundred acres abutting hundreds of acres of Fort Collins owned open land. A trail system had been installed years before, with a suspension bridge over the Poudre River for access to the trails. The Poudre ran through the Center, so riparian lands – river, wetlands and marsh – wove its natural tapestry throughout the Center. There were many treed areas and areas of open grassland. And glorious views of the Rockies from the eastern side. Deer roamed the grassy center areas, owls nested in the trees, foxes and rabbits teemed throughout and there are a large number of blue heron nests on the south side – a rookery...or heronry. The heron nests numbered thirty-five during my time there, and they were just below the old Rigden homestead that was on the site. Plants of many types filled the waterways and woodlands; some native species as well as a host of invasive species. It was a place I was in harmony with from the first time

I stepped foot in it. As I arrived at the Center my cell phone began ringing; Carolyn saying she would be a few minutes late. So I ambled over to the river and watched the water flow sinuously over the rock bed. It was dusk by now and the play of light on the water keep me entertained until Carolyn pulled into the parking lot.

As she stepped out of her car I got a sense of caring and compassion resonating from her. I liked her right away. I have had reactions like this to many people during this lifetime and have learned to listen and heed these intuitive teachings from within. She was a woman of average height with a clear smile and dark hair. I guessed her age as forty – but am notoriously bad at that. She was hefty, but not overly large; a problem I had wrestled with my whole life.

"Hi. I am assuming you are Carolyn. Am I right?" I asked.

"I am. And so you are Jim," she smiled back. "Thank you for meeting with me. I am sorry for being late."

"No problem," I said, "you gave me time to sit with the river and the water. What better way to end a day?"

"I can see we will get along well," Carolyn smiled broader.

"It's not too cold, so we can sit on the bench by the river if you like," I offered.

"Perfect," Carolyn agreed.

We walked back to the river and sat below a beautiful spreading grandmother Cottonwood tree next to the river. The Cottonwoods had been disappearing from the riverways in this part of Colorado – the Front Range – for many years. When we humans began changing and controlling the paths of the water we eliminated the conditions the Cottonwoods need to prosper. They require periodic flooding to remain healthy and tall and that is one of the things humans seem unable to abide. I continue to hope that the species we have crippled will begin making comebacks as we learn to better live in harmony with the Earth Mother. As we stop trying to do that which we cannot anyway – control her. This is a hope and belief I will never abandon. And will continue to work towards as long as I am to be walking the Earth Mother's realm.

This is a teaching I will delve into more as we go along. You will see it appear, I am certain, as we travel ahead together. It may appear, as it is now, by me stating it or it may appear through the stories of my journey I share. Control is the epicenter. We humans, especially those brought up in Western cultures, have an innate need and desire to control: ourselves; our world; our families; our pets; our jobs; our possessions and on and on. The reality is we cannot control anything. We may affect things for a short period, but they eventually shift to where the universe wants them. This is especially true around our possessions. What do we possess? When you truly understand the answer to this is "nothing" you can begin to move out of the control trap. These things I can speak of through hard, painful experiences. Experiences I will share so you see I speak not just from reasoned thought, but rather through contemplation grounded in experience. I will leave this for now, but invite you to explore these ideas as we move forward.

We both sat and listened to the sound of the water moving by us, with no words for several minutes. Then, from me, "Shall we just enjoy this place for a while before we speak Carolyn?"

"Yes, that is a good way to start. This is a beautiful spot," Carolyn agreed.

And so we sat with nature surrounding us not needing to begin our conversation quickly. I would come to understand this as a common way to begin a meeting with many indigenous people as I walked more in their ways. But for now, for me, it was simply the beauty of the time and place surrounding us that had prompted my question. Many times, as I meet with people of various cultures, I have begun with a question, statement or action that was in tune with their customs. This was through no planning on my part, but rather some inner guidance that has allowed me to connect before we connect. Connect in a way to which they are accustomed and comfortable. And, likewise, I have watched people connect with me with similar beginnings. This is another wonderful gift from the universe, if you remain open and aware for its guidance. Actually, my plan for this meeting was to ask about the Native

American students and how the Center might help, then share the story of the Center, offer a visit to the students and a program if they wished and then offer a meeting with others in our college if that felt needed. I had a plan – simple and flexible. Of course, it went nothing like that. There is another Native American saying that I remember, and quote often. It is...

"Do you want to make Great Spirit laugh? Then just make a plan."

I have found that every plan I have ever made has always gone differently than I envisioned. Now, after so many years of fretting over my plans being changed by outside influences, I go along with what presents in the moment and simply allow the process of "what is to be" evolve. If I do make plans, I always envision them as a starting point for a project or event and welcome changes as they occur.

And so we sat and got to begin to know each other while saying nothing. The water trickled by, singing softly over the round river rocks in their flow path. Listening to water move has always relaxed me and raised my spirits. As has the sound of birds – any bird, any time, any place. They sing to my spirit like nothing else ever has. As I was sitting enjoying the water chorus, the frogs began joining in. Many frog voices from the pond behind us. I do not have a trained musical bone in my body, but these frogs sounded like they were singing in three-part harmony. I was content and about to speak again as four blue herons wafted their way just above us. Honking briefly as they spied us, but then moving serenely past us as they sensed no threat. They banked left and headed towards their nesting area below us.

We were now long into the time of darkening skies and so I turned to Carolyn and asked, "Shall we go back to the building we parked near or talk here into the dark?"

"I am comfortable and the big Grandmother (moon) will light our way back. Okay?" she asked.

"Yes, great. My choice too. Carolyn, how may I help with your students? What is it you are seeking? I could invite them to the Center or give a slide presentation on campus or provide a program here."

"Jim, those may be helpful, but let me tell you what I am dealing with. We have a large number of Native students here at CSU. They come because of the University's emphasis on natural resources and its location in the mountains. Our department works with them to provide whatever support we can. It's very hard on many of these young people. For some, it's the first time they have been away from their families and their rez (reservation). As well as the customs and ceremonies they are used to. And they are surrounded by non-Native people who don't understand their needs or ways while they are immersed in courses and learning styles they are unfamiliar with. And so, almost sixty percent drop out after a semester; over seventy percent by the end of the first year. I am trying to find ways to retain more of these students, so they can earn degrees and then take them back home to help their people. This place you run is full of nature and amazing energy. Look at what we had come to us in this short time we sat here. Programs and presentations would be wonderful, and much appreciated, but I am hoping to discover other ways to connect with them here."

Wow, throw away the plan I had made. This was much more of an issue then I had realized and I had no idea what to offer her as we sat here. I felt completely unprepared for this. And I felt my offers were not only inadequate, but showed another non-Native offering non-Native ideas for Native students.

"Carolyn," I began "I'm sorry. I did not mean to insult you by offering things you already get from faculty just put in another setting. I don't know much about Native American culture and so I spoke before I asked."

"Those words sound very native to me, Jim," she smiled at me as she spoke. "No apologies, you did ask. That is much more than many do. If time out here and talks around the nature here are what we have to do together for the students, I will be happy with that," she continued. "Anything that helps us better serve these students is a big help."

My brain raced as I tried to think of other opportunities we could offer. Ideas came, and were quickly discarded for one practical reason or another. I had yet to learn to lead and create with my heart, not my head. If something begins in the heart the head will come in and play its role as needed. But for now, I was brain centered and so I was stumped. I did all that I could in the moment and asked, "Carolyn, without thinking about whether it's doable or not, what would be your highest desire for what we could do here for your students be? What is there that is different that we might create?"

"Oh, I'm not sure. That's a great question and I'm not sure of the answer. Let me sit with it a minute." And so, once again, we went silent for a few minutes.

"Jim, what we don't have is access to any place where we could offer ceremony as the students are used to back on the rez. We bring in Elders to speak with the students, but it's usually on campus. And we can't provide what they need to do any of our traditional ceremonies. We have a good number of Lakota students, for example, and no place where we can provide any Lakota ceremonies."

"What would you need Carolyn?" I asked.

"Well, a place along the river where we could build a sweat lodge – an inipi – would be a great thing. And a place we could share the traditional meal afterwards. But, I don't think the University would ever go for that."

"I thought we were not going to worry about what 'can not be', but rather what you need," I said, "So what would this entail? And how would this be used?"

"The inipi, the sweat lodge, is where we sing, drum and pray to Great Mystery and Great Spirit. Like our church, but much more. It is a cleansing ceremony that has been handed down for long generations within many tribes, especially the Lakota. Rocks are heated for hours before the lodge is to begin and then brought in—usually seven at a time. In four different sessions – what we call doors. The medicine person leading the lodge pours water over them and leads all that happens. I have seen amazing healings occur. I have heard brave men weep and weak women roar. It's very powerful. The lodge is built with willow branches and covered by hides or blankets. But I would introduce you to others to tell you more of this," Carolyn instructed me. Then, she added, "I don't think the University would allow it to be built here."

"Well, Carolyn, I was asked to run this Center and get more use of it both on campus and with the local community members. And, if I see properly, there are churches on the campus. And a worship building for all to use. Why is this different? If we are to move this ahead I believe I need to make the decision based on what I have been asked to do. I was not told to ask permission for everything done, especially if it has educational value. Would other, non-native people ever be invited or provided lessons around it?"

"I think so, but we need to bring in lodge leaders and speak together. And I would like you to meet Lawrence Little Thunder, President of the Native American Students. Would that be okay?"

"Sure. Where would be a good place to build this? What would you need? Would the site need to be off-bounds to general visitors? Sorry, probably too many questions. But this feels right to me."

"Along the river is best. The rocks from the river would give us those to heat. And somewhere off the paths, so it is respected. The rest we could talk about when we find the right place. And we have been working with people in your department for a while on other lessons, a couple of years at least, so we are not unknown to them."

"Why don't we meet here again tomorrow and identify some possible locations? Does that work for you?" I asked Carolyn.

"Yes. If you are certain, we will meet tomorrow. I will see if anyone else can come. Okay?"

"Anyone you wish. You all need to lead this. I know nothing. My job for now is to assess which sites you pick might work well for the Center."

"What time works Jim?"

"How about one o'clock?"

"Good, I'm free from noon to four tomorrow. Thank you, this will be good."

"Thank you Carolyn. This will be good for everyone."

6 | Next Steps

I HAD A CLASS TO TEACH THE NEXT MORNING AND THEN A GROUP OF students to meet out at the Center. The Center now had a small – VERY small – budget from our department. I added 'staff' from volunteers within our College of Natural Resources. They provided site work and some programs. And had a couple of faculty – those involved with service-learning – bringing classes out on occasion. Slow growth, but growth. I showed the students around and invited them to my office to speak more if they were interested in joining our 'crew'. And, after they left, realized I had two hours before I was to meet with Carolyn. I decided to roam the grounds and do some initial scouting of sites for the inipi, as well as look at some zoned-use areas I had been thinking of suggesting to Ron, my department chair.

I swayed my way across the suspension bridge and on into the heart of the Center. It was a beautiful day, about sixty-five and sunny with no wind. My tee shirt was all I needed. That and a large bottle of water. I began following the large loop trail to the south of the bridge. A group of five whitetail deer loped across the fields to my left. Their gentle motion reminded me to slow down and be gentle with myself. I have always enjoyed watching deer move and I was used to the whitetail back East. Here, in the mountain west, mule deer were the native species. They are a little smaller without the telltale 'white flag' of a tail. The whitetail were, however, squeezing them out of some of their native lands. We had both on the Center's grounds and I hoped the mule deer – mulies – would remain dominant. As the deer disappeared under a copse of trees I continued on. As I reached the bottom of the loop I headed across country into an area I wanted to designate as untrailed and unopen to the public. A place where the wildlife could roam without the disturbance of humans.

A light breeze began to come in from the west, off of the Rockies. It felt good as it played with my hair and ruffled my shirt around me. There was talk of some weather coming in this evening from that direction. The Front Range of Colorado – the area just east of the Rockies and west of the open grasslands – is a great place to live weather-wise. In the summer cool breezes often come from the west, as they were now, which helps on those clear, cloudless days. And in the winter most of the storms also come from the west over the mountains. When they do they most often 'jump' right over the Front Range and fall out in the far eastern Colorado grasslands. Only the occasional storm coming from the east can cause any real snowfall. These storms hang up on the mountains behind us and the white dumping commences. When it gets too hot in the summer, you drive twenty minutes up into the mountains to cool off. And when you want snow in the winter, you drive the same route. These weather patterns are a great gift from Father Sky. Anyway, I continued to walk, enjoying the breeze enfolding me. As I reached the river through the wooded area I walked I saw the beaver family at work. Odd they were out in the daytime, but I saw them often mid-day. With no real enemies on this land and few people venturing off the trails, I assume they felt safe enough to gnash and cut in the daylight. They routinely altered the nature of this portion of the river and the ponds alongside it. There was nothing to worry about with this behavior as they had been doing this work for millennia as a natural component of the environment here. I sat and watched them for ten or fifteen minutes as I half wandered in a dreamlike state.

I felt the breeze lessen as I focused in on the birds in the trees just beside me. There songs soothed me, even as I tried to place what species they were. I was somewhat adept at this, as an amazing naturalist had led many walks I participated in where she identified all the birds by their songs alone. It was a fun game for me, and one I engaged in often. A loud buzzing of bees came into my awareness a few minutes later and I arose to explore the source of it. Some twenty paces through the trees I found a huge, ancient decaying stump alive with a swarm of bees exiting and entering in a pattern only they understood. I made a mental note to send someone back with red flags later. These swarms appeared once in a while, and I did not want someone approaching too closely for a better view or a picture. So many people, especially those not often immersed in nature, conduct themselves as if they were in Disneyland, certain nothing can hurt them. I have watched this in many places in the natural world. It is a matter of awareness and being present to what is around you. I've seen people approach bears who were feeding for pictures; people putting babies on the backs of buffalo; people approaching bee swarms and on and on. I would often say something in warning and, more often than not, would get a curt dismissal. So I soon learned to be silent and hope for the best – whatever that best might be. Actually, my concern was more for the animals than the humans. The humans could be expected to know better. Once, while talking to Tom, a ranger friend in Rocky Mountain National Park, I asked him how they dealt with this.

"Jim, I deal with it pretty much like you do. I try to politely educate and warn. I speak about the nature of undomesticated wildlife and their behavior when threatened. And how these animals can often outrun a human when angry or scared. And they usually thank me and stop. Then I'll move on and, when I return, I see them doing the same foolish things. At that point I worry about the animals. I don't ever want to have to shoot a bear because some human provoked it into attack or menacing behavior," Tom told me.

"Good, Tom. I thought maybe I was being too judgmental and negative about some visitors. I'm glad to see you experience the same problems," I replied.

"You know, we have a name for this sort of human foolishness: 'natural selection'," Tom said with a big smile.

I began to laugh as we watched a tourist across the field from us begin to look around to see if anyone was watching and then head across an area marked "Do Not Approach the Elk" straight towards a large herd of elk, camera swinging from his hand.

"Jim, I'll catch up to you later. Duty calls. Someone else who I guess can't read. Or maybe can't think," Tom joked as he headed towards the encroacher.

I mentally came back to my current place and time with a smile on my face as I remembered this talk with Tom and realized I needed to head back to the parking lot to meet with Carolyn.

As I retraced my steps and approached the suspension bridge I saw Carolyn coming my way with a man I did not recognize beside her. She waved and smiled as I, once again, navigated the side to side motion of the bridge, noting some planks that needed to be replaced very soon.

"Hi Jim," Carolyn said as I came up to her, "This is Michael, a leader in the local Native American community." She nodded towards Michael as she spoke and I reached out to shake hands. Michael had a very soft handshake, something I had noticed with a few Native American men I had met. I made a mental note to ask a question around this later.

"Welcome, Michael," I said as we shook hands.

"Thanks, Jim. Can we walk to some possible places for this lodge Carolyn tells me about?"

Quick and to the point with his question. "Sure, let's begin with a location I saw today as I walked. I think it has all Carolyn mentioned and it is off the trail, so will not attract as many curiosity seekers."

And so we headed down the river on the side opposite the main hiking trail. We pushed through some high grasses and reached the spot I had seen just a few minutes before. The location was on the banks of the river just above a bend in its course. It was up about four feet above the water's channel and was less prone to flooding. There were five big trees screening it from obvious view from both the trail and the fields beside it. And high grass all around. Down below it, and just visible, across some marshy ground stood the old Rigden farmstead. There was an abundance of round river rocks in the water at this location – the type Carolyn had said were needed for heating for the ceremony. I now also saw, as I looked around, a large amount of old deadfall, which would provide firewood for some time.

"I think this has what you need and some privacy as I said," I repeated as we neared the site.

"This looks great Jim," Carolyn beamed. "Are you sure the University will not complain?"

"I suspect they won't even be aware it's here for a long time. We still remain one of CSU's and Fort Collin's best kept secrets," I replied.

"Yes, this is good land. The energy is strong. It welcomes what we wish to do," Michael said softly as he quietly and smoothly walked across the ground. "This is a really good thing you are doing. Many thanks Jim."

"I am doing what the University asked in bringing in more users and groups Michael. But thank you."

"May we begin constructing the lodge soon Jim?" Carolyn asked.

"Whenever you are ready. We need to talk more about how we keep people away from the area until they are invited and where the various pieces will be – fire, lodge and so forth. I will need this for the report I give our department," I answered.

Carolyn and I discussed all the aspects we could think of over the next couple of weeks. And Michael told me he felt we need a medicine man to pour the water in the rock people's lodge (inipi or sweat lodge) who would be open to non-native people being invited to some lodges or other ceremonies. This would help with University acceptance of what we would create here. I totally agreed and left it up to he and Carolyn to bring who was needed.

We agreed on a day the building would begin. Here is my writing from the past about this building and my first lodge.

7 | First Sweat Lodge/ White Man Bakes

My first joining in a Sweat Ceremony—Rock People's Lodge—is over. I did not terminally embarrass myself, pass out from the heat, or inadvertently say something only an insensitive white man would utter. These, and other similar worries, were my big concerns going in. What I came out with is a sense of inner peace and calm—and a connection with my own spirituality—I have not felt in years. This doesn't mean I am comfortable of my acceptance at future ceremonies. Nor do I feel I have any large portion of understanding of what a Sweat means to a Native Indian, or might mean to me. I do know a new cultural awareness, and a kernel of understanding at a very basic level, had sprouted.

Over the years I have traveled a lot, met people of many cultures, worked and played with them and been invited to ceremonial events. I have never been very nervous about attending any of these. This past lack of nervousness may be because I knew the people well, may be because I grew up mingling with people of many cultures back East near Philadelphia, or maybe because the interactions were in other parts of the world, far from home. Today, for whatever reasons, I was nervous about attending a Sweat; a new feeling for me. I did not know these people, or their culture, well. (Hell, I still don't know if I should say Native American or American Indian or Indian.)

I was also worried my invitation was just a 'political nicety', or necessity. I run the Center and had offered the land to house the Sweat Lodge. This Center, the Environmental Learning Center, a 206 acre nature preserve, and the organizations to which some of the Indians involved with the Sweat Lodge belonged, the Native American Student Association and Student Services, are both part of Colorado State University. My concerns about a political invite were due to the fact that State Universities are political beasts.

The people composing our organizations had begun working together, sporadically, on educational projects two years before the Sweat Lodge was discussed. We had begun doing so because there was a long Native American history on the lands of the Center. Indians of many Nations had lived within its boundaries for generations before the arrival of European settlers. Spiritual sites, like the Council Tree, where meetings and ceremonies attended by many Nations were held in the past, also dot its landscape. The Poudre River, lifeblood to Indian and white cultures throughout the area's history and into its present, also snakes its way through the land. With these, and other, interconnections between Native American peoples and the land of the Center, when a Sweat Lodge was requested, I enthusiastically approved it. Land was chosen for the Lodge's location by Native American spiritual leaders, and plans for its construction were discussed. A week before the first Sweat, several staff members of the Center had offered their help to clear the land and build the Lodge, including myself.

I SHOWED UP EARLY on the chosen construction day and found many Indian people already at work. I knew a few of them slightly, but most not at all. Some of the workers noticed my presence as I approached the site, but no one said anything. I wasn't sure how to proceed— didn't know what was correct. Do I go on in and introduce myself, or wait for someone to approach me? Luckily, as I hesitated, Carolyn Fiscus, Director of Native American Student Services, whom I knew, arrived.

"Hi, Jim. Thanks for joining us. Come meet some people," Carolyn smiled at me.

My sense of feeling out of place receded as I walked into the site with her. Carolyn introduced me to several people, discussed what we would do, and left me to work with Michael, a leader of the local Indian community.

Michael and I chatted for a moment, and then he gave me work instructions. The people around me were talking about the Lodge, an upcoming Pow-Wow, and the frybread someone would bring later. With my Italian heritage, and Mediterranean derived olive complexion, I have never felt very 'Anglo' when working with people of other cultures; even when working with the Garifunda people of Belize, a race with African roots. But today I felt very 'white'—very 'other culture'. Soon, as I got into the work of clearing the land and carrying river rocks to the site, my feeling of otherness lessened.

Just as my back started to whine from hauling too many rocks, Lyman Yellowhair, the religious leader of the Sweat, arrived and Carolyn called me over to meet him. Lyman was not an imposing man physically (middle aged, average height, long, graying hair, and dressed for work like the rest of us), but a presence of teacher (?), healer (?) seemed to be cloaked about him.

"Jim, this is Lyman Yellowhair. Lyman has agreed to be our religious leader. He will be making offerings as we build today and leading the Sweats later. Lyman, Jim is the person who has given us this land to use."

Lyman smiled as he spoke, his voice soft, but compelling, "Nice to meet you. This Sweat will be of great value to the Indian community. It's good that it can be here. The Indian people of Fort Collins have looked for a site for a long time without success. Thanks for giving us this place."

So much for my white stereotypes of Indian 'medicine men'—regal, stoic, physically large, stern...ad infinitum. I couldn't help but think of the Catholic priests of my own childhood as Lyman spoke. The same cadence, the same inner comfort his voice generated in me.

"Good to meet you, Lyman. Thanks for the kind words, but this land is not mine, or anyone else's to give. None of us own it, your people or mine. Hopefully we all can use it and take care of it."

Damn! I sounded, at least to myself, like a political hack, spouting politically correct verbal hash—even though I meant every word.

I quickly knew I didn't need to worry about my little speech as Lyman began to laugh, turning to Carolyn, "I thought you said he wasn't an Indian!"

Carolyn laughed back, "Maybe it's rubbing off already."

Lyman turned back to me, "Jim, let me tell you about the Sweat Lodge."

Carolyn went back to work as Lyman walked me around the site, telling me about the layout of the lodge, the fire pit and the altar. He made clear to me that this Sweat would be built by his tribes' ways; other tribes constructed their lodges differently. I began to build a personal understanding of what I had only read in the past: There was no one Indian culture or set of beliefs, but many Indian cultures and ways. I was learning as we went, having my Indian myths, thankfully, clobbered. After a while Lyman went off to his work, and I began gathering firewood.

As we took a rest break and drank a ritual Indian drink—Diet Pepsi—some of the Indian people spoke with me, while others had little to say. It dawned on me that some of them were probably as unsure about what to talk to me about as I was with them. Maybe some thought I did not belong here. I hoped that was the minority. Whatever the mix of pro and anti white people, I continued to feel less out of place. The sweat on my back dried quickly in the cold air, and I relaxed both physically and mentally. As we pulled ourselves back to our feet, another Indian walked in. Back rushed my mental stereotypes.

The newcomer was tall and thin, with long, straight, black hair and a ramrod posture. He wasn't smiling, in fact, appeared stern. He was young, I guessed early thirties, but had the demeanor of someone older. His facial structure was definitely Indian; to me more so than most of the other Indian people present. At least my white man idea of

Indian. If I met him anywhere I would know before we spoke that he was Native American. As someone who, by my appearance, is always picked out on sight as Italian-American, I was sure this man also knew his impact on people. This was the only pre-meeting common ground I felt with him. His 'presence' had immediately captured my attention, and cranked up my 'feeling white' quotient again. People began calling out "Hello, Lawrence," so I knew this was Lawrence Little Thunder, President of the Native American Student Association.

Lawrence nodded to the group, may have said one word I missed, and surveyed the scene and the people. He walked over to Lyman, shook hands, said a few words, and then walked to the clearing that had been made for the Lodge. He carefully considered the Lodge site, the firepit, and the river behind it. Carolyn and Lyman joined him and they all spoke. Even as I was doing my job, gathering wood, I watched them closely, interested in what they were doing. I admit I was also fascinated by the picture these three Indian people painted against the backdrop of the land their people had inhabited for so many generations. Time, past and present, folded together in my mind, and became one. This current use of the site made perfect sense, fit into the environment, and was as much a part of this land as were the trees and the animals on it.

With a rush of awareness I woke up to the fact that my attention to these people's business, and my mental musings, might be obvious, and considered rude. I quickly shifted focus to my firewood; glancing around, fearful people would be pointing accusing fingers at me. No fingers were pointing; no looks saying 'insensitive lout' met my glance. In fact, the only one who seemed concerned about his demeanor was me. Everyone else was going about their chores; smiling, laughing, grimacing, swearing—depending on the type and intensity of the job. Damn those old movies and books about Native Americans and improper-proper behavior with 'the People'! The rush of blood infusing my face began to recede to its proper channels.

Mentally chastising myself for my stupidity, I put my concentration and energies into the work at hand. As I yanked some dead cottonwood limbs toward the firepit for cutting, Carolyn called out to me, "Jim, can you come over here for a minute?"

"Be right there," I called back as I wrestled my load into position. I wiped my hands down my jeans and started over to the group of three now by the river. As I was walking to them, someone by the Lodge site called to Lyman for advice. He left, leaving Carolyn and Lawrence waiting for me.

"Jim, have you met Lawrence Little Thunder?" Carolyn asked as I drew near.

"No, I haven't," I responded.

"Lawrence is President of the Native American Student Association on campus," Carolyn spelled out as I reached them.

"Nice to meet you Lawrence," I said as I reached out my hand. He took my hand with a firm, short shake, looked me straight in the eyes, didn't smile, and said, "Hi." I had had my first impressions of Lawrence from a distance and now had my impressions as we met to meld with them: a man of few words—and a Native American who did not want, and had no time for, white people here at the Sweat Lodge. He probably would be happy to have this white man roasting over the fire he was to build here shortly. I wasn't sure what to say next; as I felt Lawrence was studying or judging me. Things to say did come to mind. Unreal things generated by Lawrence's contemplation of me like, "Hi, I'm a white man" or "George Armstrong Custer was never one of my heroes," as well as slightly more realistic comments like, "I'm really not here because I'm a political ass" flashed through the paths of my brain. Carolyn came to my rescue again.

"Jim runs the Center and is the person who has worked with us to get this site."

"Thanks, this is a good site," Lawrence said sincerely, but still with no real emotion I could read. "I need to work on the firepit, thanks again," Lawrence said as he moved away. Our words were few, and I was still sure he had no need for a white man here, but I sensed an honesty and straightforwardness from Lawrence I appreciate in people. I liked him immediately. As he walked away, Carolyn and I also returned to our tasks.

I continued to cut, haul and chop as the morning wore on. Other non-Indian people from my staff at the ELC arrived, so I was no longer the only white worker. By now it didn't matter to me, as I was now comfortable with what I was doing and where I was. After a few hours we had cleared the land, cut and stacked firewood, piled river rocks and dug the firepit and Lodge pit; it was time to begin building the Lodge.

Lyman explained to the non-Indians what he was doing as he cut one inch diameter willow saplings to build the frame. The Lodge is round, a spiritual shape for Native Americans and would be formed using the saplings tied with sinew. Twelve holes were made in the ground, in a circular pattern, using a pointed stick. Tobacco was then put in one hole, and a prayer said. This was done at each hole. The sapling ends were put in the holes, then bent two at a time to the center, where they were tied together with the tough sinew. Other willow saplings were then woven through the uprights, parallel to the ground from bottom to top, for support. Over this frame were layered blankets, and a sapling holding blankets put in place as a door. Lyman told us buffalo hides were the traditional covering, but were very expensive and difficult to get now. A small, round altar was lined with river rocks between the Lodge and the firepit. The door faced the altar and firepit behind it, all facing west to the setting sun. We were told other tribes face their Lodges east, to the rising sun; a matter of tribal custom. By mid-afternoon the work was done and we sat with food brought by family members, along with more Pepsi.

Lyman and Lawrence came and sat with me on a log by the firepit. We unwrapped our food while making appropriate 'pained fatigue' noises like 'woo' and 'ah'. "I'm ready for this food," Lyman said as he tore into his frybread and cheese, "It could be animal droppings and taste good."

Lawrence and I laughed and agreed. "When do you want to hold the first Sweat?" Lyman asked of Lawrence.

"Next Sunday would be good if you can come," Lawrence answered.

"Sunday is good. We will start to heat the rocks at four," Lyman agreed around his food.

"Jim, you have been a big help to us getting this land and helping us build," Lawrence said turning to me. "Why don't you come and Sweat with us?"

"That's a good idea," Lyman chimed in.

Talk about total surprise. The man who I thought found me unwelcome here building the Sweat just invited me to his people's first ceremony. Well, my Indian myths had taken a shot through the heart today, so my belief in my ability to judge people's opinions might as well take a fall, too.

My thoughts raced through practical considerations as I debated my answer. Didn't I read that Indians Sweat naked? As a middle-aged man, with a waistline that has expanded over the years, I can't say this appealed to me at all. My experiences doing things naked, especially with a group of people, had a very short life span during my long-haired, fringed coat, hippie days of the 60's. I wasn't comfortable then— I would certainly be totally uncomfortable now. On top of that, it was cold and supposed to get colder by next Sunday. But, if the price I had to pay to attend the ceremony was to strip down with a group of men and go into the Lodge, shivering in the cold air—so be it. At least it was dark and warm, during the ceremony.

There really was no decision, I knew my answer as soon as they asked, "I'd love to come, if you are sure that it's okay for me to be there."

"Of course it's okay. You are welcome. It's good for both peoples when we sweat together," Lawrence answered back.

"Good!" Lyman smiled at me, "Come at four and see how we heat the rocks."

I was feeling honored at being invited, and looking forward to this new experience.

Deborah Waudena, who I knew from past projects, was sitting off to the side of us. She heard my answer and came over. "You've been a big help. I'm glad you are Sweating with us."

Did I hear her right? This was a coed ceremony?! I was stripping with men and women? My angst went up, my stomach down.

"Thanks, Deborah. I'm honored to be invited." I hoped my smile wasn't as thin as it felt. I noticed Michael, eating off to our other side, had a Cheshire cat grin on his face. Was this related to my discomfort or was I getting paranoid?

Deborah walked over to Michael to talk about the Sweat as Lyman, Lawrence and I sat finishing our lunch. I mentally jerked and squirmed over the dress code for next Sunday, but I couldn't think of a good way to bring up the matter. Please, let one of my Indian myths hold true—let loincloths be worn at ceremonies.

Finally I spoke up, "What should I bring on Sunday?"

"Bring a towel. It's hot during the sweat, but cold when you come out," Lyman answered me.

Damn, nothing about clothes, or the lack thereof.

Everyone seemed content with all that had been accomplished at the site, but it had been a long day and we were all drained. We policed the site, trudged back to the storage sheds dragging tools behind us, said our good-byes, slumped behind the wheels of our cars, and headed home.

My body ached and my limbs felt like whales, but I felt good about all I had learned, the people I had met, and the expanded cultural partnership begun at our Center. If I could just squash the picture stamped on my mind's canvas of this middle-aged white guy standing naked at an Indian ceremony, shriveled in embarrassment, this would rank as a great day.

I went out to the Center early the next morning to present a nature program to Cub Scouts and found Rob, an ELC staffer who lives on-site, downing a steaming coffee by the picnic pavilion. Rob had worked with the group on the Sweat Lodge the day before, so I walked over to compare impressions.

"Hey, Rob. Did you sleep well after yesterday?" I asked in greeting.

"Not bad, it was a long day. I'm glad everything got finished, I need to study today and couldn't have helped again."

Like most of us, Rob wears many hats at CSU: He is a graduate student, works in a computer lab and is ELC staff and site management.

"Yeah, I know," I answered back, "I have a list of things I have to get done today. I hope I can squeeze in the football game."

Rob got animated, "You mean the Dallas-Philadelphia game? I'm going to break for that! Why don't you come back and we'll watch it later."

"No, I meant the Philadelphia-Dallas game," I joked back (my team-his team), "I'll try. I'd like to. It would be fun to watch you squirm as we pound you guys. I'll call you by noon."

"Good, but it won't be me doing the squirming," Rob laughed at me.

Talking about squirming gave me the perfect chance to bring up what was, I admit, the other reason I wanted to chat with Rob. Rob was an easygoing guy, in his mid-twenties, who had grown up on a ranch in (as he says) the middle of nowhere—New Mexico. We got along well, and talked often, so I knew I could quiz him on the Sweat.

"Rob, were you, or other ELC people, invited to the Sweat next Sunday?" I asked.

"Yeah, Lyman asked me, and I think a couple of others," Rob replied.

Great, now it was Indian men and women, and people who worked for me at this skin ceremony. It was definitely time to find out the dress code. My fear was still that it was either informal—naked, or formal—with shoes. I hoped Rob knew. It might determine whether I attended or had to take a two-day business trip to Tibet.

"How do we dress for this?" I asked, in what I hoped was a matter-of-fact, off-handed way.

"Just swimsuits and towels for the guys, and nightgown-type things for the women," Rob answered easily, not knowing he had just lifted the Great Wall of China from my back. "Did you know that historically only Indian men Sweated?" Rob continued, "And that the whole ceremony was done naked, even in the middle of winter?

Lyman was telling me. But this is the 90's, and he said he thought Indians should adapt so women, and non-Indians, could participate comfortably at some of the Sweats. That's what he's doing at this one. He may lead some future Sweats traditionally."

"No, I didn't know any of that," I said, "I just realized I hadn't given any thought to how we dress," I continued, lying through my teeth, sure my nose was growing an inch a minute. "I'm glad you found out more than I did. Anything else we need to know?"

"I didn't know how to dress either, so I just asked Lyman. I don't think we need to know anything else, just show up and listen." Rob ended on a practical note.

While I had worried and stressed over the 'nakedness' issue, and my inability of finding a 'proper way' to ask about this aspect of Sweat protocol, Rob had "just asked Lyman." What a great reality check! Rob had, with a few words, reminded me the only incorrect, or stupid, questions were the unasked ones. I have been an adherent of that tenet for years, often reminding groups I spoke to that they could ask any questions at all and then had forgotten the principle myself. Well, it wasn't something I'd forget again as I interacted with our Indian partners.

SWEAT SUNDAY WAS cold—biting cold. There was a two-inch cover of icy, glittering snow on the ground and even at midday, the air flowed articly over any patches of exposed skin. At three, I donned my beachtime swimsuit under heavy jeans, tugged my insulated Penn State sweatshirt over my dense flannel shirt, and tied my winter hiking boots over two pairs of thermal socks. Glancing at myself in my bathroom mirror, the Michelin tire boy instantly came to mind; but at least I would be warm before and after the Sweat.

Grabbing my largest, thickest towel I waddled out to my Jeep, shoehorned myself behind the wheel and headed out to my indoctrinary Sweat—fervently hoping most, or all, of the ceremony outside of the Lodge would occur around a blazing fire.

A pick-up truck with a dream catcher hanging from the mirror and a Chevy sedan with a feathered staff laying across the front seat were the only vehicles in the Center's parking lot when I arrived. There was not the usual contingent of bikes, cars and vans present that deposit the hikers, birders and photographers who normally populate the Center on weekends. The cold must have kept them home next to their fireplace, watching the Broncos battle the Raiders. Hopefully, the Sweat participants that the truck and car had delivered had the fire dancing in the firepit. I pulled my Jeep next to the truck, rummaged under the driver's seat for my pair of rabbit-lined gloves, picked up my towel, mournfully turned off the engine with its associated heater, and stepped out.

Here in Fort Collins we don't get a lot of cold, biting weather, or ice and snow in the winter even though we are at 5,000 feet elevation. This Front Range area of the Rockies is somehow protected from much of the weather that pounds the high country just behind us to the West by those same mountains and by the plains to our East. The worse of the winter storms seem to skip over us after exiting the mountains and land out on the Nebraska plains. I'm sure the meteorologists have scientific explanations for this; I just know the effect—we miss the worse of it. Not so today: The wind is beginning to pick up, the mercury must be dropping quickly and more importantly to me, it's damn cold: The sun, partially cloud impaired, has not even set yet. Keeping on the move will be important today, so I start walking over to the river where the trail to the Lodge begins.

Playful gusts of wind smack me in the face and neck, my two body parts most exposed to their attack. Even in my carefully constructed personal cocoon I am already cold and shivering. I unfurl my towel and twist it around my neck to block one port of entry to the frigid air. I think of an historic line from my own culture as I cross the unprotected open ground to the river trail, "Caesar, we who are about to die, salute you." The only problem with this line in relation to todays' experience is its context: These words were shouted to Caesar by the gladiators as they went into battle in the arena, and I did not feel like a gladiator eyeing his enemy, but more like a human sacrifice approaching the abyss.

Mentally leaving ancient Rome as I turn up the river trail, prickly seeming snow crystals crunching underfoot, my mind searching for anything to stop it from considering the climatically unpleasant present, lands in my own past, I walked on. Father O'Malley, an ancient, stoop shouldered, tradition confined, Irish priest from my boyhood Parish slowly stands up in my memory. Father O'Malley was a good man, with an obvious mission to 'tend his flock' in a fashion that made it possible for all of his sheep to be herded to Heavens' Gate. His thick Irish accent and mild manner made him the stuff of priestly stereotypes. His one big fault, in my opinion, which I did not understand until I was much older, was a product of his time and upbringing—there was no church but the Catholic Church, no God but the Catholic God.

This all remembered, I could hear Father speak to me of today's weather woes, "Ah Jimmy, sure to be this cold and wind are God's penance for your attending this pagan ritual. You forget my son; God will have no false idols before him. The eternal fires of Hell await those who leave the path of the Holy Church and the Holy Father in Rome. Pray with me and return to the teachings of the one true Church."

I hadn't thought of Father, or the beliefs he typified, in many years. For me religion and spirituality had long ago become a personal matter, but my musings on Father reminded me we all have some grounding in our past, even as our beliefs change and evolve. It also reminded me to show proper respect as I entered my Indian acquaintances 'church'.

My left foot slides back and my body lurches forward as I jerk to the present tripping over a snow-hidden root on the trail. I do an unaesthetic dance step as I catch myself before I drop. So much for reminiscing, I need to watch my footwork on the icy path. As I near the Sweat site I can see a thin line of smoke escaping the clutching fingers of the winter naked branches of the Cottonwood trees around it. My spirits lift knowing the fire is started, even if it's still in its infancy. One more thought comes as I approach the turn-off to the Sweat Lodge: I'm going to be a comic sight to the Indians present, wrapped in my layers of coverings, while they with their cultural background and innate ability to withstand the extremes of nature, will be standing around in swimsuits with a blanket or ceremonial robe, draped over their shoulders. Not this time, Jimbo. Italians all have big noses and can sing; Indians are all stoics and can stand the weather. No cultural myths or Hollywood visions win this round! They will be just as cold as this non-Native American boy; some, like Lawrence, who must weigh 60 pounds less than me, probably much colder. I smile inwardly, (it's too cold to actually do it and expose my gums), as I turn in to the site.

Lyman comes up to me as I arrive, ceremonial robe draped over his shoulders. His robe, however, covers thick clothing. He is as enshrined in thermal-ware as I am. Gotcha, myths!

"Welcome, Jim. It's a fine day for a Sweat," Lyman greets me.

"Thanks for the welcome, but I think you're way off base on the values of the day," I answer Lyman as we shake hands. Lawrence, who looks like he gained forty pounds with his coverings, comes over from the firepit and joins us.

"Glad you came. I thought the weather might stop people," Lawrence says as we shake.

"I can't say I didn't consider it, but I think I have on enough warm clothes to survive," I reply.

"We need to prepare," Lawrence tells me as he turns back to building up the fire in the pit. Lyman begins to set a painted buffalo skull on the altar and rams feathered staffs in the ground to each side of it. I stand to the side near the fire and watch, unsure if I should do anything. Twenty-eight river rocks are placed in the fire and covered with more firewood.

Reminding myself to ask questions, I toss out, "What can I do to help?" I'm told to bring some wood closer to the fire. This doesn't take me long, and soon I am standing by the fire again. Feeling a bit like a fifth wheel, I'm getting ready to ask what I can do next as others begin to arrive. Over the next hour, the day's participants have all gathered: Twelve Native Americans and four ELC non-Native Americans.

Those of us from the Center get no directions, so we stand near the fire and discuss what we should do. "Let's gather more wood so we're not just standing around," the ever-practical Rob suggests. The fire was growing rapidly, and the firewood pile shrinking in response, so his plan made sense.

"Should we gather more wood, Lyman?" I call over to him.

"Yeah, that's good, we'll need more for the rocks and more for us," Lyman calls back, so we head off into the trees around us.

I am working the area to the south of the Lodge, pulling deadfall free from its capturing vines, banging the pieces on the ground to knock off the leeching pieces of snow and ice, and piling them off to the side. After I have a fair sized pile of limbs, I lean them against a tree one-at-a-time, and stomp them into burnable-sized lengths. I'm breathing heavy in the cold air as I work, burning my lungs, but at least I'm stoking a spreading inner fire that warms me. I re-stack the wood and encircle the first load to bring to the fire in my arms.

The firewood pile, re-growing as others bring in more wood, is stacked on the north side of the firepit. I approach from the south side, juggling lengths of wood that feel like they are wiggling trying to escape their fate, and begin to cross to the pile between the altar and the firepit.

"Don't walk there!" several strident voices call out at once. I stop dead, dropping the two liveliest pieces of wood. What was going on? Was I going to step on something I couldn't see through my bundle? I lower my load for a better view as Lyman walks over.

"Jim, walk around behind the fire." I turn and do as I am instructed, add my burden to the pile, and start to stand, feeling totally confused. "Jim, we never walk between the Lodge and the fire once the altar is set. We walk around behind the Lodge, or the other way, around the fire," Lyman explains as he follows me over.

"Sorry, Lyman," I apologize as I straighten up, "I meant no offense, but no one told me that. I'm afraid my knowledge of Native

American customs is really thin. You'll have to tell me what I need to know."

"No problem," Lyman returns, "You couldn't know that. We just reacted when you headed that way. I'll talk about the Sweat and our customs, before we begin."

My first mistake made, I went back to work. I was sorry I had goofed, but I can't say I felt too bad about it—I couldn't be expected to know what I was never told. I was sure our group of non-Indians would make more inadvertent errors, but Lyman's attitude seemed to indicate he expected that and we would learn from them.

By six the fire roared skyward, and the river rocks set throughout its embers glowed like molten rubies. "It's time," Lyman said simply, and everyone came to the fire. "I'm going to talk about the purpose of the Sweat, and what will occur during the ceremony, for our non-Indian friends here tonight," Lyman explained to all. "First, let's prepare ourselves. Men take off all but their swim trunks, women all but their nightdress. Keep your towels with you, you will need them as we Sweat."

A small tent had been set up to the side and some people took turns changing in it. Others, like myself, had their swim trunks entombed as their bottom layer of clothing. Those of us in that condition went into the trees along the river and began to strip down, hanging our things from branches or folding them over a tree trunk.

I have never undressed so quickly, dancing in step as I peel off my layers. The wind, surely laughing at my insanity, whips up enormous goose bumps on each newly exposed piece of my flesh. The last step was taking off my shoes and socks. "This is nuts" I think, as I yank them off and quickly stand up on the snow before I lose my nerve. Then I run back to the fire, shivering, shaking and sputtering like a car with 200,000 miles under its wheels. I have never felt a fire feel this good. With my towel wrapped over my shoulders, I stand as close as possible without actually walking into the pyre, stepping from foot-to-foot and turning from front to back, trying to gain some warmth. I wonder if this is how Indian ceremonial dances got started.

As we wait for everyone to re-gather around the fire, I ask Lyman, "Lyman, the Sweat Lodge is pretty small. Does it get really hot in there? I'm not a big sauna person."

"No, don't worry, I don't run a hot Sweat. If will get warm, but not too bad. Use your towel on your head if you feel too hot," he answers me with a serious, concerned expression. By now the rest have arrived back at the fire, 'dancing' much like me. "I am going to make the blessing to the Four Corners now with tobacco," Lyman says as he digs into a small, leather pouch by the buffalo skull. He holds the tobacco to the North, South, East and West, one at a time, and says some words in his native tongue. He scatters the tobacco to each direction as he finishes. Next he holds up the buffalo skull to the heavens.

"The buffalo has great meaning for us," he explains, "It provided us with food and clothing in the past and so we honor it at our gathering here tonight."

As with the tobacco, he raises it to the four corners and prays at each stop. "I will sing an ancient song of my people and then we will purify ourselves with cedar smoke and enter the Lodge," Lyman continues to explain as he replaces the skull on the altar. "The Sweat is a ceremony of my people meant to help you cleanse your body and your mind, get in touch with your spiritual being, and pray to your Great Spirit. We will enter the Lodge from the North, women first. They will move around the Lodge pit and sit along the South wall. Then the men will enter and sit along the North wall. I will come in last and say a prayer. Seven rocks will be brought in, one-at-a-time, by the fire tender. He will circle around the Lodge with each rock, and pass it in from the South. Each rock, in turn, will have cedar and sage put on it and a blessing made. When the seven rocks are all in, we will close the door and I will pour the water. As I do this we will pray and sing together. After twenty or thirty minutes we will open the door, let the air cool and bring in seven more rocks. There will be four doors, so that in the last there will be twenty-eight rocks in the pit. When we close the door the second time, I will lead a prayer and then each person may speak, or pray, in turn as he or she wishes. You do not need to speak aloud if you do not wish to. This will continue through the third door. The fourth door will be a time of prayer and singing together. If it gets too hot you can ask to leave at the end of any door. After the four doors we will all come out and pass the pipe around the fire. After that, we will eat and talk."

Lyman went to the fire and began gathering embers into a can. I walked over to Michael and asked about the food. "Guests usually bring food to the Sweat. We thought you would bring some," Michael filled me in, "Didn't anyone tell you?" Unfortunately, no one had told us and we hadn't brought any. My mind cranked quickly for a solution.

"How about if we all go to Old Chicago for pizza afterwards. We'll treat," I ask Michael.

"Yeah, that's great," Michael agrees.

I was now sure we needed to open a better dialogue between our groups so there was nothing else we didn't know, or were not told, in the future. Nothing some quick communication wouldn't solve. I was thinking maybe we were embarrassed to ask about, and they were embarrassed to bring up their expectations of us, as Lyman bent to pick up a fan of eagles' feathers from the altar.

He held the feathers in one hand and the smoking can in the other as he fanned the smoke over himself telling us, "I am now purifying myself for the Sweat. I will also purify each of you before you enter."

We entered the Lodge as proscribed, the rocks were brought in and blessed and the door was closed. Sage was passed to each of us as Lyman led a prayer. After his prayer we were all instructed to rub the sage on our bodies to cleanse it and then put it on the rocks. As we lay the sage on the blood red stones the air filled with their burning fragrance. Lyman then poured water over the rocks as he prayed. Dense, aromatic steam quickly filled the Lodge.

"We give thanks to the Grandfather for letting us meet and pray together tonight," Lyman began. "We thank the spirits for their blessings and guidance and for these friends who join us tonight," he continued. "Now we will pray together and then I will chant. Any can join as they wish," he explained to us.

After the prayers and two chants Lyman spoke to us again, "This is a good place for our Sweat. It is on the banks of a river. That is a spiritual place for us and a place we need for the stones. It is also in a natural area and our people value nature." Sounds of approval from the participants greeted Lyman's words as he spoke. He continued, "We thank our friends with the ELC for offering this place and will hold them in our prayers tonight. Jim, will you say some words for the Center?"

Whoops, I didn't know I was supposed to speak. "We are honored by your friendship and by being invited as your guests here tonight. Having the Sweat Lodge here is very important to us. Those of us who work at the Center believe the environment is made up of nature and the people of an area combined. Working with your groups has helped us learn another way of seeing things, while we add a part of the culture back to this land that had been lost. You have our thanks." I was pleased to hear the same sounds of approval as I spoke. Lyman poured more water and fresh clouds of steam billowed up.

We were only ten minutes into the Sweat, but streams of my own sweat already cascaded off of me. Talk about extremes; from almost frozen to death outside the Lodge to sautéed during the ceremony. What had Lyman told me with a straight face? "I don't run a hot Sweat." He had had his fun; any hotter and I would dissolve into a viscous pool like Oz's Wicked Witch of the West! He was right about one thing—I was praying. I was praying he would get on with the ceremony so we could throw the door flap up and let some breathable air in. At this point, I didn't know if I could even make it through the second door.

"I will pour the water again and we will sit with our thoughts a few minutes before I open the door," Lyman broke into my revere with.

I quickly tossed my towel over my head, breathing through its fleece, as he again tipped water on the rocks. More steam and more heat jumped out of the pit. I prayed some more, "Please let me live through this time in the boiling pot and I swear I will never boil a lobster again."

After a few minutes Lyman called to the firetender to open the door. The flap went up and cold, sweet air snuck in as roiling clouds of steam raced out.

We all sat flushed, hair and skin matted by sweat and steam, and chatted for a few minutes while we cooled off. I wanted to stay—and I wanted to leave. I finally decided to go at least one more door.

Lyman called out, "Bring in the rocks," and the firetender began to bring in the second set of seven. Again the door was closed and Lyman poured the water as he prayed.

"I will begin the prayers and then Michael beside me will go next. We will move around the lodge from there," Lyman told us as the steam gathered anew. "I will sing to The Great Spirit softly in the background as others speak. You may speak or pray as you like, or ask the others to pray for you or someone else," Lyman continued, finishing his explanation. Lyman began his prayer, asking for peace and healing for all people and for Mother Earth, the sustainer of us all. He spoke of personal problems and the spiritual help ceremonies like this gave him to conquer them. His words were intense and heartfelt and I was moved to examine my spiritual self as he spoke. As he finished he began to chant softly, pouring more water, and Michael began his words.

As the turn to speak came around to me, my words came with little thought. I spoke of my wishes and desires for people to find a harmony with nature. I spoke of how ceremonies like this helped people of different cultures find an understanding of each other. I asked the others to pray with me for my sister who was ill. I spoke until I knew I was done. Those before me had been honest and open and I had done the same, feeling good that I had shared with all present. Each took their turn around the circle as Lyman chanted and poured.

It was even hotter than the first door and I panted to drag air into my lungs, but my physical discomfort didn't stop me from being deeply moved and at peace with myself as I listened and prayed. Many of us spoke for quite a while, making it a long door. Finally, Lyman called a pause as Deborah finished speaking and asked the firetender to open the door.

I wanted to stay for the final two doors, but the effects of the heat were winning out over my wishes. I was feeling light-headed and my stomach churned. I had not eaten since breakfast, a mistake I would not make again if I was invited to another Sweat. My disc damaged back was also nastily making its presence felt, causing spasms down my legs. I asked Lyman's permission to leave the Lodge, which he gave.

Stepping out I gingerly entered the frigid air, waiting for its polar swat, but I couldn't even feel its icy grip with my body temperature so elevated. Steam poured off of my body as I began to cool down. I must have looked like an alien from a B grade 1950's science fiction movie. I pulled on my jeans, sweatshirt and shoes and told the firetender I needed to walk and stretch my legs, but would be back soon to help with the fire.

I STARTED OFF AT a bold pace with snow on the ground, toward the suspension bridge that allowed access over the Poudre River to the Center's wildlife preserve. I was still hot and sweating as I looked up at the bulbous full moon breaking free of the clouds. It really was an incredibly beautiful night, especially now that my super-heated body eliminated the cold as a negative factor for me.

A Blue Heron, our Center's symbol, took off from the riverbank and arched over my head as I neared the bridge. I watched him majestically wing his way to the top of a cottonwood tree as I crossed the river. I was now in the nave of my personal church; alone, under the stars, with nature all around me. A Great Horned Owl eerily hooted from his tree perch to my east as I struck out along the trail. I have always felt good about owls and enjoyed seeing or hearing them, maybe because of their storybook representations I was exposed to as a child. But I would not mention this well-sighted raptor when I returned to the Sweat. Different animals or acts of nature were signs to Native Americans, both good and bad. I had been warned of this sign—owls were a harbinger of death for Lawrence's tribe. I was glad I read owls differently than Lawrence so I could enjoy his call and not worry about its meaning.

After a brisk twenty minutes of walking I decided to head back to the Sweat. I startled a small herd of whitetail deer drinking from the river as I retraced my steps, making me wish I had more time to hike, and promising myself I would return tomorrow night to pick up where I left off.

The rocks for the fourth door were being brought into the Lodge as I arrived. Everyone was glad to see me, fearing I had passed out on the trails. I told them I was fine, but would not push my luck by re-entering the Lodge. I would stay outside and help tend the fire. The door closed as I gathered some branches to feed the flames. The rocks were all in the Lodge now, so the firetender and I didn't have to move them around, keeping them crackling hot. Our only job was to keep the fire stoked high for the duration of the ceremony. We listened to the chants and prayers coming from inside the Lodge and communed within ourselves, feeling no need to speak. After thirty minutes or so, Lyman called for the firetender to open the door and again the flap was thrown up.

I had donned my coat when I returned to the Lodge since my steam-induced temperature had dropped drastically again. Now the others would have their chance to cool down in the brittle air. Everyone came out, one-at-a-time, their bodies pumping steam as mine had before, and gathered around the fire. Lyman picked up the feathered pipe from the altar and began to stuff it with tobacco. Once full he lifted it to the four corners, saying a few words at each stop as he had done with the tobacco and buffalo skull before the Sweat. Then he lit it up with a burning twig from the fire, took a deep inhale and passed it to Lawrence on his left. It made its way around the circle as Lyman spoke about the Sweat, saying it had been a good sharing. We all thanked Lyman for leading us. Those of us new to this ceremony also thanked him for taking the time to teach us. All were invited to meet for the pizza Michael and I had discussed, and most agreed to come. The fire was burning low now and I began to spread the ashes as the others dressed.

When everyone was dressed and had gathered up their belongings we started up the trail to our cars and the food I would now welcome. I walked beside Lawrence in order to ask a few questions as we left.

"Lawrence, can we pay Lyman something for leading the ceremony tonight?" I asked.

"No, it's wrong to ever pay a holy man for his services. Some charge tourists for Sweats now, but they are shunned by us. What is customary is giving tobacco, American Spirit natural tobacco. We can also give him a few dollars for gas since he comes all the way from Denver," Lawrence answers.

"I didn't know about the tobacco, but I will give the gas money if that's okay," I respond.

"That's fine. I'm sure he will appreciate it," Lawrence replies as we drew up to the cars.

Calls of "see you at Old Chicago, bring your appetite" ring out as we load into our cars.

THIS FIRST SWEAT of mine is an experience I won't leave behind now that it's over. It re-opened wide a spiritual door in me that has been partially closed for a long while. Lyman invited me to a future Sweat over pizza, and I look forward to it with pleasure. My biggest surprise of the night was that I expected to see and learn the differences between our cultures' religions, but what I saw was how very similar, at their heart, they are. The trappings and the deities' names may be different, but the goals seem the same to me: To be at peace with yourself, your fellow people, the world and your Creator, whatever his/her name may be.

8 | What Makes Jim Tick

You know how I began my life's walk early on as I shared a short bio at the beginning of this journey. Now I feel like I need to dig into how I see myself and how I react to others, myself and situations I am in or around. It will help you understand some of the things yet to come on my road. This really makes me feel vulnerable and uneasy, even fearful. Because if I am to do this I need to be as impartial and honest as I know how.

I will relate what I believe has motivated me at different times and how I see myself now. The hardest thing anyone can write about, I believe, is themselves – especially the warts and wounds we all carry. And yet it is essential if you are trying to pass on anything you wish 'those who see' to fully understand.

When I arrived at Colorado State I came as someone who still hid a large part of who and what he was. Someone who had learned to fear letting people see too much. I had run my own businesses and learned to function as a warrior. A way I now understand I had walked in many past existences. I may visit past lives and my thoughts on them later. But, for now, I just ask you to accept that this is part of my reality. I was a strong ally of those I trusted and believed in and a fierce enemy of those who attacked my inner circle or me. I am an emotional person, and that holds through to the present. I attach strongly to people or ideas I see as true and worthwhile. This has been mis-read by some and used against me by others at times.

I quickly began to open up and use my skills and gifts at CSU, some of which you have been reading about thus far. I was so engrossed by new people and projects of worth that I forgot the word 'no'. I said 'yes' to virtually everything I was asked to take part in. My life and work became one, which is not necessarily bad if you keep balance. I did everything hard – work, play, learning, and teaching. My motor was running all the time. This continued for many years and it is only in the recent past after some life-changing events, that I have begun to address it. When I had time off from my projects and the people I worked with, Bonnie and I would go off and hike or travel. I had forgotten, all too often, how to sit and rest.

When I attracted people around me to work on some project or program my ability to read the untapped energy and skills of these people led me to evaluate them and effectively assign positions and responsibilities based on that. This was all sub-conscious then. I did not realize I was functioning in that mode. And since I drove myself hard for good causes, I expected the same from others. I allowed time for fun and rewards, but always looked to be moving on the work in front of us as quickly as possible.

Since I could see the broad picture when looking at some issue, I would share my plans to reach our goal in terms that I understood – but terms that many could not. I did not accept that anything was impossible and many times accomplished work considered impossible by others. Always with the group working together, but with me as the guiding spirit. I carefully shared responsibility and credit, but found this sometimes backfired. I believe some people felt I was giving them credit for something I had initiated or guided. This totally confused me.

As I said earlier I wanted to be liked by everyone, although I was also unaware of this at that time. And I wanted to help people, especially young people, who I saw great potential in moving ahead; sometimes faster than their spirit was ready for.

Now after going through some amazing successes and harsh attacks, I am learning to be a peaceful warrior and learning that not everything needs to be done immediately. This has helped me heal and allowed my gifts to open to new, higher levels. And has now allowed me to start sharing what I have learned – an intention I have had for many years.

My leading from the heart approach has allowed me to attract the people and resources needed for tasks and so I welcome this gift. Especially now that I moderate its functioning. And my willingness to put aside work and 'play' as a group has kept people engaged and involved with what is being worked on.

Ron, my department chair, once told a group that I lead like Abe Lincoln – from within. I know he meant it as a slur (since he had once likened his style to George S. Patton), but I took it as a huge compliment. In fact now, with all the shifts and changes about us, I see that only through the work of circles of people can anything be truly accomplished. The time of individuals carrying the load and doing most on their own is done.

When I stayed in balance and in acknowledgment that it was Great Spirit using me as a tool to accomplish work or assist someone with their healing or have a successful business, these things naturally occurred. Each time I spoke about what I had done or thought myself responsible for my successes, they fell or I was removed. This is a key learning to understand and accept. Those who do not will remain on the rollercoaster of existence.

My passion for the non-profit missions I was involved with allowed me to move them ahead to completion. My ability to see things others could not allowed me to view projects as complete before we had begun. And my connection to people and ability to attract them allowed the teams to form as needed. My emotional side permitted me to be a very good teacher and to find new ways to engage students left behind by conventional teaching methods. My personality and gifts have served me well. It is the balance I lacked before, which caused disharmony at times. Balance is an easy word to understand, but a difficult road to walk. I believe I have finally begun to achieve balance in all I do.

I am certain this is enough dissection of "Jim" by Jim. I'm sure if others were to hold the scalpel they would find me too easy on myself. Still others would chastise me for being way too hard on myself. I am, like all two-leggeds, an intricate mix of talents and skills and always, a work in progress. I am emotional, passionate, caring, giving, nurturing, creative and able to produce results: Offset by demanding, ego gripped, unsure and unforgiving. I accept them all as I look for the best balance to do what I am and do. Remember – no destination, only a journey.

Now that this section is written I can take a breath, put my clothes back on and begin to walk forward once again.

9 | Invited on the Red Road

"I went to a holy man and asked him for help. He told me to get on the Red Road. Pray to Wakan-Tanka (Great Spirit) to help you walk the Red Road."
—Dr. A.C. Ross (Ehanamani), LAKOTA

ONE MORNING HAL, WHO LED THE BELIZE PROGRAM, STOPPED BY MY office to chat. I had been doing some more fill-in teaching for Hal as my time allowed.

"Jim, can we talk about the Belize program a bit?" Hal asked.

"Sure Hal, what's up?"

"I wanted to know if you would like to lead the twelve week course with the students down there. It will move all around the country and they will be learning about the nature and the culture there," Hal answered.

Wow, I would love it. But what would Bonnie think? And my teaching and ELC commitments?

"I would love it Hal. But I have to think it through."

"Okay, we can talk later. See you."

I met with Ron and discussed the opportunity Hal had presented. He was less than pleased. I would have to sacrifice my stipend and he was concerned about the project we were involved with around the Center.

So I told Hal I couldn't do it, but suggested a graduate student in my place. Hal offered me the chance to go down and teach for three weeks out on the cayes (small islands) during the course. Perfect, this I could do.

And so I was about to go to Belize, a natural wonderland. A country which has put two-thirds of its land and water in nature preserves. I couldn't wait to get some time in down there. Little did I know I was about to meet some Belizeans who would introduce me to those who would become my Mayan teachers. And later, would lead to my Garifuna teachers — those who will teach me the healing ways of their African heritage. And these to my aborigine teachers from Australia. All a circle, all connected.

As I was preparing for the Belize trip — shots, etc. — I continued other work. I had taken on a young graduate intern for the Center and as a TA (teaching assistant) in my classes. Sharon was mid-twenties and she and her husband had just come to CSU. He was in another college of the University and she had enrolled in our college and department. I really liked her energy and passion around nature. Bonnie and I offered them the option to stay with us until they found housing, but a friend's tip provided them an apartment quickly.

This is the beginning of another lesson I have had to repeat often. As I said before, I get passionate about people, especially young people, whom I see promise and potential in. Part of my wishing to teach and 'pass on' what I have learned. This has worked well many times with learning going both ways and some good young people going out to do necessary work. At other times it worked well for a while, then all types of problems would arise and I would find myself under attack. I see now it is primarily their inner energy field and spirit I can see and know there is great promise there. I'm not always as good a judge of their maturity and intent. But, I did not know that at this time.

Sharon quickly became an asset at the Center. She had an outgoing personality and the desire to work hard at learning what she wished to know. People were drawn to her. I spent a lot of time working with her, as I did with a small handful of other students. I realized, also later on, that I also received good energy from the young people I worked with. It helped me keep up with the large volume of requests coming my way.

I continued to attend inipi ceremonies and other native ceremonies, when asked. I felt like I had found my home in these gatherings. And found my spiritual path; I listened and learned as I prayed and sang. The Pow-Wow held each year at the University was approaching and Lawrence, with whom I had gotten progressively friendlier, asked if I would help.

"Sure, Lawrence, what do you need?"

"Would you serve on the security detail with me and some others? We are there in case of trouble, but mostly to direct visitors and assist those in need," he answered.

"Done," I agreed.

The Pow-Wow was another amazing happening for me. Lawrence's little son danced, as did many native students I knew. The regalia added to the beauty and meaning of the two days. After the event, I was thanked by several for my help. I didn't feel I had done much – unless eating frybread and staring raptly at the dancers counts – but realize that sometimes 'just being' makes a difference. In fact now in this time in our human history, just being is critical. It is often all I need to do in order for things to go in motion around me. When unsure how to proceed, I offer just being as the solution until clearer signs come.

At the inipi the week after the Pow-Wow, Yellowhair called me aside.

"Jim, thank you for all you are doing. I see you wish to learn more. I would teach more if you like," Lyman said.

"I would love to learn more, Uncle. But I am a white man – is that okay?"

"With some, yes. With others, no. But now is the time to share our teachings and ways with the four colors. And you are only white on the outside," he smiled back. I would hear these things many times as I walked the good red road and share them now with others. "Others will also show to teach you. You are a bridge person. You will share what you learn and what Spirit allows you to become with people who would not ever meet or understand me," Lyman continued.

"I do not understand Uncle. I wish to learn all I can. Your way has become my way. But the rest is not clear to me," I said, truly confused.

"Don't worry. You will understand when the time is right and you need to," Lyman rejoined. How many times I would hear this over the course of my journey! And over the last few years, I actually understand it in my soul. And now—sometimes say it to others.

I had no idea to what I had really committed to Yellowhair when we spoke. The demon 'I'm Not Worthy' started appearing. What was a fortyish, pudgy, white boy from back East doing trying to learn the ways of the Native American people? What did I have to offer? And other such 'gunk' to clog up my joy over being asked.

I met Lawrence the next day as he wanted to ask about going to pick up his bald eagle in a few days from the Fish and Wildlife Department. It was my 'eagle time' as I also had to drive to Pueblo to pick up another eagle—a mounted bald eagle for the University. I had gotten the paperwork done through the U.S. government and so my department would now have this glorious bird to use in educational programs. I immediately starting telling Lawrence about my fears of being unworthy to learn more than any other visitor to the ceremonies.

"Jim, your spirit is what invited the question. You know my story, so why do you question? You and I will learn things together as the elders are teaching me the ways," Lawrence shared.

I will not share much of Lawrence's story, as that is his story to tell. But I will relate some of it, as it is a story I have heard similar versions of it from a number of people of various colors and cultures. And a story I have heard Lawrence share with others.

Lawrence grew up Native American, hating white people from an early age. One more young native boy with 'culture anger' – for what was done to his people in the past. Something I totally understood then, as I do now. He got into trouble often and finally, was convicted of a crime and spent time in prison. He began to understand the ways of his people while there. Then he found out he had white blood through his father. I have trouble beginning to understand how that might affect someone – but I am certain it was intense. Later, as he and I began to walk as brothers, he shared with me that I was the first white person he had ever trusted.

In part I also share this small portion of Lawrence's story because we all need to release these personal, tribal and inter-cultural hates and angers. We need to let it all go, put it behind us as a race. Not forget it, necessarily, but release the emotional charge in it, which blocks us from moving forward. Virtually all peoples can point to times they were persecuted or wronged. Some more than others – but that is a matter of degree. The time of the joining of the four colors coming together in harmony rather than hatred and fear, has been foretold in the stories of many races and that time is upon us now.

"Okay, Lawrence, I hear you. I will do whatever is asked and learn whatever I am taught."

We spoke of his eagle and I agreed to drive him down south to get it. The eagle is very sacred in the Lakota tradition. Their medicine people are allowed to carry their feathers, talons, etc., for their healing work. Lawrence had a request in at that time for an eagle when one was killed through some mishap or old age. This he wanted for his staff and other ceremonial pieces.

I walked outside to my car and headed south to Pueblo, where I was to pick up the eagle. It was a beautiful day, as are so many on the Front Range and I enjoyed the ride down. I got to the Forest Service office about eleven and presented my federal permits and University ID card. They brought out the eagle and to my total surprise, it was mounted on a five-foot tree stump. This might be difficult to fit into the back of my Jeep. And I needed to go up into Rocky Mountain National Park so I could drop off some brochures at the visitor center there.

I carefully carried the eagle to the car and slowly worked it into the back of the Jeep. It was a tight fit and anyone sitting in the front passenger seat would have needed to be careful of a side branch reaching out their way. But he was aboard and ready for his new work teaching the local students of Fort Collins. He had been standing on his mounting, for a number of years in the Forest Service office before we heard he was ready for new assignments. I spoke a prayer of gratitude to Spirit for the gift of this bird. And thanked the eagle for coming our way. For now, I had 'Teaching Eagle' with me.

I put a sheet over the eagle and his perch as best I could. This was to protect him from the direct sun and to cover him over and thereby avoid any questions if someone spotted him, as it is illegal to possess an eagle, or her feathers, except with special permits as I described. The Forest Service staff had me leave my permit with them, telling me a permanent one would be mailed to my university office within two weeks. A couple of small branches also crossed over to the driver's side of the front seat, so I had to carefully manipulate my way behind the wheel. I thought about doing the Park another day, but it was between Pueblo and Fort Collins and it was such a beautiful day, I decided to go ahead with my original plan. And so I drove up past Boulder and headed towards Rocky Mountain Park on the southern access road. I cracked the windows a little as it was heating up, but it was not warm enough to turn on the air conditioning. And I enjoyed the sights, smells and sounds as I drove. The sun was slanting in through the front window as I climbed the road up, creating prisms on the dashboard and seat. Mostly purple and yellow as I remember it, but with other rainbow colors thrown in. As I continued to climb from 5,000 feet near Boulder to the 7,500 feet in Estes Park, some clouds began to join me. The prisms were suddenly gone, so I watched the clouds create animals and trees above me. Western clouds are nothing like the gray, blanketing, menacing clouds I grew up with in the East. Most times they are well defined, white and fluffy. Thus a discerning eye and spirit, can watch them make different shapes as they mosey across the sky realm. I loved this immersion in the picture show the Father Sky provides and would sit whenever the clouds appeared and watch for a while. Today I drove and watched, without stopping, as I was to meet Bonnie at four and still had stops to make.

I stopped at a great little café in Estes Park to get a bite to eat. Estes Park is the gateway town to Rocky Mountain National Park. It is on the east side of the Park and there are two entrance roads out of it. I liked sauntering around town and along the creek running through it. But today I simply ate, rewedged myself back behind the wheel and headed for the Park. I stopped at the entrance kiosk and presented my annual pass to the ranger on duty. I did not know him, which was not surprising as I knew maybe twenty staff people of the couple hundred there.

I smiled, "How are you doing today, ranger?" I asked.

He did not smile back, but simply said, "Okay. Where you heading?"

"I'm going to go to the elk meadows for a short walk and then to the museum and the visitor center," I relied.

"Go ahead" was all he responded.

Boy, not a very friendly ranger. I had not run into that before. And wanting to know where I was going. Oh well, maybe they were doing a quick survey and he was having a bad day, I thought as I drove on in.

I drove in and up the few miles to the open fields the elk often roam in. I couldn't see any as I parked in a pull-off, but I saw some large birds downhill to my left. I was ready to stretch my legs so I quickly grabbed my binoculars, got out of the car and started across the open fields towards the large, arching trees where I saw the birds circling. I only had on a tee shirt and was comfortable. I drank some water – with visions of the earlier hike to the ranch on the west side of the park in my mind – and strode forward. I got to the trees in about ten minutes, but the birds were no longer present. I sat and enjoyed the breeze serenading me through the cottonwood branches as I watched the leaves change color as they danced.

Still having stops before heading down the Big Thompson Canyon towards Fort Collins and home, I got up and started back for my car. As I neared the car I saw three ranger vehicles pulled over, with lights flashing. I hoped no one had gotten hurt or no animal was in peril. Four rangers were walking around the area and looking across the fields I had traipsed on the way out. I had circled around coming back and was walking on the other side of the road now. Well, I guess I would know what happened soon, as I was only a couple of minutes from my car now. Another learning experience I felt certain, no matter what had happened.

As I came closer to my car I rounded the ranger car behind it. The four rangers all turned and looked at me. Without smiles, without a hello or how are you. I looked past them to my car and could clearly see Teaching Eagle sitting up tall on his perch surveying all around him. The sheet had slipped, or blown, off of my mounted eagle friend and so he was there for all to see. I now understood the behavior of the ranger when I entered. The sheet must have already fallen off and he, after asking my destination, had called the enforcement rangers. I was right; this would be another opportunity to learn.

I did not know, or even recognize, any of the rangers – two men and two women. No greetings here.

"Where did you get that eagle? Are you aware it's a federal offense to have an eagle? Why is it here in the Park?" the older male ranger of the group began shooting me questions.

"Yes, of course I do know it's illegal to have an eagle or feathers. Unless you have a federal permit for a specific use. Which I have to bring this eagle to the Environmental Learning Center of CSU for educational programs," I answered. "And I am here, in the Park, because I am dropping off some brochures a couple of places before going back to CSU. I decided to stop and take a short break and walk. I had the eagle covered, but the sheet must have slipped off."

They lightened up, but only slightly.

"Okay, show us your permit and University ID," the same ranger requested.

Oh nuts. The permit. The permit was sitting on someone's desk back in Pueblo. "Sorry, rangers. The permit is back in Pueblo where I picked up the eagle. The Forest Service people had me leave it. A permanent one will be sent me from the Fed," I shared.

"You do know it is a federal crime to have an eagle in your possession without a signed permit, don't you?" the ranger repeated, as if he had not heard a word I had said.

"Yes, and I have a signed permit. The Forest Service staff took it, as I said. I'm with CSU and the permit is for educational use. How about calling your office and asking for Ray, your assistant director. He can vouch for me," I explained again.

"Ray is on leave. And we can't release you with this eagle without seeing the federal permit," he continued.

"Ranger, I hear you. But you are not listening to me. How about calling the Forest Service and they can confirm what I have said? Or my dean in the College of Natural Resources?"

"We have no authority to do that. We have authority to ask to see your permit or call in the police," he stated as if reading from a rulebook.

This was getting humorous, if frustrating. What else am I to say to these folks?

Then one of the female rangers spoke up, "Joe, why can't we call someone at the Forest Service and ask. He has CSU identification," she added into the dialogue.

"Nope. Linda you are fairly new at this. We are federal employees and we need to follow the rules set down for us. Especially in a case like this where possessing an eagle IS a federal offense. You can serve five years for that. If he has no permit we will need to call the police into the matter. They can decide whether to arrest him and whether they will call the Forest Service or hold him until someone produces a legal permit."

"Joe's right Linda," the other woman ranger chimed in, "We don't want to risk our jobs by letting go someone transporting an eagle and then finding out, he lied his way out of it," she finished.

"I gotta agree with them, Linda, the best crooks are the smoothest liars," the final ranger added.

I couldn't believe this now. I was uncomfortable when they kept the permit in Pueblo and considered going straight back to campus with him, but thought the sheet would be a good alternative. If I had been paying more attention, I would have seen it slip and would not be standing here now. Oh well. Coulda, shoulda.

Joe went to his car to call the state police. Not even the locals, but the state police. This was making me very nervous now. As he sat hunched in his front seat calling out, a Park service truck pulled over. I'm thinking 'don't they have anything else to do here but harass a graduate student'?

Over walks another ranger I did not know and asks what is happening. He is told the story as I stand listening and immediately agrees with Joe calling in the state police. Then Joe marches back over.

"I got hold of the staties. Their officers are tied up right now, but one can get here in a couple of hours. We are to hold this guy until they arrive. Let's go back to our office and wait there. You will also be more comfortable there Mr. Petruzzi. Please follow us," Joe says solemnly.

Ray got in his car and waited for me to follow. And so I did, with one other car behind me. I came up to the park often and had met a lot of their people as our department was known as 'the ranger factory' – providing many rangers for parks around the country. Now here I was in a legal scuffle over an endangered bird. Species I was committed to helping preserve. How ironic.

We went back to their headquarters, a place I had needed to stop to leave brochures, and pulled in front. I was thinking I might be held for hours while this got sorted out and might even have to call my department chair to help me as we headed in. I looked up and there was Frank, a supervisor I knew and liked from several meetings, standing with a huge grin. I turned as Joe began to grin and just started laughing.

"Okay, you got me good!" I spoke around laughs.

Set up. The ranger at the entrance station had reported the eagle and my name from my pass and Frank was there to get the call. And they decided to have some fun with the CSU guy.

As we all laughed and I shared some of my thoughts of doom and gloom and my surprise at the rangers' stubbornness at hearing my story we sat and had coffee and doughnuts. They had created a good story. And I bought it. And would not forget it. I'd get even with

Frank another time but for now, I was completely enjoying the way I was duped.

As I carried on along the red road I was to learn just how important stories are. And what great teaching tools. Stories are remembered, especially if they are well told. I have already shared some in this journey we are on together and am certain others will come as I write.

After a while I left my brochures – one of which was about an endangered species program I helped sponsor (more irony) – and headed back to CSU to deliver my friend the eagle to his new home. I hoped my trip with Lawrence to get his eagle was not as eventful as this one and would be sure he copied his permit before we left campus. I could imagine some state police officer pulling over a native guy and a white guy with an eagle and no paperwork. No need to tempt fate, I would be certain we were prepared.

I dropped off the eagle at my department and walked across campus to meet Bonnie. We were going to a talk together by a visiting paleontologist. She arrived at the same time I did, as she had been leading a geology tour up the Poudre Canyon that day. This was another piece of the cash flow Spirit was providing us so we could continue our work without resorting to day jobs that would rob our time and energy. After the talk we stopped by the home of two faculty members in my department. They were both on my academic committee and had become friends of Bonnie and mine. Hank and Linda both taught in the department – she tourism and he taught statistics. They were also to come to Belize and be teachers in the program at the same time I was there. They were going to do sections on ecotourism and visitor norms out on the Cayes – the islands along the coast and next to the reefs. We had a couple of drinks with them and Hank and I talked about my Masters' work.

During this time we found ourselves drinking more often than was our custom. This went on for about a year and then, as I walked further into Native American spiritual teachings, I ceased drinking entirely and Bonnie decided to do the same.

We left and headed home, where our dog welcomed us with great enthusiasm.

This is a good place to speak a little more of the relationship Bonnie and I shared. I do so not because I particularly enjoy sharing these things, which cause me to look hard into the mirror, but because I have come to understand the significance of how we walk with each other. Each of us with whom we walk over our life.

Bonnie and I shared the love of nature, as I have told you, although with different areas of emphasis. This was an excellent benefit to us, as we did not need to be proficient in all aspects but rather, we 'shared' the knowledge between us. This is a pattern that would repeat with others I worked with later. Where we went our own ways was in the spiritual road and work with indigenous people. And, as I also said before, in our focus on what was success. For her, a job that paid well and provided all needs; for me, a job that fulfilled and enriched. Neither right nor wrong – just different. Bonnie always said she did not have a religious or spiritual bone in her body. And so, she never participated in my work in those areas. And no interest in the work and learning I was doing with my Native American friends. She never attended a lodge, or any other ceremony, except Pow-Wows and talks on campus. She did go on one project trip to Belize I later made and swore she would never do so again. I will share this trip and its issues later in this journey.

I realize now looking back, how much I had to learn and do in the areas Bonnie did not wish to be part of. And I needed to do this walk alone, with only my teachers and guides as support. Doing it otherwise would have altered what I was to understand and become. This is very difficult for me to write, but totally true. Bonnie had some deep issues around her birth family and was unwilling to do work around them. She dismissed them as 'the past', 'forgotten' and similar statements. I now see for her to step on the spiritual road would have forced her to look at these things deeper and begin to work them through. This is so for anyone I have seen step up to a spiritual road. It certainly has been, and is, for me. There is great joy and enrichment in learning the way of the ancestors – their spiritual and healing ways. But, to balance that as all in the Universe is balanced, comes great responsibility and hard, personal inner work. If you are given understanding, gifts and powers, Spirit expects to use them through you and to walk the road ahead for the good of all. I have seen many over the years in great torment and despair as they have accepted the gifts but not used them in the best way. If you are new to these ways, I suggest you give plenty of personal time to considering these facts. If you are on this path already, whether behind me or in front of me, I suggest continued self 'checking' in this arena if you don't do so already.

Bonnie and I walked our thirty-two years together always attempting to be in balance in our own respective work, our work together and our support of each other's passions. Sometimes we were successful, sometimes in conflict. Less conflict as we walked further ahead – a sign of growth to me. In our early years together, we were jokingly called the 'battling Petruzzis' by family members. Yet our arguments and fights set the stage for the long road we walked. And we stayed the course until we could reach better balance between us.

Until I experienced the near death part of my journey well beyond my CSU days, Bonnie and I both believed in and trusted Western medicine. Doctors, of course, understood and knew the answers to all maladies. That was why they had studied medicine. Our roads split dramatically closer to the end of our walk together, when I no longer had faith in this system and she clung adamantly to this belief. As I had alternative and spiritual healing approaches used on me and I began using those given me with others, I understood the difference between curing and healing – at least in my mind. I have come to learn that Western medicine, all too often, focuses on a cure for a disease. Using drugs, surgery, chemicals, radiation and other intrusive means to stop the pain. When the pain ceases, they consider the patient cured. What they have actually done is deal with the symptoms, not the causes. Often they have driven the causes deeper and, when they surface as they always do, they are often much worse than they were at an earlier time. Alternative medicine and spirit healing attempts, when done with integrity, to address the causes. When you can face the mirror, deal with what causes your pain and come to peace with it, you are healed. There is nothing to come back and bite you like a rabid dog – the causes are dealt with and gone. This is harder work because you have to walk into the pain to work with it, but the more complete way to release it. Why this schism in working on disease – or dis-ease in the alternative way? Western doctors have been trained this way. And many have come to believe they know and understand more than they actually do. Some have begun to approach other, less intrusive, methods, but the majority stays with what they know. I will share a story in a moment, which I was told to help me understand the difference between symptoms and causes in the Native tradition. Bonnie, as said, never left her belief in Western medicine and it was a huge weight on my soul that I could not effectively use any of my healing ways with her. But as with everything, this is a choice we each make. As we do with so many aspects of our lives. In the past, these things pained and saddened me, now I accept the road each chooses – helping where I can and releasing those I cannot.

Two Bears, who will enter this journey very soon, passed this story to me. He became a primary teacher and guide to me in Native American ways and later, as many of my teachers, a brother on the good red road.

There was a young brave, Pointed Arrow, walking along the banks of a river one day, enjoying the beauty of the day and the sinuous motion of the river. He was allowing his spirit to roam as he connected in with the Earth Mother and listening to whatever Great Spirit might have to pass to him. He suddenly saw a large leaf floating down the river and could see motion in it. He looked carefully and saw there was a baby in the leaf, being carried along wherever the river might bring him. He kicked off his mocs and pulled his shirt over his head and dove in to rescue the baby. He swam out to the leaf and captured it and the baby it protected, with his left arm. He slowly and carefully wended his way back through the lapping water to the shore. He lifted the baby onto the bank and climbed out beside him. The baby looked up at him and smiled and laughed, not seeming to be in any distress at all. The brave stared down at the baby wondering how he could have gotten in the river on that leaf. Could someone actually do something so harsh? He was bewildered and as he stood pondering this and wondering what he was to do with the child he noticed another large leaf floating downstream. Once again, there was motion in the leaf and once again, a baby in the leaf. Quickly moving the baby he had rescued under a tree and out of the sun, he jumped in to save the second baby. He got the second baby to the riverbank and saw it was a little girl, also smiling and gurgling. The brave was tiring from the long swims and the emotional impact of what was occurring here. Was this the end he wondered? He sat next to the babies breathing hard and checking them for any injuries, as a white couple approached.

"Hello friend," they called out as they approached, "We see you have your babies with you on this beautiful day," the woman finished.

"These are not my babies, yet they are now with me," he said back. And so Pointed Arrow told them what had happened and how the babies came to be with him.

"That is unbelievable," the woman spoke, "Who would send babies down the river?" "And what will you do with these little ones?" the man asked.

As they spoke of what to do, the woman looked out on the river and saw two large leaves navigating the current.

"Look, there are more!" she cried out. And so the brave and the white man jumped in, while the woman stayed on the bank with the babies already rescued.

After pulling out the third and fourth baby the three people sat and continued to question what was happening. As they did so, a minister and two other people approached. They shared the mystery of the floating babies with this new group and, just as they finished, three more leaves appeared upstream. These babies were also rescued and the group again convened and spoke their confusion and concern. Four more people approached as they spoke – a rabbi, two Native

Americans and a young black man. As they approached six more leaves were spied. Some of the group jumped in to save them; others tended the babies on the bank.

Pointed Arrow walked back a little distance from the others and watched what was occurring. More babies were appearing all the time. And more people gathering, who were saving them. Each baby was being brought to a safe place, yet how long could this continue? And so, as the six new babies afloat in the river were pulled up on the bank, Pointed Arrow turned and began walking up the riverbank.

"Where are you going," the Rabbi yelled out, "There are babies to save here." Pointed Arrow nodded and continued walking away.

"What is the matter with you brother?" one of the Native American people on the bank asked, "How can you walk away from this?"

Pointed Arrow again nodded and continued to walk.

"There is a special place in hell for those who do not serve their brethren. And if you walk away from this problem there will be a place for you in it!" the minister yelled in rage.

Pointed Arrow looked at them all and walked back towards them far enough so they would hear him speak. "Friends, I am sorry you are angry with me or think I am not acting in a good way. I rejoice you are here to continue saving the babies coming down the river. This needs to be done, but I see I need to go upstream, however far I need to, to find out where the babies are coming from." With this he nodded their way once again, turned and headed upstream.

And so, Pointed Arrow worked on the symptom of what was wrong – saving the babies – until he became aware he needed to go find the cause. If you just deal with the symptoms, at some time they will continue to reappear. If you seek and face the cause you can eventually put the dis-ease, the unbalance, to rest. And, as I remember asking Two Bears, "Two Bears, is this not also a reminder not to judge others?" And his reply, with a sardonic smile, "Very good, nephew, you will learn the ways well over time."

I have heard a variation of this story, like so many others, from other people of cultures different from the Native American. And again, value it since stories finding their way into many ways of life always seem to bear universal truths within their tales.

The day after my eagle adventure I reached out to Two Bears, a medicine man whom a graduate student suggested I contact. I told him of the work I was doing with the Native American students, Lawrence and Yellowhair. He said he would be in Fort Collins that day and would like to meet. We agreed to meet at noon for some lunch at the Center.

We met in the parking lot and shook hands – softly. I had asked about this soft handshake and had been told that Native American men do this to show no animosity and to allow no ego of a powerful handshake to enter this greeting. I have been careful to be aware of this since and share the reason for my soft handshake with others I meet.

We decided to walk to the inipi – sweat lodge – site and eat there. Between us we had cheese, fry bread, raw veggies, sliced ham and water. We spoke about the beauty of the day as we walked to the inipi site. There we sat under the over-arching grandmother tree and spread our respective foods for sharing.

"Jim, I have heard of what you are doing with the students and about the lodge here. It is good work. You are to be thanked for this," he began.

"Just doing what I can. No need for thanks. The gifts I am receiving in learning new ways are a huge bundle to me," I responded.

"Good answer. Yet you must be willing to accept thanks when given it without feeling ill at ease," he replied.

He had me. I extend thanks and recognition easily to others, but did not at that time, accept it well.

"I will remember that Two Bears. And I am grateful for your appreciation."

"So you wish to learn more of the Lakota ways." Not a question, but a statement as if he already knew I did.

"I do. The first time I attended an inipi ceremony I felt as if I was home," I spoke, "It was the first time I was comfortable with a spiritual practice. Growing up Catholic was not good for me. I never 'got it'. It was too dark," I finished.

"I would be honored to teach you whatever I am able, if that feels right for you," he said simply. I was floored. Why this middle-aged, Italian East Coast boy again assaulted my consciousness.

"I would truly be honored," I told him, "Whatever you are willing to teach me."

"Good," he nodded solemnly at me, "Learning what I, and the others, have to teach you will be a good thing for you. I sense this strongly. Yet with this, comes a great deal of responsibility and work. Once you step fully onto the road and accept what Spirit gifts you, He will expect you to use it."

"I accept that, Uncle," I answered, not fully sure of what I was accepting, but trusting in this road.

Two Bears sat for a few minutes, looking at me and then looking to the skies. He said nothing. I sat quietly and still and waited – something I had already learned when working with my Native American friends. Then he looked me squarely in the eyes and spoke "Jim, I am glad this speaks to you. But I want you to spend a few days with this offer, talk to Great Spirit and your spirit guides and be certain you are willing to accept the pleasant and the unpleasant pieces of walking the road. Many will not be happy to see a white man learning, others know it is the time. Other non-native people have walked this area before you and have experienced the acceptance and rejection I speak of. Will you honor this request?"

"Of course, Two Bears. I am not sure who my spirit guides are yet, but I will ask for their guidance whomever they are," I replied.

"Ah, you have strong animal spirit guides. They will become as brothers and sisters to you as you learn the ways. And you have a powerful teacher in the spirit realm. He has already spoken to me about this," Two Bears smilingly told me. "Let me share this, also. I was waiting to see if I was to do so and see that I am. I have been told when I am to work with certain people in teaching the ways and ceremonies of my people. Usually it is young Lakota people I am guided to. But not long ago I was told I would be teaching a white man from the east. And that he would be red on the inside as he carried the spirit of the four colors within him. I thought this meant someone coming from the east of the medicine wheel – the place of new beginnings. And the place of youth. So I expected a young white man just starting out. Instead I see a white man before entering middle age, but truly on the east direction of the medicine wheel as you begin a whole new way. And to be certain this sometimes dense two-legged truly 'saw' you, you are also literally from the East of Turtle Island. And so I welcome your arrival and give thanks to Great Spirit for allowing us to teach each other. We will speak in a few days," he finished.

And so, with wonder, doubt, joy and fear in me I felt as if I had been truly invited to walk the red road and learn the ways and ceremonies of the people whose spiritual path was home to me.

"Everyone got to find the right path. You can't see it so it's hard to find. No one can show you. Each person got to find the path by himself."

—Charlie Knight, UTE

10 | Two Feet, Many Roads

I was actively engaged in many projects and programs by now, trying to balance each day as I went along. I had not yet and would not for many years, learn how to say "no". So, when asked and I thought the cause a good one, I always said "yes".

Learning when to say yes or no as we are asked to serve is something I counsel all to address when they come to me. Each is equally empowering for the individual and those who ask. Yes I will, is not good nor is no I cannot, bad as I was raised to believe. You must honor your own energy and body first, then decide what it is you are to do. If asked, Spirit will always guide your decision. As long as you listen carefully for the answer – the butterfly wings of the earlier story.

But for now, I was often consumed by my teaching, students, studies, projects and learning from my native guides. I will not go into detail in all of these as you might well fall asleep and that would not help us along on our journey together. But some will enter what I write as their lessons will be helpful.

I continued to groom Sharon in the operations of the Environmental Center and what I saw as possible growth and expansion. Sharon was the graduate student who had become an assistant to me there. I loved her energy, wit, personality and potential to be much more later down her road. And so, as I have done many times, I spent a great deal of time mentoring her. She wanted to learn every minute and was always game for whatever was occurring. I loved her as a daughter and was certain she would be one who serves as she matured.

There were a few others I was mentoring in different realms, in a similar fashion at this time. One was an undergraduate student, Jess, who had spent his life in northwestern Colorado, where his father was a ranger in a park there. He was very intelligent, quick and focused. I began working with him on management and leadership areas, since that is where his gifts and interests rested.

AmeriCorps, a government program providing young people the chance to serve community non-profits, came to the Center when I began partnering with Brian, who would become a great friend over many years, and who was the director of this program for Northern Colorado in getting these young people working together with CSU students and local high school students.

The AmeriCorps program brought another mentor, Bess, a young woman who led AmeriCorps teams. Bess was young, probably early twenties, and had served two years as a Corps member before becoming a team leader. I allowed her great leeway in how projects were planned and implemented at the Center. I often, intentionally, offered her little advice on problems until she worked them through first. And a couple of other students whom I knew, intuitively, I was to work with more intensely than others.

While I spent extra time, energy and emotion on four to six 'shining star' students at any given time I also spent a great deal of time with the students in all my classes. I had, happily, learned where to put forth extra effort and where the students were taking advantage of my willingness to be flexible. Gullible is probably – no, certainly – a better word. Now, when there was a delivery date for some work or cut-off date on a project, I held firm. A good lesson for me!

With most of the students I focused on the time we were to spend together hoping it was rewarding for each of us. For a couple, it was not so. They became very painful, disorienting lessons for me. Lessons, once again, in how different I was from most, how my emotional connection could be misread or taken advantage of, and lessons in understanding that just because someone has gifts I can see does not mean they will take advantage of them.

Sharon was to be my first lesson in this and a very hurtful, confusing one when her attacks came at me. I would repeat these actions of mine and the thanks and attacks from those I befriended as mentees several times with several non-profits before learning to adapt how I interacted with them and they with me. I would also have to learn they had to decide their own walks and that I could not alter or control that. That is not part of my job on this walk through life. Control I have spoken of before. It amazes me in how many ways we humans try to control everything around us. Walk knowing you control nothing and you walk easier and softer.

Students stopped me every day and thanked me for the unique opportunities I was giving them, faculty congratulating me for my classes and work at the Center, my department chair shining on me as I made him look good also, other organizations thanking me for my work and recognizing me with awards. I was like a kid released to play. I felt no fear of showing what I was and what I could do. Of allowing my emotions and feelings to come through. As projects were completed that many thought impossible, I began to think I could do anything if given the time to work what I saw before I began. If you read ego growing here, I confess to being guilty. I thought this was me doing these things, me accomplishing what I attempted, me, by applying past skills, being the grand builder. Not God working through me and guiding my every step, even though I sent gratitude His way every day. Well, as I have said, I would learn the hard way.

I spent the next couple of days doing my own class work for my Masters, teaching and with my spare time, sitting along the river under the trees asking for guidance as per Two Bears request. I went into the old 'not being worthy' and 'why me' doubts many times, as I would many times after and still do, at times, today.

I met Lawrence on the morning we were to go and collect his eagle. He was excited by this blessing and ready to get started. So we hopped in my car and headed south down Route 25. It was an uneventful trip down and, happily, back.

As we approached the house he shared with his wife and two beautiful kids, he asked me, "Jim, would you like to spend some hours with me Saturday around the fire by the lodge and help me with the eagle?"

"I would be happy to do that. What time do you want to start?"

"I would start a fire at dawn and then we can sit and do some gratitude ceremony to the eagle and Great Spirit. We would then prepare the eagle and again pray. From that point we would begin removing the feathers and after that, the talons and head," he told me. From Lawrence I considered this 'ask' a huge honor as he most often did things alone.

"I will be ready. Shall I bring anything?" I asked.

"No," he answered.

The next day I drove to meet Two Bears in Boulder. I had to attend an early meeting at the Audubon offices in Boulder in the early morning around another project I had volunteered for, and was grateful Two Bears would be nearby so we could talk more.

Two Bears and I embraced, left shoulder to left shoulder, as is the custom with men who know and respect each other. We sat over coffee and began our talk.

"What has come to you Jim?" he asked.

"I wish to learn all I can from you. All you are willing to share. I am uncertain what medicine I am to learn, but will be a hollow straw allowing what comes in and sending out what I am asked to," I answered.

"Good," he replied nodding.

And so our journey together began. I was now learning from Lawrence and Yellowhair and had a teacher in Two Bears. I felt overjoyed about this, but also a little fearful. That seemed like a good balance to me. Two Bears suggested we go into his lodge together and then talk afterwards. Just he and I. I quickly agreed and thanked him. This lodge would come in about a week and, in the meantime, I would be in lodge with Yellowhair and an invited group. An interesting group. Yellowhair had asked me to invite people of different faiths, cultures and walks to a lodge so we might share. I thought this a wonderful idea, but was unsure who might accept. I had no need to worry as each I asked was excited to share in this way. And so, on the day of this lodge we assembled by the fire so Yellowhair could explain a little about the lodge before we all got ready to enter.

The group ready to hear Yellowhair speak before the lodge was: A white Presbyterian minister, a Rabbi from a local synagogue, an African American graduate student from the University of Colorado, a young Japanese woman who had been working with the local schools, a woman who was a rancher, an African American woman who taught in the Denver schools, Lawrence and myself.

Yellowhair, who was a very unassuming man, welcomed everyone gently but with much emotion. He spoke of the tradition of the inipi and the ceremony we were all about to share. And he spoke of the Chanunpa, the sacred pipe, and how White Buffalo Calf Woman had gifted it to the people so many generations ago. And how all Lakota ceremonies flowed from this pipe. He spoke of the heat in the lodge and the necessity to face yourself and any fears, which might arise. And finally, he spoke of how he looked forward to sharing with such a mix of people and faiths after the lodge over our meal together.

The lodge was a hot one, with the rocks all red and ready. Each lodge is different, although the preparation for each is the same. Sometimes the lodge seems very hot, other times it seems almost cool. I could not understand this until I was taught that it is the energy of the lodge and those in it that brings forth what occurs within. And the energy of the rocks and fire, which vary each time. Often I have felt we had a very hot lodge when the intention or work within the lodge was big.

As we sat talking over the meal waiting for us in the small cabin at the Center I was most taken by everyone's agreement around the similarities of the teachings. I remember the minister saying how he expected something very different from his faith and instead realized how similar the prayers and feelings were. This would be the first of many diverse lodges provided by Yellowhair and other water pourers over the years. Youth lodges, lodges for CSU administrators, a lodge for international students and so on, were requested and honored. This became a strong teaching component of the lodge and something the leaders of CSU could understand.

I was preparing myself for the trip to Belize as I was doing my other work. Bonnie was going to go back East to spend some time with her mother while I was gone. She was deciding what to take as she helped me decide what to bring to Belize. The students had already left for their twelve weeks there and the student I had recommended, Rob, was the group lead. I was reading books and talking to people who had already been there. I was excited to the point of exploding over this opportunity and counting down the days to 'lift off'. I met with the two faculty members I was traveling with and we discussed what they would teach and how I could help provide for needs on the ground.

I was also now partnering more heavily with the Northern Colorado AmeriCorps and Youth Corps program. Two AmeriCorps and one Youth Corps groups were at work at the Center several days a week. They planned and implement projects and we at the Center provided programs and guidance for them. In so doing, my CSU students were working with the corpsmembers, mentoring as they worked together. A group, led by my friend Bill a teacher of at-risk youth from the local Alternative Schools, had joined in this partnership also. Between us we created an Integrated Education Initiative to provide some structure around what our various student groups were doing. This spread quickly and soon we were teaching in the schools, the university and in the field with each other's classes. And the various student groups were mentoring and teaching each other on many levels. This morphed into a complete Service-Learning model, with the young people taking the lead and we teachers providing guidance and counsel.

Soon community service groups began joining these efforts and the Center's opportunities began to soar. This partnership reinforced for me how important it was to all learn and share together – elders; youth; teachers; students; community members and so on. In the 'old' way of community—where each is recognized and honored for what he or she brings to the circle. This work continued throughout my time at CSU and was, as most things are, as much or more of a teaching for me than for those we served. A partnership with the Colorado Visitor Center and the Forest Service had also been crafted, where each would have some space in this building. Another elaborate project that I was asked into – and accepted.

I had also become one of the team attempting to raise money to add a building on the eastern side of the Center. This group was meeting with potential donors and working on the design of that building. Trying at my prompting, to include input from many user groups. I also served in the Colorado Wetlands Initiative as a committee chair and several other programs and projects in the region. And still other work I have not listed.

Why share this 'list' of engagements – of time an energy commitments? Partly so as to give a clear picture of what revolved around my space as I began my work on the spiritual road and partly as a demonstration of someone out-of-balance. All the projects I entered were good and worthwhile endeavors, but I had not yet learned to speak 'no'. Between traveling and doing programs with Bonnie, teaching, taking my own courses and working on my thesis, running the Center and my spiritual learning I was working every day – and many evenings. I slept five hours a night at best and ate on the run. I was happy and excited by all this work, but was running my mind, body and spirit at full throttle all the time. This is not sustainable. As unsustainable as constantly pulling resources from the Earth Mother with no thought for the future.

I now speak to all who seek me about this balance or lack of balance before I do any other work with them. Especially for any wishing to learn more about the spiritual path. In honoring yourself first, you can better absorb whatever you need to know on the path of Spirit.

11 | Honoring the Eagle

I MET LAWRENCE ON 'THE DAY OF THE EAGLE' CEREMONY HE HAD ASKED me to be at with him. He already had a fire roaring – small fires never seem to materialize for any ceremony, they always leap and roar – and he was sitting, cross-legged with the eagle before him. I sat, also cross-legged, across from him.

"Aho relative, we will start now," he welcomed me in his usual to the point way. "I would like it if you would open this with a prayer of gratitude," he continued.

"Not sure that I know any Lawrence."

"You know many, just create it," he smiled at me. I knew he was testing me and that was fine. We tested each other in this way as our bond together grew.

And so this was the first time I was asked to lead a prayer or teaching off the top of my head. Actually from the bottom of my heart. This is the way I now most often work, allowing Spirit to speak through me when I am asked.

It went something like this, "Great Mystery. Great Spirit. It is I, Jim, your imperfect son here to give thanks for the eagle my relative, Lawrence, has been gifted for his medicine. We sit here around this sacred fire grateful for the glory of this winged one. I ask that you hear Lawrence's prayers and requests for the use of this bird so he may move forward with his learning of the medicine of his people. Eagle, winged friend, I thank you for allowing us to use your feathers and parts now that you no longer need them. I ask you to send energy from your new perch in the spirit world as we do this work together today. Aho, Mitakuye Oyasin."

Mitakuye Oyasin is all my relations.

Mitakuye Oyasin – all my relations – is meant to remember, honor and welcome in all to whom we are related. That means all, everywhere – in the broadest sense. All two-leggeds, four-leggeds, winged ones, finned ones, creepy crawlies, and so on. All creatures are related and connected in the spider web of the Earth Mother and, I now realize, throughout the universe. In this way no creature is more or less than any other—each has its work to do towards the whole.

Those who consider humans (two-leggeds) better, smarter, more 'deserving' than any other creature walk in ego. And, probably, fear. Those who believe humans are the only creatures of our sort in the universe are welcome to that belief, but they then cut themselves off from such a huge part of the 'web' of existence. I will develop this thought more as we journey—as my understanding of it has grown over my walk. And I will speak more of the web of which we are all a part.

'Aho' is another word heard often around Native Americans and certainly, their ceremonies. It is used in various ways with nuances of meanings, but the meaning easiest to understand is that which I heard Yellowhair use with groups. That is that 'aho' is most closely related to 'amen' or 'right on' or 'just so'. It is used to give emphasis to what is being said.

"Good one Jim." Lawrence spoke. "Your prayers gain more heart power all the time. Good to see this. Let's smudge ourselves, then the eagle, and then I wish to speak to the eagle before we begin. Ask his permission again and give him thanks. Would you do the smudge please?"

I picked up the large shell, which held the sage we were going to smudge with.

Smudging is an ancient ceremony meant to cleanse and protect those smudged. It is used before every ceremony in the traditions I have learned. Sage is the sacred herb used for this cleansing, sometimes with red cedar and osha – bear root – also added. Smudging of houses and other buildings is also often done. To cleanse and clear the space lived in or space ceremony is to be conducted in.

Lawrence stood, facing me and waited as I lit the sage. As it leaped into nice flames in the shell I fanned these flames out with the eagle feather Lawrence owned and allowed the aromatic, white smoke to spiral towards the sky. I then fanned the smoke over Lawrence with the feather from head-to-toe. As I finished smudging his front I touched the feather to his head and said 'aho' so he would know to turn. I then smudged his back in a similar fashion. With another tap he left first his left foot, so I could smudge his sole, then his right. Then, finishing with "Aho, Mitakuye Oyasin", I handed the shell to Lawrence and he smudged me in the same fashion. Handing the shell back to me, he sat as I smudged the eagle and the space around us. With this complete, I added some sage to the shell, laid it next to Lawrence, and sat across from him, with the eagle between us.

"Grandfather Eagle," Lawrence then began, "I thank you, once again, for gifting me with your Earthly robes here when you dropped them to enter the Spirit world. I thank you for honoring me in this way. And I again ask your permission to use these robes in making the sacred staff I need for my medicine work. I will use this staff and the feathers always in a good way, to pray for the healing of all the people.

"Ho, Mitakuye Oyasin" he finished. "It is done. We are permitted to begin now," he added.

Lawrence began slowly, gently and carefully pulling the feathers from the eagle. As he did so he passed them to me and instructed me to smudge each, thank them and lay them to the side. We worked at this for a couple of hours until the job was complete. We then had many feathers laid out and a true 'bald' eagle before us. His robes Lawrence spoke of were both his feathers and his physical body. When we die – pass on into the Spirit realm – we "drop our robes." We release the physical body we no longer need. In the way of all my teachers – indigenous and non-indigenous alike – we do not die, we move into the Spirit world where our work continues. When needed, we return to this material world for more work on ourselves and with others – as a two-legged or not, as Spirit wishes.

Lawrence laid the carcass aside and began to clean each feather. After a few of these he asked me to assist. As we cleaned each we laid them on red cloth he had brought for this purpose. Then he smudged the carcass and began to remove the talons and head with a sharp Bowie knife. When this was done he cleaned these, smudged them and also laid them to dry. We had been working now for about four hours and my stomach was grumbling. Lawrence laughed as my stomach spoke loud enough to be heard.

"We can go eat when we are done, but not while we work. Okay?" he asked.

"Fine with me. At least we have water," I answered.

"Let's pray silently as we sit and wait for the eagle to dry. Then we will wrap him up and close this eagle ceremony," Lawrence shared.

And so we sat inhaling sage, feeling the heat of the fire and praying, each in our minds and hearts.

After another thirty minutes Lawrence checked and was satisfied that everything was dry. He laid out another piece of red cloth and began laying the feathers in it. He added sprigs of sage as he went. He would fold the cloth over the feathers so they did not rest on top of each other. When they were all encased, he wrapped the talons and head separately and then added them to the feather bundle. More sage was added and then he ripped four strips of cloth – one red, one black, one white and one yellow. He carefully tied the bundle with the four colors and inserted yet more sage through the knot.

The four colors are another important piece of this Spirit Road. They can represent many things depending on their use. They represent the four directions of the medicine wheel. And they can represent the four colors of people. All other colors of humans being a mix of these primary four. The four colors will enter our journey here often as we travel ahead.

"One more thing, before we go," Lawrence said. "We need to smudge the remaining carcass and bury it in a good way."

And so we smudged the carcass and buried it some fifty feet from the inipi under a Cottonwood tree. We added a prayer and gathered the eagle bundle and headed towards our cars.

Lawrence invited me for a sandwich, which I quickly accepted. As we ate, he told me he would work on the staff and we would then welcome it and smudge it together.

With that we finished our meal and I headed home, tired and a bit sore from my many hour cross-legged position, but feeling great peace and thanks for this day with Lawrence and the eagle.

12 | Into the Lodge of Two Bears

Two Bears called me that night and asked if we could do lodge together two nights hence. I agreed and thanked him. And so I was now to begin my learning from Two Bears.

I met Two Bears about 6 PM the night we were to sweat together. It was a clear, star-strewn night with a three-quarter moon smiling down on us. A perfect night for a lodge. It was cool – about forty-five – but not cold. And no wind blew. Two Bears had already started the fire and had put his ceremony pieces on the altar. He had a beautiful staff, adorned with eagle and other predator bird feathers. He had stuffed his buffalo skull's mouth with sage and placed it facing the lodge on the altar side nearest the lodge. His drum was sitting to the right of the skull and two rattles around the altar circle above the drum. His Chanunpa was to the left of the buffalo skull; the stem nestled in between the skull and the horn. His bone whistle sat below the pipe. The smudging bowl was to the left of the skull, full of white sage, red cedar and bear root. I asked permission to put my drum on the altar and he nodded agreement. I laid it next to the smudging bowl – shell.

"We will go in at seven Jim. The rocks will be good and hot. We will do four doors and I will share what I see about our work together and what is ahead for you in the fourth door. You will also be able to share your feelings or anything that has come to you. Or not, as you wish and Spirit guides you. If we need to bring things forward at other times I say let them come. This is a new way for both of us. You have been in many lodges now, but this is different – teacher and he who wishes to learn," Two Bears said.

"I have no expectations Uncle, I am ready for wherever you lead us," I replied.

"I guide, I pour, but Spirit surely leads us tonight. That is why I have a general idea of what we shall share, but no plan. You have already learned 'want to make Spirit laugh, make a plan'. Let's not make him laugh tonight."

I tended the fire, adding wood whenever any of the rocks showed through the burning logs. And replacing any burning logs which fell away from the pyre. My hair was singeing and smelled of ash and soot quickly, but I felt honored to be allowed to tend the fire. When I was not picking up the pitchfork to leverage burning logs back on board or adding new wood, I sat quietly across from Two Bears. He sat with his Chanunpa in prayer and I honored his space.

Before we enter the lodge here together I will speak a little about my teachers, brothers and sisters on my walk. You have met some already and more will follow as we move further on this journey. Even now I am amazed by the number and diversity of teachers I have had, teaching me so many different ways. And the way Great Spirit has allowed me to combine these ways at times in order to teach or act as a healing guide for others. And yet I should not be amazed. We each have our gifts and part to play in the web of the universe. Some know all there is in certain, specific areas, no matter what area we speak of: medicine, science, arts, or...the spiritual road. Others are taught much within a broad spectrum, such as I have been. There are times and places for each. For now, I am to share what I have seen and learned. Some of you may walk this road after me, some have already walked it. Others of you may see one or two areas you wish to walk in. As Spirit guides us, so we walk if we follow the reason for our being.

Many of my teachers have sat with me in the physical plane: the one we, as human beings, live in. As the teachers you have met with me here so far. Others are in the spirit world and teach in a different way. But just as powerfully. And, as you will see later, some teachers of that spirit world have shown themselves to me in the physical plane or invited me to the other. Some in wake time, some in dreamtime. These trips I will also share, as I am to hold nothing back. You will, I believe, be able to distinguish one teacher type from another although, sometimes, it is even unclear to me.

Now is the first time I am sharing much of this walk of mine. As we are about to enter this lodge I begin to share things told me I did not understand, or things that scared me, or things that empowered me. I have shared some of these with a few, such as the writing I included from my first inipi, but most I have kept to myself. Kept to myself for fear of ridicule, fear of being seen as different again, fear of attack by those not wanting me in some of these places learning what I have learned. I release these fears and doubts now and simply take you on this journey with me as I tell of my walk. Those who wish to doubt, fear, question, ridicule or attack are free to do so. It is about them, not me if they chose to do so. Those who embrace, enjoy, awaken and question as they read make this all worth sharing.

Just before seven Two Bears arose, stood with his Chanunpa held up to the heavens, muttered a few words softly then looked at me as he lowered the pipe.

"It is time. I would like you to help me with the rock people," Two Bears instructed me as he put his pipe back on the altar.

"What shall I do, Uncle?" I asked.

"For this first round, I will carry the rocks and I would have you brush them free of ash with the sweep over there," he said pointing to a space a few feet from the fire pit.

"Certainly, Uncle."

We carried in the first seven rocks for the first door. They were a good size and they all glowed bright red. No pikers here! When the rocks were nestled in the shallow hole in the middle of the inipi,

I entered as Two Bears motioned me to. I sat to the side of the rocks across from the door. Two Bears entered and sat to the right of the door, as is the custom as I have most often seen it. He had brought in his drum, a rattle for me and some sacred herbs for the rock people.

Two Bears put some sage and herbs on the rocks, welcoming each into the lodge and thanking each Grandfather rock for bringing their energy and wisdom for us. Then he opened to the seven directions – east, south, west, north, Father Sky, Mother Earth and Great Spirit (within us and above us).

"Nephew, do you wish to voice your intentions for this lodge?" he asked me.

"I would like to ask Great Spirit to give me whatever understanding I might need as I start this work with my Uncle here. And to allow me to use whatever I learn for the good of all creatures and the Earth Mother, who is my strongest connection on this walk," I spoke.

As I spoke Two Bears began pouring water on the rocks. The rocks began to sing and spit as the steam bellowed up around us. He poured ladle full after ladle full until I could not see my hands before me. And then he began to drum a song of opening as I added the voice of the rattle I held. He sang with the drum in that way I have heard so many elders be able to do, as if the drum, the rocks hissing and their voice were all one. Which, of course, in many ways they were. Sweat poured off me as he sang, longer and longer – much longer than most lodge songs I had heard sung to that time. Then he stopped and poured more water. We sat in total darkness and silence, but for the rocks crooning away, for several minutes.

"This is the first lodge of many we will share together as a circle of two," Two Bears broke the silence with, "I also asked for guidance for both of us as you spoke your intentions. You have been in many lodges with several different water pourers and so have begun to learn much of the ways and the reasons. Yellowhair is a fine teacher and I am sure he is teaching you a great deal. He understands, as do I, that the time is now to begin to share our ways with those of the other colors. As it is for them to also share theirs. And yet many argue against this. They say it is Indian only, as it has been for so long. I believe it is their fear and ego talking, but I do not judge them. I can only do what I do."

He poured more water as he ended these words. Then, "I am glad you asked to be a student of the ways. I see your heart is good. I will sing a song of gratitude and then we will close this first door with silent prayer."

He again drummed, and I rattled (yes, my insides as well as the rattle I shook) and he lifted his voice in another ancient song. Again, he sang long and then poured once more as we silently prayed. Then, asking me to join him, together we loudly said, "Mitakuye Oyasin" and he threw open the door flap. Beautiful, cool, fresh air rushed in and steam escaped in a huge cloud.

"Follow me from the lodge and we will get more rocks for the second door," Two Bears instructed.

We left the lodge, respectfully speaking "Mitakuye Oyasin" as we passed through the door. I again took the sweep, ready to brush the rocks free of ash.

"We will bring these seven in the same as the first door. Then I will rest as you bring in the rocks for the last two doors. It's time for you to carry the rocks anyway," Two Bears told me.

"How do I know which rocks to bring in?" I asked.

"Ask the rocks" was my only answer. So we brought in seven more rocks for the second door, I replaced the burning logs that had been moved and laid new logs where needed. Then we re-entered the lodge as before.

The second door was not quite as long as the first, but even hotter. Two Bears songs were powerful and he taught of the bison herds and what they had meant to his people. Then, before his second song, he said we were to sit quietly and connect to Great Spirit and our hearts as he poured 'a little more water'. A little more water was at least twenty minutes of ladle after ladle. I don't believe I had ever sweated so much. I could taste the wet, smooth, cool water we would drink after the lodge. But for now, my throat was parched, my lungs raw and my skin aching. Finally, he began his second song and I sang along as best I could. I was still learning songs and flopped on pronunciation, timing and intonation often. But my heart was in it. I then exited the lodge to bring in the rocks for the third door, the healing door.

I carefully moved some burning logs aside as I had seen other rock carriers do in order to bring out seven rocks. Two Bears was right, I had no trouble choosing which rocks to bring. They seemed to just come up in my head each time I approached for the next one. I had to stop, put down the pitchfork so I could brush the rock, and then pick it up again and reach it through the door and onto the pile already inside. I had the seven in place in about ten minutes – and only dropped one on the way to the door. Then I remade the fire and approached the lodge door.

"Fill this here bucket," Two Bears said from inside as he handed the bucket out to me. He had poured a whole bucket – a large bucket – in just two doors, when it usually lasted the entire four doors. Must be trying to bake the white boy, I thought with a smile. I handed the full bucket back in and asked permission to re-enter the lodge. Two Bears gave it and I took my place while he pulled the flaps back over the door. And so we were ready for the healing door.

Two Bears again set to work pouring ladleful after ladleful of water on the rocks as he prayed. Again the steam was so thick I could wiggle my fingers before my eyes and see nothing. Two Bears then began putting several herbs used for healing mind, body and spirit on the rocks. He asked the herbs to provide us whatever healing we needed here tonight. As he added some herbs he spoke of how his teachers had taught him their use and how to best find and gather those he needed. Things he would later share with me. The air was wonderfully aromatic and I breathed in deeply as I also silently asked for whatever healing I might need. At the same time I asked for the healing of all and the healing of the sacred hoop, wherever it was broken. After a while Two Bears drummed and sang and I realized I sang along much louder then I usually did. I no longer worried about any gaffs, but knew spirit and heart going in to the music was all that was really needed. More ladles of water followed. I had not lain on the floor for cooler air tonight, nor pulled my towel over my head as some do for relief. I did not even realize this until that moment. Big medicine, as Yellowhair liked saying, was happening for me in this lodge tonight. We sat quietly, once again, each silently praying as we breathed deep. Water kept falling on the rocks from the ladle of Two Bears, so they hissed and sang louder by the moment. They glowed red and, in places, were black where a lot of water had struck. We sat a long time in this fashion and I suddenly realized just how great I felt. And, I was not hot! I knew it was red hot in the lodge, but I did not feel it. I was soaked in sweat and it puddled under me, yet I did not feel the heat. I marveled at this. The towel I had wrapped around me was fully soaked and my hair plastered to my skull but I felt fine. As I realized these things I gave thanks and just enjoyed the moment.

I never felt hot again in a lodge from this time forward. I sweat and get mighty thirsty, but not hot. At times I am elated or sad or get visions or feel fear or experience dark, quiet beauty. But...not hot. And I understood, sitting in my pooled sweat, what Yellowhair and others had been teaching me about the heat in the lodge. You face your fears and issues when you are in a lodge and it is these which drive your autonomic nervous system to tell you how hot you are. And why many, especially newcomers, have to leave the lodge, sometimes in panic. As I had left my first lodge in fear and confusion. In future lodges I often had heavy issues I wished to release, but did not fear what was happening. I was reminded how reading things and hearing things are good ways to learn but, for me, nothing approaches experience for real understanding.

After another song, I splashed out of the lodge for the rocks for the fourth, and final, door. As I reached the door Two Bears again handed me the bucket. He had poured an entire bucket of water in this one round.

"Uncle, should I find a bigger bucket?" I jokingly asked.

"It is good you still can make jokes. This is a powerful lodge," he responded with a chuckle. The powerful part he had not needed to tell me.

I brought in the final seven rocks, each red hot as those that had gone in before. They sizzled and hissed as they joined their brothers in the lodge pit. And I filled the bucket for the third time – to the brim! I passed the bucket to Two Bears and again entering the lodge, pulling the flap shut behind me.

"Now we will begin to really pour water," Two Bears solemnly spoke "and cleanse as completely as possible before I speak what I see for you. And how we are to work together." "Relax, sit quiet, keep your eyes open and let come whatever will until I begin the song," he continued, "Let the heat move through you in a cleansing way, do not let it overwhelm you."

I never shared how I was not feeling the heat and was not completely in understanding about this yet, anyway. So I followed his directions as he began to ladle water on all twenty-eight grandfather rocks. The rocks really began singing now – in a hiss, pop, whine, sizzle joyous way. I sensed many other presences in the lodge with us, something I became more in touch with over time. The ancestors, guiding spirits, animal guides and others often join us in the lodge, especially when invited in and their help asked for. It was just the two of us humans here, but I felt a full lodge around me. This felt good and comforting, not fear inducing, as it was the first time I sensed it many lodges back. I thanked all present for being there with us as I silently prayed.

After pouring for several minutes, Two Bears put the ladle in the bucket and we sat in the total darkness, each in our own thoughts. Suddenly I felt as if Two Bears and I were one – connected in spirit. I sensed his energy as we sat across the rocks from each other. This was the first time I was aware of this connection. I now see a person's energy as we first meet and have a good sense of their 'being' before we speak a word. But, back in this lodge, I had not yet developed this gift. Time is meaningless in the lodge, as it is, I have learned, everywhere, but I believe we sat for about fifteen minutes before Two Bears picked up his drum. It felt like two minutes and two hours had passed at the same time. This time had provided the space I needed to integrate some of what I was feeling and 'seeing'.

Two Bears almost leaped into song as he beat the drum and I shook the rattle. I felt a presence telling me to be calm, be peaceful, do not fear anything now or later. Telling is not the right word, it was just 'in me', in my awareness. I sang as best I could and felt empowered again as I did so. We sang many times longer than I was used too.

And, suddenly, Two Bears stopped. He poured four more ladles of water on the rocks, asking continued guidance from the four directions – east, south, west and north – as he did so. Then we sat silently once again. Silent except for the continued singing of the rocks. I was certain ten pounds of sweat lay around me and wondered how much water remained in my body, even as more exited my pores. I felt clean and fresh in spite of this profuse sweat.

"I would speak now, if you are ready to hear," Two Bears said as he broke my revere.

"I am ready to listen whenever you are ready Uncle," I responded.

"Good," he said, "I told you how I was now to teach all colors our ways now as the prophecies require. And how I was to work with a white man from the east. I am certain you are that one and I have been preparing myself to be with you and any who follow later. This is no small work. It is important we begin preparing for the time of change to come. And, I feel you have been preparing for your walk with me. This is good. I will share more now about what I have seen, some of it now, in this lodge as we sit together. Nothing I speak is to build your head big. Nor is it to put fear or doubt in your heart. As we move ahead together more will follow, but this is what I am to pass to you for now."

He paused and placed some sage and cedar on the rocks and, as their smoke wafted up, he inhaled deeply, as did I.

"Nephew, this road you are about to step more firmly on is a hard road to walk at times. A joyous, fulfilling road, but a powerful, difficult road in many ways. You will be welcomed as a brother by many, especially those who do not only see the outside color of those they look at. And others will throw rocks and spit at you. They see their own fears, but you will be the target. This is so for all of us, no matter our outer coloring. You have much energy and many gifts to tap as you learn. And you will learn from the four colors as you go forward. You carry the four colors in you and have a strong red inner spirit. This I saw the first time we met. This others have seen, as they have spoken to me. One of your ways will be to carry teachings, teachings from many cultures, to the white people. Those who need to hear will hear you. And give you thanks. Those not ready will also ridicule and point the finger. You will need to stay in balance and true to your spirit as you do this work. You will also learn how to best use the healing gifts you possess – some from me, but I see a large amount from the South America peoples; And others from around the Earth Mother. You will have great joy and fulfillment in learning all these things; yet will be tested at the highest levels at some time. It will be then that you truly decide to step up into your power or move aside."

Two Bears paused and let a minute pass. I was wondering 'does he know these things or suspect them'?

"Do you hear me nephew?" he asked.

"Yes, Two Bears, I hear you clearly, yet I do not understand much of it. I am not as much afraid as confused," I answered.

"I would have been worried if you said you heard and understood all at once," he continued, "There is much to take in, in what I speak. I will also guide you in the way of the Chanunpa if you feel that is a road you must walk. You know the pipe from your lodges, but I will guide you in the responsibilities of the pipe if needed."

"Uncle, I continue to wonder why a middle-aged, white guy from the East, brought up Catholic, is here in this lodge hearing your words. And I really doubt my worthiness to learn all these things. Yet I respect your words and what you are told by Spirit, so I will do my best to honor you and all I learn."

"Let us finish with a song to Great Spirit and then sit and connect a little more with the Earth Mother. After that I have made some fry bread and chili. We will eat together and maybe tell some jokes. We have done enough work for today and I want you to always remember the road must always have fun and joy along its way."

When we left the lodge and walked up to Two Bears' cabin I was surprised to see it was nine forty-five. I thought we were in there for a much shorter period of time. This is another phenomenon that still repeats to today. I feel as if an hour has passed in a ceremony, only to find out it is three hours later.

I started the hour plus drive home about eleven and Bonnie was waiting to hear how it went. I told her of the lodge and Two Bears' words to me and that I would now be learning from him on a regular basis. "I still don't see why you want to spend so much time with this religious training," she began, "but if it's what you want, you need to do it."

"It's not religious, it's spiritual. Why do you keep throwing 'religious' at me? It is my way to connect to the universe and my God," I came back with, more than a little heated.

"I don't have a religious bone in my body and spiritual seems like some made up thing to me," she responded, also heating up.

"Let's drop it before we are in an argument," I suggested. And, of course, we didn't drop it. The argument escalated into other areas of conflict. And then it was over. We had both spoken our words and so we both apologized – as we often did – and discussed plans for the trip we were to take the next morning.

As an emotional being, quickly affected by the moods of others, I still walked in joy or anger many times during a day. I had not yet learned balance in this area either. Actually, I thought it was the norm and, for good or bad, I still believe it is for many in our culture. Bonnie was not as emotional, but strongly opinionated and not afraid to voice her opinions. It worked for us – allowing us to find center ground and good solutions most times. Yet, today, I wish it had been different. I remind myself, at the same time I may regret some past interaction, that we all do the best with the tools we have at the moment. Had I evolved other 'tools' at that time, I would have applied them. By continuing to move ahead and evolve in a good way we honor all we have done, even our mistakes, in the past.

13 | With the Earth Mother

THE UNIVERSITY WAS ON BREAK AND SO WE HAD DECIDED TO TAKE a week and head over to northwestern Colorado, a sparsely populated, beautiful natural area of the state. I had spoken to my friends at the U.S. Forest Service, which allowed us to spend the first two nights in a cabin in the middle of nowhere. We were also going to be scouting out new locations to take people on Bonnie's geology field trips. We were, as we often did, mixing pleasure and business.

We arose early the next morning and began heading out of town so we could enjoy the ride in the morning light. First, we stopped at Hank's, just north of Fort Collins, for breakfast. This was always a fun breakfast place for us. An interesting mix of people were usually here: University people, locals, ranchers and tourists. It bustled any time of day. And they had some of the most decadent, delicious cinnamon buns I had ever eaten. We ordered two, along with a serving of bacon and eggs we would share. As we worked on the buns, a local rancher I knew waved from across the room. He was Tom Cox, a true character of the west – a role I know he loved. I smiled and waved back then went back to my bun, sipping my hot, strong black coffee between bites.

"Jimbo, how you doin' pard?" I hadn't noticed Tom get up and come over as I ate with attention on my sticky, gooey, hot bun.

"Good, Tom, how about you?" I asked.

"Well, you know, too much to do and not enough sunshine to do it in," he chuckled. Tom had a thousand of these lines, one for every situation.

"Where you all headin'? Bonnie, right?" he asked.

"Yes, I remember you from that meeting at CSU Jim was at. Good to see you again," Bonnie answered him. "We're heading west for a week."

"Over around Steamboat Springs," I answered his other question.

"Hell, boy, you went west when you came to Colorado. Now you're headin' over the hill," Tom said, loudly.

It was almost always loudly with Tom. He would have made a good stage actor. Over the hill meant up and over the pass that the Poudre River flowed down. Over to the western slopes of the state.

Tom was one of the ranchers who had attended a three-day meeting of ranchers, university faculty, environmentalists and Native American people I had arranged to discuss land use and protection. He came angry, loud, opinionated and rarely quiet. Yet he managed to come to a place where he saw some areas of agreement between the groups. Still thought the rancher way was the WAY, but was willing to at least listen to others. He had thanked me for the chance to be there afterwards and was always pleased to see me around. In spite of the fact I disagreed with many of his ideas on land use, thought he would be more at home in a comic book than on the range and found him often over-bearing with his demeanor – I liked him. He was real – real, at least, in his world.

"You old ranchers love to tweak the Eastern boys, don't you Tom? Maybe it's just a function of 'old'," I said straight-faced.

"Damn, if you keep that up it will be harder for me to twist your horns. But it's good, I like competition," he laughed.

"Hey, did you hear the forest service was talkin' about raising our grazing fees again?" he asked.

"Tom, when you pay so little to use the land we all own to make money on your cattle, I don't see how you can complain," I said, the continuation of many talks we had had.

The grazing on public lands issue is big in the West. What I said to Tom was true, but the other side of the argument was that costs of beef and beef products would go up as fees were raised. No issue has one side. If it does, it's not an issue.

"Alright, not today. I ain't goin' there. You two enjoy your meal and trip. Jim, I would like to see ya when ya get back. Okay?"

"Sure, Tom, call or you know where my office is," I consented.

"Fine day, Miss Bonnie" he tipped his over-sized western hat her way and ambled back towards his table and the two grizzled old boys sitting with him. As he moseyed across the room, eyes everywhere turned to follow. Tom had a handlebar mustache that was a prizewinner; a black felt 12-gallon hat, spurs and leather riding breeches. Today all topped off by a red and black checked flannel shirt. I watched at least three people snap his picture and smiled because I knew he was aware of it and loved it.

"Well, this should be an interesting week if running into Tom is any indication," I said to Bonnie.

"You do seem to attract some...what's the right word...unique people to you. But then characters attract characters I guess," she smiled broadly as she spoke.

We chatted, laughed some more about Tom's manner, and finished our sticky buns. Then a trip to the restrooms to clean off the sugar before we gassed up and headed west.

We headed up the road alongside the Poudre on this bright, very warm morning. We talked about rocks and wildlife as we twisted our way upward. About ten miles from the base of this road we saw a parking area to our left. The river was to the right. We pulled in and parked and, after taking a look at the trailhead map, decided to take a short hike before heading to the cabin. To get to the trail you needed to cross the road and then cross a small walking bridge over the Poudre. The Poudre was running nicely and we listened to her sing as we crossed. On the other side the trail bent to the right and upward. We moved forward and began noticing some wildflowers as we walked. After about a half-mile the number of wildflowers exploded. A meadow full of them stretched out in front of us as far as we could see.

"This is beautiful!" Bonnie exclaimed, "Why have we never heard of this trail?"

"There are so many great hikes and I don't think too many come this way," I answered.

"Let's take our time going through them. Or at least I am. If you want to go at your fast pace I'll meet you when we leave these behind," Bonnie said.

"No, I'll take this one slow also," I agreed.

As we got a few hundred feet into the flowers suddenly, seemingly out of nowhere, another explosion occurred. Butterflies. Thousands of butterflies erupting out of the flowers and grass, seemingly dancing before our eyes. "This is unbelievable," Bonnie said breathlessly. "I don't think I've seen this many butterflies in my entire life."

"I know I haven't," I exhaled. The butterflies danced and floated and dipped and rose for a good twenty minutes as we watched, totally captivated. They literally bounced off us at times; with a touch so light you could never truly feel it. Finally they were either down or had moved off and we decided to head back to the car. Anything else we might see on this walk would now be completely anti-climactic. I had not yet heard the story of the brave and the butterfly from Two Bears. If I had I might have questioned myself about what they were telling me. I did not understand signs and messages at a conscious level yet – but I did understand the gift of such outstanding natural sights.

Time, I believe, for another side trail here on our journey together. Signs and messages. I have come to be awake for things in nature, in my interactions with people and in my dreamtime that are telling me something the universe wishes me to know. I have met many who walk in this way. Perhaps you do. I have avoided some pitfalls by paying attention to signs and have also collected some assets I may well have missed without them. If you believe, as I do, that everything in the universe has a reason and a purpose, then it makes sense that the purpose of some is to leave subtle messages for others. Nature has provided many of these for me. Native Americans have a whole system of meanings attached to animals, plants, rocks, the elements and the like.

I have often found these to be accurate when I experience one of these creatures or elements. The trick is to balance what you see and what you infer from that. Ask your spirit guides and your own heart about the importance of what you have seen. I have met people who attach meaning to everything they see. That dilutes the power – if everything is a sign, then nothing can be a sign. On the other extreme side I have watched people looking at some remarkable happening and then dismissing it as 'odd'.

Balance – once again, balance. Added to balance is repetition and multiple elements. If the same sign keeps appearing, like a red-tailed hawk over you three days in a row near noon, begin to ask yourself what this is trying to tell you or teach you. Or if you see a huge lightning bolt come down through a tree on which an owl sits, you may want to explore the connection of these elements.

Then there are visions. Signs and messages are different than visions in my world. A vision opens before you in pictures, words or both in wake-time or dreamtime. At least, this is how I differentiate them. I recognize signs and messages coming at me almost daily, but I have had three visions – really three parts of one vision—through this entire walk I am on. Some never receive any vision. We each have our roles and mission. As with signs, I have had people tell me visions are 'bunk' and they would never have one because they don't exist. They are correct in part – they will never have one. What you put out, comes back. Others speak of the visions they have almost weekly. No judging but, maybe, these are signs? As with most things on the spirit road, there are no rights or wrongs, no one-way. Your heart and spirit will guide you if you allow them and, over time, what is 'so' becomes more and more clear.

This I can only tell you, it is not something that can be captured well in words. And now I sound like so many of the elders who have taught me...'Hmmm. Words don't work here. You will know when you need to know. You will understand when you need to understand'.

So the joke is on me and I need to apologize for each time I thought 'why can't they just give me an answer or a way! Just say it!'

Back to Colorado and heading up the Poudre. We crossed the pass about an hour and a half later, with a couple of stops so that Bonnie could explore some interesting rock formations along the way. The road we were to head up towards the cabin came into view. It was a dirt road that quickly turned into a dirt track and soon after a rutted, rock-strewn track. I knew it would be fun in our Jeep. Soon after arriving in Fort Collins I had released my 'back East' car – a mini-van – and bought a Jeep. After all, we wanted to get into the backcountry, didn't we? That was the argument that had won Bonnie over to the idea.

We drove the five miles to the cabin in about a half hour, lurching, sliding and tilting our way along. The cabin was rustic – two small rooms and an outhouse. But right in the middle of nowhere. There were some newer cabins down the road further, but all were empty at the moment.

We took out our bag, hiking shoes, water and food and put them in the back room. Then off we went for a hike through the woods. As we headed up a heavily treed hillside, I sensed elk near-by. This was that gift of sensing animals before I saw them and so often spotting wildlife before anyone else. Or spotting wildlife you could easily miss – high in a tree, under a shrub or along a riverside. I still thought it was just luck and good eyesight however and, for that time, this served me well. We followed the faint trail I thought I could see and, in about ten minutes, we came into an open space with five elk standing twenty feet away just staring at us. We enjoyed the moment, then slowly backed off so as not to disturb them.

This animal spotting sense sometimes produced interesting results. At one time, at another forest camp with two CSU faculty members, I was asked to help find deer. These two were hunters and had licenses for does. I am not a hunter and find no logical place in this world for guns. I am not a vegetarian either, so I can't deride hunters too loudly. But killing a magnificent buck or bull moose just to hang its head on a wall is hardly an evolved human trait to me. Having to hunt for food I get. But trophies – no, sorry NRA buffs.

I went with these two and quickly sensed large animals. So I led the way for about three miles over some rough, steep terrain. And found them their herd. A small herd of elk. What a shame they had deer licenses. They muttered and cursed all the way back to the cabin. Then we played poker and drank some beer as they laughed at my 'prowess'. The next time I was out with these two, they had elk licenses and so I found a large herd of deer – including one buck with a huge rack. This became a joke in the department – "Jim can always find game, just the wrong kind." In fact I believe this was put into effect by the animal spirits that now protect me, letting me see and feel the gift, but not providing game for sport alone.

We started a fire in the small indoor fireplace and heated up some food. Then we took it outside and ate under the huge pines all around us. The way food always tastes best – outside, sitting on Mother Earth with Father Sky above you. Then I chopped some wood for the night. The cabin would need some heating, as the dusk temperature drop would make it cold and drafty.

Then we settled in, talked a while and Bonnie soon wanted to read her geology book, so I wrote in my journal.

I kept a sporadic journal at best. Some days – or weeks – I only wrote a few lines. Sometimes a couple of pages and other times nothing for long stretches. No reason to this, I simply was learning to follow my inner voice. This also held true for photographs.

We seldom took pictures – whether in Europe, Central America, the wilds or anywhere else. After our first trip to England, we even stopped carrying a camera. Again, I can not tell you why exactly, except it seems, for me, what I was to see and learn needed to be 'in me' and not just recorded by mechanical means. Later, as my road continued, I never missed having these 'things' as I could go inside and see and hear all I had walked through. I thank Great Spirit for this gift each morning.

The next day we hiked, sat by a nearby pond and meditated and simply enjoyed all the Earth Mother was showing us. That night, with our fire leaping high and hot, we listened to the abundance of night animals and birds offering to sing us to sleep. Coyote whine, owl hoot, woodpecker up late, a snuffling, groveling sound around the perimeter of the cabin and the far off screech of a hawk out hunting. We slept soundly with this serenade in our ears and souls.

The next morning I awoke early, as I always did, and went outside to make coffee at the fire pit there. And I almost walked into the six elk browsing outside the cabin. I edged back in and woke Bonnie. We cracked the door and watched these regal animals until they moved off slowly. Then we ate, drank camp coffee, and repacked for the trip to Steamboat Springs.

Our trip to the Steamboat area was relaxing and informative. Bonnie decided to offer a three-day geology tour there in the near future and I offered to come and speak of the plants and animals we would see. And there were lots to see.

One morning we arose early and drove south of Steamboat. I looked to our left and saw a big, lumbering black bear a few hundred yards down the stream we had just crossed. We pulled over and watched her forage for some time. She looked our way and, after a while, must have felt we were safe as she looked to a copse of trees, made a harrumphing sound, and welcomed her two cubs to her side. We watched them all for over an hour — neither they nor us in a hurry to leave. I then thanked them and we moved on. We had multiple encounters of this sort during this trip, as I would have from here on out.

One day while in Steamboat, we decided to drive southwest from town. We often just drove to see what we would find, stopping for hikes whenever we were moved to do so. Not paying attention to any map we found ourselves, many hours later, driving along a river with a series of large ponds dotted along its course. In the big cottonwoods lining the banks were eagle nest after eagle nest. This went on for miles and we watched some twenty bald and golden eagles as we drove. We were open-mouthed, as we had never heard of this nesting place—and with so many eagles present, although not nesting at this time. We pulled over, pulled out some lunch, and watched the eagles come and go for over two hours. This was one time I would have liked a camera.

Finally, we had to leave to get back to Steamboat and some folks we met for dinner. The interesting part of this eagle day is we were never able to find this place again. We looked for waterways on maps and drove to them. We tried, over the years we were in Colorado, to drive as many roads as we could which might connect to this spot. Logic can't explain this – we were there, we sat and watched for an afternoon, but then we could never find our way back. We were there when we needed to be, with the eagles, and did not need to return again. This my spirit told me, not my mind.

Eagles have continued to be a power animal for me to this day. And would have special significance far into the future beyond this day.

We traveled back home to Fort Collins and Bonnie packed for her trip back East, while I taught, took classes and readied for Belize.

I drove Bonnie to the airport in Denver the end of the following week. She was looking forward to time with her twin sister and I was glad she had it...and I did not have to be there.

I had never gotten along with Bonnie's twin. There was no common ground between us and she, in my mind, was the 'evil twin'. Our dislike of each other was enormous and I had not yet learned to ignore and avoid. I was still a warrior male, so I attacked each time she insulted or belittled my beliefs or me. Such wasted energy, ways we all need to drop. She, and my reactions to her, were great teachers – I just wish I had learned the lessons quicker.

I took part in two inipis while I awaited my flight day to Belize. I spoke my intention to bring the spirit of our lodge circles with me while I traveled. And was told, by those in the lodges, to bring their energy with me as well. This all matched my still limited understanding of 'we are all one' and so I felt empowered to widen the circle.

14 | Belize: Red Road to Road of Many Colors

I MET UP WITH MY TWO MARRIED FACULTY FRIENDS, HANK AND LINDA, AT five AM the morning of our flight to Belize. We had a graduate student willing to drive us to the airport, so we loaded up into his car and headed south down Route 25. We chatted along the way, but I heard little as I was so hyped up by the trip before me. I would be working with the students, checking on Rob, the graduate student lead and working with Hank and Linda to support their teaching sessions. I was not teaching this first trip, as I would often on later trips.

Hank and Linda were an interesting couple. Bonnie and I got along well with them, but Hank's strong opinions often irritated her. Hank was a 'my way or the highway' guy and made no bones about it. Linda was softer, but also very opinionated about how things should work. They were fun to be with, but they liked to drink – often. For a couple of years Bonnie and I joined them too frequently in this past time. But, as I said, they were fun to be with and, when away from their university stress, quite fun-loving.

I will now add just a short entry here about Belize so you have some understanding about the land and its people. Belize is a fascinating country located in Central America, immediately south of Mexico. It is the only English and Spanish speaking nation in Central America. Travelers from North America can reach Belize in about two hours by air or a couple days by road through Mexico. Originally settled by the Maya, this diverse country is a former British colony and its people consist of Latinos, Creole, Maya, Garifuna and thousands of settlers from myriad ethnic backgrounds including European, North American, and Asian. For me, one of the most intriguing parts of this diverse population is that each group sees themselves as Belizeans first and Mayan, English, etc, second. A lesson many diverse countries, like the U.S., could learn from.

In addition to the diversity of its people, it is a place of incredibly varied natural wonder and ecosystems of many types – from wetlands, to cayes, to uplands, to forest and jungle, to marine environments and others. This makes it an unequaled place to learn from and about nature and culture. These were the things I was thinking about as I lined up at customs.

We went through security quickly – remember those days? – and boarded our flight to Houston. You had to go through Houston to get to Belize. In Houston, we boarded a Belize Air flight to Belize City. Free food and drinks on all Belize Air flights at that time. I took advantage of the food and Hank and Linda the food and drinks. In Belize City, we checked through customs and were met by a six-foot plus black man with a huge smile and outgoing personality. This was Richard Belisle, the Director of Natural Resources for the country and husband to Ann, the in-country director lead for the Belize Program the students were in.

"You are the CSU group?" he asked as he approached us.

"Yep, that's us," I answered.

"It is so good to have you here," he smiled as he shook our hands, "The students look forward to you arriving. I thought we would drive up to Belmopan and spend some time with Ann. You can stay with us tonight or at a room at the Bullfrog. Then tomorrow we will get you to the students and we all will go to the cayes. Okay?" Richard said.

"That sounds fine Richard," Hank answered for us.

We headed out of the airport after grabbing our bags off of the cart being wheeled in from the airplane. Customs was easy. We got in line, Richard waved to the customs agents, and we were passed through. As we walked outside all my senses came alive. The sights, sounds and smells of a tropical climate came flying my way. A lot different from the Colorado Front Range. Hank and Linda seemed not to notice as we headed towards Richard's car. We had talked on the plane and I was surprised that Linda, who taught tourism in our department, had never been outside of Canada and the United States. And Hank had only been to a few places, mostly for conferences that were housed in large hotels. I thought this would be an eye-opening trip for them.

We jammed into Richard's car and headed down the paved highway towards Belize City. This is one of the two paved highways in Belize – the rest are an adventure in dust, mud, rocks and ruts depending on the season and weather.

"We need to go to Belize City for some supplies, but first we stop for something cold," Richard explained as he headed away from Belize City.

We drove a short distance and pulled into an open-air bar and café – Belize style. That's with lizards on the floor and beautiful birds flying through the patios. It was an old, small place run by a small, round jovial man in his fortys.

"Hey, man. What you havin'?" he called to Richard as he led us in.

"Good rum and good local beer. What would you like?" Richard asked us.

"Beer for me," I answered.

"I'll have a rum and coke and a beer," from Hank.

"Beer's fine," from Linda.

"Four Belikin and a rum and coke. Dark rum," Richard told the barkeep.

"We produce our own rum here, the dark is best," Richard turned back to us as we sat, "And the beer is Belikin. The Belize beer."

The drinks came and Richard asked for some fruit and cheese while we all settled back. The beer was good – smooth and cold. We all drank quickly as we were parched by the humidity we were unused to. Richard ordered a second round, which we drank slowly. "How do you like Belize so far?" he asked.

"My senses are working overtime and my sweat glands relearning how to work overtime," I answered him with a smile.

"It seems very colorful," Linda contributed.

"This is just the edges. Many eye, ear and nose treats are coming," Richard shared.

We finished our drinks and snack, thanked the barkeep, eased into Richard's car again and he headed us to Belize City. We drove through some economically depressed areas as we headed to the center of town.

"Look at this poverty and filth," Linda commented as we drove.

"You can't expect much from third world countries," Hank told her. I thought, oh boy, this will be an interesting time here with these two. They've already looked, seen and judged and we haven't even gone thirty miles yet. But I said nothing and just enjoyed the smells rolling in through the open windows.

We stopped at a food store and Richard loaded the boxes the clerk brought out to him on top of the luggage. Then, with a full car, we headed north to Belmopan, the capital.

Belize City was the capital until the Belizeans tired of constantly rebuilding after each hurricane – the majority of which hit Belize City in its coastal location. They built Belmopan inland, but I always felt most still considered Belize City the real capital. We bounced up the other paved road to Belmopan and arrived a couple hours later. We drove to the Bullfrog Inn and Hank and Linda decided they wanted to stay there. They asked me to stay also and I agreed.

We dropped off our bags and headed over to Richard's house. It was a small, modest house on a residential street. With a small fenced in yard and several cars and vans pulled in front of it. Some of the students were here, while others were still in northern Belize. We got out to a bunch of hugs and hellos, some sunburned bodies and an assortment of nicks and scratches. We met Ann as she came out to greet us.

Ann was Canadian by birth, of French ancestry, and she and Richard had been married for about twenty years. A thoughtful, often solemn woman of short stature but tall presence.

"How was your trip?" she asked.

"Fine, no problem," I answered, being the closest to her.

"You sound Belizean already," she jokingly said.

As we begin walking this trip to Belize I will tell you I could write another whole book about my work and the teachings I received while there and in the surrounding countries. Again, if it's needed, that is another book I will write down the road. Here, in this journey, I will tell some of the stories and share some of the contacts and teachings I received. Part of me is saddened by this, as each culture I have learned from deserves full respect in what I share. Yet that would blossom this book into something too large to carry and too much to read. It's better if we journey together many times, learning more from each group of teachers as we journey together in the future.

I spent the evening over dinner at the Bullfrog Inn with Hank, Linda, Richard and Ann. We had a good talk about the program and the students. At one point Ann shared that Rob was a nice young man, but maybe needed a little more control in his actions with the students. Hal had asked me to check on this aspect of the program before I left CSU, so I was now tuned in to the need for this. I spent the night in a small, un-airconditioned room at the Bullfrog listening to music from the outdoor patio and, later, the frogs and night insects. I slept soundly and got up refreshed at five am. Sweaty, but refreshed – and a cold shower took care of the sweaty piece.

For years, I had slept little. Pretty much from my twenties until the last few years. If I slept five hours – that was good. Then on occasion, I would crash for several days. My waking time was always filled with those things I am passionate about, as I have been sharing with you. This is not a model I would ever suggest. It was part of the reason for my collapse much further down the road. Action, motion and brain noise were just another addiction – another means to not go inside and deal with the inner person. I have found, with almost everyone who seeks me out as a healing guide, that each has his or her addiction or addictions. Drugs, alcohol, food, sex, action, and physical activity – the list of these addictions is as long and varied as are we human types. Some people these excesses take out of the game and move them to the spirit world and others deal with them – fight them – their entire lives. Some of us come to finally accept them for what they are, stop fighting and start listening and learning. This is not easy. There is no roadmap, but there are ways and means to begin dealing with whatever your addictions are. And to stay aware and awake so that new excesses do not replace those we manage to release. I offer that no one can truly walk the spiritual road in all of their power if they do not address their demons.

Facing these things that would block us is also a journey, as new excesses can creep into our routine at any time. Each week I inventory myself and examine my balance. And usually find some excesses I need to address – before they take over and grow. This helps us stay in tune with mind, body and spirit – the other area where balance is critical.

Richard picked us up and we went back to his house, where Ann had made a nice breakfast. After checking for any banana – a fruit to which I have a potentially fatal allergy – and finding none, I dug into the food with great appetite and enjoyment. I had eaten bananas since I was a child and had them each morning on my cereal. Suddenly, in my late teens, I had to be rushed to a hospital where a tube was inserted down my throat. I was swelling up and could not breath. Later, after many medical tests, it was shown that bananas were a fruit that could kill me the next time I ate one. And now here I was in Central America, where bananas and their by-products were everywhere. I still don't understand this strange allergy, but work on it energetically quite often.

Allergies, in the energetic healing world, are all about emotions. I still work on releasing old emotional blocks and wonder if, one day, my allergies will cease. I am curious to see how this evolves.

After breakfast we loaded everyone's gear, the food and some boxes into one of the field vans of the program. Then the students and our group piled into Richard's car and the van. And off we headed to Belize City to catch a boat to the cayes. We would be on Ambergris Caye in the town of San Perdo for ten days. From there to Caye Caulker. The cayes, or islands, are great places to learn about the reefs of Belize, as well as many of her cultures. The Belize reefs are the second largest in the world, with only Australia having a larger system. Ambergris allows buildings of only two stories and only walking or golf carts to get around. A short boat ride takes you to the Hol Chan Marine Preserve – which Richard also was in charge of.

Belize has preserved about two-thirds of its lands and waters. Yet they only have a small handful of people in their natural resource department to monitor the use of these lands. It is quite a problem – one that Richard wrestled during the years he was the director. On future trips to Belize I would do some research around tourist uses of Hol Chan. This is the way much of the study of the protected areas is provided to the Belizean staff.

Rob and most of the students had been in San Pedro for five days ahead of us. The remainder of the students were now coming with us. We got to the docks and Richard went to negotiate with one of the boat owners to get us to San Pedro. Richard was coming with us and would stay for three days before returning to Belmopan. After a few minutes of animated negotiating, he came back to us and told us to begin unloading everything on the pier next to three boats, which would take us over. The boats, which take people to the various cayes, are fairly long, tapered powerboats, capable of good speed across the open waters. They hold about a dozen people and some gear. With our group, a couple of Richard's staff and all the supplies we were taking with us we needed the three boats to make it work. So we unloaded the car and vans and waited as the crew loaded everything on board. They were paying close attention to the weight distribution as the stowed bundles in multiple places on the boats.

Two of the students wandered off as the rest of us watched the loading process and chatted with Richard's staff about the marine preserve. After about twenty minutes the gear and supplies were all loaded aboard and the captain of the lead boat called us together so he could also distribute us, by weight, amongst the boats.

"Everybody line up over here, next to the lead boat," the Captain ordered. The students slowly started moving ahead, some still with small bags in hand.

"First put any bags on the ground. They go in the boat, not with you," the captain continued. Some started to gripe about this and I stepped in.

"People, bags on the dock. It's not optional. If anyone has any medication they need over the next two hours, stick them in your pockets. Otherwise, the directions were for all gear on the dock." Some frowns and grumbles, but everyone complied.

Once everyone was lined up, the Captain spoke again, "Is everyone here?"

One of the students spoke up, "Jen and Steve are not back. They said they were going to the post office."

Of course, we had asked no one to leave the group as the boats were loaded. All listening, but two had opted not to hear. I went over to the Captain with Richard.

"We need to get going," the captain told us, "It's two hours over, unloading and ninety minutes back. We need to be back on that schedule for another group I have coming."

"Sorry Captain, I will go look for them," Richard offered.

"Richard, I think we need to look at another way here," I suggested. "You told me Rob was having trouble with discipline. Students doing as they wished. That's too dangerous here. Let's set an example right now," I concluded.

"What do you have in mind Jim?" Richard asked.

"Captain, can you start loading everyone on board knowing the two missing are average weight and height?" I asked.

"Sure, but we still need to go soon," he answered. "I know. Let's tell the students if they don't make it back, they will be left behind. And mean it. We won't tell them, if that happens; I will also remain and book space for the three of us when another boat goes out. And have them pay for it with their expense money," I relayed to Richard and the Captain.

Richard began laughing as he spoke, "I like this very much! This story will go through all the students by tonight. Ann may not be happy, but she is not here. Are you okay with that?"

"Sure. I was asked by Hal to do what I could about safety and security and how the students were behaving. I will have no problem telling him what we did, and that it was my idea, and why we did it." I confirmed to Richard.

"One more thing, Captain. If they make it back in time, can you work it so they will be seated up on the bow of the boat? Together on the small front, triangular seat?" I asked.

"Sure, but I usually don't use that space for people because they would get soaked." The captain answered as he began to smile. "Are you Belizean, mon?" he asked with a chuckle. Richard was laughing and wrapping his arm around my shoulder.

"No, but part of my heart is quickly becoming Belizean. Wet I want, as long as they will be safe," I said.

"Plenty safe and plenty wet," the Captain ended our discussion of the plan.

We went back to the students and told them we would begin loading and would leave Jen and Steve behind if they did not make it back by the time we were loaded. That caused some quick response. "You can't do that", "What will they do?", "How will they get there?" and so on, began coming all at once.

"Hey, people," I began to answer them, "This is not a game here. This is a group effort and when directions are given, there is a reason. It's too dangerous to go wandering off. This is a country totally different than what you are used to. And people have their jobs to do. The captain needs to be back for his next load. Jen and Steve will have to find a boat willing to take them and pay whatever it costs. That's the way it is going to be."

The Captain began picking out students and assigning them places on the boats. Richard's staff sat where instructed and Richard went and stood by the wheel of the lead boat. After another twenty minutes, we were almost ready. The engines were fired up and started to warm. These were fast boats and would soon be skimming like flat stones across the surface of the water. I was about to step off and wait, when I saw the two truant students running down the dock next to us.

"Let's make the point again Captain. Can the first boat pull off?" I asked.

"John, go. Right behind you," the Captain called over to the pilot of one of the boats. The first boat pulled away from the dock, revved its engine and began moving into the channel. Steve and Jen were now waving wildly, but I pretended not to see. As the second boat made ready to pull away from the dock, I looked up and pointed towards the laggards. The Captain looked and nodded grimly – trying not to smile. Two minutes later, Jen and Steve reached the boats panting.

"You were going to leave us!" Jen yelled, almost in tears.

"You ignored Richard's directions and we needed to get the group to San Pedro. The Captain has a schedule. The whole group and the captain and his crew can't be disrupted because you two decided to do as you pleased," I answered.

"We only went to the post office and on the other docks," Steve panted pleadingly. "We would have been stuck here."

"You would have found another boat and paid for it I hope. If not, you would have called Ann for instructions. No more talk. You already have everyone late. Get on where the Captain directs," I sternly ended. The Captain directed them to their soon to be 'wet seats' and we took off.

As we headed out of the docks, the boats moved at a slow pace. We watched Belize City unfold before us as we headed across her length to reach open water. I sat, next to Richard, and sucked in the sights, sounds and smells. The boats continued at their leisurely pace so as not to disturb or injure the marine life beneath us. After about a half hour we reached the open expanse of water between the mainland and the cayes. The engines now roared and we rocketed across the top of the water, bouncing as we went. Spray began rolling over the bows each time the boats dipped in a swell. Our two roaming students were quickly soaked to the skin. Richard nudged me and smiled his huge, glorious smile. Then he shook his head, eyes twinkling and looked down so his reaction would not be too obvious.

Hank and Linda were in another boat. We had not included them in the discussions around the missing students. As faculty of the University, I had not wanted to put them at risk of disciplinary action. As a graduate student who also taught as an instructor and ran the non-profit Environmental Center, I was in an interesting place as per university policies. Added to that was the fact that my funding streams came from several university sources. This was at different times, a curse or a blessing. I was not 'faculty' and so did not always follow faculty guidelines. Yet I functioned as student, faculty and Center director. So when the University did not appreciate something I did, they tended to arbitrarily use the rules from any of the areas to reprimand me. Or reward me when they were pleased with results. A great learning experience for me in learning to walk many roads at once.

We passed two other cayes on our way to San Pedro. One was Caye Caulker, where we would spend time later on this trip. There were multi-colored fish of all sizes passing below us and multi-colored birds of all shapes winging over us. What an amazing place I was already finding this to be!

We pulled up to the dock in San Pedro two hours after leaving Belize City just as the captain had predicted. Some of the other students were there to greet us and help move the supplies to the camp. After everything was unloaded, we thanked the Captain and he left for the remainder of his rounds.

Our two wet students approached me and apologized for their behavior – promising not to wander off again. I was certain some of the other students were already sharing the story with those in San Pedro before them. Nothing is faster then the student grapevine and I was counting on that.

The faculty working with the students had left two days before we arrived so the students had two days to relax and enjoy before Hank and Linda began their sessions. We got to the base camp, which was a large open space with a few small cabins on the perimeter. The students' tents were set up in various groupings and the cook tent was near the back of the space. Everything was unloaded and the new students set up their tents. A few minutes later Rob showed up with a few of the other students.

"Hi all," Rob said in greeting, "How was the trip down?"

"Good, Rob. Is everything set up for my lecture tomorrow on the visitor norms?" Hank asked in his usual need-to-get-to-his work immediately way.

"Ah, we don't have a place or projector yet. There was a problem with the hall I thought we would use," Rob answered.

Hank frowned, obviously not enjoying this answer. Hank is a researcher; born and bred to gather data, sit at his computer analyzing it and writing papers on the result. And he was very good at it. Linda was the same, although not at quite an extreme, making them a good match.

I was an applications person – I wanted to look at studies, talk to people and rolling my sleeves up, use what I had learned in a good way. This was a good balance between Hank and Linda and myself.

"Well, we need to start tomorrow so I get in everything I need to teach," Hank continued – as he would until he felt certain his 'teaching space' was secured.

"Ah, I'll see what else I can do," Rob said, flustered and embarrassed.

"Hank, let me stop in some of the local hotels and see what I can uncover," I offered.

"Great, would you do that Jim?" Linda asked.

"Sure, I can give it a try. After we get done setting up here," I answered.

The four of us chatted a little longer, then Hank and Linda went to the cabin they would occupy to unpack their things. This meant, for Hank, his computer and papers first – everything else second.

"Rob, how is it going? Where are the rest of the students?" I asked. I had noticed only about half the students were around the campsite.

"Okay. But some things have been a little difficult. The students were all supposed to be here when the boats arrived, but some have gone off to the beach and into town. I told them to only go in groups and to always have one of our Belizean guides along, but some have not listened."

"What can I do to help? Anything you want me to talk to the students about? Anything I can do for you?" I asked.

Most of the students knew me from taking my courses or from work at the Center and my rapport with most was good, so I wanted to support Rob however I could.

"If you could talk some more about safety and let them know this is not a vacation time only, that would help. I might be too close to them in age and that hurts my credibility I think." Rob was thirty so his thought about the age issue was a good one. And, being such a kind, mild-mannered man didn't help when trying to be an authority figure.

"Sure, let's call a circle tonight and we can all chat. Okay with you?" I asked, wanting his permission so he saw I wanted to support, not supersede his authority.

"Yeah, we can try. They've been going off to the bars and community parties a lot at night. Makes me nervous," Rob agreed. What he said – and what was implied behind the words – made me certain I needed to get a sense of what was going on.

"Let me invite them later. I'll think of some reason," I told Rob, "For now, let me see if I can get space for Hank so he can relax."

"Awesome. He needs the space for the next three days. I thought it would be easy, but I haven't really found anything," Rob admitted.

I asked one of the Belizean guides, Danny, to take a walk into town with me and told him what I was looking for. He agreed – mentioning that a cold Belikin would really taste good. I told him it would be on me and we started out.

The first inn we stopped at had no space that would accommodate the group, so we had a Belikin and went on to the second down the road a block. The owners were not in, but the staff person told us to stop back later if we had no success. I thanked her, ordered two more Belikins, and sat drinking with Danny. Two locals Danny knew came in, so I ordered two more Belikins. Two Rastafarian, Rasta, looking guys – full dreadlocks and clipped Creole speech.

The Rasta movement is a black movement that rejects Western ways and promotes black culture and, sometimes, violent behavior. I would find that many, especially in Belize, affected the look without really being a part of the movement.

"How you was Danny mon?" the taller of the two, Frico, asked.

"I be good mon," Danny answered, matching their lingo. "Dis my mon, Jim from Colorado. He be good mon," he said, introducing me.

"Jimbo mon. Good day," he said to me as he reached out his right fist, knuckles forward. This is the Belizean equivalent of a handshake, especially between men. Each reaches out the right hand, fisted and the fists are tapped together.

As we tapped knuckles I said, "Good day to you mon. Good to meet you."

"You been makin' him be Belizean Danny mon," the other Rasta, Big, laughed. Big, naturally, was small. He stood about five foot six and had a rooster swagger when he walked.

As we spoke I liked the humor in his eyes and words and realized my discomfort at first sitting with three black Belizeans, two in dreads, I did not know. Unconscious judging and typecasting, I realized. Happy that at least I had realized it.

"He be brand new, mon. Being Belize takes time to work da magic," Danny told him.

"We work on him mon. Bring down to the town rag Saturday night," Big said.

"Yeah, mon. We do dat," Danny agreed.

We finished our beers and said goodbye to Frico and Big, promising to be at the town party on the weekend, and started back down the road and strip of small hotels coming up.

"Danny, let's hit the big hotel down the end there," I said looking down the line of hotels.

"We can try, but that's the big tourist hotel here in town," Danny answered.

So we walked to the hotel and, I was happy to learn, the manager was in. I introduced myself and talked about the project and the student needs of a place to learn. He liked the idea and the fact I promised to mention his hotel to the program leads, so he walked us into the rooms he had for meetings. A few minutes later, he had agreed to the largest room, his projector and screen his staff would prepare and a computer hook up for Hank to bring up his images. Then he asked about food. I told him we would take the students back to the camp for lunch. He offered to provide sandwiches and fruit for the group, to which I said 'yes' in a heartbeat.

And this for all three days. I had not yet learned about intent, trust and manifestation, so I thought I had done an amazing job. I sure had plenty of ego issues to work through – so many, I'm surprised at any successes I had until the point I began to deal with the big S energetically superimposed on my tee shirt.

With this done, I asked Danny if he wanted to get some lunch. Really a rhetorical question, as he had been talking about his empty stomach for an hour or more. So we headed to a little Mexican restaurant down one of the side streets. We ordered a dish of shellfish, vegetables and herbs I had never had before. And big glasses of water, since it had gotten hot and we both were feeling parched. As we waited for the food I asked Danny how he felt things were going with the students.

Danny was an interesting man. He was a mix of Mayan and Garifuna (African) blood, stood about five foot ten and was muscled like a prizefighter. He also seemed to know everyone, saying 'good day' to almost all we passed on the streets. And he took his job seriously, according to Richard and Ann. When students went off by themselves without a guide, he followed along behind them in case any trouble arose. It was not like Belize was a dangerous place, especially by developing world country standards, but young, gullible students were easy targets for mischief. Especially given that most of the students had never been outside of the U.S. and certainly never in a country such as Belize.

I knew Danny had been sizing me up – still was, as he looked me squarely in the eyes as he evaluated my question. "Pretty good mon, nobody has gotten into bad trouble. Two cuts in the mangrove, but the local doc fixed them up," he said in a measured fashion.

"Danny, I'm not looking to point fingers or blame anyone. I care about these young people – many are my students back at CSU. And Rob is my friend. I suggested him for this role. But to help and support him and know how to work with the students, I need some square talk," I said, knowing I had to put my cards on the table.

He took a long drink and as the food arrived, waited a minute before speaking.

"Rob is a good guy. I like him. The students like him. You know, everybody likes him. But he has trouble getting the students to follow his directions. Yesterday, two of the girls went off by themselves. Not cool, mon. And they met two Belizean guys and agreed to go out on their boat with them. The guys came on strong and they were lucky not to be raped or messed with. And at night, too many are going off drinking without telling anyone. None of us guides (there were two others besides Danny) can help anyone if we don't know what's goin' on mon. They tell Rob mon, they are adults and can do what they want. But they don't know this place. Last night four of them got into a near fight at the Rasta bar the other end of town. Some tough guys there. Tonight there is talk of many groups goin' drinkin' and partying before the session begins tomorrow. I am worried about it." As Danny shared all this, my brain was working through some approaches.

"Danny, I won't share any of this. But thanks, it's what I need to know."

We ate our meal and began heading back to the campsite, pausing to say good day to everyone Danny knew. When we got back I went to Hank and Linda's cabin to have a chat. As the faculty members teaching next, they had responsibility for the students also. I told them what Danny had told me, but deleted who it was I heard the stories from. Then asked for any thoughts they might have.

"I worry about tonight and this drinking you heard about. I'm afraid this behavior will escalate and Rob will lose even more control," Linda correctly worried.

"And, as the adults here, we have some of the responsibility for the students welfare," Hank added.

"I think we need to do something about tonight and then begin to meet with the students about their behavior in the broader sense later," I suggested.

"I totally agree," Linda said.

"How about this. I saw an antique truck in town with old signs painted on it. What if we buy cases of beer and have the truck deliver it after dinner. Then we can have Danny have a couple of his friends come and play guitar. The students will be drinking, but at least it will be here where its safe," I thought through as I spoke.

"Great idea. We will buy the beer if you can take care of the guitar players," Hank said.

"Done," I agreed.

"I don't like them drinking either, but it makes tonight safe and gives us time for more planning, so I agree," Linda chimed in.

So I rounded up Danny, told him our plan and headed to town where we rented the truck and a driver, bought the beer and told them to put it on the truck and tracked down two guitar players Danny knew well. Then back to camp once again.

I found Hank and Linda poring over a paper they were working on and told them the camp party was on.

"Oh yeah, Hank, with the student problem I forgot to tell you we have a great space for your lessons, with your electronic needs being taken care of and lunch for everyone."

"How did you do that?!" Linda said amazed.

"I just went in to the hotels and began asking. No magic. Got lucky," I answered her.

"Perfect, thanks Jim," Hank said and I left to take a short nap.

Before dinner, I asked Rob to take a walk so we could talk a while with no one around to see or hear us. We walked through town and out into the mangroves, sitting on the trunk of a beautiful spreading tree of a variety I was unfamiliar with. I had spoken to a few of the students I knew well just before this and had gotten stories similar to the ones Danny told, but I didn't want to make Rob feel like others had pointed the finger at him. He didn't need any more reasons to cause his confidence to sink even lower. Thinking it through, I decided to approach Rob the same way I taught, by asking questions and seeing what came out.

"So, Rob, how goes the journey so far?" I asked.

"It's really been a great experience, but much harder than I thought it would be. I am having a lot of trouble getting the students to listen at times. Maybe I'm too young or just too nice. I could use some help," Rob said dejectedly.

"Hey, first time doing anything like this. Are the students safe or are you worried about that?"

"Too many go out without asking and getting a guide. Then they tell me they are adults and their free time is theirs to use. Almost had real trouble with two of the girls and some Belizean guys. But I'm not sure what to do to change it. They know you and respect you. And they like Hank and Linda. Maybe you all can talk with them. If Linda would meet with the girls that would really help, too. As a woman she can say things I'm not comfortable with."

"Good idea. I'm sure she will," I answered him.

"Rob, I did hear a lot of the students were planning on drinking in town tonight. I heard some talking earlier and asked Danny what he thought. He doesn't like it at all. What do you think?"

"It's not good, even in groups. If they drink too much, or say the wrong thing, a fight could break out," he agreed. "We've planned a party with Hank and Linda. Hope that's okay?" I asked.

"Perfect. It will keep them here. But there may be problems if you bring in drinks or beer. They are a legal age here, but not by U.S. standards," Rob said.

"I know," I agreed, "But if we don't bring in beer, at least, I think they will sneak out anyway."

"Right," Rob agreed. So I told him the plan and he thanked me for any help I could give him.

Then he added, "Jim, we have a couple real problem students. Especially Jonathan. He's not from CSU so you don't know him. He questions everything I say, gives the staff a hard time and goes off whenever he likes. I've tried to speak to him, but he ignores anything I say."

"We'll meet with Hank, Linda and Richard tomorrow and talk about how we can approach the students and then let's see what happens. Let me know if this guy acts up again and we can talk about it," I said.

"Okay, good," Rob finished as we got up and strolled through the mangrove swamp on a narrow, winding trail, back to camp.

As we entered camp we passed a student I didn't know and Rob introduced me. It was Jonathan – so now I knew who he was.

Dinner began at six and I arrived early with Richard to chat with the cook and other staff members a bit. I thanked each for their hard work and Richard asked about any needs. After a few minutes we got our plates of chicken, rice and beans and a fresh salad and sat at one of the tables. Hank and Linda joined us as we dug into our food. The students were lining up and getting their dinners served. Same as ours, plus some big wedges of good fresh bread.

A minute later we heard some commotion. Followed by yelling at the head of the meal line. I got up, with Danny and another guide, Raphael, an older Mayan man, to see what was wrong. There he was, Jonathan, yelling at the cook.

"When the hell will we get something different to eat!? The same crap every night! Chicken and rice and beans! I'm sick of it! My parents paid a lot of money for me to come here and I expect real food, not chicken and rice and beans every damn night!"

As he finished this he threw his plate on the ground. Everyone stood silent – in shock. Up stepped Raphael, right into his face – five foot eight facing six foot one.

"Son, I hear what you are saying. We do the best we can here. The cook and I both serve the same thing to our families each night – but without the chicken."

"And sometimes without the rice," the quiet, mild cook added from her place behind the serving line.

I watched tears well up in many eyes with these simple words. I know they were in mine. But Jonathan seemed confused and still angry. I'm not sure he understood the basic truth in these words. So I grabbed him by the shirt and pulled him to the side. Hank and Linda could see my anger, so they came over and took him off to be spoken to.

Danny said to me, "Jim, that's his third time with behavior like this. But this is worse. I hope something is done."

After talks with Jonathan, and then talks with Richard and a call to Hal, the program director back at CSU, Jonathan was sent on one of the boats, with one of the guides, at dawn the next day to reach the airport for the one flight out. The end of his Belizean trip. And a perfect lesson for all the students – not that any other ever did anything this outrageous.

A little after seven the antique truck came rumbling into camp. I had not realized it operated on steam, which had it come huffing and puffing like an old locomotive. The cases of beer were on board, as were the guitar players. We called the students in and told them we all needed to stay in camp tonight so we had brought the party to us. Everyone had a blast and no one got drunk or out of control. The next day, we spent the morning talking to the students together, and then in little groups, about their twelve weeks in Belize, Rob's responsibility, their responsibilities and opened to a good sharing amongst all. This was no silver bullet and issues continued to arise, but it certainly helped.

We 'adults' – whatever that means – all felt good about having diverted a night of drinking and possible trouble and our subsequent talks with the students. I felt like I had done my part in supporting Rob as best I could, but hoped I would be comfortable leaving after my three weeks.

What we didn't know, and I would not be told for four years, is that Hank, Linda and I were 'blackballed' by CSU for providing beer for underage students. For me, no one ever asked me to explain and no one told me of this decision. So I created my own 'stories' for why I had to get funding from the department, other sources or the Belize program every time I went to work in Belize from then on. Looking back, it's another great lesson about not creating your own reasons for why things have happened. Accept them and move with what you have.

I will skip the rest of the ten days in the cayes, saving it for another day, and move us into the interior – to the Cockscomb Jaguar Preserve. The Jaguar Preserve is the largest of its kind in the world. This preserve covers 150 square miles of rain forest, crisscrossed by many trails. It is truly tropical, with over 100 inches of rain a year. And an unbelievable haven for wildlife of all types.

The day after we arrived I went with one of Richard's staffers, Jon, to meet a very old Mayan man, Roberto, who lived in the jungle near the preserve. He was to come to talk with the students one day and Richard wanted to see him about that. We found him, at eighty plus years of age, out in his field working. We had brought water and fruit along and we sat with him to talk. He had a large smile – almost too large for his small frame, which he was unafraid to use.

Roberto was leathery, golden brown from the suns rays and slightly stooped from age. His eyes and smile, however, spoke thirty, not over eighty. He offered some nuts he had in a pouch on his side and so we three sat eating fruit and nuts while we talked. He and Jon talked about the Belize government, the scarcity of money and people in the natural areas and their respective families for some time. I listened and ate. Then they talked about the logistics of getting Roberto to the students and came up with a plan. Jon said he needed to change one of the tires on his truck and left me to connect with Roberto while he went to deal with this.

"How long have you lived here, Roberto?"

"Over eighty years amigo. My whole life. I plant, learn the medicine of the plants and roots, and practice the spiritual ways of my grandparents grandparents. It's a good life."

"I think Richard told me you are Mayan."

"Yes, my people built great cities in these lands. In Belize, Mexico, Guatemala and elsewhere. The culture grew until it was time to step back."

I found this an interesting way to present the Mayan history.

"I have also heard my Sioux friends speak about their people going back to old ways with less grandness."

"Ah, you know some of our red brothers and sisters from your country. How do you know them? Are you Native?"

"No, I am Italian by descent. But I have worked with the Native American people at Colorado State and have begun to learn from some of their medicine people. It has become the spiritual road I will walk for now."

"I have always wanted to meet some natives from America. We have much in common and much we could share. I think it's good you are learning from them. And good they are willing to teach you. If you come to Belize again, I will bring you to some Mayan people who would welcome you and share Mayan ways if you would share the native ways you are learning."

"I know very little yet, but am always happy to share anything I do know. And I know I will be here again. I love this place."

I was stunned I was being offered a chance to share ways with the Mayan people. I thought it was the Lakota way I was to learn. What an opportunity if I got to learn the customs and ceremonies of two cultures.

Roberto and I sat and talked for about an hour until Jon returned and said it was time to head back. He wanted to reach the camp before sundown with the narrow, rutted, sometimes cliff hanging roads we needed to take. I thanked Roberto for his time and promised to return.

"Good. I will be here. Where else? You stay with me a while when you come."

The rest of this trip in Belize seemed to fly by, yet many, many events unfolded and many lessons were learned, especially by me. But, after our three-week stint, Hank, Linda and I were dropped off at the airport by Richard for our flight home.

15 | Time Out

Now we take some time out from our journey together and sit in circle as I share some things. I do so because I see it is now time to know these things between us. I do not mean this book to be a 'how-to' to spiritual growth nor to be a road map for anyone's life path. It is my life path and has many teachings within its words. Yet there are no signposts identifying these moments. They are not needed. Those who need to gather understandings from this journey will do so. I teach as my teachers taught me and as I taught in schools and colleges in the past – through stories and questions. This can frustrate many people, as it has me at times, but it is how we truly learn. Memorizing a list of presidents does not allow you to understand American history. Just so, having answers given you does not allow you to understand the questions or those answers.

A story to demonstrate this: While at CSU I was asked to be the keynote speaker at the AmeriCorps graduation ceremony one year. I gladly agreed. I spoke of learning by doing, practicing what you thought might work and growing through your mistakes. And I congratulated all the young corpsmembers I had worked with in doing just that.

Then they asked the young woman who ran one of the groups to speak. She came up, a small, thin young woman of twenty-four and stood silent for a full minute. Then she spoke, as she looked me directly in the eyes.

"My group has worked with you for two years Jim. We have built things and learned things I never thought we could do. And I remember how, especially in the beginning, when I asked you a question you would ask me 'what do you think'? I would get furious with you. So angry that I would go out with the group and look at whatever the question was about. And we would all talk and come up with a way to go about it. Then, since you would not help, we started doing it. And often it worked. Or, if we hit a snag, you would come by and make a suggestion or ask another question. Now I thank you from the bottom of my heart for being the teacher you are. I understand what you were doing. Not lazy, as my anger made me think then, but guiding us so we could really learn by doing it our way."

Then I was awarded a plaque I still cherish. It's not the physical plaque I cherish, but the way it allows me to remember this way of teaching.

A key point I make now – also alive in the preceding story – is do not judge. As we journey further together I ask you not to judge me, anyone else in this trek and, most importantly, not yourself. In the Lakota way, when you point a finger at anyone, three fingers point back at you. In my way, after many trials getting there, whenever you point a finger at anyone, you are really pointing at yourself. This is a key to spiritual, as well as personal, growth. This answer I do give you – if you judge yourself or others you will not move forward. This is in part because judging others brings on fear and anger, the two things that can stop we humans dead in our tracks. You have seen judgments of others I have made already and there are more to come. And, most often, I was wrong. Please, feel free to accept or reject the things I will share, but work in your spirit not to judge them. You will find if you work on this judging tendency we all have, your path will be smoother and you will travel much further in less time.

I said we would sit in circle and I would share some things. I opened this chapter that way because, as I sit here writing, I see you who will read this gathered around me in circle. This is a circle at work — me writing as guided by my inner voice and spirit and you reading for whatever reason brought you to this book. And I see this is a circle of change — male and female, the four colors, old and young, awake and beginning to awaken. When you finish this book the circle will not close, but will move ahead in some way I do not yet see. Maybe in other books. Maybe in some connection on the web or through meetings. Maybe some totally new way. And each in that circle will have opportunities to teach and to learn. How these things are to work I don't know, nor do I care at this time. When more is needed, if it is, it will come. I do not know how many are in this circle either — how many have been guided to this book. Fifty or fifty thousand makes no difference and is also not my job to concern myself with. It may not even be published and so I only write for myself. That too is perfect if that is what Spirit wishes. It has taken me many years, with still present backslides, to reach a place where I not only understand, but also accept, these unknowns.

You will see clearly how surrender and trust have evolved in me over the years as we go forward. Many of us say we surrender and trust in God or the universe, but few can actually walk there. It is one of the most difficult things for a human to do — truly and completely surrender and trust.

Not long ago, I had a vision for a daunting piece of work Spirit has asked of me. Many pieces of smaller visions over the years came together in this and I began to doubt my ability to walk this road and the truth of the vision itself. I worked hard in my spirit to stay in that place of surrender and trust I have cultivated through my hardships and losses. I did a Chanunpa ceremony that night to focus, center and ask for further guidance. I clearly heard Spirit say to me, "Do you surrender and trust?" And I answered in my prayers, "Yes, Great Spirit, I do." And again I heard "Do you truly surrender and trust?" Again, as I prayed through the pipe I answered 'yes' — but a little slower. A third time the voice spoke in my heart "Do you TRULY SURRENDER AND TRUST?" I answered back, "I am an imperfect human learning better how to surrender and trust each day. I am doing so at the best of my ability now."

With this I felt no more presence and finished my pipe off. I felt relieved to know I still had a lot of work to do in the surrender and trust area, but that the more adept I become at it, the easier the road I need to walk.

I offer you the chance to practice your own surrender and trust gifts as we walk here. Go beyond just not judging anything I have to say, but attempt to surrender any doubts or skepticism that may come at you and trust that whatever you need to get from this journey, you will get. Ask yourself three times the 'do you truly surrender and trust' question and, each time, go deeper for your answer. These are tools that will serve you well in many areas as you walk your road.

I see it is also important that I share a little about the space I occupy as I write this. I think this is so you can 'see' where I 'see' our circle formed together as I write. I sit in my office looking out the window at the hummingbirds darting to and fro from their feeders in Page Springs, about ten miles south of Sedona, Arizona. I am living in a small house in the desert in what is an oasis – circled by natural springs, trees and bushes. Seven ponds are a short walk below my place and Oak Creek just a little further beyond them. A flock of red-winged blackbirds – thirty or more – are sweeping in over the ponds to feast on the black oiled seed laid out for them. They are landing with great energy and attacking the seed with gusto. Across the parking area sits a red-tailed hawk in one of the trees, waiting for his chance at lunch.

It's a cold day for Page Springs, no more than forty-five degrees, even in February and the birds are particularly thankful for the repast left them. A large bullfrog sits by the edge of the small pond fed by the springs, eyeing the birds with great interest. About a week ago my partner, whom you will meet later, watched the bullfrog leap up and take a finch for dinner. I did not even know they were capable of this, but the feathers floating on the surface of the calm water verified that they could and did. Sedona is a place of amazing natural beauty, as are so many of the places I have been guided to live and serve in. Its red rocks are world renown for their energy and striking visages. As is the spiritual and healing energy of the region. Many are drawn here and many pushed away by the power of this environment. It is, in most of its environ, very masculine energy, but where I reside with the water and plants abounding, is a haven of feminine energy. It is in front of the house, next to the small pond with the always-running spring filling it, beneath the arc of the birds that I see our circle now formed. Be welcomed to hear the spring gushing, the bullfrog croaking and see the birds of many colors darting as you read on.

We have traveled a fair distance since we began walking together, yet I am surprised that we are still visiting the Jim in his early days on the spirit road. For a moment I worried about how long this was getting, then released that fear knowing it started when it needed to start and will end the same way. This is a book, which I may have said earlier, that I have felt the need to write for almost ten years. Yet, until a few weeks ago, I was unable to do so. I accept that now the time was right and so the way became open for me to begin.

To this point on my spiritual path things have gone along fairly well for me and those around me. But things always change, as you will see, and there is balance in all. But, at this time, I was basking in the glow of success and good fortune.

Bonnie's cancer had not reappeared over the bi-annual tests she received, giving us hope we would have the time we requested of Spirit.

For the most part, people liked me and wanted to be involved with work I did. I was constantly being praised and thanked by many groups and individuals. I felt free. Free, for the first time in my life, to be myself and let my skills show. Free to try new things and experience teachings in the classroom and the inipis. Free to let my softer side show through with little worry of what others might think. I was amazed how good I was at so many different things. How effectively I could lead others — and have them follow me. And surprised at the successes I had achieved.

When you stoke your ego to an out-of-balance point, the universe will adjust it for you. And I was stoking my ego, I can now see, with a gigantic shovel. Telling myself the ego was not for myself, but for the projects I believed in. Yet then, how can I explain how amazed I was by all the great work 'I' had completed? Not the work Spirit had allowed to flow through me, but the work I did. Ouch! It hurts to even write this. And the more people praised and thanked me, the more projects I said 'yes' to. I was becoming a 'praise' junkie – needing the 'fix' of recognition more often all the time.

Then, the element of control. We can control nothing, but I had not learned this yet in any way – even a small dose. So, if I was so successful at all the things I was doing, didn't that mean I knew the best way? This made my stated opinions strong – sometimes too strong. And, when they often proved to be correct, it generated animosity towards me.

To balance this building ego was my teaching way with the students. I was learning more ways to empower them and get them involved in their own education all the time. I was on the board of several service-learning organizations and worked with other proponents of this approach within the University. Every project I was a part of and my work in the classroom were guided by my heart – with my head following after. This was, and is, my strongest tool and biggest problem.

Some students I worked closely with, like the young woman with the AmeriCorps group, were grateful for the emotional and intellectual connection we shared. As were most of the students and co-workers I interacted with. Some, however, misread my openness and personal approach as a means to 'get something from them' – product, sexual favors, 'stars' on my resume, etc. Still others used this openness and sharing spirit to attack me for hoped for gains of their own. Some tough lessons are about to begin.

As many of us do, for a long time I took credit for my successes and blamed my failures or any attacks made on me on other people.

Then, after time, I began blaming myself for anything that was going wrong in my life. Slowly, practicing no judgment, I have learned to accept that at any given time I did the best with what I knew and understood at that moment. There is never any one party to blame for anything. When something does not go as I wish it now, I stop and look at the whole picture with all its players. And either see another way to proceed, which may have results I can better accept, or offer best wishes and walk away.

No more attacking as in the past when I felt attacked. No more battles of words. That is truly no longer the way, if it ever was. This keeps me out of the dark and in the light as well as I am able to stay there. It is a different kind of warrior then I was in the past, a warrior of good energy working in the clean, white light of the universe. Many of you, I feel certain, have also made this choice. Many of the rest of you, especially those of you just beginning your spiritual walk, will most certainly have this growth experience before you.

As our circle rises and stretches our backs, shaking our legs and feet, I ask you to prepare as we re-enter our journey together back at Fort Collins, some months after my return from my first trip to Belize.

"You want to know who's a real medicine man? He's the one who doesn't say 'I'm a medicine man.' He doesn't ask you to come to him. You've got to go and ask him. And you'll find he's always there among his own people."

—Louis Farmer, ONONDAGA

16 | Ripples and Waves

BONNIE AND I HAD JUST GOTTEN BACK TO FORT COLLINS AFTER A week in Utah. We had been given a lodge house in the woods to stay at, about forty miles from Salt Lake City, by a friend. We had fun times hiking and exploring an area we did not know. Yet, each day I had numerous calls for guidance from three of my environmental staff students. Sharon was most frequent, with a lot of simple questions, which did not make much sense to me. But I worried about what trouble she was having, being too emotionally attached to my key students. Jess, my male student who had been helping with some user research at the Center, also called numerous times. Jess was really intelligent – as well as focused and intent. I really liked and valued him, but many found him too abrasive. He complained that Sharon kept getting in the way of the study at the site and was giving orders as if she ran it. So here was a link – some rivalry going on. And I thought the world of each of them, so I hoped I could mediate it without taking sides. I didn't want to do this until I returned. Then Barbara, a young undergrad working in the Center's office started to call and ask if she had to report to Sharon. Oh, boy. Finally I stopped answering the calls, deciding to let them work at it, or battle through it, until I got back.

Jess had shared a lot of personal issues with me, since I was his advisor. And we had worked through some of them together. Actually, he worked them through – I just listened and guided. I knew he wanted to be in an assistant role to me, but I had given that to Sharon when I saw her skills appear and when I knew she and her young husband needed cash badly. And, so far, it had worked. Sharon had also disclosed many personal issues and problems to me and sought my help. Many of the students I advised did this and I willingly listened, supported and helped wherever I could.

Later, after a couple of major issues, I drew back from this role and would only listen to class related issues. Unfortunately, many faculty members, male and female, end up in this place after being judged or attacked for their actions. In our college, it got so bad at one point that no female faculty member would meet with a male student unless the door was open and the discussion audible to anyone walking by. And, likewise, with male faculty members and female students. I even heard male faculty say they would take no female graduate students on as advisor because the potential for charges was too high. I am happy I never went to these extremes, but I understand the fear behind these actions and can't fault the faculty who took these steps.

When we got back to CSU, I found Sharon waiting for me in the office early on my morning back. She began complaining that the other student staff members would not listen to her. We had a long talk and I had to tell her that her job was not to be the director when I was gone, but to carry out whatever I asked in my absence. We had spent a lot of time together as I taught her what I knew of running a business and the center and had become close. And Bonnie and I had spoken with her and her husband about their issues with being at CSU. Here is a case where my being close to a student angered her, as she thought she was ready to do more than she was capable of. Just a ripple, but I never saw the wave coming behind it.

My meeting with Jess went better than the one with Sharon, as he did not have as many issues around any instructions I gave during my absence. But even he said he thought I was his friend and certainly a father figure, and asked why I didn't take action while I was in Utah. We talked more and he, being a rational, non-emotional type, was accepting of my logic.

Sharon starting becoming more withdrawn and edgy over the next few weeks, missing appointments with me to work on some issue of the Center. She confided in me that she and her husband were going through some hard times. Rather than pull back, I followed my heart and tried to be there for her. I was upset that she was in obvious pain, as I was with any of the students I knew well. Bonnie suggested I let it go, that I was too available at many levels for students. I heard her, but argued that was what made me able to be the best teacher I could. So I checked in with Sharon when she missed meetings and accepted her emotional excuses. Soon she became Sam's teaching assistant in his environmental interpretation course, while remaining as a student intern at the Environmental Center. This worked, actually keeping her out of my sphere more of the time as she also had work to do for Sam.

I had offered Sharon, Deb and Rob spots on an upcoming project I was committed to do in Belize before her change in behavior. Bonnie had decided to come along on this project, paying her own way as I could not justify her being part of the team with the project being funded by my department. I continued with these plans and this group, hoping the time in Belize would help Sharon work things through in her mind. Rob, I hoped, would regain some self-image he had lost while leading the Belize Program group. The project was to do an environmental education inventory of the country: Meeting with schools, agencies and local communities – both on the mainland and on the cayes.

Richard and the Department of Education were thrilled to know such an inventory was about to be produced. They had no funding or people to undertake such a mission, yet needed to know what resources were available around their country. I had secured some funding from our department through Ron, our chairman, and some through a government grant. I was surprised I could get no general university funding support, but did not yet know about being blackballed. I had enough from the sources I had, so I worked on the planning – collaborating with Richard as I did so.

As these behavior issues were beginning, so too was some issues around my teaching and outreach work. I was becoming more of an advocate of service-learning as I continued to see how well it supported and enhanced what the students got in the classroom. I was working more with Brian and his AmeriCorps youth and integrating the at-risk young people with each of our groups. And I was being asked into the K-12 public schools to talk to teacher groups about the model. The staff of CSU's Community Service Department were overjoyed with these connections and were also promoting my work. Other CSU faculty engaged in service-learning – and there were not many—also connected with me and we did some programs together.

I had begun to learn, however, that the more visible you become in a university setting, the more people go into jealousy and anger.

Hank and Linda, both on my graduate committee, were asking why I wasted my time with this work. For them, as I have said, it was research and publish coupled with publish or die. And I did research with them, and published and presented at conferences, it just was not my primary road.

Other faculty asked why an instructor – not even faculty and without the PhD behind his name – was teaching so much and involved so heavily in the community. Two went to their respective deans and complained I was 'distracting' their students from their classroom work.

I handled this well, right? I ignored it and them. I wish I had. Instead I went into anger and justifications of my work.

Today, I would wish them well, not agree or disagree with them, and go on my way. With no anger or resentment towards them. But, with the warrior ways I knew then, I attacked back and in so doing, called in more negative comments.

A couple of years later this would go to new levels as I won the Outstanding Award for Teaching for CSU in innovative programs.

Many congratulated me after the President called me up, thanked me, and gave me my reward – but many did so with anger in their hearts. I could not see this then, as it is something alien to my nature. Ron, my department chair and friend, especially congratulated me and I found out later, resented not getting the award himself.

With my AmeriCorps partner, Brian, getting an award from the President at the same time for Outstanding CSU collaborator and educator, as nominated by me, the rubbing raw of some people was heightened. I saw, years later after leaving CSU, that Ron had actually added this award to his professional resume, knowing full well it was I, not he, who had won it. This is part of that strange, to me, university belief that anything done by people under you by divine right also accrued to you.

On the positive side, I was able to be involved in more service-learning projects thanks to the recognition the local community gave the work Brian, Bill (from the alternative schools) and I were doing.

On my teaching front in the classroom, I was getting more requests for student over-rides in my classes when they filled at the beginning of the semesters. Sometimes I added an extra class to accommodate these requests; sometimes I was unable to do so. Some of these students thought my course would be easier at first, partly my fault because I was known as a 'good guy' in the student grapevine. The reality was, my classes were often more work. The students had to learn the academic subject and implement a project in the community. And, after being taken advantage of by many students early on, I held fast to due dates and requirements. Yet, according to the majority of my students, my classes were fun and stimulating, many saying they had never had a class like them. Students who were only comfortable in the traditional classroom setting, with the instructor lecturing at them, were rarely happy with my style. I spoke about this at the beginning of each semester and usually had a handful drop my courses. This was better for them and me. I did have some students make complaints about their grades, as happened to virtually all faculty members at one time or another. I had one female student, who turned in almost no assignments; go to our chair, and then the dean, complaining I had treated her unfairly because she was a woman. And that the women who liked me were given high grades. At the same time a male student complained that I favored the women and was harder on the men. While both complaints were quickly dismissed, they scarred me in ways that are cumulative.

I was learning balance and the need to release ego and anger, but did not know it. Instead I picked up my spear and shield and fought like the good warrior I was bred to be. After all, how could these people attack me and my work? How could I do more? They need to be dressed down and taught a lesson and I was the warrior to do it. I won each of these 'battles', as I would others to come, but at oh such a high cost I would pay later. I could be the nicest guy anyone had ever met and be there to teach and support to the best of my abilities, but I could also be a fierce opponent when I or mine were attacked.

This was what my past had made me to this point and I don't judge it. I needed to learn by it, I am certain. And, as I only very recently discovered, there was something else at work inside of me affecting all I did and all I was. More on this when its time is right.

It is difficult for me to write of some of these dark moments on my walk and especially to recognize and accept my own responsibility in their creation. It is much easier to point the finger and blame, as I did then—but I say again, that is not the way of growth or the way to walk the spiritual road.

17 | Having Fun

Enough painful remembrances for now on our journey here, so I will add some fun parts of my walk to maintain balance – as we must.

One of the outcomes of my heightened exposure as a service-learning teacher and my connections to Native American students was a request to teach a field trip to the dinosaur tracks area in southeast Colorado. The request came from another department in our college. I think it was wildlife biology, but I am unsure. They asked if I would approach Lawrence and if, together, we would take eighteen students in the area of the tracks for three days.

Now this was right up my alley. The request for Lawrence to co-teach with me was because there were also some sacred Native American ruins near the tracks and they hoped he would share how his people lived and worshiped in an area like this. There was an old Mexican farmstead, long abandoned, where we could all stay. The property was now BLM land, I believe, or possibly Forest Service and we had their permission for the course there.

I approached Lawrence and he was immediately jazzed. So we agreed, began planning a three-day course and went to the host department for the funding and transportation we required.

Bonnie had hoped to go along, but she had a two-day geology course she was leading at the same time. She did suggest Lawrence and I go and scout the site before bringing all the kids along.

I thought this a great idea, as did Lawrence, so we headed down early one morning. It was a clear, warm sunny day and the ride was about three hours, so we drank plenty of water along the way. We met with the ranger on duty in the little town near the site and he gave us a key to the gate guarding the steep, winding access road down to the ranch. We spent a few hours checking out the ranch, the tracks and finding some of the Native American ceremony spots high above the river running through the site. It looked down on the dinosaur tracks, which wended there way along the riverbed. Being satisfied we had a good feel for the place, we left and stopped back at the ranger station to return the key. We talked with the ranger quite a while above the site and all it had to offer the students. Then, now about seven in the evening, we began heading back.

The last ninety minutes towards the site was a flat, barren waste-land, so the first ninety minutes going out would retrace this boring stretch. About forty-five minutes from the ranger station we saw a small café and bar a short distance down one of the few cross roads along the way. Lawrence said he was hungry and thirsty and wanted to stop. I was tired, but also hungry, so I agreed.

We pulled into the café's parking lot and parked my Jeep alongside the two-dozen pick-up trucks, off-road vehicles and dirt-covered cars already there. I was surprised there was such a crowd, but, of course, we had seen nothing else for miles. I gave no thought to who might be there – what type of crowd – as we entered.

I was thinking about a juicy roast beef sandwich and a cold beer as we stepped inside, stepping carefully over the raised doorplate on the floor. The place was loud – really loud—with talk and music blaring from a jukebox. And filled with smoke, with a good portion of those inside either smoking or resting their lit cigarettes in ashtrays. The crowd – all rancher types; boots, jeans, bandanas, mustaches, flowered skirts, sequined belts and big hats were spread around the room as the smoke weaved through them. And in Lawrence and I walk – Lawrence with his chiseled, unmistakable Native American visage and me, his suntanned cohort. Both with our CSU Native American Student Pow-Wow tee shirts on and four color horsehair necklaces hanging from laces around our necks.

I looked over at Lawrence – he was stoically looking straight ahead with his 'I eat white people' stare he had perfected over the years. Empty beer bottles littered most of the tables, some of the patrons were dancing in a western swing in the middle of the room and most all of them were singing along to, "Mammas, Don't Let Your Babies Grow Up to Be Cowboys" grated out by Willie Nelson from the jukebox.

"Mammas don't let your babies grow up to be cowboys
Don't let them pick guitars and drive in old trucks
Make 'em be doctors and lawyers and such
Mammas don't let your babies grow up to be cowboys
They'll never stay home and they're always alone
Even with someone they love."

Followed by a rousing "eyah"… … … … …and the next chorus.

As we stepped further into the room the cowfolk became aware of us, all heads began to turn and all voices began to silence. I was not happy as a bunch of expressionless faces, many a little slack from beer and whiskey, stared at the Indian and his faithful sidekick, dumb white boy.

"Lawrence," I whispered out of the side of my mouth, "Let's just leave and stop in Denver. It's only another hour or so."

He looked at me, shook his head 'no' and headed to a table to the left center of the room. Having little choice and not about to leave the Indian with the settlers, I followed him with little doubt this would turn out bad.

We sat and a waitress came over and asked for our order.

"Two beers, two roast beef sandwiches, some fries and a big bottle of horseradish," Lawrence said, ordering for both of us. Our last meal I remember thinking.

The other patrons began talking amongst themselves again and drinking their beer, but every few seconds some would look our way, probably wondering if we were nuts or just had a death wish. One of the good old boys – forty something, spurs and jeans covered in dirt – went over to the jukebox, put in his coins and after a few seconds of whirling sound from the boxes guts, "On the Road Again", also sung by Willie Nelson, blared out.

I was thinking 'must be Willie Nelson night here in Bubbaville'. I was glad I liked Willie Nelson because most country western music bored me. If there was to be a showdown at least I would head into it hearing a singer and songs I liked.

> "On the road again just can't wait to get on the road again
> The life I love is making music with my friends
> And I can't wait to get on the road again
> On the road again like a band of gypsies we go down the highway
> We're the best of friends insisting that the world keep turning
>   our way
> And our way is on the road again just can't wait to get on the
>   road again
> The life I love is making music with my friends
> And I can't wait to get on the road again."

We stopped being the sideshow as the crowd again got into Willie's words and began loudly singing along. When everyone else hooted and clapped between choruses, Lawrence clapped along. So I followed suit. When the song was over, "Mammas, Don't Let Your Babies Grow Up to Be Cowboys" came on again. More loud singing, more hooting and clapping. We were pretty much being ignored now and so we ate our meal in peace. Maybe I was wrong and this was okay. When this song finished the machine whirled once again and the third song of the set came on. I don't know who the singer was but the title was "Battle of Little Big Horn" and I still remember some of the lyrics. I searched and found the rest of the lyrics and saw it was by Porter Wagoner.

"Have you ever heard the story of the pride of Little Big Horn
Right from the lips of someone that saw
Well, I was there on that cold and fateful morning
Watched General Custer and the bloody massacre
        There were muskets, arrows, cannonballs a flyin'
Yellin', screamin' a lot of men were dyin' there at the Little Big
        Horn.

There were one thousand Indians standing on the river bank
Two hundred calvary waited there with pride
        And I saw Chief Crazy Horse leader of the Indians
Old General Custer with his musket by his side.

Then Crazy Horse started things with a yell
That shattered the quiet of the early morn
General Custer gave out a mighty, mighty roar
        And they met at the Little Big Horn.

There were muskets, arrows, cannonballs a flyin'
Yellin', screamin' a lot of men were dyin' there at the Little Big
        Horn.

Of the one thousand Indians there on the river bank
        Five hundred Indians died in the fight
And the brave calvary that had fought there that morning
Two hundred men not a single one survived.

There were muskets, arrows, cannonballs a flyin'
        Yellin', screamin' a lot of men were dyin' there at the Little
        Big Horn.

There at the Little Big Horn.

There at the Little Big Horn..."

I had heard stories from Lawrence about the fights he had been in earlier in his life and had seen how quick he was to anger on several occasions. Now he had General Custer, the great, brave hero and the cowardly Injuns right in his face. But, at the end, he smiled and clapped also. I was amazed.

After a minute or two, Lawrence got up and went over to the jukebox. He put in coins, walked back to our table and smiled at me. I only saw a couple of people notice that he had picked some songs. After the expected whirling, Lawrence's first song began.

"They took the whole Cherokee nation
And put us on this reservation
They took away our ways of life
The tomahawk and the bow and knife

They took away our native tongue
And taught their English to our young
And all the beads we made by hand
Are nowadays made in Japan

Cherokee people
Cherokee tribe
So proud to live
So proud to die

They took the whole Indian nation
Locked us on this reservation
And though I wear a shirt and tie
I still part Redman deep inside

Cherokee people
Cherokee tribe

So proud to live
So proud to die

And some day when they've learned
Cherokee Indian will return
Will return will return
Will return will return"

"Cherokee Nation" sung by Paul Revere and the Raiders – an oldie ready in the box for Lawrence. He sang and whooped along with the Raiders, so, as I remembered the lyrics, did I. Many ignored us, a few frowned and a good number smiled and whooped along with us by the end. When the song finished, the whirl returned and Lawrence's second song began... "Cherokee Nation." This time the majority of the cowboys and cowgirls sang with us. And, when it came on for the third time, almost the whole place sang, whooped and clapped like hell when it was done.

Then an old timer, darkly tanned and wrinkled, came over, grinned at Lawrence, told him, "You got grit boy. Thanks for the fun."

Then he walked back to his place leaning on the bar.

We left shortly after and headed to my Jeep, weaving between the new pick-ups and cars that had been pulled in willy-nilly. Lawrence said simply, "Those were good roast beefs. Got to stop here some time again." He was at least right about the sandwiches.

Lawrence and I were scheduled to take the students for their three-day course in a few weeks. In the meantime, he was scheduled to attend and speak at an Inter-Tribal/Government Land Use Conference in Denver. It was coming up in a few days and he had asked me a while before to come as part of the Native American attendees, as an environmental impact consultant. I had asked him if that would go over well with the other tribal people and he assured me it would. So I had agreed. We would be in Denver for two days and attend breakout sessions as well as the main speakers agenda. Lawrence was speaking for Native American youth as President of the Native

American Students Association at the University. He was going to speak to preserving the land for the young and the young after them and not destroying it with high impact mining and drilling. I was curious to hear what he had to say and was pleased he had included me. Hopefully I would also get a chance to voice my opinions in the small sessions.

When we arrived at the conference we were given a brochure, which included all the speakers, their topics and all the attendees for the tribes and for the U.S. government. As I looked through it I remember being surprised and a little overwhelmed, when I found mine was the only 'white' face in the tribal part of the brochure. This was something I would get use to over time, as it was often the case when I worked with indigenous people in different parts of the world. It gave me the wonderful opportunity – and understanding – of what it felt like being a minority, if only in a small way.

Lawrence was speaking to the assembly fairly early in the program. The person moderating the talks and introducing the speakers was a man with the Department of the Interior. A non-native man from Washington, D.C.

Several agency people spoke first – I remember someone from the BLM and a woman from the Bureau of Indian Affairs.

Then it was Lawrence's turn. He walked to the podium with his stoic look once again firmly in place, but without the sometimes attendant frown. He was about to teach me and, I believe, everyone in the room a fine lesson, totally unplanned and therefore even more effective. As Lawrence reached the podium on the stage, the host shook his hand and began to introduce him.

"Ladies and gentleman, the next speaker is the President of Colorado State's Native American Student Association, Mr. Little Thunder. Mr. Little Thunder is...ah...Mr. Little Thunder, what do you prefer to be called? Native? Native American? Red? Indian?" he turned and asked Lawrence.

Lawrence paused, slowly looked to the host, cracked a smile and said, "Why not call me Lawrence? After all, that's my name."

There was dead silence for a few seconds, and then laughter broke out on the Native American side and quickly spread throughout the audience. Lawrence's words cracked the serious demeanor of all present before that and reminded everyone we are all the same, all people, regardless of our color or culture.

The rest of the conference was uneventful, except that I got to meet many new agency people and Native American attendees. And got to experience the disapproval and anger emanating from some of the native attendees. As Two Bears had warned me to expect as I walked this road. Being a sensitive this reaction bothered me, even though I fully understood the source and reasons.

Bonnie and I did some exploring of new areas, for us, east of Fort Collins over the next weeks in between our classes and my teaching. We spent a lot of time – and much more later – in the areas of the old grasslands. Something about these lands attracted both of us. The home of the buffalo before the settlers killed them off in order to drive the Native Americans away. Tatanka – buffalo in Lakota – are amazing and resilient animals. Strong and powerful, yet graceful of movement. They did, and still do, talk to my spirit.

Bonnie had planned a two-day drive to northwest Colorado to check out some rock formations for a course she was writing a paper for. I was able to go since she had picked a weekend.

We left on Friday night, drove 'over the hill' and took a room in a small motel between nowhere and no place. The next morning we headed out to the formation she wanted to explore. It was a warm, sunny day with a few puff clouds slowly scudding across the sky.

After she was done at the formation we decided to head out to areas unknown. I can't remember exactly where we ended up, as we never used maps when we explored this way, but we were on a high ridge following a bumpy, two-lane road. We saw a van stopped in the drive lane up ahead, so we slowed and then stopped behind it.

Some two hundred feet in front of the van was a surging, waving, undulating sea of black. We could not make out what it was, so we approached the four people standing alongside the van. There were several others in the van peering out the front window at the black wave.

"Howdy," I called out as we approached, "What's up ahead?"

"Howdy," a middle-aged man in western garb answered back, "We are trying to figure out how to cross them without killing them."

"What are they?" Bonnie asked.

"Tarantulas," the man answered, "On their annual or bi-annual – I forget which – migration. They can cover miles, thousands and thousands of them, and might take hours to cross the road. Or, if they stop, as they sometimes do, we could be here through tomorrow. And we don't want to drive across, killing hundreds as we've seen some people do in the past."

The black sea now became even more fascinating. I went back to the car and got our binoculars. With them to my eyes, I turned the adjustment knob and, sure enough, he was right. Thousands of the mild, tame, very fragile, but sometimes scary looking tarantulas. I gave the binocs to Bonnie and she took a look.

"Oh my God, I've never seen anything like this. Or even heard of such a thing," she exclaimed.

"Not many see this big a wave, but smaller waves sometimes cross highways and many are killed," the man responded back.

"I got an idea," he continued, "I have some sixteen foot boards on top of the van I'm bringing to my ranch. What if we take turns holding the boards on the side of the road the critters are coming from and, as the road clears and they move to go around the board, we can edge the cars through? What do you think?"

"Good plan. Let's try," I answered. "I'm Jim and this is my wife, Bonnie."

"George and my wife, Thelma," he introduced back and we all smiled and nodded.

Then he introduced the others and we pulled down the boards. There were eight of the boards strapped on top and we brought down two.

Then I had a further idea. "George, what if we take down five boards? Then we all work at it. We work our way out slowly placing four boards in a row, one after another. Then wait for the tarantulas to clear the road before slowly edging the cars forward. As we clear the last board, we take it up and move it to the front. The fifth board we use, if we need it, to gently sweep the tarantulas aside if they just sit in the road. Doable?"

"Sounds like a plan," George agreed.

And so we took down the boards and I headed out into the tarantulas with Bonnie with the first board. We had to slowly shuffle our feet forward so we would not squash those we were trying to pass in peace.

It's interesting that one of the world's largest, hairiest and to some, scariest spiders is also one of the most fragile. Many fear them, as they seem to most spiders, not understanding their nature and value in the web of life. You can pick them up and have them crawl on your arms and legs without any worry. Yet, if you were to drop one from just a couple of feet up, it would explode on contact with the ground. Soon we had tarantulas eight-footing it over our feet as we were engulfed in the black wave. It was an interesting feeling, both physically and psychologically, as we became part of their dance.

"This is amazing. I'm glad we ended up here. I can almost feel their energy all around us," Bonnie said as we eased further out.

"I can feel their energy at many levels. It's almost like I can look through their many-faceted eyes. I wish we could just sit among them and see what would happen," I answered back.

The process worked, if slowly, and after about an hour, we had both vehicles about half way across the eight-leggeds parade ground. The two people driving the cars had no interest at all in joining us and our furry friends on the ground, so they simply waited for directions to slowly slide forward.

Suddenly, as we stood holding the boards in place as we straightened up to stretch our backs, the wave changed composition. As if to aid us the tarantulas in front of us began moving in, almost like the neck of an hourglass, getting thinner where the cars and we were. Within ten minutes we were across.

We shared a few more words with George, waved goodbye to all and went on our way. Although I have seen small numbers of migrating tarantulas twice since, this is the only time I have seen this phenomenon and may never again. What a gift! Even now, I can close my eyes and watch the small, furry black army march before me.

"But the Great Spirit has provided you and me with an opportunity for study in nature's university, the forests, the rivers, the mountains, and the animals which include us."

—Walking Buffalo, STONEY

18 | Time for More of the Red Road

MEANWHILE I CONTINUED WITH MY LEARNING FROM YELLOWHAIR AND Two Bears. In lodge with Yellowhair and Lawrence I learned much about the meanings and uses of the ceremony, as I did about other sacred Lakota ceremonies as we sat around the fire before and after. I was often the firekeeper and rock carrier, so I was busy before and during most ceremonies. I soaked up all I was told and all I observed like a sponge. I was like an empty cup looking to be filled with new knowledge and understanding. With Two Bears, I was learning about the sacred Chanunpa, White Buffalo Calf Woman bringing it to the Lakota people many generations before and the other six ceremonies, which derived from the pipe. For those who know nothing of this story I am adding it below, as the Chanunpa and White Buffalo Calf Woman will play large roles in my walk as we move ahead. These versions of the story – of which there are many, yet all very similar – are from text adapted from *Return of the Bird Tribes* by Ken Carey (Talman Company, NY), 1988 and the other as told by Joseph Chasing Horse, Sundance Chief of the Lakota Sioux.

"We Lakota people have a prophecy about the white buffalo calf.
How that prophecy originated was that we have a sacred bundle, a

sacred peace pipe, that was brought to us about 2,000 years ago by what we know as the White Buffalo Calf Woman.

The story goes that she appeared to two warriors at that time. These two warriors were out hunting buffalo, hunting for food in the sacred Black Hills of South Dakota, and they saw a big body coming toward them. And they saw that it was a white buffalo calf. As it came closer to them, it turned into a beautiful young Indian girl.

That time one of the warriors thought bad in his mind, and so the young girl told him to step forward. And when he did step forward, a black cloud came over his body, and when the black cloud disappeared, the warrior who had bad thoughts was left with no flesh or blood on his bones. The other warrior kneeled and began to pray.

And when he prayed, the white buffalo calf who was now an Indian girl told him to go back to his people and warn them that in four days she was going to bring a sacred bundle.

So the warrior did as he was told. He went back to his people and he gathered all the elders and all the leaders and all the people in a circle and told them what she had instructed him to do. And sure enough, just as she said she would, on the fourth day she came.

They say a cloud came down from the sky, and off of the cloud stepped the white buffalo calf. As it rolled onto the earth, the calf stood up and became this beautiful young woman who was carrying the sacred bundle in her hand.

As she entered into the circle of the nation, she sang a sacred song and took the sacred bundle to the people who were there to take it from her. She spent four days among our people and taught them about the sacred bundle, the meaning of it.

She taught them seven sacred ceremonies.

One of them was the sweat lodge, or the purification ceremony. One of them was the naming ceremony, child naming. The third was the *healing ceremony. The fourth one was the making of relatives or the adoption ceremony. The fifth one was the marriage ceremony. The sixth was the vision quest. And the seventh was the sundance ceremony, the people's ceremony for all of the nation.*

She brought us these seven sacred ceremonies and taught our people the songs and the traditional ways. And she instructed our people that as long as we performed these ceremonies we would always remain caretakers and guardians of sacred land. She told us that as long as we took care of it and respected it that our people would never die and would always live.

When she was done teaching all our people, she left the way she came. She went out of the circle, and as she was leaving she turned and told our people that she would return one day for the sacred bundle. And she left the sacred bundle, which we still have to this very day.

The sacred bundle is known as the White Buffalo Calf Pipe because it was brought by the White Buffalo Calf Woman. It is kept in a sacred place (Green Grass) on the Cheyenne River Indian reservation in South Dakota. it's kept by a man who is known as the keeper of the White Buffalo Calf Pipe, Arvol Looking Horse.

When White Buffalo Calf Woman promised to return again, she made some prophecies at that time

One of those prophesies was that the birth of a white buffalo calf would be a sign that it would be near the time when she would return again to purify the world. What she meant by that was that she would bring back harmony again and balance, spiritually."

Joseph Chasing Horse

After the brave returned to his camp – another version of what White Buffalo Calf Woman shared.....

"The brave hurried to his tribe and the chief, after listening carefully, built the camp as she requested, convinced his people would receive teachings from one who lived amongst the stars.

That night, as she approached their camp, the people were amazed at how young she was. Without speaking a word, she walked seven times around the central fire; as her feet touched the sand, all who watched felt her prayerful reverence for the Earth. Few could look into her eyes. Those who dared saw pools of perfect blackness and saw themselves as they really were, naked and revealed. When she spoke at last, her voice was like the song of waters singing upon the rocks, like the song of birds calling above the meadows.

Seven times I have circled this fire in reverence and in silence for it symbolizes the love that burns forever in the heart of the Great Spirit. The same fire that warms the heart of every buffalo, every sage hen, every eagle and every human being. This fire that burns at your center is your love, and it is right, at times, to express this love sexually. This passion, if uncontrolled, roars like a wildfire and can destroy everything in its path. If tempered with wisdom, this same passion can fuel whole generations, warming a thousand lodges through a hundred snowy winters and give its power to your children's children.

Those, like the young man whose bones now lie underneath the moonlight, who think first of the sexual expression of this fire and only secondly of the spirit behind it, lock themselves into cycles of suffering and illusion. These cycles were unknown to you years ago, but now weaken your vitality and drain away your power.

White Buffalo Calf Woman then taught them to harness the power of this creative force and reminded the people of the Sacred Hoop and how to gather power and focus it within its circle of commitment. In the warm atmosphere of that circle, the power of love builds like a storm until suddenly the circle can hold no more and explodes in the conception of the new.

She pulled a burning branch from the flames and spoke, "My tribe is the Fire Bird, we are the Winged Ones of Heaven. Your people have forgotten the most precious thing, your connection to the Great Spirit. I have come with a fire from heaven to kindle again your memory of what has been and to strengthen you for the times to come."

She drew a pouch from her side and took from it a sacred pipe. The bowl was round and of red stone; red for the pathway of the Sun. It represented the circle of the Sacred Hoop, the cycles of giving and receiving, of inbreathing and outbreathing, of living and dying... White Buffalo Calf Woman filled it with the finest tobacco and in that simple act, honored all the plant world.

She held the pipe aloft and addressed the people, "This pipe will help you remember that every breath you take is sacred. Your life is lit from that same fire that burns in the heart of the Great Spirit. Your flame, your individual human life, can light a greater fire...the flame of love in another's heart and so bring consciousness to the Earth. Keep not the love that burns within you turned towards your self and your desires but give away that fire, that it may burn bright in the helping of each other."

The pipe was passed seven times; the first smoke honored the people's highest thoughts, prayers and aspirations and was a breath of gratitude to the Great Spirit. The twelve eagle feathers hanging from the stem of the pipe allowed the tribe's thoughts to fly high above the world of their little selves. The tribe was instructed to remember always that every living creature was a sacred being and to know this especially while mixing with other tribes whose ways were different from their own.

A second time the pipe was passed in love and reverence for the Earth, our Mother; for the grasses that clothe her and feed the people; for the rain clouds that fill the streams; and the blue skies that protect us all. The third passing thanked the four-footed ones and the feathered ones, the buffalo and the hawk and the fishes, and all the creatures of this good Earth. The fourth time the pipe was passed paid tribute to the many tribes of humankind and saw a blending of all the races into the harmony of the rainbow. When the pipe returned to her she paused....

"Honor all creatures as your sisters and your brothers for all are sacred parts in the body of the Great Spirit. Each one is holy. Live your life in harmony with the way of balance and you will know peace and joy. If ever your hearts should feel heavy within you then smoke a fifth time, asking for the guidance of the great beings of the spirit world. Ask that spirit to help you make the clearest choice. In time you will come to know that spirit as your own true self. When you invite spirit into your life, you help yourself far more than if only concerned with your own affairs. Human beings are not fully happy or healthy until they serve the purpose for which God created them."

White Buffalo Calf Woman then explained how the sixth smoke was sent to the six people whom you would most like to see especially blessed. The seventh smoke must always be taken in silence; for it was offered to the Great Being from which all others sprang. For that sacred mystery at the source of life, it was better, she said, to have no words.

After the seventh smoke was completed, such a unity was felt by those present in the great teepee, it seemed in that moment as if there was but one present. In perfect stillness, the silence spread like warm water, dissolving the last traces of disharmony from the heart of the Sioux."

Return of the Bird Tribes by Ken Carey

Many believe that the buffalo calf, Miracle, born August 20, 1994 symbolizes the coming together of humanity into a oneness of heart, mind, and spirit.

"Miracle, the Sacred White Female Buffalo Calf, was born on the farm of Dave, Valerie, and Corey Heider near Janesville, Wisconsin during the morning of August 20, 1994. Not an albino, she was considered to be the first white buffalo calf born since 1933. Furthermore, she was extremely important to the religious beliefs of many American Indian and Canadian First Nations tribes.

The Lakota, Dakota, and Nakota Nations (known collectively as the Sioux) were considered Miracles' primary spiritual guardians and she played a pivotal role in the fulfillment of their most revered prophecies. However, her place in the prophecies and beliefs of many tribes made her a highly sacred symbol to many of the American Indian Nations across the continent. She was seen by a vast number of people as a symbol of hope and renewal for humanity and for harmony between all peoples, all races, in our world today.

Although not American Indian, the Heider family came to view Miracle as a special gift, which belonged to the hearts of all people. Commercialization was not allowed. They opened their farm to visitors free of charge seven days a week so that people could visit Miracle at the pasture fence. For safety reasons, visitors were not allowed into the pasture. Miracle was, after all, a wild buffalo as are the rest of the buffalo on the farm. Many people came to offer prayers in her presence; some came simply out of curiosity. Whatever their reason for visiting Miracle and this simple farm, thousands came and few people left unaffected by their time there."

From http://whitebuffalomiracle.homestead.com

I was thinking of the story of White Buffalo Calf Woman as Two Bears loaded his Chanunpa and placed it, leaning, on the buffalo skull by the altar as we readied for another lodge together. We had been meeting around fires and in lodges as often as he had time, since we were in the lodge where he had agreed to be my teacher. I tended the fire, adding wood where needed and moving burning logs as I felt was the way. Soon, I brought the bucket of water, which was placed to the right of the door in the lodge – the place the water pourer sits. Then we entered for another ceremony together and another step on my road. "Tonight I feel we must do things in a different way here," Two Bears began, "We will open the pipe as we begin and then see where Spirit guides me to take us from there. I do not know why this is, but it is so. I feel we will do four doors, but not the traditional doors of the lodge. This is a first for me and I give gratitude to Spirit for allowing me these new understandings today. Bring in the rocks, nephew."

I carried in the seven rocks and then, at Two Bears' request, handed him his Chanunpa. He had been busily moving the rocks I brought around in the fire pit with the deer antlers he had for this purpose. He had only done this in the third and fourth doors in the past, making certain there was room and connection for the rocks of those doors to fill. This time, he arranged them in some pattern he must be seeing in his mind or heart. Then I entered, lowered the door partway, as he asked, and awaited his words or directions. In the past, he had always lit the pipe, smoked it into a good burn, and then passed it to me. I would draw in the smoke seven times, for the seven directions, and then pass it back to Two Bears. He would finish the tobacco and empty the ash on the rocks with prayers and thanks. You do not inhale from the pipe, but bring the smoke into your mouth, then exhale. You envision the smoke going through you cleansing you as you watch the physical smoke head skyward. As it does so you ask it to bring your thanks and prayers to Great Spirit. The tobacco really, most often, contains little tobacco. Rather it is a mix of sacred herbs and a little tobacco. Herbs most often collected by the pipe carrier from sacred places. Tonight, he handed the pipe to me, unlit.

I was unsure what to do, so I sat silently holding the pipe cradled in my left arm as I had seen Two Bears do and waiting for instructions. Several minutes later I still waited. "You've waited long enough nephew. I don't think it will light itself," Two Bears said without any chuckle.

"You want me to light the pipe Uncle?"

"I passed it to you. You are holding it. We need to open it. So, please fire up some sage and light the Chanunpa so we may start. Get it burning hot and then pass it to me."

I did as told, asking permission of the pipe and Spirit as I did so, yet feeling unworthy and a bit afraid it would not light in a good way for me. But it did and I drew on the stem until the tobacco burned hot and the smoke coiled up to the heavens. Then I touched it to my head and heart and passed it to Two Bears.

"As I take seven puffs, begin a prayer to Spirit asking guidance," he instructed me.

I did a short prayer of gratitude and then asked guidance as Two Bears smoked. Then he passed the pipe back to me and he began a prayer, thanking Spirit for sending this white student and asking further guidance as I smoked the tobacco down to ash. I held the pipe towards Two Bears, but he told me to offer the pipe to the Earth Mother, the Father Sky and then Great Spirit, after which I was to empty the ash onto the rocks.

"Good. Now put the pipe back out on the altar and come back in and we will close the door," he instructed further. I did as I was told, silently thanking the Chanunpa as I placed it back against the buffalo skull. After I closed the door Two Bears again spoke. "Jim, we will do the doors of the lodge now but, after a song and thanks in the fourth door I will quietly beat the drum and we will do some journeying together. You have heard of this from several of we Lakota. Now we will see what comes of it together. I will drum the heartbeat of Mother Earth and I will speak more of our journeying before we begin."

I had heard quite a lot about journeying, especially from Lawrence, but still had trouble distinguishing journeying from meditating. I sat quietly in each lodge in the healing door and the fourth door and waited for whatever might come. Often images would come to me, but usually unclear or as if far away. Sometimes just a peaceful blackness engulfed me and I would hear birds or waves or wind. Tonight we would actually focus our intent on this journey. I admit I was not as totally engaged in the first three doors as usual, anticipating the fourth door of journeying to come.

"Nephew, you lost some of the power of the lodge tonight. You seem unfocused. Did you want the fourth door so much you missed all you might have received from the first three?" Two Bears asked as we prepared for the fourth door. Busted. For many years, until the gift of seeing these things also came to me, I was amazed how many of my teachers and elders in general were able to know what went on inside another.

"Sorry Uncle. What you say is true," I answered.

"You do not need to be sorry to me, it is you who lost some of what you might have received. Release that now as a good lesson learned and we shall begin a song of cleansing."

After a song, more water poured and sage and cedar added to the rocks, Two Bears spoke again, "As I beat the drum slowly, in the beat of the Earth Mother, open all your senses, breathe in the sacred herbs, feel the heat of the steam and ask your guides to come to you. Ask your spirit animals to come to you. Ask eagle to carry you high so you may see. Open the eye of your far vision, the eye of your forehead, and see where you are taken. Let any fear run out of you like the water of the stream. And any doubt be taken away by the Mother Earth. Always travel with your heart, not your mind. Your spirit may leave any time, it will know how to return, and I am always here to guide. When it is right I will lay the drum down and join you, or go my own way, as it will happen and be."

As I always did when meditating or connecting with the spirits, I relaxed my body first, then asked my mind to empty and allow the heart to take over. I inhaled deeply of the sage and cedar and began connecting the beat of my heart to the beat of the drum. The drumbeat of the Earth Mother's heart is a simply one, two – pause – one, two – pause – and on. It is low and steady, as the beating of our own hearts. Time becomes meaningless when you begin to enter this state of relaxation, opening the heart and spirit and connecting with Mother Earth, Father Sky and the spirit realm. Sometime after we began I asked any animal guides willing to take me to where I needed to go so I might see what I needed to see to come and show themselves. My eyes were open in the pitch-blackness of the lodge, as is my way. In a moment I saw an animal approach, as if from a great distance. As it neared in my mind's eye and hearts perception I saw it was a wolf. It came and sat beside me. Suddenly I was sitting in a field of high grasses with clusters of trees visible in all directions. In the far distance I could see snow covered mountaintops rising off of the flat grassland were I sat with my wolf guide. I could see a clear blue sky above and my senses told me it was summer, although I could not feel temperature or air blowing. The wolf, Sugmanitu tanka in Lakota, sat, looking me in the eyes. I could feel his power and strength and the calmness of his spirit. He did nothing, made no sound, as we both sat facing each other.

In most of my journeying, connecting to spirits and visions during my walk, I usually see pictures and colors and designs. Sometimes whole vistas, sometimes storylines as if watching a movie. I rarely, until recently, had spirits or animal guides speak to me. Sometimes I would hear their thoughts, but not as if through voice, rather in straight connections between our spirits. Others I know have the opposite experience. It is not the means that is important, but the messages.

After a time I thanked, in my mind, this wolf brother for coming. He nodded, still staring me in the eyes. I then asked if there was somewhere he would lead me. He rose, holding eye contact. As I rose he turned and began a slow walk in the direction of the mountains in the distance. We walked through the high grass together and I could feel these long fronds swishing around my legs. We passed by trees and small ponds as we walked. A small herd of deer appeared to our left, looking up at us as we passed, and went back to grazing, knowing we were no threat. After some time walking in this way I wondered where we went and what I was to be looking for, if anything. Or was this journey with my four-legged guide the message I thought I sought. As these thoughts began to come I again asked my brain to relax and let the heart lead. The wolf looked back at me, then to the skies, then back at me. I stopped and looked up, seeing only clear skies and pulsing globe of the sun. We were near some large tress and a stream running through them and off towards the horizon. Again I reached out to Sugmanitu Tanka and asked if I were to do anything. He simply sat and again looked me in the eyes as I sat beside him.

After more time wolf looked up and I followed his gaze. As I began to follow his upward stare I could hear a loud screech above us and saw a huge eagle, with a bold white head, circling slowly directly above us.

"Is it the eagle I am to see brother wolf?" I asked through my heart. The wolf looked back down to me and again up to eagle – "Wambli" in Lakota—soaring above. I stood and wolf lay down. His part done for now? The eagle circled, ever lower, until he landed beside me. He was huge, towering beside me as he also looked me in the eyes and screeched. I found myself approaching him and stood with my left hand on his side without being aware neither of how I had gotten there nor of reaching out. There was a shift in time and scene and I next remember being on eagle, or in him, or with him – it all meshed as one – as we soared aloft.

Fear was in my whole being for, in my physical body, I have a great fear of heights. Actually, I learned many years later, I have a great fear of falling, not heights.

I felt energy and peace entering my spirit from this warrior of the skies and the fear subsided as we climbed under the power of his striking wings. We climbed ever higher and I could see in all directions. I could clearly see the mountains, as we were moving in their direction. The snow and falling water of their towering expanse. And I could see a vast ocean of water to our right. At the same time I was watching this aerial vista, I could also focus and see all things small below us, down to a field mouse running far below. It was a very unsettled, yet exhilarating, mix of images my spirit beheld. My physical body seemed to be with me on part of this journey and I ignored this sensation as it made no sense to me.

Eagle and I flew over the mountains, back over open water, and then across grasslands that appeared to have no end. As I began to feel some comfort, and a great deal of awe, suddenly other images appeared before me. We circled high and I watched a group of people on horseback chasing after a herd of buffalo. It was a hunt of the kind my Lakota friends have shared which their ancestors undertook. And then we swooped over a village – a village of over a hundred teepees and other larger reed constructed buildings.

"What is it I see, Wambli? Do we travel the past?" I sent out to my eagle guide. He screeched loudly and twisted his head from side to side. My answer was 'yes'.

While on this journey, I did not ask myself how this could be, but rather accepted that it was. This is one fine benefit of asking your brain to rest and your heart to lead. We circled this village for some period of time and then my winged-friend wheeled and circled higher once again.

As he continued to climb my fear of falling once again surfaced and, once again, I went deep inside to work on allaying it. As I did so eagle, climbed ever higher then, suddenly, leveled off and flew even faster forward. I could see little below but a blur. I tried to reach out through my spirit senses again to see what was below, but the blur remained. Then Wambli dipped and slowed dropping down lower once again. No more hunters or teepees below us now, but a landscape of short grass and desert. In the distance I could see gas pumps and oilrigs dotting the land. A minute later, four ATV's roared over a small high and bounced across the land below us.

"Are we back in the time I walk now?" I put out. And got no sound or reaction.

We crossed over what I thought was a pond I had seen earlier, but the trees around it were dead or dying and the water reddish brown in color. We flew over cattle dotted lands, but none of the great bison of the earlier scenes were visible any longer. My spirit wanted the eagle to soar back to the earlier places he had borne me to, where the grasses were high, the plants healthy, the air bluer and the bison were roaming. Yet, even with its maladies this land below us now was also beautiful.

The contrast between the two scenes eagle had brought us to visit was stunning. Reading about the land as it was and as it is now is one thing, seeing it is totally different. More real, more undeniable. As I had these thoughts in me, eagle screeched as if to concur, then again soared high. He did not fly high as long this time, if I had any sense of time to judge it, then swooped down and began circling the landscape once again. The land below us now was almost all desert, with a few, small bunches of spindly trees visible scattered around. Two ponds we crossed were almost dry, with white and blue residue around their edges. Oilrigs and gas pumps still dotted the landscape, but they were not functioning and many were falling apart. Some antelope jumped and danced their way below us, but no buffalo or cattle were now present. Everything seemed parched and barren, like some parts of the desert I have hiked in the heart of Nevada. But a sickly, pale parched look—not parched as in a healthy desert, which had always existed that way. Wambli straightened and flew into the direction of the sun. Soon, we passed over a small town – a ghost town—falling into ruin. Another distinct contrast with the village we had flown over earlier.

I thought I had the message clearly now – past, present and future. I felt like Scrooge, but on a journey of our natural world, not my inner spirit. Wambli had more to share, however, as he circled up high once again. And flipped and began circling down. Now before me were all three scenes intertwined. It was difficult for my senses to unravel the parts all being present at once. Even as I tried to sort this visual feast out scenes of another type appeared and disappeared mixed in with the eye stew. This was a scene of villages, but not teepees, small buildings made of various items, which I could not see clearly. And some desert, but also some water and plants looking healthy and alive. Then these were gone and I again looked at the three scenes at once. Past, present and future as one. The circle.

Eagle flew with me for what seemed a long time with the scenes changing (at times), yet with the mix of past, present and future holding true. He flew back and forth, high, then lower, wheeling and soaring. My fear was forgotten in wonder, even if I did not understand the meanings of much of what I saw. Finally he screeched his loudest, longest siren call and wheeled straight up, spinning as he/we went. He soared into some clouds that had formed and flew, with us shrouded and unable to see. When he began spiraling down, he cleared the clouds and I could see clearly below. I stared down into the eyes of my wolf brother from the beginning of this journey. I knew at once it was the same Sugmanitu Tanka even while he was still a dot below, sensing his energy and seeing his eyes I could not logically yet see. As if logic had any part to play in this adventure. The eagle zoomed in next to the wolf and lowered his head, a clear sign to alight. As I got off I thanked him for showing me what I needed to see. He bobbed his head four times – immediately bringing up the four directions; four colors of man; four directions; and four seasons...the medicine wheel describers. After the fourth, he rocketed up with another long, ululating screech and headed back to his primary domain, the home of Father Sky.

I looked to wolf and felt I was smiling. Wolf was large, even for a gray wolf. He was colored mostly in gray, but with brown, reds, yellows and white evident on various parts of his muscular body. He showed white around the muzzle and some behind the ears and under his throat. Red intermingled throughout his coat, especially in the front. And gray along his back, also mixed with the black. Overall, his color was stunning, and not like any I had seen before, although I had seen many wolves with mixed colors. His shoulders were broad and powerful and his hindquarters roped in muscle for long bursts of fast motion. When you looked into his eyes, you knew where his power lay. I do not know their color, and still do not to this day, as they seemed to change subtlety at times. But they were always focused, sharp, knowing, caring and watchful – no matter what color or when they were seen. Now, even stronger than when he had led me to the meeting with Wambli, I felt he was friend and protector, the guide I had asked for. He stood with me almost eye-to-eye, and I stand six foot one. I realized following him out to this place he sometimes looked up to me and other times looked straight across into my eyes. Yet I never sensed his size changing. I had more of an appreciation of Two Bears repeated teachings to travel in heart, not head. The brain would try to apply logic to what I was seeing and feeling and would probably melt down, shut down or simply pull me from this journey. My heart was simply observing all, connecting with all and avoiding any interpretations.

I sent to wolf my question, "Will you lead me back now and have me rejoin my Uncle in the lodge?" He continued staring for a moment, then turned and headed away from our direction in, towards the stream I saw earlier from up high. I, of course, followed along behind.

Soon wolf began a slow run, then speeded up rapidly. I also broke into a run, and matched him, staying two paces behind. This was a definite confirmation I was not in my physical body! In minutes running as we were, we approached the stream bank. As we neared a group of four arching, majestic willows, a wind began picking up – out of nowhere—as the air had been still up to that moment. Dust began blowing, although there was really no large amount of dirt here in the grasslands next to the stream. Regardless, dust billowed and darkened and thickened by the second. It was all around us and again, as in the clouds with Wambli, I could see nothing. No fear now, however, as I could sense my wolf brother beside, untroubled and unruffled. Soon the dust settled and, as my eyes cleared, I saw a high mesa before us. No grassland, no stream, just desert and a mesa rising out of it. I looked to wolf and he looked back, then began up a narrow, winding path that wended up the sloped side of the mesa. It was no more than an animal track, but wound up nicely to the area he seemed to want to take me.

As we crested a slight rise I could see a man on a horse in the distance, on the flat top of the mesa. He was looking out from his perch to the land below, which I could not yet see. As we drew closer I saw he was a red man – not Native American in the traditional sense – but a red man. His dress and the bow and arrow he carried were Native American, but his color was bright red, as if painted. He just sat and looked away from us as we closed in on him. There was no recognition of our presence or the noise we made coming up the rock and gravel-strewn path. Finally, we came up to him and I could hear him sigh. Down below, on the plains, was a small Native camp – maybe twenty teepees. It was this he looked at. He scanned the sky and then the land around him and, in so doing, faced us for a few seconds. And he was me. And he felt fear and anger. His fear was for those below him, his tribe, his people. He was a warrior who was now a hunter. This I knew the instant I saw it was me looking at me. Bright red face looking at olive-skinned face, but otherwise the same. My brain wanted to take back over and start doing panic flips, but my heart was well in control now and not willing to let that happen. In another minute, the red 'me' spoke to his horse and reined him down the mesa on the side opposite our approach, towards the people below.

"Wolf brother, I see me, but what are you showing me? But I thank you for sharing this with me." My four-legged guide looked at me, turned and headed back the way we had come. As we started down off the mesa, the wind again picked up and the sand and dust blew around us. When we reached the bottom, how without being able to see I don't know, we came out of the sand and into a very bright, sun-glaring land of sand, trees I did not know and birds overhead I was unfamiliar with. Not too far from us was a group of people squatting, looking at something.

We began heading towards them at a slow trot. As we neared the man closest, with his back to us, who was picking some plants from the ground, holding them up to the others while obviously speaking, then putting them in a leather looking pouch draped over his right shoulder. He was a short, wiry black man, wearing only a loincloth and a hide on the top of his head. Once again, he was black – pitch black, also as if painted that color. The others across from him were indistinct as I tried to see faces. Then, as the black man rose to gather some plants near us I saw his face. And, again, it was me. Not as big a surprise this time, but still strange and chilling. He appeared deep in thought as he picked and spoke, turning to his audience to be certain they were listening as he worked. As we watched this scene, a kangaroo appeared close to the men, then bounded off into some brush beyond them. My face now on a black native person in Australia. Are these men me or connected to me? People I know or will meet? Then I again knew not to question, but just see what my wolf friend showed. Wolf turned away and began back the way we had come, once again in a slow trot. I followed, anticipating the dust this time.

And it came seconds later. This time wolf stopped and I aped his actions, and we waited. Soon the dust cleared and I looked forward. We were in a tropical setting right next to a man studying a group of giant ferns he stood next to. A yellow man. Bright yellow in Asian-looking garb. He too, as he turned, had my face. He studied the ferns and stood touching each, one after the other, as if speaking to them. Then he made notes on a small pad of paper he carried, gathered some leaf fronds from the ferns and began moving off. He stopped, bowed to the ferns, looked skyward and was speaking. In a minute he moved off and quickly out of sight. Wolf turned and just stared at me, as if asking if I understood. I didn't. Me in different colors of man – I got that. And scenes of past, present and future – I got that too. But were all these things I was seeing connected? If so, what did they mean? Or, if not, what did each mean? After a moment, wolf seemed satisfied, turned and began walking in a new direction. Right on cue, the wind, sand and dust came up to swallow us.

This time, as the dust cleared and the wind died, we were back by the stream that this part of the journey began at. Yet it was different in some way – more green plants along the bank and clearer looking water. Or maybe I just misremembered what it had looked like. Wolf began heading upstream and I, as I was now accustomed to, followed behind.

In a mile or so I saw some buildings in the distance. Nearing, I could see they were small dwellings and some larger buildings to one side. All fairly close together, all with plants around them and a garden just beyond them. A fairly extensive garden from the looks of it from here. Further in the distance was an even larger building, with people milling around and going in and out. All of the buildings were adorned with solar panels and many had grass covered roofs, also planted. Several fire pits were beyond the buildings, which looked like small dwellings, and I could see two inipis past them. Past all of the dwellings a quarter-mile or so were a line of hills and, on two of them, wind turbines cut the air. Water ran in many places. There were at least four good-sized ponds I could see, which all seemed to be spring fed. And a creek, about thirty feet across, was running below all the buildings. A few pickup trucks and maybe twenty cars were all parked off at some distance from the buildings. The entire infrastructure was nicely separated by plants, water and paths, but also clustered together in a way that left the grounds around them all open and wild. A comfortable sight to my senses. I followed wolf into the middle of the dwellings, watching various people moving about their business. These were very diverse people, obviously of varied cultures. As we approached one of the larger buildings I could see some young people gathered around listening to a man in front who was showing some pictures and drawings. He was tall, about six foot one or two, large framed and gray haired. And he was pure white, the artist with the 'people' brush had been at work again. And he, also, was me. An older me, but me teaching. This time, however, I thought that he saw, or at least sensed me watching with my wolf brother, because he looked our way and a small smile creased his face. Then he went back to what he was showing and sharing. Wolf looked over at me and trotted back downstream.

We backtracked our initial route and, as we neared the place I thought I had first been aware of wolf coming to me, I stopped, bowed and gave much thanks to this excellent guide. I told him of how I had never experienced anything like this and how it was because of him I was able to be 'present' and feel safe. And I also gave thanks again to eagle, who I sensed wheeling high above us. Wolf stared at me, raised his head, and let out an impressive howl. A howl that went up and

19 | Fry Bread and Fried Head

I MUST HAVE MOANED OR BLEW OUT AIR OR MAYBE SHIFTED MY BODY, as I was stiff and sore, because Two Bears almost at once asked quietly, "Are you okay nephew?"

"Yes, Uncle, I think so, but every part of my body hurts and my legs feel like stone," I answered haltingly. I always sat cross-legged in a lodge or during any seated ceremony. This is a position I was comfortable in for as long as I could remember, one leg crossed under the other. I could sit this way for several hours with little or no discomfort, especially if I uncrossed my legs periodically and re-crossed them with bottom on top and top on bottom. Even as a small child I would sit watching cartoons all Saturday morning with my legs crossed this way. I thought it ironic now that I was beginning to walk the red road where sitting in this way was often the norm. A coincidence? As I no longer believe in coincidences, I must assume there was a reason for this. Some foretelling of my path? Some preparation so my body would be comfortable in this position later. I don't know, or care, but am thankful it was not a way of sitting I needed to learn as I started this part of my walk.

"How do you feel inside? Are mind, body and spirit connected? What are you feeling?" he asked, with some concern in his voice.

"Confused and a little wobbly I guess. I never had any experience like that. So much to see and so many images and colors, my head is swimming. But I think I am okay. Can we talk more about this in a little while? I need some time to just let my brain stop spinning and my heart to slow down. It seems to be beating pretty fast."

"So. Let's close with a prayer of gratitude and then go up to my place. I made fry bread earlier and we will heat the stew you brought. It smelled good as you carried it in. We can talk and share as we eat."

"Thank you, perfect Uncle. It will give me some time. I am already unsure what I saw and heard and am a little winded. The stew should still be hot — I had it boiling until I left my house and then it stays hot for a few hours," I replied to him.

"Jim, we will see when we come out under Grandmother moon, but I think it is almost two in the morning. You were gone a very long time. I have sat here for at least a couple of hours, maybe more, since my journeying ended, waiting for you to come back. I got fearful of how long you were where you went and thought to bring you back with drum, but my guides told me to be still and focus on my own prayers. To leave you be as you were protected by many and needed to finish your trip in a good way. It was important you finish — that came to me several times. So I sat quietly and waited."

I had meditated for a number of years and journeying maybe six times before this, so I knew sometimes you go where you go for a few minutes, sometimes an hour or more. Once, with two Native American students we all were off for two and a half hours. But this, if Two Bears was correct, was one long journey. We had entered the lodge before seven and so had probably started the fourth door around eight thirty. Five to six hours of journeying? In some ways it felt that long, in other ways it felt like a few minutes. I was beginning to feel anxious as I thought this through, so I went back into my heart and asked for peace and calming. Two Bears must have felt my unease.

"Relax Jim and breathe the sage for a few minutes. Then slowly move your body around. Loosen the knots, but not too fast or you may cramp. I will go out and tend the Chanunpa while I wait for you.

Before you come out, you could move to a crawling position so you don't get dizzy. Go to all fours like a wolf and wait for your body to adjust. Then rise slowly as you leave. I will be there if your legs are weak."

How interesting he described going to hands and knees like a wolf. I did as he suggested and found I was dizzy and weak, so I took it slow and easy. When I finally crawled through the door and began to stand, I wobbled and almost fell, but Two Bears put a hand on my arm and steadied me. I went to the smoldering ashes of what had been the fire and stood for a few minutes. Then I felt able to walk up the low hill to Two Bears' home.

It was late – or early depending on your perspective – as I saw from the clock in his kitchen. 2:20 in the morning. Two Bears turned the heat on under the stew and we sat at the table, a large pitcher of water between us. I slowly drank as I was dehydrated from the long stint in the lodge. As I drank I began to feel physically more comfortable and a little more mentally alert.

"Stay here tonight. We need to talk and you do not need to drive, as tired and drained as you are. Will Bonnie worry?"

"No, I told her we meant to journey and I did not know when we would leave the lodge. Two friends from back East are with us for ten days, so she and Pat are going to Denver today, anyway. Dick will watch TV and read his papers. So, thanks, I think I will stay."

"Good. Let's just eat quietly for a while. This will give you more time to do some inner work. For your spirit to work before we speak of the lodge."

"I like that. I don't even know where to begin inside, let alone speaking yet. So I will not think about what came and just let my inner being do as it will."

We sat, enjoyed the stew and fry bread and continued to refill the water pitcher, as we both needed to hydrate. We spoke a little on my work at CSU and the work Two Bears was doing with some ex-cons down state, but no mention of the lodge or the journeying. When we had our fill, we took the water and our glasses and went into his small living room area. Two Bears built a fire in the fireplace and burned some sage in his bowl, with which we smudged ourselves thoroughly, and then we sat – in two overstuffed, comfortable chairs to speak.

"Jim, as we speak of our journeys, you are free to speak as you wish or be silent as you wish on any parts of what occurred. There is no right or wrong here, as with all we do. I will guide you as I am able, as is part of my role as teacher. And you are free to guide me if you feel it is right. Do you understand this? Accept it?"

"I do. But I don't know how I might guide you. I am so new at all of this I would not know when or where to guide."

"Ah, listen to Spirit and listen to your inner voice. You will learn to speak as words come. Now is a good time to start."

"Got it Uncle."

"With your permission, nephew, I will speak of my journey first. So you will see what I saw and hear what I heard before we go into your longer trip."

"Of course, Two Bears. Thank you for being willing to share. I may also better understand how to tell my story after listening."

Since it was Two Bears' journey, and so his story to tell, I will honor that and will not share it here. Except for a few points that related to me. He was told that he was to listen to my tale carefully – whatever I was willing and able to share – and remember for later, all he heard. He was to give no answers, but to ask questions when they were needed. And, as he had already told me, he was told that I was safe and protected in my journey, so he was not to bring it to an end until it ended itself. We sat, enjoying the heat from the fire and the sound of the popping, burning wood, after he finished for a few minutes.

Then he spoke, "Nephew, when you are ready to speak, I am ready to hear."

And so I began telling the story of my journey earlier. I was amazed how it came back to me as I spoke, in all its detail and even the nuances of color and patterns I saw. Two Bears listening quietly, but leaned forward in total concentration. The more I spoke, the quicker the words came. I did not know what I was going to say before the words flowed from my mouth. Two Bears looked as if he was going to ask questions a few times – once I even saw him shake his head 'no' – but, each time, I felt this, he did not speak. This had been a long journey and it was a long story to tell. As I moved through it I was no longer aware of Two Bears, but reliving the journey as I spoke. Not at the level of the original, but with my attention on what I was saying.

Finally I was finished. No more words came, so I blew out a long breathe, stretched my neck and then looked over to Two Bears. He was sitting perfectly still, in concentration, with a half frown or smile on his face – I could not tell which. And with tears on his cheeks. This threw me. Laughs, snorts, questions, doubt, understanding – any of these I would have expected, but not tears. I feared I had offended him in some way and my own self-doubts, still very strong at this point in time, assaulted me.

"Two Bears, if I have offended you in some way or said something I was not supposed to, I apologize. The words just came. I should have thought before speaking. I had no intention to offend you in any way. My respect and love for you are great. So, I am sorry for any error."

He continued to sit quietly, then smiled and looked at me.

"Jim, you will need to leave these fears and doubts behind as we move ahead. We will work with this. If I told you there was no right or wrong and if I told you to share what you would, how could you have offended me?" Two Bears paused then began speaking again, "Now leave this foolish doubt behind and let us speak. What animal did you see first? Where? How did he appear?"

"The wolf, Uncle. The big gray wolf with the multi-colored coat. He was with me the entire time except when I soared with Wambli and even then I remember feeling his presence. Actually, as I can now as I speak with you."

"Good. What other animals were strong in the journey? I know you have told the story as it was, but I ask questions so you may see the answers," Two Bears said.

"Eagle, Wambli, also was strong in the journey."

"Just so. An eagle large enough to carry a man until you were ready to understand size does not matter in these things."

I did not know what he meant about being ready, but the eagle had been huge.

"Tell me about the painted ones. The ones with your face. Who were they?"

"They were the four colors, of that I am clear," I began. "I am not clear about why they had my face. Are these people of different races I have met? Or will meet? Or teachers I will have? Or are they parts of me? Maybe people I was or will be? There are too many options and I do not see which might be true."

"Why must only one meaning be so? You are correct about the four colors of man as seen on the medicine wheel. Why were they so painted? Why not just a black man, a red man, a yellow man and a white man?"

"I don't know Uncle. Maybe so this imperfect human would be clear about them being the four colors of man."

"Good answer. It may be so," Two Bears responded to my words. "What do you see in the part of the journey Wambli guided you on?"

"I see he flew in both time and space. Past, present and future and different locations as each presented itself. I think I see that he stayed longer in some places than others. Maybe because he was aware when I had seen enough. And I also see I had to face my fear of heights, in order to see more than my fear before me."

"Excellent," Two Bears beamed at me. "Especially your awareness of the fear part. For fear is the only thing in the universe that can truly stop us from moving forward. We must be vigilant and work on our fears each time they arise. Sometimes this is quickly done, sometimes it requires much time. When we conquer fear of anything that stops us, we are ready to continue the journey around that issue. And, yes, it is the circle again, the circle of past, present and future. Does this travel with Wambli relate to the travel to the painted people with wolf?"

"Maybe, it feels like it does, but I don't see the full connection. It's unclear to me."

"How does it feel like they are one?"

"I don't know Uncle. Well, the circle I suppose. The four colors circle and the circle of past, present and future for one thing. The land, the Earth Mother, was strong in both trips."

"Good. So there are some connections and maybe many more when they come to you. Maybe it is but one journey and not two. But you will see," Two Bears said, giving me more questions, but no answers – as he said he would.

"What did it feel like as you took this journey? From your heart now, not your head."

"It felt as if I was there, not in the lodge. And that got stronger as it went forward. My senses became more alive as the trip continued. Yet other things were different than real time. I was on eagle and with eagle at the same time. I could speak and hear wolf, yet no sound was made – except his howls later on. Once, with the painted white man, I felt we were seen or felt, but the rest of the time I felt we were invisible observers. When I returned to the lodge it was fast and I did not feel it coming. It took a few minutes to even remember where I was and why."

"So. I offer this may be 'a' real world, but maybe not the only real world. Why did the painted white man see you and wolf, yet no others did?"

"I don't know Uncle. Because it was near the end of the journey? That makes little sense – as if any of this does. I don't know."

"Good. Sit and rest a few minutes. I need to walk under Grandmother Moon and the star nations and ask my guides if we, or I, are to go farther now. Are you okay?"

"I'm fine. I'll drink water and try not to think too much."

I was joking, but Two Bears responded with, "That's a good thing when dealing with spirit work. Very wise." He was very serious, but I also thought he might be letting me know my joke was actually a good way to go.

Two Bears returned in about fifteen minutes, carrying in some chips, salsa and three plates – one a Spirit plate. After each lodge, when we eat together, first we prepare a plate with a little of each of the foods, which we bring outside to honor Spirit. I was surprised to realize I was hungry again, especially after the stew and three fry breads I had wolfed down earlier – pun intended.

He sat, put chips and salsa on the Spirit plate, which he then put next to the sage bowl. Then put chips and salsa on his own plate and settled back. I took my plate and, after adding chips and salsa, also settled back in my chair.

"So. I have permission of the spirits to share some with you. And permission from the Earth Mother and Father Sky – as I felt this was important. Will you hear?"

"Yes, please Two Bears. I am confused, yet excited, by what I saw and what we are speaking of," I answered honestly.

"Good. First, another question. You have journeyed before. What have you seen and felt in those times?"

"Ah, well, they were different. Once I remember seeing just black and some other colors mixed in at times. I felt very calm and peaceful. Almost like floating in dark water. I think that was the first time and it was much like when I meditate. Once I saw grasslands and thousands of buffalo in all directions. The grass blew and the buffalo moved slowly. Each of these lasted maybe thirty minutes. Once I was high in the air looking down on animals. I seem to be blown by the wind. I remember animals looking up at me. And then I was back – suddenly. The other times were similar. Maybe two others."

"So. This time you journeyed far and high. You saw a story. A story not done yet. A story you must not try to understand fully yet. This was more than a journey. You had a vision – and a powerful one. You saw many things and many others also appear in the trip. Many claim to see visions, few do. I had a vision around my purpose many years ago. The only one of this life I have had. Most, when they have a vision, have it around a specific purpose or thing they will need to do. Yours was circles of many types in many times. No one thing you are to do. At least not yet. I see that more will come to you over time. There will be big work for you to do later. Speak when you are ready," Two Bears finished.

Speak? I did not know what to say. "Why would a beginner on this road – a white, middle-aged beginner – have a vision. If there is big work, why would the vision not come to you? You have walked the spiritual path your whole life and are ready to do things now."

"Visions are for those to whom they come. Each of us has a role, as we have spoken. My role is not yours, nor yours mine. I shed tears because I realized how broad a vision this was as you spoke – even before, as you journeyed, I knew this was more than a journey. Why would you seek to give your vision to me if Spirit sent it to you?"

"Sorry Uncle, I meant no disrespect. I understand what you are saying. My fear and confusion spoke."

"It's good to see that and speak that. I took no offense – I never will as we work together and expect the same from you – I only wanted you to question why you spoke this. You did so well."

"I am trying to understand about this vision. And you saying it is a broad vision."

"It has past, present and future. It has you in many colors and many places. It has strong animal guides. And it has not told you to begin something specific now. Why did you receive it? Why does any- one receive a vision? And why does your color or age matter?"

"I hear you Uncle, but I feel like I see no meaning in what I saw. I don't know what to do with it. What do you see in this? Will I un- derstand as I think, sorry – feel, it through?"

"I am not to tell you what I see in this. That is not for me, it is not my vision. There is more I may be able to share at a later time, but not now. Will you understand this vision? You will when the time is right."

"That is something I hear from all my teachers all the time. You will understand – or know – when the time is right. If I live long enough and acquire the wisdom to become an elder, do you think I'll sit and say that to those who ask me questions?" I asked, a little testily I fear.

But Two Bears smiled and answered, "Yes, you probably will answer in this way. Because by then you will understand this answer."

"There is no way to argue with that Two Bears. I will remove my foot from my mouth now, with your permission," I smiled, any anger gone.

"Permission granted. I will say this. Your primary spirit guide will be wolf – the one who led you. He has always been there, but you had yet to ask him in. And all the wolves will welcome you as brother and protect you as one of theirs. Eagle will also be a strong guide. He will take up when you need to 'see high'. And buffalo, Tatanka, will provide grounding and strength when you need it most. Speak to them often, especially wolf, and ask their help when you need it. What else do you have to ask?" he finished with another question.

"I am unsure if it is accepted for me to ask this, but I will as you have allowed me to speak with no right or wrong. Does a white person ever learn the ways and carry the Chanunpa? I have felt it in my space since the first lodge with Lyman."

"Ah, I was not going there yet, but you have asked and I will answer this. Yes, some non-Natives carry the Chanunpa in a good way. And many have just allowed themselves to pick one up, not understanding and so suffering all that will go wrong. If the Chanunpa speaks to you, you are to carry one at some time. This is a huge responsibility, one we would have to speak about at length. And we will, but not now. For now, ask White Buffalo Calf Woman for guidance. Do you know the story of how she brought the Chanunpa to the people?"

"Yes, I do Uncle. I will ask her guidance and ask again in our next lodge. And I wait to hear and understand more. Yet I feel strongly this is to be, if you agree and are willing."

"I do. You will carry the Chanunpa well. But you will carry it differently in some ways than most of us. You will know and honor all of the ways as we teach you, but you will add some things for your work I do not see clearly yet. It will come when it is time," he said cracking a huge grin. "And you will learn and share other ceremonies also. You will be one who brings teachings to those we would not reach. This is all good. But enough for now. Let's get some sleep."

This vision caused me to attempt to 'figure out' its meaning for several months. I got nowhere with that and, after time, it faded into the background of all the things I was doing. A couple of years ago it resurfaced in fuller memory as other pieces came to be – but that's for later. Except to note that even as I write this for all of us on this journey together, the clarity with which I remember and again see this vision has sharpened even more. As with everything we do – when we think we are doing it for others, we also do it for ourselves. The importance of the circle in all that was (the past), is (the present) and will be (the future) throughout the universe was, however, something that grew in my consciousness as I continued my walk. And is something that now guides much of what I do, share and teach. Because the circle of life and the medicine wheel, which represents it, are central to my walk, I will spend some time discussing it.

20 | Teaching of the Circle

"All life is a circle."

—Rolling Thunder, CHEROKEE

I SAID I HAVE LEARNED AND TEACH BEST AND, I BELIEVE, MOST EFFECTIVELY through the use of questions. I break that tradition in this chapter as I speak of the circle – and yet I also hold true to it by asking you to ask questions of yourselves as you travel this with me. And to accept that I will also ask questions of myself, and you, along the way. I do so because this is the center – the core – of all else. Anyone trying to undertake anything alone will be hard pressed to move it ahead. Will, in fact, most probably fail. The time of 'I' is over. It no longer serves us. The way of the circle is the way of creating new and manifesting whatever will now be needed. The time of the 'we' is dawning. Not just any circle, however, will suffice. And so, as we stop and rest from our journey for a few minutes, I ask to be allowed to offer some of what I have seen and been told about walking in circle.

My circles were continuing to grow and the number of circles I walked in to increase at CSU. I was learning the power of the circle in creating ideas and manifesting visions and dreams, but I was just a babe when it came to truly understanding the nuances of walking in circle. I understand much more now and have seen circles create the impossible and circles spin without growing. Now I am no longer a babe in the understanding of circle, but maybe have moved along to late teen. As the change in our planet continues to happen quicker and chaos becomes the norm, I am led to look into circle constantly in order to expand my understanding and share what I have seen and been told – by my guides, by the ancestors and by the actions and effects of myself and those around me. If you are reading this book, you are awakened or beginning to awaken, so you have an understanding of what I am saying here and what I will share in this part of our journey. As always, some of you may have an understanding equal to mine, some of you may have walked further and some of you may now just begin to consider what you read here. Each is where he or she is meant to be at this moment and each with the ability to consider and accept more or not.

As I said, I understood the synergy of circles then – the sum is equal to more than the individual parts or, for you math-oriented folks, 1 + 1 = 3. That is, if each is allowed and willing to bring his and her part to the circle and the entire circle willing to let all the parts come together, what is created is bigger than these parts separately. There is the individual energy of the parts and the cumulative energy of their combined essence. Added to that is the power and energy that the guiding spirit of each and the will of the universal order brings to this sphere. The parts vary – one may bring higher math skills, another the overall vision, another the ability to raise resources, another the ability to mange the whole, and so on.

In the best of circles you begin by asking God—or the universe or whatever your sense of this energy is – to send those with the parts that are needed. Then if you truly surrender and trust, these people – or thing – will begin to appear. That is the easy part; walking ahead, all out of ego, all willing to lead or follow at any time, is the difficult part.

I have been part of many circles that have created and manifested visions thought by most to be impossible. A beautiful thing to watch when the individuals and the circle get 'in the flow' and the pieces seem to just drop into place. Some were my visions manifested, some the visions of others. Yet in each there was, for me, a flaw. The flaw was me. I was a strong leader, especially when I was truly passionate about some vision or idea. I was willing to do whatever was necessary to bring the vision to fruition for the common good – the good of humans, animals or the planet. And I could, at times, effectively follow. But if I saw the process going off-track – in my opinion – I stepped back in to right it. Hail the knight in shining armor! I am not judging myself by writing this, but I am stating what I now see to be truth. Probably because my intent was pure, the visions to be manifested worthy and the circle was created and the parts used, each vision did manifest, usually even quicker then I thought possible.

Then, when the creation reached a point of sustainability, my leader is 'I' approach caused me to be ejected from the circle, usually in an emotionally painful way. Sometimes I would fight my expulsion, sometimes just walk away in confusion, anger and disbelief. I see now I had done my part in the circle, used my skills of attraction and leadership, but had then walked as the leader rather then one of the circle. When I could finally see and accept this, I was able to further accept that the primary reason for my removal from a circle was me. So that the circle could continue to grow, but in the new way – as a whole of equal parts. Not with 'a' leader, the mode in which I still functioned.

Now, more than ever before in our short human history, I have been shown that the only work to flourish is the work created by this higher level of circle. Anyone trying to manifest a vision as the primary leader accepting help only from others, is now doomed to an inability to move ahead. This applies to everything – business, politics, education, spiritual visions and all else you might wish to add to the list here. This is hard for most humans to accept, especially males trained to lead and fight for a good cause, but I assure you it is so.

Look at our universe, our solar system, our world and we as human beings and you will see the circle is the primary component of each. Galaxies circle throughout the heavens above, our planets circle our primary star, the sun. Our suns, moons and planets are circular and rotate in a circular fashion. Water, the blood of the Earth Mother, moves through various watercourses, evaporates and falls again as precipitation so it may be used by plants then put back into watercourses – and the cycle repeats – a perfect circle. The blood of our bodies' function in the same way, mimicking the way of our planet. Each existence we experience, whether one or many depending on your beliefs, is also a perfect circle – from birth, to growth, to maturity, to aging, to death. Cultures start, grow, rise, attain power, lose power, weaken and die as new cultures take their place. The examples are endless, in fact, in the Native American, Mayan, African and other traditions I have been gifted to learn, the circle is in everything. Everything there is, is a circle, with no beginning and no end. Human thought, especially in Western cultures, has bred the belief that things have a beginning, a middle and an end. Look at all in you and around you. Is this so? Is it then, truly about the destination and not the journey? If so, what do you do once you reach the destination? One answer to this is you stop growing. If you are 'there', what reason could there be to learn more and advance?

Why is this circle of equal parts so important now? My answer is there are many reasons, but the primary one circles around this time in history we all occupy. All is now in chaos: politics; the elements; the climate; financial institutions; economies; businesses; our bodies; our minds; and our spirits. We are at the time of choice – accept the crashes that are here and coming. Our choice is to change our ways and be reborn like the Phoenix of myth or walk the road of the dinosaurs before us. It is that simple and that complex.

In the teachings of many cultures I have been exposed to, especially the Mayan and the Hopi, this is the time of the Fifth Earth approaching. Most have heard of the prophecies of 2012, but I don't think many understand their true import. Many have sensationalized these prophecies, out of fear and greed, calling up the old images of the haggard old man walking through the streets carrying his sign with bold, shaky letters exclaiming "THE END IS NEAR!"

What the prophecies talk about, as my teachers in this world and the spirit world have led me to understand, is that we now live on the Fourth Earth. The Earth before us, the Third, was controlled and directed by the feminine. And, after change was not welcomed or accepted, it collapsed and this Earth evolved – one controlled by the masculine. We all see what males have made of this Earth. The Fifth Earth needs to be a balance of the masculine and feminine where true circles of equality may form and prosper. This you can read in many books. And, it is true. Yet I have seen there is so much more.

Equality of the circle goes far beyond the balance of masculine and feminine – although that is a very strong spoke in the wheel of the circle. It means balance between the four colors – red, black, yellow and white. Balance between the ages, from youngest to oldest. Balance and equality between cultures and beliefs. Rich and poor. And all other degrees of balance and equality your mind, and heart can list. By achieving this balance and equality of all parts, we will be able to move into the Fifth Earth, a world of harmony, love and peace, without the total destruction and turmoil Hollywood depicts. Those who will be able to understand and manifest these changes are those who have awakened, have dealt with their egos and fears and have surrendered to Spirit their willingness to embrace the changes. If this invokes images of the sixties or simplistic images of everyone holding hands singing "Kumbia", sorry, it is not so. It is a very real, very much needed, evolution of spirit humans must now chose and enact. If this sounds "foo-foo" to you, look inside and ask yourself why you find it so.

It is, in fact, the most difficult, most challenging change the human race has, or will ever, experience. Those humans here now, at this critical time, are here for a reason as the Mayans teach. Many are choosing to go through the fear and doubt of awakening in order to play their role in this change. Many others are staying and will stay; blithely unaware that anything of this magnitude is occurring. And many others are becoming aware of what is going on but are allowing their fear to drive them into anger and denial. Those who do not, or cannot, make the shift will not be able to become part of the Fifth Earth. There is no right or wrong here, as there is nowhere—simply choice, conscious or unconscious, by each person.

As I watch, and function in circles, I see the number awakened and conquering their fear growing by the moment and this gives me great hope that the Change, the Shift, will occur with the least amount of chaos necessary. If enough do not reach this willing awakened state, the chaos and changes will intensify, also as predicted in numerous prophecies. Whether you choose to accept this interpretation of the prophecies and what is currently occurring around all of us is for you to decide. Ask yourself more questions. Ask your teachers and spirit guides for affirmation or rejection. Then go into your hearts with all you see and hear. However you understand and accept the current changes, the circle is a dominant force without which no endeavor will now prosper.

How do we create these circles of equals? I will list some of the things I have been shown are necessary, but also being certain the list is much longer. Add to it, as you will. Each addition, each new thought strengthens the power of the circles growing and about to grow.

1. Work on yourself. It is impossible to be in a circle of equals over time if you have not done the inner work to accept how the circle functions.

2. Begin working on yourself by understanding and accepting there are no more prophets, no more gurus. Following them automatically creates leaders from whom others expect all the work.

3. Stop worshiping saints and prophets of the past and begin working on yourself so you will one day join their circle.

4. Work on releasing your ego. This is anther step that sounds easy, but is difficult. The first step is admitting you have an ego. The next is to examine what you do and ask your heart what guides it – ego or service.

5. Work on any fear in your being. Fear is the one thing that can totally stop our growth.

6. Stop pointing fingers and judging. You only judge yourself when you do this. As you put out this energy, so it will come back at you.

7. Accept all creatures as equals – no matter how many legs, wings, or fins.

8. Bring the Earth Mother and nature into all you do. Without connecting in a good way with the Earth, humans cannot exist.

9. Prepare yourself to be unwilling to do anything 'for' somebody and totally willing to do something 'with' somebody.

You will know, by checking in with your inner spirit, your highest self, when you have done adequate work on yourself to prepare for the circles you are called to enter. Not when you are done, as we are all always works in progress, but when you have reached a point to move forward. If you are open to walking your road in the best way and ask Spirit to show you which circles you are to enter, they will appear to you in short order. In the meantime, look at the circles you are already a part of. Are all the parts accepted as equals? Does each person lead and follow as the task before the circle requires? Do the circles attempt to reach their goals with integrity? If some of your circles are functioning in the ways I described above and some are not – what differences do you see in each and the results each is achieving?

When the circles you are to be a part of start to appear, explore their energy and operation before becoming a spoke on the wheel. Be as willing to say "no" as you are to say "yes". You must honor yourself, and your willingness to join, before you can honor the others of the circle. I have found that if many circles ask you in at the same time, the ones you are not to remain with will drop away of their own accord.

As you begin to do your work, remember all is a journey that we learn from as we walk. None of us will suddenly get it all, make all the right choices or understand the way of the Fifth Earth without hard work and trial and error.

I provide these suggestions and lists as a guide, not hard and fast rules. This way of sharing what I am to share is not the way I prefer, but it may help some as a takeoff point. I hope so. Now, in my way, I will speak of my own trail on the circle road.

I spoke of how I functioned in circles in the past – and how, eventually, each spit me out. My work done, my 'leader is me' methods no longer acceptable. Many times I walked this way, learning a little each time. Some of these you have seen already in what I have written, more will follow. Then, five years ago, as I walked through loses and pain, I asked Spirit to show me where I was to serve. Almost immediately a group formed with me. I may share more about this later. We created an organization dedicated to teaching how to work in the 'we' instead of the 'I'. We all learned how truly difficult this was as we created the essence of how this circle would work together. One dropped out, not able to accept that he would no longer be the leader of the circle. Others were unwilling to put forth the energy it would take to develop and implement this work. At the same time other new people appeared to join us. We began workshops and retreats where we practiced this 'we' approach and had success with sharing the model and learning and growing ourselves. Then, after a period of time, we disbanded and now share ideas as we do our work in many parts of the U.S. For me, I was drawn to Arizona and the spiritual mecca of Sedona. I knew only a couple of people slightly and asked Spirit again to guide my path. Within six months, five different non-profit circles asked me to join their teams. These were also from various places around the country. During that same, time a small group of us in Sedona created another non-profit to preserve land in a manner that would be in harmony with the Earth Mother. So a sixth circle had manifested. Now, a year and a half later, I remain with three of these circles. And I have watched and become aware of how my understanding of circles of equality achieve while circles led by one fall or stumble ahead.

One of these circles was a support non-profit for a company developing renewable, clean energy. The leader of the company was brilliant in design – in seeing the vision for how these methods would work. Yet he was out of integrity, lying to investors and needing to control everything. His ego would not let him empower others to lead in their areas of expertise. And so, the non-profit circle collapsed and the company staggers along, barely able to pay its bills. I released this circle with hope for the awakening of the visionary leader so his work might succeed. And I released the circle of the non-profit support group as not being necessary until those supported could move into circles of 'we'.

Next was a cultural institute, set up to bring peoples of many cultures together to learn from one another and to share the teachings of ancestors to all who would listen. The young man running it was well intentioned and hard working, but he also suffered from ego, as well as lack of self-esteem. He was being guided by the voices of people looking to feed their own egos and, therefore, guiding him to mistakes. This, too, collapsed—hopefully, with some new blood, to rise again like the Phoenix down the road. Once again I watched a circle controlled by a few cease to function.

The fourth circle I still walk in. It has come together around the vision of a close Native American friend of mine—a man I consider a brother. His is a wonderful vision, which I totally support and intend to do what I am able to help manifest. Yet my friend, at time, suffers from pride and often vacillates in decision-making. He has given himself the title of overseer of the non-profit – a title which defines how he sees his role. He tries to do the majority himself, as I have so many times in the past. Yet he is making strides to move more into true circle, so I wait and serve as best I am able.

That is my role in many things at this time – to just 'be'. I am unsure why, but do not question the teachings of my guides on this. In this circle there is, again, a man of great visionary power and great artistic gifts who has difficulty accepting that his gifts in other areas are much less evident.

The fifth is a non-profit formed many years ago to promote world peace and understanding. The woman running it has great gifts and, now, is learning to work with a circle. She struggles to move from the 'I' to the 'we', especially difficult for someone who has been functioning mostly solo for many years. It is an ongoing piece of work for she and those of us who have formed around the organization, but it is moving ahead as we learn and create together.

The sixth, the land conservancy I mentioned, is running in the 'we' as well as I have seen it ever work. Not perfect, we have a long road still to travel, but well. It had taught me patience, something I lacked in the past. And taught me that, when using the skills of all, forward motion happens – even when it is not always obvious.

There, enough circles to consider as we move forward. Now, with the permission of our circle, I will step back on the journey with all of you. Thank you for listening and considering the importance of the circles of life. Look for them if you will, as we walk forward and look for them all around you in all you experience. This will aid you in understanding circles and entering them in a good way.

21 | **Back to Belize**

I WAS VERY BUSY WORKING ON MY MASTERS IN NATURAL RESOURCE Management and Environmental Interpretation for the period of time after the lodge in which I received the vision. I immersed myself in this, my teaching, running the Center and taking playtime when Bonnie and I would pick places in Colorado or Wyoming and go exploring. Just to see what new things we might stumble across.

The environmental project in Belize was coming up, slowly but steadily, and I needed to focus some time and energy there. I was communicating with all the parties in Belize, but felt at a disadvantage because I had only spent three weeks there and only seen a small portion of the country. I had the funding lined-up and was finishing the paperwork with one of the small family foundations involved, when I realized I did not understand part of what they were asking for. So I gave my contact with their organization a call to discuss their needs.

As we spoke, I shared my wish that I had had more time on the ground in the country, but that I was certain our team of five could accomplish the list of promises we had made. The contact woman thanked me for clarifying and responding to their requests and told me she would call if anything further arose. If not, I would have the funds within a week. Bonnie and I had also added some geology and wildlife tours to our days to pay for her expenses on the trip.

The next morning the foundation called back. She said she was happy to inform me the grant had been approved and they looked forward to our report when we returned. Then she brought up the lack of time I had to date in Belize. She, at the direction of her board of directors, offered me the funding to spend two weeks in Belize – a "familiarization trip" she termed it – before I brought the team down for the project. They were able to fund two people; my wife and myself if I so chose. I had not been fishing for this – had not even considered it an option – but was rather being honest about any obstacles we might have when she had asked that question. Yet here it was, offered without an ask. I thanked her and the board and accepted the offer. I went home to discuss the option with Bonnie.

When I got home, I found Bonnie had spoken to her mother and was upset. Her mother had melanoma – skin cancer—on her head and she required surgery. Bonnie had told her she would come to stay with her in her home in New Jersey for three or four weeks. I told her about the pre-project trip to Belize and my hopes she could accompany. After a talk – the need for her mother to address the cancer quickly and the need for the Belize trip to move quickly – we decided I would go to Belize alone. Since we would both be going together on the project soon anyway, it was not a hard decision to make. I decided not to advertise this trip, since some jealous remarks about how 'Jim always seems to get his projects funded' had been surfacing and I did not want to pour any gas on the flames. Besides, no university money was involved – I had secured the foundation funding on my own. So we simply told people Bonnie's mother was ill and we needed to spend some time out of town. Not a lie, but I'm glad no one asked any additional questions.

Ten days later, I was driving Bonnie to the plane in Denver and three days after that a friend was driving me over the same route. That afternoon I landed in Belize City, with one bag and a carry-on shoulder pouch. Jeans and tee shirts – my favorite wardrobe to this day. I got through customs fairly quickly – although not as quickly as when Richard was there waving to the inspectors – and went outside to look for a rental car. I needed four-wheel drive, as I expected to be off the few paved roads of the country. It turned out I needed to go into Belize City, so I took a cab and headed to the city. I found a Jeep to fit my needs and rented it for the duration, with the agreement I could return it earlier if I was going out to the Cayes. I headed out towards San Ignacio, in the mid-central part of the country a little way past Belmopan. I intended to spend a few days there learning the land and meeting some people. I did stay three days and met a number of new, interesting locals. I hired one to go with me on a Jeep tour of the region the second day. This worked well and was a process I would use many times again on future trips.

After leaving San Ignacio, I headed for the Cockscomb area to see if I could find Roberto whom I had met on my first trip. Four hours later after being stuck in mud twice, hitting a dead-end due to a bridge out and enough wrong turns to make me dizzy, I crested a hill that looked familiar. Somehow – not related to any expertise on my part – I had stumbled into the valley where he lived. Thirty minutes later I found his house, from which I could see him in his field off to the left. He saw the Jeep from where he was and headed up towards me. As he got close he recognized me and opened a huge smile. He was pleased and totally surprised to see me. Remembering me was not hard, as six foot one American white men were in short supply, especially in this part of the country. He gave me a big hug and welcomed me back to his home. He wanted to know how long I would stay and I told him until he kicked me out. He liked this and invited me in. I hauled in my bag and carried it to a small back room he pointed towards. A bed and a small table – all I would need. Then I went out and joined Roberto in the little living area of the house. He was boiling water and had brought out a sack of what I supposed was tea.

"Some good tea and herbs Jim? Will clear your body and mind after long trips," he asked.

"Sounds perfect Roberto. I brought some biscuits from San Ignacio. Want some?"

"Oh, yeah," he answered with a smile. I had stopped and bought an assortment of crackers, biscuits, fruit, vegetables and some chicken before leaving. I did not want to impose on Roberto's food supply, feeling certain it was limited.

"I brought a few other things from the market. Let me go bring them in if that is okay?" I asked.

"Whatever you brought will help fill the cabinets. Thanks."

I brought in the food and laid it all on the table. We put it away as the water boiled, Roberto simply pointing where each item went. I saw he had lots of vegetables from his garden, so I was glad I had gone easy on them at the market.

"Ah, maybe we will have chicken and rice tonight. Do you like that? he asked.

"Love it, especially if you add some beans," I replied.

"Always with beans amigo."

When the tea was made and the food put away we went and sat in the two chairs in Roberto's living area. They were fairly comfortable but, like most things in Belize, not designed for a six foot one user.

"So, what brings you back and so soon?" Roberto asked.

"I am bringing four others to do some projects here before long and wanted to get the lay of the land. And I hoped to meet some new people. I have been working with my Lakota teachers and thought I might share some things with people here. That's not very clear, but I'm not entirely sure why I did come."

Roberto looked at me smiling as he drank his tea. The tea was hot and very pungent. I do not know what herbs he had mixed with the tealeaves, but it was refreshing and energizing.

"So, you are learning the healing ways of the old ones. That's a good thing, especially these days."

"Well, more the ceremony and prayer ways, at least for now. I have been working with Lakota people and other Native Americans since I got to CSU. It was surprising how I came to meet with them, but I'm glad it happened. I know very little yet, but my spirit is welcoming all that is shared with me," I shared with him.

"Never be surprised, that is one of the teachings of my Mayan people. All things occur how and when they need to. I feel you need to learn the medicine of people who walk closely to the land, also. Maybe I can bring you to some who would welcome you. And maybe I can show some things my grandfathers' grandfathers gave to me. And I would be very happy to hear what you know from our native brothers and sisters up north."

"I will certainly share all I have learned – but I am just a child beginning. And I would love anything you are willing to share," I said.

I am not going to tell you all I learned from my Mayan teachers, nor the Australian aborigine nor the African teachers and friends later. This too I may speak more of at another time, but I will tell you of some I met and worked with, like Roberto, and the nature of what they taught me. And I hope – what I was able to teach them.

Roberto and I sat talking for hours – he about the plants he worked with and their healing ways and me about my past and the spiritual road I was now on with my Native American friends. We talked through lunch – the biscuits and tea sustaining us – and on through the afternoon. Finally, we decided we needed to make dinner and talk more as we ate.

As we prepared dinner together Roberto asked, "Would you like to do a Mayan fire ceremony tonight Jim? I could ask some of the neighbors over and show you the way of the healing fire."

"That would be fantastic, Roberto. May I help with anything?"

"Watch the dinner and clean that lettuce while I go find little Umberto. I will have him go to others and send my invite. They probably already know a white visitor is here and will be interested to meet you."

So I finished fixing dinner as Roberto went 'next door'. Next-door must have been a half-mile away, because that was the nearest farm I saw driving in. When he returned he boiled water for the herb tea and we sat down to dinner. He offered thanks to his ancestors for this chance to be on the Earth and this land. And he thanked God for all he gave him each day. It was similar to listening to Lakota prayers, but shorter and with less stylized language.

We cleaned up after dinner and went outside where we smoked some strong – very strong – tobacco rolled in natural plant paper. Roberto told me this was a type of tobacco, grown naturally near-by, that his people had used for generations. I told him how little tobacco was used in the Chanunpa of the North American native people. And apologized for not being able to smoke much of his tobacco, but it had my head spinning. He laughed and took another big puff. I hoped I wouldn't have to smoke this tobacco too often if I was invited to any ceremonies. We sat, enjoying the cool evening breezes and listened to the night birds. The sound of birds, any birds, had always soothed me and put me in a place of calm. Their songs, screeches and hoots do so to this day. Roberto saw how I was 'moving' with the night sounds and smells and commented on my connection to nature. "It is strong Jim?"

"Yes, it always has been Roberto. Nature and the Earth Mother are the pieces of this world to which I am most connected and with which I like to work and play."

"That is very good. Very good. So many now have forgotten what it is to be really outside. Even here, in our tropical country, many of our people live in the cities and forget to go out. They just forget."

"I've always thought one of my purposes in living is to help remind people," I added to his words.

"Ah. Yes. I see."

In a while he said it was time to prepare. We went inside and began collecting things from around his kitchen. I asked if I might add some sage. He agreed and I dug some out of my bag. I had brought a large bundle, making me nervous going through customs. We took what we had gathered and carried it to an open space a few hundred yards from his home where many fires had been lit in the past. The area was circled in rocks of all types – river rocks, lava rocks, crystals and many I did not recognize. This brought up the continued connections of so many people as it looked much like the fire pit where we heat the rocks for lodge, but without a hole for logs.

He laid what we had both carried over to one side and took out a large bag of white flour. He began making a large circle around the burning area. It must have been thirty feet across. You can figure the diameter – I'm no good at math. Then he went around this circle again, this time with sugar. When he was done, he bisected the circle twice, creating four equal quarters. This he also did with flour and sugar. He then took blue and red powders and poured them along both sides of the bisecting lines. Then he told me we would wait for whoever came. Here it was again, not only the circle, but also a medicine wheel of sorts. Shortly we saw some people coming our way from three different directions. In another fifteen minutes we had a group of eighteen people, plus Roberto and I. A few children, women and men made up our fire circle gathering for tonight.

Everyone had brought things with him or her. I saw many bunches of flowers and bags full of leaves and containers of all sorts. Everything brought was laid beside what Roberto and I had carried out.

"This is my friend from Colorado and the university there, Jim," Roberto began in introducing me. "Welcome all who have come. We will do a fire ceremony tonight in the Mayan way so Jim may see how we do this. And we may all pray together and heal together. Jim learns from the Native people in the United States and I see he has good medicine to bring here with us. Let us all say our names as we stand around the circle so we are a family tonight," he finished.

We spread out around the flour and sugar circle Roberto had poured and each said his or her name, starting with Roberto and going to the east from him – the same way as speaking is done in the Lakota lodges.

Then Roberto began instructing people to place, pour and shake out the various things they had brought. He asked me to lay the sage where I felt it was needed, so I put large handfuls in each of the four directions. People began laying the flowers around the circle and along the bisecting lines. Others were putting herbs in various spots inside the circle. It was a maze of color and texture being created. Designs began to appear amongst the ingredients of the circle. It was becoming more beautiful and elaborate by the moment. Chocolate was unwrapped and also put into the growing design, as was sugar cane and feathers. Then the candles were brought out – over a hundred of many colors. These were also added to the design. It was a round collage of foods and herbs, flowers and feathers and powders. It took well over an hour before everything was worked into the design. It was truly a work of art, a work we had created together.

Then Roberto began to teach about the Mayan fire ceremony, for my benefit I am sure. He spoke of how this tradition went back more generations than any remembered. And how, when lit, the smoke and fragrances would bring our thanks and prayers to God. And to ask God and the Earth to allow the people to stay on this land and use it for only good things. Then he spoke of how each would also take any pain or illness they had and put it into a candle, which they would add to the fire to release these ills. Then, as the fire burned the offerings, all would pray.

"Jim, would you do a prayer of opening for us tonight?" Roberto asked me, catching me totally by surprise.

"Ah, sure, I would be honored," I answered his request. And so I opened the ceremony to the seven directions, asking Great Spirit to listen to all our prayers and ease us of any illness we carried at the end. I felt like an outsider, but I also felt my prayer was well received.

"That was a powerful prayer, amigo," Roberto complimented me, "I am sure we all are grateful. Let me now pray as we light the fire. Raul and Mary, will you please light all the candles within the circle first?"

The two he had called forth entered the circle carefully and went around lighting all the candles. Then Roberto began a prayer to his people of the past as he emptied some rum on the circle. He lit four dry sticks and passed them out – to three around the circle and one to me. He motioned us to light the circle. The rum was a great fire starter and the blaze spread quickly, jumping up into the night sky. When Roberto was finished with his prayer one of the older women began to sing a song and soon everyone joined in. I hummed along feeling that was appropriate.

We stood around the fire after a few songs and each said a prayer, silently or aloud, and put their candle into the blaze. We all sat down then to wait for the fire to burn to ash. Roberto asked me to speak about the ways of the Native people I knew and to share, if I was willing, what I thought of this fire ceremony. And so I began to tell some of the things I had spoken to Roberto earlier. When the fire was done, we all headed to Roberto's to share some food before we broke up for the night. I thanked everyone for allowing me to be part of this ceremony and one of the young men said, "Big white, thank you for what you had to tell us." This nickname would stick over my many visits to Belize and I was okay with that – I always knew who they meant!

The next morning Roberto was up early, as I was to learn was his daily custom. The sun had yet to make an appearance and I smelled strong coffee as I lay in my bed. I got up, washed my face and went in to greet my host.

"Morning Roberto – I think."

"Yes, a good morning. Let's take our coffee out and say good day to the sun."

As we watched the sun rise over the stately trees below the house Roberto offered, "I would begin to teach you about the healing plants of the jungle today if you would be happy with that. But, first, there is a little work in the garden you could help me with."

"Happy to help. The only problem is that my knees are killing me this morning, so kneeling down might be difficult."

"You have bad knees?"

"Yeah, and getting worse each year. Some days they are fine, some days they scream at me."

"We need to go up country one day and meet Umberto. He lives in the jungle, near where the howler monkeys live. Do you know of them?"

"I heard of them, but have not seen them."

"They are more to hear than see, but we will stop there on the way. Umberto is very old and knows all the healing ways of the plants, dirt and trees. He will like you. Maybe teach you a few things, eh?"

"Wonderful, you just say when."

So we went out to the fields and did some weeding and diverting water to plants that needed it. Then Roberto showed me how to thin some of the vegetables and re-plant what we took around the edges of the field. We were done in a couple of hours and went to the house to wash up. We grabbed plenty of bottles of water and headed out to my rental Jeep. Roberto kept telling me to turn just before we needed to, so we made a lot of hard, fast rights along the way. At one point we crossed a chasm on two narrow wooden spanner boards. I did not think I could do it as my fear of heights rose in my throat, but somehow I set the car in motion, gripped the wheel with pure white knuckles and made it over. All the time praying there was another way back. There was not and we would repeat this lunacy later in the day.

Finally Roberto told me to pull over where there was a clear spot along the rutted dirt trail we traveled. I congratulated myself for my foresight in renting a Jeep. Of course it was still 'all about me' and 'how clever I was' and 'how I was always able to think ahead'. No recognition that I was being guided and no thanks to Spirit for providing what I needed before I knew I needed it. I still had so, so much to learn and understand. Still do, but now I at least recognize the fact. I guess that's growth of awareness, at least.

Roberto started showing me plants of all types. I took pictures and made quick notes in my pocket notebook as he did. He showed me what to mix for certain maladies and what for injuries. He showed me roots for infertility and leaves to ease pregnancy. We kept at it for hours, drinking water and eating more biscuits when we got hungry. Roberto laughed at my pronunciation, but praised my sensitivity to the plants and roots. He said he saw how I was connected to nature, like I told him the night before. My back was aching and my knees throbbed, but I did not want to stop. I began to limp enough so Roberto noticed.

"Jim, let me make a mix of roots and some bark from this jungle-vine tree. It will help your knees and back until we get to see Umberto. Okay?"

"I'll eat the bark off the tree if it would take some of this pain away, Roberto."

He gathered three different leaves, the bark from one tree and some moss from another. He told me their names and waited while I took pictures as he did this. Then he ground them together in a small mortar and pestle of wood that he carried. He then prayed over the mix and also asked Mother Earth to make this food strong. I noticed he had called the natural medicines of the jungle 'food' several times.

"Why do you call the jungle medicines food Roberto?"

"Wait, Jim. Let me finish here." He took the smashed powder he had created and poured it into one of the water bottles we carried. Then he shook it for several minutes.

"Drink this, my friend. Take a good swallow, then sip it as we walk. I kept some powder and I will make you a tea tonight, also. Tell me when it begins to work. These plant gifts we call 'food' because they are food for our bodies and our minds and our spirit beings. They are gifted by God and the gods and kept strong by Mother Earth. Then, when we need some, we give thanks for the food feeding whatever we need fed. Not thanks for medicine that only hides our pain."

Wow, the symptom and effect teaching again, but from a Mayan in the middle of the jungle. The circle is truly connected throughout this world we walk and throughout the universe. I learn this more clearly with each lesson that comes my way.

"Well, I am giving thanks for the food feeding my aching joints before I feel them working. This is a Lakota practice – to give thanks, knowing what you ask is coming, before you receive it."

"Ah, I like that. I will start doing the same. I am showing you many things today, but it is only a little of what the land gives us here. In the forests are many things to use to help to heal, other things on the edge of the forest and others in the open spaces. Some of the old ones have studied many, many years and find new things still. If you come enough I will teach you and I know others will when they see you, then you will know what to make for yourself and others. But don't share what to use with many. There are many people who would not use these things right. You need to meet Rosita, the plant lady, sometime. She has studied plants for many years and teaches others. The people who make drugs have tried to buy her secrets, but she tells them nothing."

"I would love to learn more, thank you. And I will be careful what I share with others. But most of these plants and roots and such don't grow in the United States, so I could only use them here."

"That is why you will know Umberto. I can teach you a lot about all the medicine foods we make here; Umberto will teach you what to see in plants so you can use what is near you. He will show you what to look for and how to use it. Not a certain plant, but the heart of that plants energy."

This amazed me. That would mean you could find healing plants anywhere things grew. Or at least some healing plants. I was fascinated to meet Umberto. We had been walking as we talked and now Roberto stopped to show me some broad-leafed ferns and talk about their use. Suddenly I realized most of my pain was gone. In maybe thirty minutes. "Roberto, a lot of my pain is gone. I didn't even notice until we stopped."

"I noticed your limp stop a mile back. Now sip the mix every hour or so and drink plenty of water in between."

We spent the rest of the day filling my head with new healing mixes from the plant world. I had very little pain in my joints, even though I was repeatedly bending and kneeling to look at certain plants Roberto was showing me.

Then, at dusk, we started back. Unhappily, for me, we had to cross the 'chasm of impending doom' over the planks once again, but I found it easier this time, knowing what was there.

The next morning we got up early, ate and did a couple of hours work in the garden again. Then we got into the Jeep and headed to the howler monkey preserve. It took about two hours but the roads were dry, if choppy, and we had no problems. The howler monkeys, actually baboons, welcomed us with loud, long screeches. They swung through the trees over our heads wailing down at us, probably not wishing to be disturbed any longer. Soon we left to go find Umberto.

We found Umberto about an hour later, after Roberto asked three people if they had seen him – the third giving directions, gathering plants in the jungle. We parked the Jeep and walked over to meet him.

"Umberto, this is Jim, a friend from Colorado here to listen and learn. He works with Native people there. I wanted him to meet you and you him," Roberto said introducing me.

"Jim, this is Umberto, an elder with a lot of wisdom. He has walked the jungle longer than he remembers. He is a Keeper of Medicine in my people's way. He knows the plants and their parts. And he knows the ways of healing by working with the spirits," he continued as he introduced Umberto to me. "Umberto, do you have time to be with us for a while?"

Umberto was a small, thin man, slightly stooped, but very robust looking for his advanced age, whatever that age was. I am no good at guessing ages, but Umberto was certainly advanced in years. His face was wrinkled and tanned dark brown, as were his hands and legs. Yet his hands were very smooth, like someone decades younger. His energy, as I was beginning to feel and see energy much clearer in those I met, was strong and bright. My sense was he was a man who would not waste time on the unnecessary, but would give time where it was deserved. From the moment we approached him and during the time Roberto was introducing us, he studied my face, tilting his head to the left and then the right, but always looking me straight in the eyes. I returned his study by also looking him straight in the eyes, nodding my head and smiling.

"Yes, I always have time for you my friend," Umberto said to Roberto, "And I see I have time for your friend here also. He is real. You see things and go places, don't you...name again?" the last part spoken to me.

"It's Jim, Umberto. I have gone many places and over the past few years, I have seen a lot and am beginning to learn how to live a spiritual life. Roberto has been teaching me some about the healing parts of the jungle plants. I would welcome anything you have time to tell me. I have begun to learn some healing ways through spiritual practices from my teachers, but don't know much about the plant people, yet."

He nodded as he continued to look at me. Then he looked to the sky as he wiped his head with a bandana. Then he took a drink of water from his bottle, wiped his mouth, and looked back at me.

"The ways of healing are best used by taking what the Earth gives us in plants or rocks or water or animals and using them with Spirit ways. One without the other is just a shadow. But I asked you if you saw things and went places, because I see you do. You did not answer this as I asked it. I did not mean on the Earth we walk, I meant in many places. Do you see and travel?"

He threw me. I am always fascinated by what some elders see in a person. I used to think they were guesses based around the person's energy or vibrations, probably because I was learning to sense these things and so it made sense to me. As I am now more attuned to things I see in people – not with my eyes, but through my spirit and heart – I understand that some older elders can see these things clearly, as if printed on you.

"Ah, I'm not sure how to answer you Umberto, but I will try. I have always seen things most people do not seem to be able to see. Things around people or animals or places. Usually it's unclear to me what I've seen, but sometimes it is very clear and I understand it. Going places...I am journeying with my Native American teachers – just beginning to learn. But I did have a long trip recently during one of these journey times and it felt as if I were there. Is this what you meant?"

"Yes, thank you. You have a lot to do in this life. But you have plenty of time, you are young. Especially compared to me. You see a lot and you will see more. Time is your friend, get to know him. Do not fear him when you use his help. And you are the places you go. That is why it seems that way," he smiled as he said this last piece. "Your body does not have to be somewhere for you to be there. You have had this happen many times, you just did not know it that way. Have you looked across a field and let your head wander?"

"Yes, I guess I have."

"What did you see and feel?" he asked.

"Different things at different times. I have seen huge herds of buffalo roaming open plains. A couple times I saw huge plants and dinosaurs moving like buildings on foot, shaking the ground. I saw a place of people and animals living on the ground with no fear of each other. I don't know, things like that over the years."

"You will learn more. I will show you some of the plant work I do. How long you in Belize?"

"Three weeks and then I'll be back soon with a group for another three weeks or so."

"Come and stay some days if you can," Umberto invited.

"Love to. Maybe next week?"

"Good. I'll be collecting for many weeks yet. Just come and find me."

We stayed for about four hours and Umberto began to tell us how all the plants and plant parts in Belize have other plants like them in many places. He taught how things repeat around the Earth and how the energy of some plants is very similar, even if they are very different plants. He said he would begin to teach me how this worked and how to know these plants when I met them when I returned next week. That's how he put it – when I met them.

He invited us to dinner and we spent another couple of hours just talking about our pasts and what we liked. Then Roberto and I began heading back to his place since he wanted to work in the fields longer the next morning.

I thought about Umberto's words quite a bit over the next couple of days, but he would not share any more of this information until I stayed for an extended time. Umberto did tell me to accept these things in myself as a gift and stop hiding it. He said you must respect and then honor the gifts you have and you can't respect them if you hide them away. He was right, since I had been hiding the ways I thought I was different – odd – my whole life until recently.

When I returned the next week, I ended up staying for five days. He taught me more in those five days then I could learn in years through reading and courses in colleges. He knew the plants as if he were one of them and that made all the difference. I would visit him several other times over the next four years, learning new things and new ways to combine healing methods each time. One of his biggest gifts was in teaching me some of the prayers to say to God and the plants before taking any for use. And also how to ask permission – as do many Native American people – before harvesting. Then he taught me several songs to sing as you harvest, with the intention of creating the healing energy of all you take before you begin to actually mix any remedies or poultices. These teachings meshed nicely with all Roberto was teaching me and all I would later learn from others. It is the energetic and spiritual part of healing that western medicine has ignored and drug companies laugh at. And why the same medicine, from different sources and means, may work or not.

The next morning Roberto and I arose early again, as was my habit anyway, and went out to work in his fields. I had taken some more of the mixture, which he had since shown me how to prepare, and my knees felt fine. No pain. After spending the morning in the fields, we decided it was time to visit the Jaguar Preserve.

"Jim, you will enjoy this place. I know it will speak to you. There are some plants I wish to teach you there and some I need to harvest. We can do this together."

"Sounds good Roberto. Are there a lot of jaguars in the preserve?" I asked.

"This is the largest jaguar preserve in the world – maybe the only. And there are many jaguars. But they are almost never seen. They often hunt at night and avoid people at all times. They are smart." He finished with a smile.

"Just being around their energy will be enough for me. And yes, they are smart," I answered.

"I have seen their droppings a couple of times, but never a jaguar. My friend, Jesus, heard one about a year ago. He hiked towards the sound for an hour, but saw nothing and heard no more. Yet he remembers the sound with big affection."

So we headed back out on the bumpy, rutted roads towards the preserve. Soon we entered, drove a little way further and pulled off. Roberto taught me more of the plants of this area for a couple of hours, then we worked together – asking permission, praying and singing, harvesting some vines and plants. These we put carefully in two sacks he had brought. When we were done he asked if I would like to walk a while. I was hoping we would get the chance to explore a little. It was mid-afternoon by this time, so we decided to walk until dusk in a circle Roberto knew, ending back at the car.

It was a wonderful walk – the terrain covered by amazing plants and vines, as well as multi-colored mosses in some places. The tree canopy varied from completely closing us in to open skies. Birds tweeted, chirped, squawked and peeped in all directions, darting across our line of sight every minute. It was a walk through a tropical paradise. We ended up walking further than Roberto had intended, as we followed some flowing water next to the trails, soaking in the beauty of the water plants and ferns along its course.

"Jim, we will have to pick up the pace a little to make the car before dark. Or, we can finish in the dark. I know the trails well and the roads here were not too bad. What would you like to do?"

"Take our time and finish after dark. I don't want to rush this," I told him.

"As I thought you would say amigo."

So we continued our walk using all our senses and enjoying the input of each. Just before dusk, with just a little shadow moving in, we rounded a bend in the trail, following the flight of what I think was a parrot. Multi-colored, for sure. We were going slowly and quietly, letting the forest do all the speaking. And suddenly, only twenty feet in front of us, a jaguar appeared – sleek black and muscled. He stopped dead center in the trail, sensed us and looked our way. He stood on all fours, shoulders hunched, eyes on us, for maybe twenty or thirty seconds—which seemed like hours. Then he bounded off. He had made no sound and we were frozen in our tracks in surprise. A few seconds later we heard a short roar/wail we knew was the cat. But we felt no fear or menace in it. As his voice came to us, Roberto sat hard on the ground – almost a collapse. I was up, but weak-kneed by this sighting. I quickly sat next to him. Roberto was crying, softly and quietly. Then laughing – then crying again.

"I've lived a long time Jim, but had thought I would never see one of the big cats. Oh, my, what strength and beauty."

"I have no words for it, either. Once, some years ago, I was driving with my wife just at dawn and a swamp panther crossed in front of our car. On a back road in the south of the U.S. But this was one hundred times the power of that sighting. He was here with us and we were with him. My God, Roberto, I want to tell everyone I know right now. Share the energy of the moment."

We sat there for a while, drinking water and talking about the big cat. Then we finally began heading back towards the car – in the dark. I was even more impressed with this sighting when I researched jaguar sightings some time later, at home in Colorado. I found the chance of seeing a jaguar in the wild is over 17,000 to one. What a gift this view of the big cat was!

I spent time with Roberto and Umberto over the next eight or nine days—watching, learning and just enjoying their company. I could have stayed the remainder of my time with them, but wanted to get back to San Pedro and explore the Hol Chan Marine Preserve, where our group coming later had committed to look at visitor impacts and report back to the preserve leadership. So I packed up and headed for Belize City, where I dropped off the Jeep and caught a boat to San Pedro.

22 | Sea Palette

THE PROJECTS I HAD COMMITTED OUR GROUP OF FIVE TO COMPLETING were: Visitor impact study in Hol Chan Marine Preserve; environ mental education inventory of the country, especially in the schools; a preliminary visit and evaluation of the site for a future national environmental education center in Belmopan; and a visit to some of the villages to explore eco-tourism opportunities.

It was a lot to attempt in three weeks, but doable if we split up at times. The Hol Chan project was near to my heart, as I had fallen in love with the reefs, waters and cayes of this off-coast part of Belize on my first trip. I hoped to connect with the Hol Chan personnel and get out into the preserved part of the reefs for some first hand sense of them. I wanted to see how this area compared to the areas I had briefly visited on my first trip. As I am an experiential learner (needing to see, hear, feel, smell and touch what I study to best understand it) this immersion in the waters around the reef was important to my understanding and final planning. The preserve is divided into three parts: sections open for recreation and use: Sections only open to Belizean fishermen and other Belizean water-based workers; and sections closed as protected preserve. I wanted to experience all three.

I found a little bamboo-constructed hut for rent, with a small bathroom and hotplate for cooking, right on the beach – part of a local Belizean hotel. I grabbed it up and moved in my gear. I had put my snorkel equipment in storage in Belize City and had picked it up when I dropped off the Jeep. I had prescription goggles that I especially wanted. The only thing worse than not getting to snorkel, or dive, would be to get the opportunity and not be able to see well. I caught some lunch at a small restaurant I remembered – conch and fritters – then headed for the Hol Chan office. It was a ten minute walk outside of the town proper and I enjoyed 'feeling' San Pedro again as I walked.

When I got to the office I found a hand printed sign on the door – 'Back soon. On the water.' That's it, back soon. I had gotten use to how time works in Belize and other Central American countries I later learned. You made plans to meet with someone – local, business person, politician, anyone – and hoped to see them sometime within a few hours of the agreed upon time. It just is. I would learn soon the best way to meet with almost anyone was set a lunchtime or early evening meeting at a bar – preferably one with sandwiches. These became my best, most productive meetings – getting to know the person outside of an office or business.

I walked back to town to the telephone office – the only place to make a call to the states. There were only a couple people in line, so I got to a phone quickly. I called Bonnie and we brought each other up to date on what we were doing. Then we just chatted for a while. I knew this would probably cost $150 plus, but we needed to connect from our respective places on the globe. When we were done we said our 'goodbyes' and I hung up and trekked back out to the Hol Chan office. The office was open – my luck! I met with their director for about thirty minutes, then sat and talked with two staff people. I had the offer of going out the next morning on one of their patrol boats and I wanted to be certain I brought whatever was needed.

I'll insert a section now I wrote soon after my excursion that morning. Hopefully it will give the flavor of what I saw and felt.

Sea Palette

As I float over this multi-colored world, I am having trouble absorbing the vast variety of shapes, sizes, and hues of its denizens. A group of plate sized angelfish hover just below me, either unaware, or unconcerned by my presence. A twenty-foot eel snakes his way through the coral just below them, unconcerned by either of us. I have snorkeled and dived many places, but have never been immersed in a natural aquarium the likes of this. Life is exploding all around me, bombarding my senses with its diversity. I purposefully stop thinking for a while and just revel in it. My fish identification chart hangs from my belt, but I don't bother with it; all I care to know right now is that the creatures below me are blue or orange, or round, or angular. Knowing their names at this moment can only lessen their impact on me.

A large sand shark is now slinking along the bottom, ever alert and watchful. As I follow him from above, I know I need to go down and swim the bottom. I suck air and dive, getting the rush I always do when I know my only air supply is what is in my lungs. The bottom seemed three feet below me from my float, but this pristine water is as deceptive as ever. I knife down about twelve feet until I am in the corals. The shark edges away, but only a few feet; I am neither food, nor a threat. There is a coral bridge a few feet ahead and I angle towards it. It's large and I can see through it, so I know it's relatively safe. I swim through, slightly scrapping my stomach on it's underside, and shoot out the other end. A hoary old lobster is atop the coral head to my right. If I weren't in the preserve part of the reef, it would be my option to grab him for lunch. The local people grab his cousins just off the coast of the Caye's only town, San Pedro, every day they are in season. I have been invited to many of these lunches, and have yet to turn one down.

I am so wrapped up in what I am doing and seeing I haven't paid attention to my lungs, which are starting to burn. I've been angling down, so I need to rise some twenty feet to fresh air. I know I've over-stayed my visit, and I'll be gasping when I hit the surface. I haven't done any snorkel dives for years, and my lungs are out of shape. I begin to pull for the surface—not too fast, heavy exertion will only make it worse—as I am engulfed by a school of purple and yellow. I don't know what they are, but there must be a hundred of them. They rise up about me, making my ascent a fairyland adventure.

I hit the surface, rip off my snorkel, and gulp the sweet air deep and long. I hang there, forcing oxygen back into my body, wonder-ing why I always have to overdo it. I chide myself for my stupidity, knowing I can go down as often as I like, but also knowing I will probably do it again.

Bernaldo's ranger boat bobs on the surface about forty feet to my port side. I like to get nautical whenever I am near the water, some-thing I don't get to do near enough now that I live in the mountains. He waves his hat and yells out,

"Jim, mon, are you drinkin' water?" The laugh behind his words tells me he knows how long I stayed down. Just another loco gringo. Chances are, he is not surprised by my obvious rapture over this place.

Bernaldo is a ranger with the Marine Preserve, and he invited me out on patrol with him today. This area of reef we are in is an area of the preserve, which is off limits to users; so it is just Bernaldo and my-self, and a lot of open sea. He wanted me to see a section of pristine reef, so I could compare it to the reef the snorkelers and divers use, and get a better understanding of the damage they do. He was right, I thought the recreational section of reef was incredible, but this sec-tion is a watery heaven. It makes my heart ache for the dead reefs I have seen in too many other countries.

Bernaldo snaps me out of my ruminations with, "Jim, snorkel a while. I am going to the reef point for water samples. Be back in an hour. Be careful, you're alone, mon, and you buy the rum when we get in."

I tell him I will be careful; but not to worry, if anything happens to me, my money is on the boat. He laughs, starts up the boat, and rockets forward, skimming the surface like a flat rock over water, in true Bernaldo fashion.

I reset my mask and snorkel and turn my attention below once again. I swim along lazily, watching the purple and yellow parade, which is only a few feet below me. I am surprised the school is still there. I don't have any jewelry or flashy accouterments on; that's the first thing you remove before going into these waters. You don't want to look tasty or interesting to sharks or barracudas.

A huge manta ray is flying the water currents below. They usually like the deeper water. I wonder why he is......quick answer: the bottom drops off below me, suddenly, to eighty feet or more. Vertigo hits me like a wave as I watch the manta drop over the edge. I know I am floating above the abyss, but whenever I come across a drop-off, I feel like I am falling. I wait for it to pass and then move forward. Vertical coral branches reach out from the chasm wall like bony fingers stretching for the surface. Every color imaginable is poured across their surface. I am certain Neptune did some of his finest work honing this reef.

As I swim back over ten-foot deep bottom, I know I have had enough with lazing along; it's time for another dive. I start to breath deep, hoping I can stay down longer without the pain. I get ready: clear my mask, blow my snorkel and watch the bottom. Shit! I catch motion and teeth, a lot of teeth, right beside me. I turn my head to look, gulping a quart of salt water in the process. My absorption in a dive made me miss the barracuda beside me, and I go into a momentary panic. His evil grin does not help, and I take another unwanted drink. I calm as we watch each other for a moment, then he moves off, leaving a foolish feeling snorkeler in his wake.

A modification of an old axiom comes to my mind: "Their look is worse than their bite." Their look, close up is, however, pretty bad.

I begin to do some dives with a school of parrotfish. I am proud of myself for remembering I am not one of them, only a visitor, and coming up as I need to. I feel I could stay here for days, as the colors and shapes swirl and writhe around me, but on my fourth ascent I see Bernaldos' boat bouncing back.

As I clamber aboard, I question Bernaldo saying I thought he said he would be an hour. "Jim, I've been gone ninety minutes." Incredible, it seemed like ninety seconds to me.

I remember clamoring on the boat, really exhausted, as Bernaldo asked, "Jim, if you're not too tired I'd like to go out a ways to where the inland caye water meets the ocean water. There are lots of fish and different plants to see. What you think mon?"

"Don't know if I'll have the energy to swim more, but I'd love to see it."

It was about fifty minutes by boat to where he was taking me, so I laid down to rest for a while – and awoke with Bernaldo shaking me. I had dropped off soundly. The swell was higher here and the boat rocked to it's tune. I decided to go in, even if I ended up only floating. But once in I decided to go under with Bernaldo. He told me of some beautiful underwater arches and I wanted to see them. He swam around until he found the general area, then we took deep breaths and went below. The arches were truly a sight to see – encrusted with plants of every color and covered by crawling crabs and long, insect-like crustaceans. We went down four or five times, and then as we swam through a large arch, I looked to my right. I almost blew out my air when I saw the huge fish hovering beside me. It looked like the size of a whale as it slowly paddled it's enormous fins, hanging in position like an air blimp. Bernaldo swam up beside me, tapped me and pointed to the left, where there was now another behemoth hovering on that side. We stayed some seconds until we needed air, then surfaced. We gulped air and went back down. Our huge brethren still just hung there, apparently unaware of our presence. Again we surfaced, gulped air and dove back down. Their sheer size made me feel tiny and the energy they exuded was something I could almost see. Then as we surfaced again, we could see and feel them begin to move off.

"What were those Bernaldo? Whales?" I asked.

"No, no whales here. Those were giant perch. The biggest I ever saw. Much bigger than any before. Something to see, huh?"

"Wow, you bet. Thanks for stopping here."

23 | Walking a Spiritual Road

As I started working and finding spiritual teachers in countries like Belize and Guatemala — countries where nature is all around you on the land and water — I began to realize how connected nature and a spiritual path really were. This is the connection to the Earth Mother through those places less spoiled by the actions of humans. As I learned about, and from the plants, I used and learned new spiritual connections. When I connected with Spirit and the Universe in the Lakota way, I had animal guides. As I entered the waters, I experienced creatures that made me more aware of my place on the planet. And so on. It slowly worked into my consciousness that there were elements within and without — of our material being — that allowed for stronger, more connected spiritual growth. This is an awareness that grows daily to this day. New opportunities and means to increase spiritual awareness and abilities — to teach, be a healing guide, lead ceremonies, etc. — present themselves if you stay open and receptive to them. And awake to however they may come your way — the wings of the butterfly delivering the message once again.

I will speak now about some of the things that have helped me, and others I have known on this walk, to begin and continue on the spiritual road — the good, red road of the Lakota way. Some may speak to you, some anger you, some confuse you, some not ways you are comfortable with. As always, that is fine – there is no right or wrong. As I told you all at the beginning – as we journey together and you read what is written, take what you need and leave the rest behind. If these thoughts and methods only give you ideas that will work for you, I will be happy that I included them here. Some of these thoughts to muse may be repeats of what was shared earlier. But why not, is all not a circle?

1. Work on the understanding that religion controls through fear and spirituality frees through joy. The way of our present Fourth Earth is control; the way of the Fifth is freedom.

2. Accept that the time of religion is past for those humans wishing to evolve: The time for spirituality is the present and future.

3. Understand and accept there are no more prophets, no more gurus. Ask for teachers and be a teacher as knowledge and experience dictate.

4. Work on any fear in your being. Fear is the one thing that can totally stop our growth.

5. Delve into surrender and trust – two words so easy to say that encompass actions so difficult to do. The more deeply you surrender and trust, the more quickly spiritual growth will occur.

6. Accept all creatures as equals – no matter how many legs, wings, or fins.

7. Honor the Earth Mother and begin consciously working in harmony with her.

8. Be willing and ready to receive. We are told we can ask Spirit for those things we need to do our spiritual work. We must also acknowledge we are ready to receive it.

9. Work on judging no one or no thing. Everything exists for a reason and purpose. It is not our role to judge.

10. Begin to seek guidance from within and without on whom you are to work with and whom you are to wish well and disconnect

from. We are not here to serve all who ask, but are here to serve those whose requests 'speak' to us.

11. Leave behind the concepts of 'good' and 'bad'. Realize there are no good and bad. Good and bad are judgments we are not meant to make.

12. Seek teachers, or accept those who appear to you, whose energies align with your own. Ask questions and answer theirs. Learning is sacred and those who teach and those who learn must select carefully.

13. Question rigorously any who come into your sphere calling themselves guru or shaman or similar. If you sense they do not recognize it is not they, but Spirit, working through them— consider walking away from them. As with those who say "I heal".

14. Accept you never will heal or create a miracle. You may be used by Spirit to manifest these things, which will occur through and around you.

15. Be willing to become all that you are – to accept all that Spirit will work through you. Never try to be less than this, but never try to be more than this either. All roles are equally important or the role would not exist.

Maybe we will revisit this list later on our journey to see if we want to add or delete anything, but for now it provides some guidelines for stepping on the spiritual path. If this seems like an easy list to master – give it a try...an honest try. I believe you will find it anything but easy. It takes time, patience, belief, understanding and trust for any spiritual work. There are no shortcuts.

It's time for a story or two to demonstrate how walking this path works – and doesn't work. Or doesn't allow one to become all they were meant to be. These are, as always, stories shared without judgment, but as learning tools. As you are seeing – and will continue to see – one reason I receive understanding from the walks of others is because I have walked in the energy they do now before them. And as my teachers often have walked before me.

I met my friend, Jonathan, about six years ago, when I attended a retreat he offered. I was invited by another friend, who also walks the spiritual road and in whom I have great trust, at a time that I was walking through my own 'dark time of the soul'. And so, not certain I was even able to travel to Southern California, I agreed after speaking with Jonathan to get a sense of his energy. Jonathan had written several books about spirituality with strong elements of self-improvement. I had read one and was engrossed in it's teachings and knew I needed to make the attempt to attend. About twenty-five people showed up and the majority were staying together in a large house of a woman who also supported Jonathan's work. We attended his workshops, participated in ceremonies together and held talking circles to explore his work and our ideas. Jonathan spoke – and still speaks – eloquently about working together in new ways, without one being 'The' leader or guru. His books present many good arguments for this and, in part, form the basis for my own exploration of circles in the new way. It was a very fruitful four days, after which many of this group stayed connected. Jonathan asked five of us to be his 'circle of elders' to promote the work and collaborative ways of working. Other retreats, over the next two years were created and the circle grew. Then this 'guiding' group suggested a retreat in Colorado of those wishing to brainstorm next steps for the group and for promoting Jonathan's ideas. Jonathan had been seeking a publisher for five years by this time – with no success. He provided the books electronically through his websites. He was confused as to why this was. We prepared for a five-day planning retreat in the Colorado mountains. Of the thirty or so now in the larger circle, eight wished to attend.

We all arrived in Colorado on the same day and drove up to our hosts' house, where we were to spend a night before the retreat. The retreat was to be in a wonderful center in the middle of nature that our host had provided. We made dinner together and chatted for a while, then played music and relaxed. When bedtime came, Jonathan and a woman of the group suddenly got into a loud argument about who would have one private bedroom that was available. I was amazed by the suddenness of it and the ego I felt flowing out. After a half hour, I got up, left and went to a local motel, not wishing to bring discord into our planning in my heart through hearing this debate. The following day we moved to the center, where each had a room and bath of their own.

We began meeting together, starting with some bonding exercises, and discussing how we were going to organize around offering retreats where people could learn methods to better work in the 'we', rather than in the 'I'. Jonathan's work would provide the basis for the retreats, with each of us adding elements where we had expertise. Jonathan became quieter as time went on and, by the third day, was obviously in emotional turmoil. He began speaking about how several circles had formed around him in the past and how each had, over time, dissolved. He then began to speak of how he considered his books to be THE important piece of anything we did. And how, as a non-profit, he would need to be the president. Clearly, his writings and his personal understanding of his own work did not match. He was in huge ego, denial and fear.

After the retreat the remainder of us, without Jonathan, put together retreats and teaching circles around the United States. Jonathan moved on and formed another circle, then, as that dissipated, another after that. Still with no publisher, still with no circle to work with. The circle with the guru as leader could no longer work, yet he was unable to see this. Perhaps his 'job' is to get the teachings out there and be Johnny Appleseed, then leave and let the circles he forms move forward without him.

Several years later, after having moved many times, he moved to Sedona, where I now live. We met on numerous occasions and hiked, had dinner, or just talked. Several times he asked me to work with him as a healing guide, yet when the time to meet came he always called with an excuse to postpone it.

Over one lunch, during a conversation where he voiced confusion as to why his retreats and books were not selling he said, "Jim, religion and spirituality are businesses. They are much more, but need to be run as and understood as businesses."

I disagreed, as I had before with him, pointing out that when you take this approach you lose the power of what you are offering. If you move to surrender and trust, putting out what you offer for the general good with no attachments to who does or does not partake, you will manifest whoever needs to be there. He always thanked me and congratulated me on this belief, but could not walk there. He moved from here about seven months ago to Colorado then, a few months after that, to Oregon. Still stuck. I really like Jonathan and respect his work, but know I cannot assist him in his walk until, and if, he begins to see the new way and then asks for guidance.

I appreciate the connection of this story I tell of Jonathan's walk as it is now and the part of my walk I am journeying with you. The part of my walk where 'I' created things; 'I' led things; 'My' skills and talents were needed – and on. And how long it took me to understand the impacts of ego and of being in the 'I'. Hopefully, in joining me on this journey, some of you will see this clearly and take the trip of understanding and shifting faster than I did.

I will pass on one other story here about a spiritual circle that I was part of for a while. I was serving with a non-profit environmental organization in the mountains of Colorado when I heard of this circle, and the woman who had formed it, from a friend who was also a member of it. It was a circle formed around the traditions of Native American people, which came together for ceremony, prayer and healing. The woman, Martha, who had formed it many years before was a white woman in her senior years. She had studied with several Native teachers and one had guided her in carrying the Chanunpa. She was, in her past, an attorney for the government, but she and her husband had retired to Colorado many years before I met them. She had always led the circle and the ceremonies, but spoke of her vision of many pipe carriers working together for the good of the circle. Their ceremonies were often on the grounds of the non-profit I was running and they wished to do more there.

Bonnie and I met Martha and her husband and went into natural areas together for walks and to connect with the water of the land. She invited us to a pipe ceremony and we agreed. We began attending the ceremonies and dinners the circle sometimes had. After a few Chanunpa and journeying ceremonies Bonnie decided to drop out. She attended other group events, but was uncomfortable with the ceremonies. This was, in part, because the spiritual way was not hers, but also in part because she became very uncomfortable around Martha. Soon, three of us stepped up when asked to be pipe carriers of the circle. And Martha continued to speak of how the circle was now a circle working as one, without a leader or controlling person.

This circle grew, yet I was feeling uncomfortable by all the 'damaged' people being drawn, but not assisted on their healing road other than through the ceremonies. I brought this into the circle and we spoke of it. Yet I felt unease from Martha. Martha had worked with the Native American people in this region for years and had contacts with other Nations around the West. She had worked on having a building dedicated to Native spiritual practices and teachings on the grounds I managed. It had been promised at one time – then the promise rescinded. Martha had also sought other places where inipis could be built, but only had one on her own property come to pass.

I may speak more of this part of my walk later, as it occurred just before my 'dark time of the soul', but for now this story is about being in the 'we', not 'I', so it needs to sit here. The group continued to meet and grow in numbers. Yet I also saw some leaving. This is always the way, so I asked no questions. I was becoming more and more aware, however, that Martha was functioning as 'Chief' at virtually all gatherings. As she was the eldest, I respected this and said nothing. I had not yet come to understand honoring the elders versus someone needing to control for egos' sake.

One week an Australian aborigine came to play the didgeridoo, for which he was known around the world, and to share some stories and teachings from his life and his people's ways. For those of you who do not know the didgeridoo, or didge, it is a wind instrument developed by indigenous Australians at least 1,500 years ago. It is sometimes described as a 'drone pipe'. Authentic aboriginal didges are produced in Northern Australia or by indigenous people who travel around Australia to gather the raw materials. Hardwoods are most often used to make didges, but bamboo is also used. The didge is played with continuously vibrating lips to produce its distinctive drone. It is a wonderful tool to assist with prayer or healing, much as are the drum and flute. If you have never heard a didge, I suggest getting a CD and giving a listen.

I offered the lodge of the non-profit's grounds for one night of our visitor's performances. Bonnie and I had heard him speak and play in the past and were excited to see him again. The night was a fantastic mix of music and talk and it ended going rather late. When the performance was done, our Australian friend came to me after carefully packing his instruments. He told me he had carried some sacred bear fat for a long time, certain he would know whom it was to go to when they appeared. He told me it had powerful healing power and strong connection to Earth Mother. As he spoke this, he handed me the container, which held the bear fat, telling me I would need this for my work. I thanked him, confused, as others more senior than I were there. But he again said it was for me. Martha was nearby and I could see annoyance and anger in her face. Later, I took some of the bear fat and gifted it to Martha. She thanked me sweetly, but I see now the damage had been done. This was a circle of 'I' – although I had not learned the words for this yet – formed from ego to feed ego.

Over time several people were 'uninvited' from this circle as, finally, was I. And it occurred at a time when I asked for some healing guidance from Martha through the Chanunpa. This was also declined. I went into confusion and anger – this is not the way of Spirit as led through the Chanunpa. Of course, from my place today, going into anger and resentment 'is not the' way. I have forgiven myself for this anger and Martha for her declining to assist me – this 'is the' way. Yet, to this day, none of the other pieces for ceremony or teaching that are sought by Martha have materialized. And I am told of other issues that have beset her. There may not be any right or wrong way to walk the spiritual road, but there are ways of following the road, which allow doors to open and other ways, which keep doors shut. Being imperfect humans, we can only do our best to follow our hearts and spirits, listen to the teachings we receive from elders or spirit guides, and walk without ego as best we can.

Words are very important in these times – as Spirit and the Universe hear what is said and accept it on a literal level. If you say "If I get the resources I need I will do the work of……", you may or may not get what is needed. If you say "When I get the resources I need I will do the work of….", you will receive what is needed if the work is true. I have personally experienced this a great deal of late and have offered this concept to others who report the same results. That is, if you have done the work on yourself and prepared yourself in all ways to walk your part. What I am saying here is not the pop, jingoistic, PR material that some have been espousing lately – "Set your intentions, ask repeatedly for what you want, give thanks before you receive it, and it will come to you". This creates the expectation that all you need do is ask your God and thank him and whatever you want – you get. Then, when you don't get it, you are told your intentions were not strong enough or you did not ask with enough power or you did not ask from the heart.

The reality is you are asking before doing the hard work to prepare yourself. Coupled with that is that you are not necessarily asking for things needed to serve as you are meant to. In our modern world all too many of us have been conditioned to expect rewards without any work or sacrifice. Some will even seem to get the rewards they ask for this way – after all, positive intention is powerful. But often the circle comes around, especially if the intention is not in integrity, and there is a heavy price to pay. Here in Arizona there is a good example of this as the James Ray case is still working its way through the courts as I write this.

So, if words are so powerful, how do you speak of yourself and your work when you walk a spiritual trail? And how do you deal with

other people's opinion of you and what you are? I suggest never saying, "I am a guru" or "a shaman" or "healer". When asked, I say I am
a healing guide or I have studied shamanic healing and have acquired
some skills. Likewise, if someone calls me, or introduces me as a shaman, I gently say I have learned these ways and am thankful Spirit sees
fit to work through me in my practices. It may sound like splitting
hairs, but it helps eliminate ego and allows us to remember that the
powers and abilities to do any healing or ceremony can be removed in
an instant if we do not honor and recognize it is not us in the driver's
seat.

24 | Mountains Call

I FLEW BACK FROM BELIZE TO COLORADO AND BONNIE, WHO HAD returned a few days before me, picked me up at the airport. My flight arrived early in the morning and we decided to go to Rocky Mountain National Park for a walk and talk before returning home to Fort Collins. We shared stories along the way, stopping at a favorite breakfast place in Estes Park – The Egg and I – before going into the park. We drove up a side road and parked at its dead end to walk up a rushing stream we particularly liked. We hiked up for an hour or so and then sat on some big, flat rocks next to the stream. Bonnie had filled me in on her mother's surgery and recovery – and on how difficult it was to spend any time with her and her self-centered ways. Bonnie had issues with her mother throughout her life, and opted to leave them unresolved. A decision we all face with one person or another. One I have faced many times and now always chose to deal with problems of this type. If they are not dealt with, they go deep inside and fester over time. For one walking a spiritual path this can block energy and intention.

We drank big gulps of water as we sat on our rock perch, as we now always did when hiking at this altitude. And we shared some biscuits we had wrapped in paper towels at breakfast. Bonnie wanted to know all about my experiences in Belize – who I met; what I had learned; how I saw the project developing.

We spent a couple of hours talking through all that had happened around me there and exchanged ideas for the project. Although Bonnie was not interested in spiritual endeavors for herself, she was always ready and interested to hear about my delving into this arena. As was I with her passion for geology, rocks, minerals and weather. It was a good fit – as we shared what we learned, but felt no need to learn in depth about the areas the other covered. After finishing my tale, she told me Two Bears had called the day before to see how our respective trips went. She told him I would be in touch after I returned. Seems he was ready for a lodge.

Then she told me she had run into Jess, who had complained about the issues that arose when I was out of town. She had asked him what was the problem and he told her, "Just Sharon again. I don't get her. She was everyone's friend, now there is something troubling her and others get the fallout."

"Jim, I am worried about her being on the project if interpersonal issues are cropping up," Bonnie told me with a worried frown.

"Yeah, I know," I answered, "But it would be politically very difficult to change things now. And she's done some of the legwork on the environmental education inventory. She would file a complaint with the University for sure if I bagged her. Besides, I want to find some way to help her through whatever is going on. She has great potential," I finished.

"You can't save everyone, you know; especially from themselves," Bonnie responded with a warning she gave me often.

"I know. But I'm an instructor and part of my job is to help these young students deal with their issues and be more successful at learning."

"I no longer trust her Jim. Too many people have had something to say and others say she goes out of her way to connect and be nice. She's a disturbed young woman. The last time I saw her husband he had little to say to me and was obviously in distress. I know you never expect people to act in unpleasant – or bad – ways, but some do. You'll end up under attack if you are not careful."

"I hear you and appreciate what you are saying. But I'm only trying to help. What trouble could that cause? Besides, we'll be in Belize, wrapped in projects. She'll do her part. I've not seen her not deliver on her work. And she feels strongly about this," I said.

I would remember this conversation very well later.

As we started to feel cramped from sitting too long, we got up, stretched, took off our shoes and socks, rolled up our pants and began walking up a quiet side stream. We stepped over and around the rocks strewn throughout the water and just had fun, putting our concerns away for the time being. When our feet started to feel numb, we clambered out of the water, dried off with a towel we always carried, put our shoes back on and began our trek back to the car.

It was good to be back in Colorado. I have been blessed to live in many places surrounded by natural wonders, but Colorado is the one place that has always felt like 'home' to me. Perhaps it will be again, if my good, red road beckons me there for a new reason.

I got back into taking my own coursework, working on my Masters' thesis and teaching my course load. I also had three or four projects I needed to catch up on. And the Center to run. Back to my, by then, usual twenty-four seven.

Bonnie and I did carefully allot a few hours a day where we could take a ride on a new road or a hike in the mountains just behind us. And we always made certain we had a couple hours around dinner for talk. Sleep, for me, was hard to fit in. Five hours a night was still my best shot at it.

After all, I had to do all of this – wasn't I being asked to? And I knew how to make things happen – could I ignore my skill and success rate? And, of course, something needed to happen as soon it appeared – would I want some meaningful project to grow stale? Besides, I was getting praise from my superiors, from the Department Chair to the Dean to the President; additional funding for my teaching course load and awards from the university and various groups I worked with. So didn't I need to redouble my efforts? When someone wanted to know about service-learning – go ask Jim. Or a good way to raise money – ask Jim. Or how to better connect with the local community – Jim again. This was not building my ego, I told myself and Bonnie and friends, only my passion for the important projects and work I was involved with. I had dealt with my ego when I ran my businesses so successfully and had a huge ego – so I had no further need for an oversized ego.

Hmmmmm…..What do you see in all of this my fellow travelers? Ah, vision is 20/20 in the rear-view mirror. Even so, I do not regret any part of my walk, for I could never have the clarity I now do without it. I thought my mission was to perform in all of these areas I worked in to honor my pledge to God – and (from this present perch) – to feel important and needed. I see now it was to learn all I was exposed to from all I met, even if the projects were important and did make a difference.

About a week after my return Two Bears called again. I had gotten so wrapped up in my 'work' I had forgotten to call my friend and teacher. I apologized, explaining the multiple balls I was juggling, and asked his forgiveness for my negligence.

"No forgiveness needed, Jim. It is not Two Bears you neglect, but the part of your growth we work on together," he answered – teaching as he spoke in a way that struck home.

"Yes Uncle. It is as you say. When may we get together?"

"I would like to do another lodge – just you and I – in two nights. Then an invite lodge for ten or twelve the following week. Can you squeeze me in?" he said with a chuckle.

"I will bring elk stew, with your permission, to both lodges. I was gifted some elk by Lawrence just the other day."

"Ah, good. Nothing like fresh elk meat. I will make fry bread for our lodge. And next week, we will ask all to bring a dish. Would Bonnie join us that night?"

"I will make the invite or you can give her a call if you wish. I doubt she will do the lodge with us, but I am certain she would like to join afterwards for the shared meal."

"That is good. I will call her and offer the invite."

That was how it played out, with Bonnie happily agreeing to the meal and talk after the second lodge – bringing along one of her famous bean dishes.

The night of the lodge Two Bears and I were to share was cold and starlit. When I arrived he already had a fire roaring, which I was thankful to see. The altar was also already laid out, with two bundles wrapped in hide and tied with the four colors, off to the left of the buffalo skull.

We started the lodge about six thirty, since the rocks were ready and it was cold outside. As Two Bears asked, we took turns carrying the rocks – two doors each. Then, after the ceremony was complete, Two Bears threw open the inipi door, asked me to stay inside, and left. He returned with the two bundles I had seen before we began. He sat and smudged them with sage, then passed them to me.

"Jim, these are for you to learn from and to begin to feel the power. Open them and we will talk."

I opened the first bundle to find a Chanunpa – beautifully beaded with ribbons attached to the stem and with several feathers attached near the bowl. I was stunned. The other bundle contained a Chanunpa bag and a tobacco pouch.

"Do not have fear, Jim. I want you to begin carrying the Chanunpa and the tobacco so you learn from it. Do not open it – that is far off, I think. But take it out and do prayers with it. And load it with sage. And smudge it when it feels good to do so. It is yours now. I said before, I see a different walk with the Chanunpa for you. I see many pipes. Or different pipes. Or pipes for different things. It is not clear. Usually we are gifted a Chanunpa when we start this path and it walks with us from then. If it is destroyed somehow another may or may not come – as Spirit's wishes. But what I see for you is not this way. We will not worry about this as Spirit will make it clear when it needs to be."

"I am truly honored Uncle," I said with tears running down my cheeks, "I will do all I can to be worthy. And I will do as you say with the pipe."

"Good. We will speak no more of this now. I would speak about one more thing and then let's go eat. I'm hungry."

"Of course Two Bears."

"I would like to take a trip. In the spring. I would like us to go to Pine Ridge, the rez in South Dakota, to Wounded Knee with you. Maybe it will be time for your Hanbleche, maybe not. We will see and we will see if you feel ready."

Wounded Knee was the site of the massacre of hundreds of Lakota men, women and children in 1890. I had not yet been there, but Bonnie and I had planned to get there sooner or later. Now it would be sooner. Hanbleche is the cleansing ceremony where you go on the mountain for four days and three nights, without water and food. You are forced to face your biggest fears during this intense time. Usually one or two will accompany you, camping somewhere nearby so they can visit on occasion. Sometimes they will come and do ceremony, bring wood for a fire and then leave. You must stay within a small circle for this time, while you pray, journey and experience whatever comes.

I had great doubts that this white boy could last through it. Well, we would see what happened by then.

"I am ready to go to the rez and Wounded Knee, but I don't know about sitting on the mountain. But I hear you, I won't worry about it – at least for now. Could Bonnie and a friend of hers come? They could spend some time in Deadwood or Rapid City," I asked my teacher.

"Of course. We may be one day or four on the rez. We will see," Two Bears replied.

When we got to Two Bears' house I took out a small package I had wrapped in red cloth – a Mayan amulet, one of three given me by Roberto.

"I brought this for you, Uncle. It is from a new friend and teacher in Belize. Roberto, a Mayan man," I told him as I offered the gift. "I feel it is small compared to your gift, but I bring it from my heart."

"That is all that matters Jim. That it be from the heart. It has power – I feel it. This I will wear. So, I see other teachers of other ways have already begun to appear. Good."

This was a busy week for inipis, as Lawrence had requested one from Yellowhair. It would be in two days and would be a sweat for Native Americans, with the exception of me. Lawrence asked me to meet him a little early and tend the fire a while. Bonnie was going to meet Lawrence's wife and help prepare food for after the lodge.

Although I don't mention people, like Lawrence, all the time as we journey here, does not mean I was not working with them on a regular basis. I just need to be selective where I lead us, so repetition does not put you to sleep. And more seriously, Spirit is guiding what events I am to guide us through. I am surprised that some people from my past I thought would have met us by now, have not. And others I did not expect, at least until later, have already appeared. Such is the nature of an unplanned trip – you go where you are moved to go and meet whomever appears. It's all about the journey, my friends.

I arrived early for the inipi Lawrence requested, as he asked me to. He had the fire burning high and hot and was putting on even more wood as I walked up.

"Ho' relative," he greeted me, "Grab some more wood. I need it hot tonight."

After we had enough wood to satisfy Lawrence, we sat by the fire and shared some water. "I have finished my staff. I will bring it to the altar when Lyman arrives," he explained to me. "The feathers from Wambli were very powerful and his claws grip the air as they are on top. Thank you again for being with me when we honored the winged one."

"It was an honor. I am glad we got to do it together," I answered – very heartfelt.

"I brought this for you," Lawrence said as he offered me a bundle – wrapped in red.

I opened it to find an eagle feather, the shaft worked with red wrappings and a loop at the end. Next to it was a dream catcher. "Thank you, Lawrence. Are you sure I am to have eagle?"

"Yes, this feather is for you. With gratitude and good thoughts. Wambli wished it so. And the dream catcher I made for you for guidance and protection. Maybe it will go in your car."

"And I brought a gift for you, also," handing him the second Mayan amulet, "From a Mayan friend.'

"Thank you, Jim. I will put it on now."

It is the custom when someone 'gifts' you that you gift him or her back. I was glad, that with both Two Bears and Lawrence, I had gifts to give them. Coincidence? A joke, of course, as there are no coincidences.

We all shared a powerful lodge that night. The rocks were red hot, so there was much steam and heat. I had already begun to sweat heavily when in an inipi, but not feel the heat as too intense. After the lodge we went to the building where food waited and feasted on chili, fry bread, vegetables and squash. And, as always for me after a lodge, several large glasses of cold, sweet spring water.

The day after this inipi Bonnie and I had lunch with a friend, Shirley. Shirley was director of an organization that was a resource for interpreters. Interpreters find means, both written, oral and acted out, to explain and describe what they see before them. In our college it was the natural resources that we focused on. Shirley was also a non-traditional graduate, as was I. Read 'non-traditional' as 'older'. She was probably around forty and a very heavy woman. She was also an excellent cook, although she often used too much fat and sugar for our tastes.

Rob, my intern from the Center, rented a room from Shirley, so going for lunch or dinner was always fun, with the four of us getting along very well.

Shirley had a great personality and the ability to talk with anyone. She was also a very creative planner. What she lacked was any carry-through. She always looked for others to do the work. And often found them — at least for a time. We had a big dinner, with multiple courses and as we sat over dessert, Shirley brought up an offer to us.

"Guys, I've got a business deal for us. Want to hear about it?" she asked.

"Sure, Shirley," Bonnie responded.

"I have a friend, actually an old flame from years ago, who owns a camp permit up in Wyoming. He runs horse-packing weeks for eight people at a time. He's fallen on hard times and can't afford the $5,000 annual fee and doesn't know how to advertise. He asked if I wanted to be a partner and I mentioned you two," she explained.

"What would the deal be? And whom would we serve? I don't want to just run another business, Shirley," I said.

"This friend, Randy, would sign the permit over to us and work for us for a percentage of the profits. I thought we could change the trips to environmental interpretation as well as recreation. And we could have some trips for CSU faculty and others for students. The students could earn credit, just like they do in Belize."

"Sounds interesting. I could add a geology section for those who wanted it," Bonnie said. "What do you think, hon?"

"What would it take, Shirley?"

"Randy has sold all but two of his horses, so we would need to buy horses. Maybe $6,000. Plus the $5,000 annual fee and maybe another $2,500 in supplies. Advertising I'm not sure, but I think we can get some coverage through my contacts around the country. And we can promote it through other universities."

"Where is the camp?" I asked.

"It's at 14,000 feet, right behind Yellowstone. Randy goes out of Red Lodge over the border in Montana. Then he takes the group up the highway towards the north end of the park. Up the road a way he parks in a pull-off and the next sixteen miles is by horseback."

"Let us think about it for a couple of days, Shirley," Bonnie said, "See if we could swing it if the idea appeals to us. Okay?"

"Sure. I told Randy I'd call next week. That okay?"

"Perfect," Bonnie answered.

That night we had a long talk about the offer. We had just gotten a $15,000 settlement from an insurance company for some of Bonnie's treatments when she was dealing with her cancer, so we had the money if we wanted to try this. Our big concern was Shirley's inability to do what she committed to do. We knew we would end up with most of the work or we would all have to agree to hire someone. We mulled it over for two days, then decided to go ahead. It was too unique an opportunity to pass up. There were only a handful of these permits in that region of Wyoming and they never became available. So we called Shirley and told her it was a go. And we set times to meet and begin planning. She suggested we all go up to Wyoming to meet with Randy and purchase gear and supplies in a few months, before the summer season set in. In the meantime, we could start promoting the trips. The places we needed to go to pursue the different opportunities coming our way were mounting up. Luckily being with a university, there was plenty of free time. So it was to Wyoming to meet Randy in the spring.

25 | Belize Projects Unfold and Explode

THE FIVE OF US HEADING TO BELIZE TO UNDERTAKE THE MULTIPLE projects we had scheduled met at the CSU carpool at five on the morning of our departure. In addition to Bonnie and I, we had Rob, Sharon and Deb. I had told everyone to bring just one bag or duffle bag, plus we had a bag of materials we would not be able to get in Belize. Ron, my department chair, had arranged for a van to get us to Denver and another grad student, Carl, had offered to drive us down. Everyone was excited and more than ready to get started, as we had been planning and coordinating with people in Belize for months.

Bonnie was excited, but also a little nervous – backcountry camping in the jungle was not her cup of tea. She loved hiking anywhere and exploring new places but, at the end of the day, was very pleased to find a motel room. There were no guarantees on where we would stay on part of this trip. She was, however, looking forward to the trip and I was happy she was coming, especially with the way Sharon had been behaving for months now. It would be good to have an older woman along for counseling or advice if needed. And I knew she would really enjoy the new geology this country had to offer her.

We made our flight in plenty of time and were on our way to Houston as we ate breakfast – back when you actually got a meal on a flight. There we went boarded our second flight to Belize City.

Richard was at the airport smiling and waving, rushing up to give me a bear hug as we got to the small terminal. He then hugged Rob, who he knew well from Rob's time guiding the students in Belize. I introduced him to Bonnie, who also got a hug, and then Sharon and Deb – more hugs.

Richard drove us to a van rental office in Belize City and we picked up the van we would use for our land-based projects. Richard asked if I remembered the way to Belmopan, where we were to spend a few days, since he had some meetings to attend near Belize City. I assured him I did and invited him to stop with us for a snack at the bar and café I mentioned on an earlier trip. He immediately agreed and we drove the twenty minutes to this, our first stop, following Richard. We talked and ate for an hour or so and then Richard left for his meetings. We got back in the van and headed to Belmopan.

We were all talking, joking and laughing as we drove up the road to Belmopan. Sharon, however, was relatively quiet for her. Suddenly, after Rob made some joke about how we might have to cut our way through the jungle, she attacked him, yelling at him that he was harassing her and she would not take it. Everyone went silent. She and Rob were, from all appearances in the past, friends – something I always consider when putting together a group like this. She started again, yelling how he had been harassing her for months. Rob, the gentlest soul you could find, was stunned. He stammered out that he was sorry, but asked what she was talking about. As another rant started, Bonnie stepped in and told her we were all joking and laughing and that there was no comment directed at any one person, nor had anything been said by Rob that harassed anyone. Sharon shut up, but with obvious energy that wanted to explode. The rest of us began talking again, but subdued. When we got to Belmopan we went to Richard's home and met with Ann. Sharon was now all bright and light – smiling and getting Ann to like her, as she was so good at. Bonnie and I talked about the crazy behavior in the van, then talked to Rob after which we all decided to let it go for the time being.

We stayed two nights in Belmopan, then moved to a cabin the natural resource people used that Richard had secured for us. It was in the jungle, but near many schools and communities we needed to visit for the environmental education inventory. As we were driving to the cabin, Sharon again began berating Rob over some innocent comment. This time Deb started supporting what Sharon was angrily spouting. Bonnie again put a halt to it and told the two she wanted to talk with them when we got to the cabin. We all remained fairly silent for the remainder of the trip. Bonnie was mad, as I could tell from her body language and the frown she wore. When we arrived she took the two young women into the cabin and asked Rob and I to take a walk—which we gladly did.

We walked for about an hour and I questioned Rob about any trouble he had been having with Sharon that I was unaware of. He seemed truly confused and assured me there was nothing he knew of. They had been friends, working on projects together for the Center back at CSU. I was certain he was telling the truth – his face would have given him away in a minute had he been lying. We went back to the cabin and Bonnie was waiting to speak to me. So we went out into the trees around the cabin for a chat.

"Something's going on with that one, I guarantee it. Deb apologized for saying anything, but thought everyone else was teaming up on Sharon. When I pointed out we were not attacking her, but stopping her ungrounded assaults on Rob, she shook her head 'yes' and went silent again. Sharon said Rob's been sexually harassing her for some time and his jokes and sexual innuendos in them were making her furious. I told her we were all in the car together and no one felt any such thing and, as a woman, I certainly heard none of that. I also asked why she had not made a complaint at CSU if he had been harassing her. She said she didn't want to cause him trouble. So I asked why would she start ranting now, here on a project, where this type of behavior would affect what we all were able to accomplish. She angrily told me that she heard what she heard. I asked if something else was wrong. Were there problems with her marriage, that she told us about, troubling her? She told me that was none of my businesses or anyone else's. Jim, there is something going on in her head. I know it. Almost like she wants to cause a schism in the group. She has this calculating look in her eyes, even when she seems so furious."

"Ah, great. This is not a good start. I'd like to help her through this, but I won't condone her attacks on Rob. And I won't let her affect what we have promised to do here. I'm going to call a meeting after dinner. What do you think?"

"I think you have to, but watch out for her. She is up to something. You know, I also saw some negative looks from Ann when we picked the girls up this morning. I would not be surprised if she was creating her drama there, also." Sharon and Deb had stayed at Ann's, while Bonnie, Rob and I got a room at the Bullfrog, since there was not enough room at Ann's house. And, now that Bonnie said this, I remembered the look of disapproval. I put it down to the fact Ann did not resonant to me, especially after I had reported the behavior issues after my first trip down. I'm certain she took this as a personal offense, even though it was only the safety of the students I was worried about.

"I hear you. I'll do the best I can. Back up my play please. Let's get these projects done and when we get back to CSU I'll talk to Ron about what's been happening with Sharon."

Bonnie agreed and we joined the others. I told everyone I was calling a meeting after dinner to discuss any issues or concerns anyone had. Then we left to visit two organizations and two schools. We gathered the input from the people we met, with me dropping Sharon and Deb at one school to observe classes and meet with the teaching staff and Bonnie, Rob and I visited the non-profits. When we were all done we headed back to the cabin for dinner. Sharon was almost silent during dinner, occasionally smiling when someone spoke to her. Then we sat around a small fire for our meeting.

"Okay, everybody," I started, "I want to give everyone the chance to clear the air, voice any issues or concerns, or talk through any obstacles you see in front of us. We have all committed several completed projects to various agencies and communities here. And I, for one, intend to deliver what we promised to the best of our abilities. And each of you has made that commitment to me before you were brought on the team. There are no rules in this circle, except to wait until someone speaking is done and to say what you need to while respecting the others in the circle. Okay?" Nods all around. "Anyone want to start?"

"I'll start," Rob said sheepishly. "I don't know what I said to make Sharon, or anyone else angry, but I apologize for whatever it was. I thought this was a group of people who liked and respected each other and that's how I hope it stays. These projects are important here and not work the Belizeans have money for."

"Thanks, Rob. Anyone else?" I said.

"I don't find the arguing of the past day worthy of anyone here. I've spoken to everyone and I don't see where it's coming from. But I know we can't accomplish what Jim's leading us around if this sort of behavior continues," Bonnie said with feeling.

"I guess I'm the bad one again," Sharon began, "I don't like being called names, harassed or made fun of. And I don't have to take that. If it happens any more, I'll continue to speak up."

"I don't know what you heard, or think you heard, Sharon," I began, "But I certainly heard nothing of the sort. And we have all been together so far, so any inappropriate words or behaviors would have needed to be in front of us. If I hear or see anything of that nature, you won't have to speak up because, as project lead, I'll take action at once. So far I've only heard inappropriate words from you. If you have other complaints, bring them to me – or Bonnie, if you prefer. But no more yelling tantrums in the car or anywhere else. Understood?"

This was not where I wanted to go, but I was angry and I needed to put a stop to the outbursts.

"Okay," Sharon said with no conviction.

"It seems to me everyone is picking on Sharon and that does not seem right either, Jim," Deb spoke up.

"No one is picking on Sharon. Sharon's here because I value her work, as I do everyone else's I invited along. But it is her behavior that is causing problems at the moment. I've not heard anyone else yelling or accusing or I would be calling them out also – including myself. Who else needs to air anything? Or is there more to say on this piece?" No one spoke so we closed the circle and prepared for bed.

That night mosquitoes and tiny gnats got into the cabin in large numbers. We did not have any netting, since we thought the cabin would make that unnecessary, so we were well eaten by the morning. I have since learned that, when in the jungle or even on the cayes to eat a lot of garlic for a month before I arrive there and keep eating it while I'm there. This helps greatly with the number of bites you get.

"I look like hamburger and feel worse," Deb complained at breakfast.

"I know, my legs are half eaten too," I answered. "We will pick up some netting today so we have some protection tonight. Tomorrow we'll head to the eco-lodge, where it won't be a problem."

"I guess we had to give a little blood for the project," Sharon smiled at us. She had been light and happy since we all arose – more like the person we knew in the past.

"Hopefully no more," I said.

As we got ready to leave for our appointments, Bonnie called me aside. "I don't trust this new, happy Sharon any more than the calculating one I saw yesterday. Stay alert," she told me.

"Okay. I hope you are wrong, but I'm not sure you are."

We completed our work that day and, the next morning, we packed up and headed to a small, family run eco-lodge located between Belmopan and Belize City. From here we could visit the Belize Zoo, known for it's educational components, the jaguar preserve and a number of schools in this region.

As we drove there Sharon piped up, "Sam's here for a project of his own. And I think he's staying at the same lodge for a week. That should be fun."

Sam was the person running the Environmental Center before I was asked to take over – the one I spoke of earlier. Not one of my fans, feeling I had conspired to remove him from that post. Oh, well.

As we stopped for gas, Bonnie asked me, "How did Sharon know Sam was here and staying at the same place? He has no love for you."

"She is a TA for him, so she would know. I'm more interested in why no one said anything to me about it. And why he just happens to be at the same place at the same time," I answered her.

"Sam is a plotter, user and conniver – you've said so yourself. If she's hooked up with him this could give you a lot of problems here."

"I can't believe she would have anything personal to do with him. He is a user. I hope not. She has a lot of ability and energy, she doesn't have to plot against people and things like he seems to think he does. It doesn't seem like we are able to talk to her about it though, so we'll just watch what happens and I'll work to keep the project together. I still wish I could find some way to help her. She has such great potential."

"You keep wanting to 'save' everyone from themselves," Bonnie started in. "You get so emotionally attached to everyone and everything. Hon, you can't save everyone. It doesn't work that way. I wish you could see that, you would save yourself a lot of disappointment and pain. But I guess that's who you think you need to be."

"I know, I hear you, but I work on emotion – brought up that way and it has worked well often. I just hate to see resources wasted – people or organizations. And I do care about people, but maybe you're right – sometimes I care too much. Well, it's out of my control here."

Working from the heart is a powerful way to do your work, but, as I've learned, sometimes difficult. I am an emotional person – by heredity, how I was raised and my natural inclinations. I will share some of the times this has worked in a good way so you may see how these things balance. Actually, I've found it most often works to the benefit of all but we humans tend to remember the problems, not the positives. Becoming perceptive about where you can allow your emotional side to come through – where it won't be mis-read or abused – is what we need to learn.

We got to the lodge and found Sam had arrived before us. I gave everyone a couple of hours to relax and then called a meeting to discuss our next steps on the inventory. When the time for the meeting arrived, Sharon was a no-show. The rest of us had a coke and chatted for a few minutes.

After twenty minutes I asked, "Does anyone know where Sharon is? We need to get this meeting started so we can head out for our appointments."

"She went off for a walk with Sam a few minutes after we got here," Deb told us.

"Let's get started, she can catch up when she arrives," I decided.

Sharon wandered in about an hour late – just as we were finishing the meeting. "Sharon, the meeting was scheduled an hour ago. Did you forget? We are ready to leave in fifteen minutes," I spoke.

"No, I lost track of time. Sorry all. What did you all decide?"

"Too late to go over things again. Everyone – we all need to be present, on time, for any meetings or appointments. Please honor this for the good of all of us and the project. Deb, will you fill Sharon in as we drive?" I asked.

"Sure. We can sit in the back of the van," Deb agreed.

Later I took Sharon aside and asked how she could show up an hour late – knowing we had appointments after the meeting. She promised to be more careful and would be certain it didn't happen again.

The next day we were to meet at eleven in the morning to discuss more logistics and what we had gathered to date. This time neither Sharon nor Deb were present. Rob went to check on them and found they had left the lodge to go into San Ignacio with Sam and a Belizean friend at nine. I was furious, as were Bonnie and Rob.

We drove in to town, as it was on the way, and checked some of the cafes. Rob found them eating lunch with Sam and his friend. I came in and lost my temper big time. I asked what the hell they thought they were doing? Asked if they wanted to be part of this project or be removed right then? They could stay with Sam, at their expense, or get a lift to the airport and go back to Colorado now. I was not in control. The dark side of my emotional being, while possibly deserved, did the project no good.

They were in shock – sitting stone-faced, probably fearful. Sam just stared. He never argued anything face on – it was his way. They both began stammering how sorry they were and that they did not want to be thrown off the project. With semi-controlled anger, I told them if that was the case they had five minutes to get to the van that was parked up the block.

While this scene kept the two women on the project team, it heightened the tension amongst the group to even higher levels. Looking backwards, it would have been smoother had I just dropped them at that point.

Over the next few days, we managed to accomplish all we had scheduled, but both Sharon and Deb were unpleasant to be around except when we were with those we were working with. On the third day Sharon again lashed out at Rob for no valid reason. I drove us back to the lodge and called an immediate circle.

"Okay, Sharon, I don't know what is going on with you, but it's enough. You have been a problem from the beginning of this venture. Now it stops. Deb, I don't know why you have bought into this behavior either, but I think you are following a poor guide. You both have a choice now. Leave the project and fly home or stay on your own or I will allow you two to finish the school inventory out of here. Sam can drive you or you will have to rent a car. We three will go off and do the Belmopan project and then go to San Pedro to work with Hol Chan," I finished severely.

"We still want to be part of the whole project," Sharon said, interestingly speaking for both of them.

"Sorry, that is not an option," I answered.

"Then we will work with the schools," Sharon again decided for both of them.

The remainder of the project time went smoothly, with the three of us completing the work in Belmopan and with Hol Chan. And we enjoyed ourselves during our free time, without the issues and problems generated by Sharon. I contacted Sharon and Deb twice and was told they were collecting all the information needed. Since I could not be in two places at once I accepted their word and hoped for the best.

When we got back to Colorado I jumped into my work and some geology excursions Bonnie had lined up. I met with Sharon two days after everyone had returned. She told me she thought it best if she just worked as a teaching assistant for Sam and not be a student intern at the Center. I agreed, glad I didn't have to release her from that role. I had a talk with Ron, my chair, about what had occurred and the way Rob had been treated. He offered to look into it. The next day, Ron came to my office and the next level of waves began. Sharon now claimed it was not Rob sexually harassing her, but actually me. But she had no one to tell this to. And she told Ron she had already apologized to Rob and hoped to be friends again. She also refused to turn over the information and data collected from the schools after she and Deb were working on their own. Not having ever been in such a situation I asked Ron what the best course was. He affirmed it was nonsense, but politically the University had to follow up on all complaints of this sort. He asked me if I knew what was going on with Sharon and I told him about her time with Sam and Bonnie's certainty they were having an affair.

"Oh, great, now we have his manipulations going on too. I see the pattern now. This is exactly how Sam operates when he wants to attack someone who's wronged him. I'm glad Bonnie was part of your team down there. Rob is Mr. Nice Guy – wants everyone to like him, so his backing will be wishy-washy at best. But Bonnie was there and can tell the full story. Oh, yeah, Deb came to me and said she had no issues and was not part of any complaints. The sheep following the wolf – until they get turned on."

"Yeah, that's about right. What do I do next?"

"It goes to the Ombudsman for review and she will meet with the parties. I'll make sure Bonnie is on that list. She takes classes here too, so they can't deny her testimony. Meanwhile, watch out for Sam. Avoid him as best you can. So will I," Ron instructed.

It played out as Ron thought, with Sharon having to admit to an affair with Sam and Bonnie telling of her interactions with Sharon and the unfounded assaults on Rob. The complaint was dismissed. But I still felt the knife in my back. I wasn't used to this, although I knew it happened every day in the schools. When just a few try to use the system for their own profit, everyone suffers. Like so many places in life.

Two weeks later Ron called me in for another chat. Now Sharon had complained that I was stalking her and had found cigarette butts near her house, so she knew I was also staking out her house. He told me he knew it was nuts, but to try and not go anywhere alone until we could deal with this. And, if I did, to call him on the cell phone so he could testify to where I was, should it be needed. I felt trapped in some insane sci-fi movie. How could someone get away with this sort of behavior? But I did as Ron suggested.

Bonnie was furious with Sharon and wanted to go give her a tongue-lashing. I told her what Ron had advised, and she got even madder. But she agreed Ron knew best, having been through similar things with many faculty members.

So, another complaint and another scheduled meeting with the ombudsman – a week out. The ombudsman called me and advised me to stay away from Sharon at all costs until this was sorted out. Then she apologized for the system and for me having to work through all of this.

Three nights later Sharon and Sam over-played their hand. I got a call at home at nine PM from Sharon. She told me she was at the Center and there was a problem with the roof on the visitor center. She thought it might collapse. She pleaded for me to come out and see what we needed to do. I knew she was staying with Sam now and had been told she left her husband. So I knew – even with my gullible nature in those days – this was some sort of plot. Bonnie wanted to go with me, but I told her that she, as a witness, would probably not work twice. She agreed, so I called Rob and Shirley and asked them to accompany me. We drove out and I went to the house door—the house Sharon was sharing with Sam. Sharon came to the door with just a raincoat loosely draped around her and a menacing smile. Rob and Shirley rounded the corner of the house so Sharon could see them and her smile turned to fear. Shirley asked what she was trying to do and Sharon just stammered. Sam came to the door and asked why Shirley and Rob were there. We three shook our heads and left.

The next day I filed a complaint with the ombudsman and Sharon's complaint and mine were viewed jointly. She and Sam were reprimanded and Sam was told by Ron to vacate the house on the Center's grounds. Sam and Sharon stayed at CSU, with Sam teaching and working on his PhD and Sharon going into another department. But, a couple of years later, they got married and moved to the Midwest. I heard from someone that a year later they divorced and went their own ways. The drama had come full circle – but I did not understand these things then. Instead I felt anger, the need to attack back and complete confusion about why someone would orchestrate something like this. So I had counter-attacked by remaining in the drama, something I would not do now. Happily, it did not make me cynical nor move me out of my heart.

More frequent were outcomes such as the one with Sally Manless. Sally was a high school student in one of Bill's alternative school classes that was working at the Environmental Learning Center with AmeriCorps members and my CSU students. The ELC was becoming more and more popular with teachers throughout the educational system. Bill was spending a lot of time with Sally and three or four other students who had suffered abuse while growing up. Bill was a great example of working from the heart and allowing his emotions to show, yet also knowing when to draw lines and require outcomes. Bill was the first man Sally had trusted in her life to that time – as she told me a couple of years after I met her. She and her mother had been abused by her father – physically, sexually and mentally. Finally her mother found the courage to leave and was forced to change her name and go into hiding due to her ex-husband's threats. She changed her name to Manless – no man would ever ruin she and Sally's lives again. One heavy load for Sally to carry. As she worked more with the groups, and realized Bill and I were friends, she slowly began to speak to me and ask questions. And began to interact slightly with some of the male students.

After some time of the diverse groups engaging in service-learning projects at the Center I was invited to attend an international service-learning conference in London, England, and present the partnership we had all created. I proposed that we bring a group – Bill and one of his students, Brian from AmeriCorps and one of his members and me and one of my CSU students. Together we would present the model, with the students taking the lead role. The idea was quickly accepted, but there was no funding to make it happen. I could secure some funding from CSU for my student and myself, but we had four others to bring. Together we wrote grant proposals and, after about three months, had the money we needed. So we began working on the presentation and a display we were going to set up at the conference. And we started getting all the documentation we needed and booking flights. Suddenly Bill realized Sally, the student he had chosen, could not get a passport. There was no documentation of her birth and the name change later only made it worse. To use her previous name could open a means to locate she and her mom.

I offered to drive her to Denver and see what we could do at the office that handled passports. We had little luck at first but, after two trips with Bill to Denver and four with me, we thought we were making headway. Then, out of the blue, her request was again denied. And now it was just three weeks before we were to leave. Brian had already had to drop out due to a report he had to deliver in Washington, so he had named his assistant director to fill his spot. We didn't want to lose another of the starting team, especially Sally. Bill and I both knew this could be a breakthrough opportunity for her to realize good things could also happen in this life. Tom, my student going, suggested we try a political approach. Not knowing how to do this, I called our senators office and told Sally's story to his aide. She promised to bring this to the senator quickly. And she did – within a week we had Sally's passport. The conference and our time as a group in London were stellar and on returning, Sally thanked me for being the second man she could trust. A year later, she graduated from high school and entered Brian's AmeriCorps program. Two years after that I was happy to write her a letter of support – along with many others – and see her off to college. College was something she had always said was beyond her abilities to reach. A year later, she called so I could talk to her boyfriend of three months. Then, again, she thanked both Bill and I for showing her anything was possible, even a boyfriend.

And so we have the balance that appears in all things. Yet the pain of the less successful attempts from the heart can easily stop us from walking that way again. It is good to go inside to see this and simply count the successful and unsuccessful episodes before leaving your heart behind.

26 | The Four Colors – Plus One

"There's a deep wound in people-that they have been so cut off from the source of their being, their mother, their Earth Mother."
—Francis Story Talbott II (Medicine Story),
WAMPANOAG

I WAS LEARNING MORE ALL THE TIME FROM MY NATIVE AMERICAN and Mayan teachers. On my next trip to Belize, I met some Garifuna people and was invited to gatherings they were having. The Garifuna were originally brought to Central America from Africa as slaves, much as in the U.S. Many, however, later migrated to Central America of their own free will according to what they told me. Before long I met with Anna and Bob, a married couple who practiced spiritual healings of their people. We met, odd as it sounds, in the post office in Belize City. I was confused by the postage I needed to buy to ship some materials back to CSU and Bob walked up.

"Need some help, mon?" he asked.

"I could use a little. I need to send these three packages to Colorado and I don't see any indication on the stamps about which are for overseas. No one's at the window and I need to get along to meet some people," I explained.

"No problem. Let me see. Okay, use three of des stamps and one of des and you will be fine, mon. You could buy the more expensive ones for quick post, but it is only a name. It will take ten days anyway," Bob directed.

"Thanks. That's a great help. I'm Jim, from Colorado," I said.

"I am Bob from Belize," he smiled back at me. "And this is my wife, Anna," he went on as Anna approached us. "What you doing in Belize, Jim mon?"

"I'm with Colorado State University and I come here for a number of things. Sometimes bringing U.S. students, sometimes to work with the agencies and schools here and sometimes to work with some Mayan and Hispanic friends on my spiritual growth."

"Ah, that sounds busy, Jim. Do you enjoy this wonderful land too?" Anna asked.

"In everything I do, Anna. I love nature and try to honor it, and the Earth Mother, in all my work – and play."

"Very good, Jim," she continued, "We also have a strong connection to the Mother beneath us. Our parents had this in Africa and we have it here. It does not matter where you are on the Earth, the Mother of us all knows you."

"Beautifully said, Anna," I complimented her – and meant it.

"I would like to hear more of what you do, Jim," Bob said. "Would you come to eat with us?"

"I have to meet some people in the Education and Environment Department soon, but would love to have dinner with you after that, if that is okay?"

"Perfect," Anna picked up the thought, "We will draw you a map. You come when you come. We don't make special times to eat. We will eat when you come."

"Thank you both. I look forward to talking more. What may I bring?" I asked.

"A big appetite, Anna is a great cook," Bob said. "You are a big mon, so this should be easy for you," he finished, again with a smile.

"That's no problem, Bob. I have eaten very little today. And I am big, so I could use some filling. Some of my Mayan friends like to call me "Big White". I'll try to live up to my name when we eat."

"Big White, I like dat," Anna laughed out loud.

They drew me a map, we hugged and I went off to my meeting.

My meeting was set for two PM and everyone arrived by three – unheard of for meetings in that part of the world! It was the equivalent of everyone being early. The meeting went smoothly and quickly, after which I excused myself from getting a few Belikins with some of the attendees because of the dinner I was invited to.

I began heading towards Bob and Anna's place, trying to think of something to bring. A fresh flower merchant solved my dilemma. I picked up two big bunches of multi-colored flowers – a plant rainbow – and continued on my way. I arrived at their place about five – flowers in hand and smile on face.

Their house was a small clapboard house in, I believe, the north side of town. It was neatly painted white and flowers sprouted all around the small yard. A two-foot fence was across the front, with ferns growing all along its length. It was 'comfortable' to me the moment I saw it, but I felt bad about bringing flowers as they had them all around the house. Well, I thought, it truly is the thought – the intention – of any gift.

I went up and knocked and I heard wooden floorboards creak as someone approached the door from the inside. Bob opened the door with a big, welcoming smile. Bob is a tall man, probably six foot, lean and muscular. He was, I guess, in his late fifties when I first met him. His skin was dark black, almost luminous. Anna was smaller, about five foot eight, also lean and very attractive. She was probably a few years younger than Bob and her skin was light brown. In Belize the colors 'mix' a great deal – adding spice to the four colors of the medicine wheel. Bob saw the flowers I carried in both arms and yelled over his shoulder, "Anna, come see, Jim is here. And look what he has brought! How did he know?"

Anna walked out of the kitchen in a brightly colored housedress and apron, wiping her hands on a dishtowel.

"Ah, my! Look at these beautiful flowers coming to make our home happy! We love flowers and plants Jim. We have them grow all year outside and now we have their joy inside. Thank you so much," she finished as she took the flowers from me. She began gathering jars and tins from cupboards and putting flowers in each. Soon we had six bunches of flowers around their cozy living room.

"We have a mix of Belize and Africa tonight, Jim. Rice and beans, salad, and lentils and spice and meat. Good for you?" Anna asked.

"Sounds wonderful."

We had a belly-busting dinner and then took strong cups of coffee back into the living room, where we sat for some talk.

"Tell us more of what you learn from the native people of your country and our Belizean Mayan people," Bob asked. And so we talked for a couple of hours about what I was doing and learning and what they had learned from their elders.

"Where you staying?" Anna asked when we took a break in our spirit, nature and religion talk.

"I'm at the blue hotel near the post office we met at. I was going to stay a few more days then wander up north," I answered her.

"Why don't you go get your stuff and come stay here. I think we have a lot to talk about," Anna offered.

"Great idea, if you want, Jim," Bob added.

"I'd love to if you have room."

So, with Bob along as it was night and not the best time to wander around some parts of Belize City, I went and checked out and moved to their place. For the next two days we had a fruitful time, sharing teachings, stories and jokes. Then they asked if I would like to meet some Garifuna elders.

"Absolutely. I am always honored to meet elders and listen to whatever they wish to share," I answered enthusiastically.

"We will go towards Belmopan tomorrow and then visit Momma and Pa John. See how long we stay. See if they want company. I think they will be interested to meet Big White," Bob chuckled.

The next morning I rented a car – a Jeep once again – and we headed up the Western Highway towards Belmopan. About half way to Belmopan we turned off on a narrow, rutted dirt road and drove for some ten miles to a small group of houses. Houses made up of whatever offered itself for use – some clapboard, some woods I did not recognize, some sheet tin and some logs. We pulled next to one of the homes and Anna got out, went to the door and knocked. A young black girl answered and Anna spoke with her for a minute, then went inside. In about ten minutes she came back out and told us Momma would be happy to see us.

The inside of the small house – actually, more large hut – was full of African art and things from nature – feathers, horns, rocks and plants. Sparse furniture was in the main room, a table with three chairs, two stuffed chairs and a cupboard. There were three other rooms I could see, all small. One was a bathroom, the other two were bedrooms. In one of the stuffed chairs was a large, imposing black woman decked out in a billowing print dress, a colorful turban-type head covering and feathers hanging around her neck. She was very old and quite heavy. And she had a big, beautiful smile. "Welcome friends," Momma waved at us as she spoke.

"Good day, Momma. It's too long since we were together," Bob greeted her as he approached and gave her a hug.

"Good day, Momma. It is good to meet you. My new friends here were kind enough to bring me here. I hope we are not interfering with your day," I spoke.

"How dat? I don't climb da hills no more and I don't run wit da dogs no more, so nothing to get in the way of," she laughed at me. "I am happy to meet you. Not many people come here other than family and my friends. Anna tells me they call you 'Big White.' That's funny, I like that. Some call me 'Big Momma.' I know. That's good for me. Where you from?"

"Colorado, Momma."

"Why you come to Belize?"

And so I briefly shared my tale of meeting people and learning their ways. How I had done this many places around the world, but now I look to learn more of their spiritual ways.

"Ah. So you would learn of some of our Garifuna ways, eh?"

"I would be honored to learn whatever you or others would teach me. I try to bring into my heart all I learn, put the pieces together wherever they fit, and use what I know to do my work. I am still a baby in the spiritual ways, but I am a quick learner," I answered her.

"That's a good way to be. I would spend time with you and I know Pa John will too. Little Eta went to go get him. Will you stay with us a while? We only have a small room, but you would be okay there. I like you study nature and the world around us. We could tell you some things and I want to hear about what you have got in dat head and heart," Momma asked straight out, right up front.

"I would love to stay here. Maybe I could return in a couple of days when I leave the home of my friends here?"

"Good. I ask you bring some food. Okay?"

"Certainly, Momma. Give me a list before we leave today," I agreed.

"Good. Now, let's talk a while. Pa John will be here soon unless he is with his niece."

We talked for about ninety minutes about Spirit, spirituality and cultures. Then the door opened and a small, wiry, slightly stooped, dark brown man entered. He was old, but moved smoothly across the room. I found out later he was over ninety – how far over he did not know, as there were no records. This, of course, was Pa John.

"How you all is today," a surprisingly young, strong voice almost boomed out of his small frame.

"We all good John," Momma answered him. "You remember Bob and Anna and dis here be Jim. From Colorado."

John said hello to Bob and Anna, giving a hug to each. Then turned to me and grasped me in a strong bear hug. With his voice and the strength of his hug, I would have thought him to be much younger than his years. "Jim. Good day. It is good to see you."

"Good day to you Pa John," I said. "It is also good to see you."

"We been talkin' John," Momma began. "Jim here going to stay with me for a while. He works with Native American people and other people who walk in spirit. We have much to talk about and I knew you would be here for that."

"Goodness me, yes. When you comin' Jim?"

"In a couple of days, Pa John."

"Call me Pa or John, no need for Pa John. That came from a granddaughter long ago."

"Let's sit some more. I will mix some roots and flowers and make a tea for pure energy and strength. Okay?" Momma asked.

"Yes please, Momma," Anna responded.

And so we drank our tea with the mix Momma put together and talked at length. We talked of the use of plants and animals in healing; the different ways of medicine people; the Catholic Church's distain for Garifuna and Lakota ways; the connection of our minds, bodies and spirits to the universe; the connection of the Earth's creatures and more. Then Momma asked my feelings on the Earth and nature. This kicked off the main part of our talk that day.

"We will need a lot of time for me to express all my beliefs and feelings about the Earth Mother and all upon, under and over her. It is my passion in this walk – the connection of humans and the planet and nature where my primary role sits. No matter what else I do."

"Yes. I knew this," Momma began. "As it is with me too, Jim. Always has been so and will be so. And is too for John here and many people here in Belize – not just us African people. There is no spirituality without the Mother in our Earth and the nature she provides. Dat is my belief and I see dat it in many people who are still close enough to nature to remember dis thing."

"This is all true for me, also," John chimed in. "Without the nurturing of the Earth, we are nothing. Without the assistance from the Earth in our healing, we can do nothing."

"This is why we brought Jim to you," Bob began. "We have had many talks and we knew you all were the same on this. If you allow it Momma, we will also come when you three talk. We can drive up for a couple of days at least. Sleep in our car."

"And we will also bring food Momma," Anna added.

"No sleepin' in cars. Jim will stay here or with me and Bob and Anna with Pa John. No problem," John invited. And so our group was set for later.

"I agree with your wise words, Momma and John. I have seen that connection between healers and worshipers and the Earth Mother in many cultures still connected to her. I believe this will need to be the way again for all humans if we are not to become dinosaurs," I returned to our conversation.

"And if we do not embrace the Mother of the Earth again we will deserve to become like the dinosaurs," Momma added.

We talked until after midnight then, at the kind invite of Momma and John, agreed to stay until the morning. The three of us who had traveled here were tired and the road is dark and can be difficult at night. We went so late, in part, because of the tea mix Momma had made. We all felt full of energy and did not realize how late it was until someone looked at a clock. I went with John and Bob and Anna stayed with Momma, as her extra room was larger than John's.

THE CHANCE FOR another side trip from our journey together is calling to me now. We have traveled some distance together thus far and have further to go. But, with as far as we have come, I know you see the connection of spirituality, nature, the Earth Mother and all creatures — especially humans. We are all connected — all one — intricately in this sense.

You also begin to see the four colors I was working with — black, red, yellow, and white. Or some of them I have mentioned thus far. While I traveled before Bonnie and I moved to Colorado, I was observing and learning about the natural places in many places around the globe. And I was meeting with, talking to and learning from people of many cultures and races — although not yet about their spiritual ways. I was 'in training' for my walk to come. Soon I would meet with, and begin to learn from, aboriginal people from Australia and some Celtic teachers from Britain. Yellow has only entered my circle in limited ways — to this day. I have read about the spiritual ways of the yellow races, attended gatherings and spoken with some who walk that road, but no teachers of the yellow spiritual paths has emerged for me. Either that is not a path I need for my work or they have yet to appear. Whichever it is to be will be what I need to continue my road. Trust.

Some I have learned from and worked with have also been brown or olive skinned or other shades of the four. Remember, in the four colors of people, all other colors are mixes of some of these. Does that mean their spiritual path is a mix of various ways? I don't know, but have thought about that often. If that were so I would be painted in many hues with the number of spiritual ways I have been guided in.

These four colors are important – the medicine wheel does not exist in so many cultures without a reason. Yet the fifth color is, to me, even more important. It is the heart, the glue, and the color that allows all the others to flow, connect and do their work in a good way. With the conversation at Momma's house, and all I have written thus far, you know this color already. Green. The color of the Earth Mother. For the Red man or woman to do his/her work, green must infuse their red ways. So too for the white, black and yellow. It needs to always be present or the work done is much less than it could be. And, without the green liberally splashed into spiritual work, there is no sustainability. Those still closely connected to the Earth Mother understand this and honor it in all they do. Others have strayed from this understanding and so go into fear and confusion when events occur they cannot explain with their science.

The Earth Mother will continue to walk with us on this journey, teaching as we go along. Although I feel very fortunate to have had all the human and spirit teachers and guides, who have provided me the knowledge I need to fulfill my life's work, I am even more thankful that the Earth Mother has taught me all that she has. These teachings have come through ceremony and journeying, through the plants, through the animals in all realms, and through the landscapes of her natural world. From my beginning, as a small child, I have been drawn to the natural world. My father's love of the outdoors provided the opportunities to be in nature from an early age and feel the connection between everything of nature and myself. And, once I committed to Spirit to step up and serve as he wished at the onset of Bonnie's walk with cancer, the connection became more direct and powerful – with the added spiritual connection taking things to a new level.

Many humans speak about how we have abused our planet with our ego-based, consumptive ways. The doom and gloom group speaks of how we are about to become extinct. Those who feel everything in the natural world is here for humans to use – or misuse—as they will, continue to deny the natural crisis building around us. I believe, from all the Earth Mother has shared with me, that the choices are all ours. We have not, and cannot, destroy the Earth Mother – short of blowing the planet apart. We can scar her and cause disease in her systems, the symptoms of which then reflect in our bodies, minds and spirits. As several teachers have told me – as well as the Earth Mother herself – everything we do to the Earth, we do to ourselves. If we partner with the Earth Mother in a good way, the fruitful outcomes of this show in our planet and our bodies. If we mistreat and abuse the Earth, we suffer the pain and disease ourselves. Yet thinking we will 'kill' our planet and so, in the process, also die, is more human ego. We may well pollute and disrupt our planet to the point we, as a species, will disappear, but the Earth Mother will then correct and heal herself over time. Time – which means nothing to Her or the universe. If enough of us work with the Earth Mother in integrity and balance, a place for humans will continue to be provided by her. How many people is that? What percentage? That I have not been shown, so I do not concern myself with it. I simply see, and have been shown, that in working on our inner selves as spiritual beings and working with the planet and its creatures around us, we will evolve and prosper. For me, that is enough. I follow this twin road, which is really one road, each day to the best of my abilities. I seek new learning each day to promote this walk. And I reach out to others to share what I have learned and welcome them on this road beside me. From earlier – do not try to be more than you are, but do not try to be less than you are either.

How will this change and shift we creatures of the Earth and the Earth Mother are going though turn out? I've had many people asking me this and my answer is – we will all see together. I have my thoughts around this, but they are simply my thoughts. When I share what I 'think' I am careful to define that. When I am taught the ways and prophecies of many cultures and am taught by my spirit guides, I report that. When we begin to see similar or connected stories from people of diverse cultures, I know there is truth within the words. When my spirit guides or Spirit teach me I am not shown the 'destination', only the journey we humans need to walk to return to harmony. From that point I assume it is back into trust – if we trust in the outcomes of our good actions, they will manifest.

How do we become better stewards and partners of our planet? There are shelves full of books offering practical advice on this matter, but I will write next what the Earth Mother wishes me to relate around this question.

Some ways are easy – if we do not allow ourselves to become lazy or unaware of things around us. Think about each thing you do that has an effect on the planet. Remembering all things are connected in this web of life, ask yourself each time you take an action, "What effect will this have on the others of the web?" Throwing recyclable items in the trash because it is easier or less expensive. Throwing garbage in the trash rather than creating a compost pile. (As I caught myself doing twice yesterday.) Buying things with unnecessary packaging. Owning three of anything, when one is enough. And on and on. The basis is being mindful and learning to live more with less.

Yesterday I paused to walk with Onyx, my black Labordoodle, along the creek to hear the birds, feel the breeze and touch the water. Oak Creek is a short walk from where I live, across fields and through groves of trees in land managed by the Fish and Wildlife people. When we got to the creek, Onyx shot for the water and dove off the bank with joy in his energy. I threw him sticks until my arm hurt, then decided to walk the mile along the creek trail to another trail we could take home. I had my bag over my shoulder to carry water and carry out any trash I might see as I always did. We had walked this trail about four days ago and I had picked up any trash I saw then. This time, as we reached the end of the river trail of a mile, I was aware the bag seemed very full. As we headed back home I felt instruction in my heart telling me to list what I had collected. So, when we arrived back home, I took out the trash and looked at what I had. Remember, brothers and sisters, this is one mile of trail – a relatively unused trail – that I had cleaned four days before.

Here is the inventory:

2 beer bottles

3 sandwich wrappers

2 beer cans

1 water bottle half full

1 empty water bottle

1 powerade plastic bottle

1 ball of tin foil

11 cigarette butts

1 small wheel cover from a bicycle

1 plastic container

Is this mindful stewardship of our home? I know we have all seen this, and much worse, and hopefully some have also cleaned the trails, but have we gone beyond anger or judgment to ask the Earth Mother why this is and what we need to do about it?

Okay, we have all heard or read or seen pictures of our natural areas as 'trash cans' a million times. But have we listened? The Earth Mother taught me long ago there is no difference between one human throwing one plastic bottle on her or BP, in it's greed, flooded the Gulf with oil. The only difference is in scope and this means nothing to her. Both actions are out of integrity, both are unsustainable. Yet, all too often, we rant in rage against the BP's of the world as we throw our bottle on the ground.

One good guide for all actions humans take is the native teaching of seven generations. I have been taught this many times also and many of you may know it, but sharing it together reminds us of its importance and relevance today. Before you do anything – a flower you wish to pick, a rock to take home, a big car you buy, a program you start – you ask yourself "What impact will this have seven generations from now"? That is to say – how will this affect our children's, children's children? How will it affect our Earth? If the answer is it will have a negative effect, you do not do it. You find another way or abandon it. I take this out into nature with me at all times. And, when I see a rock I wish to take home for study or teaching, I ask myself the question of the seven generations. If I see or feel no negative impacts from my taking the rock, I then ask the Earth Mother's permission to take it. If I am given permission – either in my heart or through signs – I then look for others rocks like it and pass over the first seven I see. This again allows for the seven generations that follow. I take the eighth and, if there are not eight, I take none. This may all sound extreme to you, yet it is not. It becomes second nature as you walk each day. And it will help with the balance between humans and the Earth Mother so lacking. Sometimes to reach balance you must pull hard in the other direction.

I can list all of the things humans have been doing in a unsustainable way – building houses larger than we need; driving cars with fuel guzzling engines; buying two, three or four cars; eating foods from threatened species and pages more if I wished. Our ego has pushed us away from the natural way into a materialistic way. All of us taught the 'to own' – to possess – 'is success'. Now we strain the capacity of the Earth Mother to tolerate these excesses. We all know these things – have talked about them for years. But talk and walk are two different things. The time for talk is nearing it's end, we now must all walk what we know to be in harmony with each other and our planet. If not, the Earth Mother will adjust for us. And Spirit may reconsider how, or if, we are to evolve. I know we have the capacity to live in the sustainable way, I have seen it in action in many places. We just need enough of us willing to make the changes needed. Many think these changes will cause pain and hardship, when in fact they create joy and relief.

Changing how we walk with our natural world by cleaning our inner and outer 'nests' will not, however, provide all that is needed for a richer walk of spirit. Connecting with the Earth Mother does not just mean behaving in more sustainable ways. We need to go out into nature and speak with her and her creatures. That does not mean everyone needs to walk as I have, seeking nature in hard to get to places around the globe. You can go to a park, a river or your own back yard. How many people do you see going from home to car to business and back? How many rarely leave the cities? If you find time to regularly go off into nature and sit quietly and listen, you will hear. I can guarantee you that much. If you go for walks or hikes and watch the nature around you, you will see. Immersing yourself in the natural world is a prerequisite for many things, including our own healing. You will see more of this when we rejoin the main trail of our journey.

Consider tonight, when you finish reading, or tomorrow if you are reading at night, going out into the natural world with these perspectives and see what you see and feel. Go out in your heart, but bring your mind along for documenting. Talk to a tree, smell a flower, ask for permission...or whatever moves you. Later, I will offer ways to shift the senses and, as I like to teach others, smell a rock, feel a flower's aroma, touch a thought and be connected.

I continue to walk with the four colors of people, in congruence with the green of the Earth Mother, the blue of Father Sky and the white energy place I do my spirit work and connect with Great Spirit. The colors are but symbols, but the elements of our journeys they represent are essential to walking the good red road. We will probably speak more of white energy work and black energy work further on.

I thought this chapter was complete, so I began the next last night. During the night the Earth Mother spirit told me it was not complete, more needed to be said. So, for the first time I go back to capture whatever now comes through me.

The spirit and energy of the Earth Mother is powerful. It is power all who wish to walk a spiritual road and awaken fully must connect with – on an ongoing basis. Not like going to church on Sunday, then walking out and back into our old ways. After connecting with all the aspects of nature around you – from two-leggeds to rock people – psychically reach out and connect with the Earth Mother. Or, do so as you are aligning with the natural world around you. For some new at this it is sometimes easier to connect with nature, then the Earth Mother. Try both ways and see what works best for you. If this connection with the natural world has not been a strong part of your walk thus far it will take time, patience and practice to 'hear' what you need to hear, 'see' what you need to see and 'feel' what you need to feel. As is most often the case, allow your brain to take a break and sit in back as you go from the heart. I also suggest no expectation or anticipations – just see what comes. Lessons, understandings or directions will come if you stay patient and trusting.

Not only are these connections and immersion in the nature world and the energies of Earth, as defined by the Earth Mother symbology, powerful teachers and guides, but they also help repair the disconnect most modern day humans have from all around us. In fact, this disconnect must be repaired and the natural world connected within both a physical and spiritual way before you can acquire any meaningful spiritual teaching from another human. All true spiritual teachers, especially those indigenous ones still connected to 'all there is', will tell you this. It is the Earth Mother and all of nature who are the primary and best teachers of the spiritual way. Humans who have learned these lessons simply pass them on to others, sometimes with suggestions for actions or thoughts along the way. For some, the Earth and nature, spirit guides (whether you call them ancestors, angels or spirits) and the direct connection to God (Great Spirit, Allah, etc.) are all the teachers they will need to understand their purpose and their powers. For me, these did become – and still are – my primary teachers, but I learned many 'specifics' from my human teachers. I received many teachings, which 'filled in the blanks', and many ways to accomplish what Great Spirit showed me I needed to do.

Today many people claim to be shamans, healers, gurus and the like, as I mentioned earlier on our journey. Most are not, especially if they have not learned from our planet and those humans closely connected to her. It is the other reason I never call myself a 'shaman' or any other term. Not only does it not honor the fact that it is God working through any of us, but it also can dump you in the pop culture...learn to be a shaman like me in three days or less.....just $495, plus the cost of materials.

A couple of weeks ago, as I was walking through Uptown Sedona (an oxymoron, as this is a three block strip) a young man came rushing up to me all excited. He was probably in his late twenties and just glowed with pleasure. He asked, "Are you from Sedona?"

"Yes, I am," I replied.

"Can you tell me a really good place to go sit in the rocks and meditate," he spoke so fast, his excitement so high, I had to really listen carefully to catch his words.

"There are many. There are energy vortexes, water spots and spots few know of. What are you looking for?" I asked.

"I just finished the second day of a three-day course with Shaman Bob and when we left for the day he told me I was a shaman! I had no idea! Isn't that great! He wants me to go meditate before tomorrow's last day on what I need to do next. I'm so excited! He told me, after just three more courses with him, I would earn my Shaman's diploma. Oh, my God, I can't wait to tell everyone!" he gushed out.

I wanted to say something to him so he might think about what he was being told and the motivations behind it, but clearly got from Spirit I was not to do so. So I asked, "Who are you to connect with while you do this meditation? What elements are you to seek – fire, water, earth, wind? Are you to be high or low on the earth?"

"I don't know, Shaman Bob didn't tell me any of that. I guess wherever I want. And I guess I'll meditate by being silent and see what I see," he said, a little less hyped.

So I told him of three spots, each with different energy, wished him well and watched him head off up one of the roads I suggested.

I don't need to add too much to this story to explain why I shared it. This young man was well intentioned and, I felt, truly wanted to find his path – his purpose. But look who he found – Shaman Bob. And the ability to earn his Shaman Diploma because, after all, he was already a shaman. I will add I have diplomas from various universities in teaching, theater, natural resources management and environmental interpretation. But I assure you I have no diplomas in any of the work I have mastered – to a point – in the things that really matter, my spiritual assignments from Great Spirit. I get a huge smile creating a mental picture with me asking Two Bears for a diploma in Chanunpa carrying (?), water pouring (?) or maybe just general medicine work. Or from Roberto as Keeper of Medicine. Or any of my other teachers. Two Bears would ask for the pipe back, Roberto would take back his plant knowledge and Yellowhair would sit me down for a long discussion.

If you walk the spiritual road, please people, be true to yourself and seek your guidance from places and people of integrity if you feel you need that on top of what nature and God will provide.

Now I believe we can step back on the main road once again. Permission to do this now, Earth Mother? Ah, thank you. So back we go.

27 | Spirit Teacher Appears

Back to Colorado and my days studying and teaching so we can again pick up the thread of those things I have learned. Things became ever more hectic for me as the word 'no' continued to be absent from my vocabulary. My understanding still that, if asked, you were supposed to serve. Bonnie and I did tours together, usually with four or five people. And we went on our own exploratory trips in the mountains and on the plains, often ending up at totally unexpected places. Lawrence and I were now teaching field courses for students from grade school through college – courses like Red Man, White Man, where we shared the traditions around nature and culture from our own backgrounds. Others around wildlife or plants and still others about the spiritual ways as we both understood them. They were quite popular and we tried to honor each request, sometimes infringing on our own study time. But we loved it – as did Bonnie and I our courses and seminars. I had a troop of students and experts from numerous fields providing field courses at the Center as well. And I was more and more involved with local non-profit efforts. As I wove these things, Ron asked for more of my time for fundraising for the environmental building at the Center and the plans for its construction. More manic all the time. And I was finding Bonnie and I were driving through our exploration trips, allowing much less time for walking and connecting. After all, I needed to be prepared for the next thing.

Making time for my own classes and my masters' work, my spiritual training and the classes I taught took precedence – forcing sleep to suffer even further. Yet I was enjoying every moment, thinking I was doing all I could for all I could in a good way. My trips with Bonnie and my work on my spiritual teachings were the times I could unwind and relax – in nature, the inipi and gatherings. I had no concept of what balance really means. I repeat these things so that you understand they not only continued, but also grew. It puts this part of our walk – and later ones – in context.

I am sharing some of the lessons from my indigenous teachers as we walk. Those that I am free to share in this way. Other ceremonies and teachings I may mention, but in no great detail, as these are not shared in this way. For those drawn to these ways, there are many who will guide if they are sought out. Some I work with now, I guide along the paths I have taken or send them to others more knowledgeable in what they seek if Spirit directs me to do so. I will introduce you to other elders of various cultures, as we trek forward, but I suspect I will share more of the work I have done with my Native American teachers than with others. It is the Red Road that drew me to this walk and the road I feel most connected to. Even if my Red Road is tinted with black, white, yellow, brown and olive.

The lodges with Yellowhair had become more popular with many people over time, so some weeks we requested two. If Yellowhair was unable, there were other water pourers we would ask. In this way I was exposed to ceremony conducted by many medicine people. And no two were ever identical. This was an excellent lesson for me later as I began to combine the ceremonies and teachings of the cultures I worked with.

I carried my Chanunpa with me each day – sometimes leaving it in the car, sometimes keeping it on my person. Except for Bonnie, I shared with no one it's existence. I felt it was for me to feel and understand the connection between us and did not want ego in the way. Explaining where the pipe came from and why I carried it could put me in an ego place or so I thought. Actually I think I was also afraid of 'finger pointers' and ridicule as a white man carrying a Native American spiritual tool. I always brought it to Two Bears' lodges, along with my tobacco and sage – each time placing all three on the altar. And each lodge Two Bears and I did together, he spoke more of the responsibilities of carrying the Chanunpa; how to connect to the Chanunpa; how to pray with the Chanunpa and; how to know when – if – I was ready to use this sacred instrument.

As spring approached Two Bears again brought up our trip to the Pine Ridge Reservation and Wounded Knee. I asked Bonnie if she would come and bring a friend if she wished. She decided she would enjoy the trip and did not feel like staying behind, as she sometimes did to immerse herself in her personal time and interests. She invited a woman who she worked on a lot of geology study with, Carmen. Carmen was a very friendly, outgoing, western woman, probably in her late forties. The four of us planned and prepared for what we might need, as Bonnie and Carmen would rent a car in Wyoming and go off on a geology field trip while Two Bears and I were on the rez. For once, plans actually worked and we loaded our gear into my Jeep and headed north in early May. We could find winter or spring in South Dakota that time of year, but Two Bears' kin on the rez assured him that winter had passed.

We had a fine trip together – the four of us hitting it off as a group. We stopped several times along the way for a night's rest and twice walked into natural areas at night to build a small fire, around which we shared stories. And we stopped twice to visit with friends of Two Bears'. It was pleasant to be in no rush. Finally we arrived at Rapid City, not far from Pine Ridge. Bonnie pointed to a Best Western and, in a few minutes, we had rooms for the night. The next morning Two Bears and I would head to Wounded Knee and Bonnie and Carmen would head for the hills – actually, the rocks.

The next morning was sunny and cold – a perfect day for both groups to head out. We had a big breakfast at a near-by restaurant, stopped at a car rental outlet where Bonnie rented a Jeep for she and Carmen. We had a cup of coffee, then Bonnie hugged me and sent her love and prayers with me, and we pulled out in opposite directions. Two Bears and I headed to Pine Ridge for whatever he wanted to teach me, show me or allow me to see. I had no clue what his plans were and he had evaded each question I asked – so I stopped asking.

It was not a long ride to Wounded Knee and we sat, silently, except for Two Bears pointing directions out as we drove. I was enjoying the rolling hills and cuts through rock faces we drove through, so I almost missed his finger pointing to the left. I braked and pulled onto a side road, going just a few feet to a sign – an old sign – next to the road.

"This is the sign about Wounded Knee," Two Bears finally spoke. "See where the word on top has been nailed over what was below?"

I looked and saw the sign said the Massacre of Wounded Knee. The word 'massacre' was the word he spoke of.

"The sign, when it was put up, read 'The Battle of Wounded Knee'. This was no battle. The army butchered men, women and children. So, with much anger from the people, it was changed to massacre – as it was. Soldiers from this battle were given medals and still these have not been taken back. These were hard times for white and red. For some they still are," he explained as we got out of the car.

"I will wait here," he said leaning against the Jeep, "Go and read the sign and listen to your spirit as you do so. See what comes to you," he instructed.

I approached the sign and suddenly felt something welling up in me. I looked at the sign a few moments, then stepped around it and began walking to the side – to some open grass as I remember. In a few seconds I was doubled over in pain, driven to my knees. The pain was centered in my gut and it felt like knives trying to get out. I went forward on all fours as the pain built even stronger. Then I was overcome by sadness and grief and began wailing out loud. Tears poured down my face and onto my hands. I lay down and continued to moan and wail as I also tried to understand the pain. Colors crossed my eyes – red, brown and black I remember as the primary hues I was see-ing. Then that was gone and I felt sharp pains in my back, like pointed stakes being driven in. I thought I was dying and had no idea what to do, so I asked Great Spirit to help me, as I was powerless to even move. More gripping pains in my gut forced me to focus on just bearing the pain and tears continued to roll out of me, like a faucet left full open. I was scared – no, petrified. I had never felt pain like this and did not know what was happening. After a while I began to also feel pains around my heart, like a fist closing on it. The pain was strongest in the bottom area of my heart and I remember thinking, "Is this what a heart attack feels like? Is it my time – so suddenly?"

Two Bears was not far away and I thought he must see me, yet he did not approach. This onslaught of pain and tears lasted about twenty minutes Two Bears told me later. Then everything stopped at once, as quickly as it had come. I lay panting, afraid to trust my legs yet as they felt like rubber bands. Slowly I pushed myself into a seated position – legs under my torso in the inipi position. My brain was running like a racecar trying to make sense of what had happened. And I was soaked in sweat, my shirt hanging off of me dragged down by the perspiration it had absorbed. I wasn't even sure I was still alive for some seconds until the energy of the things around me made me accept I was. My mouth was so dry I could not even swallow. So I sat, moaned softly, wiped sweat and breathed in big gulps of air. Trying to stop the panic I felt inside of me.

After what seemed like an hour Two Bears approached me with a bottle of water and a very serious look on his face. A serious look mixed with concern and sympathy. "I gave you a few minutes before I came. Here, drink slow," he said as he handed me the bottle.

"What the hell is wrong with me! Do you think it's my heart! Did you see me on the ground? You must have heard me," I gasped out in a rush.

"Yes, I saw. I did not expect anything like this. I thought this place would touch you, but not in that way. I was very worried for you but knew I could not come to you. I hold sorrow for that but I know it is so. I do not think anything is physically wrong with you, but it is your heart you feel. This place came to you as it was then. You were there now as you were then. These things happen sometimes. Not often, but they do. I begin to see why I was guided to bring you here. But not just for this I see. We need to open the Chanunpa and ask for guidance from above. This is big and I do not pretend to understand much of it. Are you able to stand?"

"I think so, if you help."

I got up and Two Bears helped me to the car. I passed the keys to him – not wanting to drive yet. "Will this happen again, Two Bears?"

"I do not think so. I do not know anyway. I have spoken about the pain that would find you as you walked more on this road and into your power. This is occurring with some now as the time of the prophecies nears. I will speak of my Hanbleche one day soon. It is the only time I had an experience like yours here. But not as intense, I think. You howled and wailed as the tears came and the pain grabbed you. Tell me what you felt, saw, smelled or tasted as this was on you."

Two Bears drove us to another dirt road and we headed up into the hills, where we could see nothing or no one in any direction. We got out and walked up a hill beside us, with Two Bears carrying the Chanunpa. He gathered some sticks along the way and made a small fire to burn sage and light the pipe. As we did this I told him all I could remember of the pain, emotion, colors and tears. Then we sat at the fire to open the pipe.

"I would like you to open this time with a prayer. And I would then like to smoke together and then sit quietly so we see what we shall see. Okay?" Two Bears asked.

"Of course," I answered, then began my prayer of intention for the Chanunpa. "Great Spirit. Great Mystery. Ancestors. I ask for guidance today – for my Uncle, Two Bears and myself. I ask this, not for us, but so that we may continue to learn how to serve in the best way. I ask for whatever you are willing to send at this time. All this I ask so we may better be able to heal the sacred hoop wherever it is broken. Aho. Mitakuye Oyasin" It was the best I could do, as shaken as I still was.

"Good," Two Bears said, then took a burning twig to light the pipe. I added more sage to the bowl and lit it with another burning twig. Two Bears passed the pipe to me twice, then he finished it off and tapped the ash into the fire with a brief prayer. After that we sat, quietly, each with a blanket wrapped around us.

I sat and tried not to think – just to feel and stay open to whatever came. I was partly successful, but confusion, doubts and fear kept edging in. I had never experienced anything like what happened and was still unsure about it not being a heart attack. Yet I physically felt nothing but fatigue now.

Understand, at this point in time, I had no belief in past lives, out of body experiences or anything like that. Not that I had ruled them out, just that I had not thought much about these things and, when I did, they were not things I could grasp. Yet I was 'gathering' experiences that defied my understanding of the world – as it had been taught to me so far.

After twenty or thirty minutes Two Bears cleared his throat, stretched and put some more wood on the fire. We only had small sticks and twigs we had gathered, so the fire had burned very low. As he added the wood new flames reached toward Father Sky.

"So, Jim, what do you need to know now?"

"I don't even know where to begin. But as I sat here I realized what you said before... 'This place came to you as it was then. You were there now as you were then.' What did you mean?"

"I meant that. You 'move around', as I was told this student who came to me would. You were at Wounded Knee in a past walk. That is all I know of that. And you saw it again today. You felt it. You were here and there."

"I don't know what I think of reincarnation, Two Bears. It has always interested me, but I don't know much about it and I'm not sure I believe it."

"Reincarnation. I do not like that word. It is past lives. In each you learn and, sometimes, they connect – or some of them connect – with the walk now. It happens when it is needed, as the meaning of teachings come when needed. We are all spirit. Energy of the universe. Not here once and gone. The universe and Great Spirit do not waste energy or teachings. To have us here once and gone would have no reason. So we come when we are needed, for the circle and ourselves. We will speak much more of this when we meet at home. Especially after today."

"I'll think about that before we sit together on it. It makes sense to my heart and spirit, but my brain is fighting the whole idea."

"Good. We don't do our things through the brain anyway," Two Bears smiled at me. "What else?"

"I guess just what do we do next?"

He looked me right in the eyes for some time, as he did on occasion, then spoke, "How do you feel now? Are you able to do something I wish you to do? Or we can stay with my relatives tonight and do more tomorrow. Or head back to Rapid City for the night and return tomorrow."

"I feel okay physically, but my brain and gut are in turmoil. No fear anymore, but...disquiet, I guess. We agreed we would stay here until you said we were done what needed to be done. So I'm ready for more today. The day's still young. Then, if they permit us, I would like to spend the night here."

"Fear stops everything. We cannot walk our road if we are in fear. So I am glad that has left you. I see that you need to go off on the land here alone for a while and see what you see. I will show you the roads to start in on and then you follow what you feel is the way. They are dirt roads to the middle of nothing and they will turn into dirt tracks at some point. You will need to pay attention to directions – where the sun is – or you could get lost. First I would have you drop me off at my friends' house. This is Frank I have spoken of. I will wait there. Are you able to do this?"

"I will give it my best. Just drive and see what comes my way?"

"Drive a while, walk if it feels right, or sit – whatever is so."

"What if I get lost? This is some big open country with not many landmarks."

"Do not enter fear again. You will not get lost and, if you did, I will know which road you started on. We would come and find you... some day," this time with a grin.

"Okay. I'm ready. I think," I said a bit unsure of my heart for this next thing I was to do.

"You must be ready and certain of being ready. If you are not we will wait for another time. I am not sure why I see this for you, but I see it strong."

"No, let's do it now. I am ready," I replied.

We drove out of the area we sat in for the Chanunpa ceremony and back to the two-lane road we were on earlier. We turned right at Two Bears' direction and drove for about a half hour, then pulled off to the side where he pointed. There was a dirt road off to the left with a number on a sign next to it, but the number had been shot off by someone doing some target practice at some earlier time. At least that would be a landmark when I returned to the road later. "Go up this road here," Two Bears instructed. "When you go in about five miles you will see many dirt roads you can choose from. Some go high, some to places of rock canyons and some low near the water. Listen to the one which chooses you and go that way. Then drive or walk or sit as we spoke before. Now let's go to Frank's, get you water and something to eat and you can start back here. Pay attention to the roads as we drive so you find this place."

So we drove to Frank's house, with Two Bears pointing out landmarks and roads along the way. Luckily for me there were not too many roads in this part of Pine Ridge. As we neared Frank's I asked, "Two Bears, what if someone takes offense with a white guy walking alone on the rez?"

"Don't worry. I doubt you will see anyone. If you do, and they ask where you are going, tell them I sent you to be on the land. They will leave you be. If you do run into a problem, just apologize and leave. But this will not happen."

As he finished, we pulled up to a weather-beaten wooden house, from which we could see another six or seven houses nearby. We got out and went to the door. As we neared the door, it opened and a tall, thin man of sixty or so stepped out. When he saw Two Bears he broke out in a big smile, whooped 'hocke he' and grasped Two Bears in a hug. After a minute, he turned to me and Two Bears introduced me. Frank reached out and shook hands, in the soft handshake I now knew to use.

"Be welcome here, Jim. Two Bears is my brother of many seasons. It is good to see him – and you."

"Thank you, Frank," I replied.

"How long you here for brother?" Frank asked Two Bears.

"Maybe one night, maybe more," Two Bears answered.

"Ah, good. You will both stay with me then. I have good elk stew for tonight."

"Good," Two Bears replied simply. And so we now had a place to stay and a place I could take off from in a little while.

We went inside the small house and Two Bears said, "Frank, my nephew here needs to go on the land soon. Can he fill his water bottle and do you have some fruit or meat for him?"

"Of course. So, Jim is your student, eh? What tribe is he?" Frank smiled as he spoke this since I look Italian or Greek, but not Indian.

"I am of the Olive Skinned Nation," I answered Frank quickly, so as to beat Two Bears to my humorous answer. Frank looked at me and then laughed. I had already learned that this answer was not only truthful, but a good one to give. With someone like Frank, who was kidding me about not being Indian, it usually got a laugh as it continued their joke. For someone not happy to see a white in a Native American group, it usually broke the tension.

"I will tell you more of my student here later brother," Two Bears said to Frank, "but I think he needs to be on his way soon."

"Let me get some meat and fruit. Jim, bring your water bottle in and fill it at the sink," Frank directed.

I filled three bottles with water, since it was warming up and I did not know how long I might be. Then I took the food from Frank, with a small bow as I had been taught, turned and headed out to my Jeep. Two Bears followed me to the car.

"You are still good for this?"

"Yes Uncle, if you see me doing this, then I need to do it now."

"Um. Remember what I said about directions. Know where the sun is when you head in and stay aware so you can follow the Grandfather (sun) back out."

"I will. I heard all you said. I have my journal so if I just sit and write that is fine. Maybe I can write about this morning. It may help me understand a little more."

"Okay. We will be here when you return. Frank is a good cook. The stew will be hot and the fry bread fresh. Be safe. Listen to Spirit within and without." With this he turned and went back inside.

I got in the car and headed back the way we had come. Except for one wrong turn, which I realized after just a few miles and could retrace quickly, I had no trouble finding the pull off dirt road with the shot up sign. I checked the position of the sun and slowly headed up the road as Two Bears had instructed me and, after about five miles as Two Bears had said, I came to four, not three, dirt roads leading off it in different directions. One went up steeply so I assumed this was the one to the high open space he spoke of. Another seemed to wend downwards and the other two went off at a forty-five degree angle from one another. I sat, drank some water and cleared my mind. I opened my eyes as a desert critter scooted across the left fork of the two roads. I think it was a desert rat, but was unsure. But I took it as a sign and turned up that dirt track. I drove another six or seven miles, crossing two dry streambeds along the way. Then the track got rocky and pitted, so I slowed down. Soon I was on a narrow road along the side of a hill or mesa, with a drop to my right side. My fear of heights – which I would later learn was really of falling – came into my throat. I slowed even more and gripped the steering wheel so hard I thought my fingerprints might imprint on it. Soon I was past this point and I heaved a big sigh, took in three big breaths and worked the pain out of my fingers. After some water, I moved on. It was truly magnificent out here, with no people in sight nor any sign of people living here. The sky was painted a deep blue, with small puffball, white clouds dotted across its expanse. The rock was red and brown, speckled with small shrubs and cactus-like plants. Coarse clumps of grasses grew in some areas, probably liking certain mineral deposits in their spots. The land opened out big, fairly flat and empty once again and I felt I needed to keep moving into it. After a few more miles I saw some hills to my left with interesting looking narrow canyon areas between them. It had really gotten warm now, but I decided this was a good time for a walk to these hills. And I thought I might find some shade between them where I could sit and write and eat my lunch. I carefully pulled the Jeep off the track, and then wondered why I bothered. I had seen no one and, if someone did come along, they could have pulled around me easily. Ah, habits die hard.

I put two waters, my lunch, some sage and a shell, my journal and pens and a book on Belize I was reading into my small, day hike sized backpack and headed towards the hills and rocks. It took me about thirty minutes to reach them – taking my time and looking around me for signs of animals. When I reached the hills I saw some denser bushes growing in the many shaded spots between them. I stopped, took a long drink of water, and surveyed the land and hills before me. I saw a place with a long, wide swath of shade, some good flat rocks for sitting and shrubs and bushes for plant company, so I headed that way. When I arrived, I laid out my lunch and journal and sat back to eat and relax for a while. I ate quickly, as is my way, drank some more water and just looked at the beauty before me. After a few minutes I decided to write a while before lying down and trying some journeying. I put sage in the shell and lit it, then smudged myself thoroughly. Then I picked up my journal. As I did so I realized all the water I had been drinking had worked its way through me, so I got up to go and relieve myself. I rounded the small hillock I was resting on and walked right into the presence of a man I had no idea was there. I had not seen anyone since leaving the road and thought I was totally alone – hard as it is to be totally alone anywhere any more.

He was a thin, fairly short Native American man sitting with his back against a small tree, looking up at the sky. He was browned and wrinkled by long years in the sun, with eyes that seemed to partially squint – also as if from sun. He had gray hair, which seemed to be tied on the left. I could see one feather tied on the right – a hawk feather, I think, but I could be wrong. He had on a white shirt tied at the throat and a vest of tan skin with some painted symbols faded on the front. His pants were dark gray sweat-type pants as best I could tell. On his feet were plain moccasins. As I walked into his space, not knowing he was there and embarrassed for disturbing him, he heard me and looked over at me. I think he said "Tanyan yaki" quietly – welcome.

"I'm sorry grandfather, I did not know anyone was here. I did not mean to disturb you. I will gather my things and move elsewhere," I said to the elder through my embarrassment of disturbing him. He looked old, but I do not know how old, with the work my years of sun and weather had on his face. I had seen no other cars, so I thought he had parked on the other side of the hills and walked in that way and it had never occurred to me to scout around to be certain there was no one else here.

"No stay, man," he began speaking again. "Did they send you to look for me?"

"No grandfather. My teacher, Two Bears, sent me out this way to see what I would see. I was eating and smudging around the rocks that a way," I said as I pointed the way I had come. "I left my car over by a dirt track I came in on."

"Ah. Yes, I sit here today to see what I need to see also. I was looking at Father Sky for a while. Is he not powerful in his beautiful robes today?"

"Yes, he is." The sky was amazing, with more white clouds scudding across it rapidly now. And a breeze had picked up, which felt good on my skin.

"I look for these cool places where the shade from Mother's plant people allow me to look out without always being in the heat. I have found this to be a good thing," he continued. "What is your name, Grandson?"

"My name is Jim. Jim Petruzzi, Grandfather. I come from Colorado, where I am learning from many teachers the ways of the ancestors."

"So. But what is your Earth name?"

"That is the only name I have Grandfather. In Central America, when I work with Mayan brothers and sisters, I am sometimes jokingly called 'Big White'."

He looked at me as he proceeded to stand, which he did so slowly, working some aches out of his body I assumed. "You have a strong Earth name grandson. You know it well, but it must not yet be in your heart enough to speak it. Where do your people come from?"

"Italy Grandfather. I say I am of the olive skinned tribe. They came to this land just a generation ago."

"They were close to the land in Italy – yes?"

"On one side, yes they were. Nomadic shepherds."

"Your energy is from that side. But you know this also if you just allow yourself to know it. Come and burn some sage with me," he finished as he reached an old stone bowl in which he had sage.

I went to him and he motioned for me to light the sage, which I did. Then he stretched his arms out – an indication he wished me to smudge him. I did this also and he turned so as to get all parts of him. Then he took the stone bowl and motioned for me to reach out. I did so, matching his slow turn, as he smudged me all around. Standing he was of average height, slightly stooped and with a little bit of a potbelly. I sensed great energy coming from him. I was not too adept at reading and feeling these things yet, but his energy was almost like a wave emanating from his body.

"What to you want to see here? How did your waonspekiya [teacher] guide you?" he asked.

"My teacher, Two Bears, did not tell me. I would walk, or drive, or sit or do what my spirit guided me to. My Uncle never adds too much detail or too many directions."

"Very good. Our Kakalas [grandfathers] need to guide, but not direct. This is the way. Only Wanka Tanka [Great Spirit] directs. He must be ksapa [wise to one's spirit]. And what have you seen or felt?"

"I was aware of the Earth Mother all day, as I usually am. Her power seems very strong here. And Father Sky and his beauty as you spoke. These hills also called me over and I to sought the shade."

"What else?"

"Earlier I was at Wounded Knee and, near the massacre sign, I fell in great pain and anguish for some time. That may have lessened what I am seeing here, Grandfather."

"No, not made it smaller, but made it bigger. You are seeing much more, but you need time and guidance to really see and understand. Have your elders spoken of this?"

"They have. I am trying my very best to learn and understand. My heart is open and my spirit reaches for all the Spirit learning I am gifted with."

"Maybe you try too hard? Don't try so hard and more will come. This is also the way. Be open. No 'kunwo' [fear]. There is much to come to you, I see this. It is you who lets it come or does not let it come. You are one who walks with the Earth Mother, so listen to her. Ask her into your heart."

"I am sorry, Grandfather. I do not know the word 'kunwo'," I said.

"Fear, Grandson. Fear. The thing we do not see, or touch, or smell but the thing that stops us."

"Two Bears has spoken of fear many times. Yet, at times I still fear. Sometimes I do not know what, but it can be strong."

"You are human, so you fear. To fear is not a bad thing, but not to look it in it's eyes can cause much suffering. Do you see?"

"I think so. Thank you for this teaching, Grandfather."

"Let the animals guide you. You have powerful animal spirit guides. Wambli [eagle] works with you, Iktomi [spider] will show you the way of the great web of life and your primary animal guide awaits you."

"Do you know what that animal guide is?"

"I see who that guide is," he answered me, without telling me. "You will know him when you are ready. This will be soon. He may come with the coming of your readiness to use the Chanunpa. Or he may come sooner. Time does not matter. Spirit does."

"Thank you again, Grandfather. I am happy we met."

"Yes, we met. If you need another grandfather on your road of spirit walk, you can ask me. Call me. Or visit me. You have teachers, but never too many for anyone."

"I will. How do I find you? Do you live near here? Will Two Bears know where you live?"

"I did not know Two Bears, but now I do from within you. No, just look for me and I will be found. Prayers can always be sent as a way also."

This was a big offer, but I knew the chances of finding his place were small, unless Frank knew him. Still, a big offer. An old Indian man being kind to a younger seeker. As I tried to be a good guide to those younger than me, I welcomed when others did the same for me. It struck me how many elders had been offering to guide me on my way. I wondered why, then put that thought away.

"I will remember this. Thank you again."

"Yes, remember. Maybe I will find you when times show me to," he said with a smile on his face.

"I am certain this white man, getting started late on this road, will need all the help he can get," I smiled back.

"Do not make yourself little!" he said strongly. "That does not honor you or your teachers. Be what you are and stand in that. White... that is your skin. And not even white, but the color of your country as you spoke. Inside you are all five colors. Honor each. Remember each. Walk in balance with all of them. You have a hard road coming at times, as will many now. Prepare for this as you can. Hard is not bad. But hard is hard. You will have illness and loss to see. Seven times around the circle. But you are strong. It will be from your ikpi – your gut – and your chante – your heart that it comes. Especially your heart."

I was confused, but was listening carefully. Then the colors hit me so I asked, "Grandfather, I have been taught there are four colors. The colors of the medicine wheel – red, black, yellow and white. You told me to honor the five. I do not know this."

"Green. The color that surrounds all of the colors. The Earth Mother color. The web the other colors move on. The fifth color," he explained.

"Why the hard way ahead of me? Yellowhair, another teacher, tells us we don't have to walk in pain. Yet I see so many do. Yellowhair walks in a great deal of pain and I know he has been tested often by the stories he tells."

"Great Spirit allows for us to learn as we need to learn it. He does not give pain, but often we walk through pain. Many times it is our choice. And it was our choice before coming to our bodies. How many walks have you had?"

"What walks, Grandfather?"

"How many life walks have you had? Had many here, on the Earth Mother?"

This question of many walks seemed to be coming at me, so I knew there was something for me to learn here. "I only know of this walk I am on now. Two Bears and others talk of many walks and continued growth, but this is new to me. If there were other walks before this, I am unaware of them."

"There were others – many others. And you hide this from yourself. But this is okay, you will understand and see when you need to. As with much of what you will learn and see now."

"I will think more on this, as I have also told Two Bears."

"Go into this, do not think about it. Your spirit will see the truth of these words. Some have had a few walks, some many. This does not make one better than the other, but it puts humans in different places. Keep learning and listening – some you will remember, some will be like smoke until you need it again. It will not be lost, but it may seem smoky sometimes."

The sky had begun to darken and I could see big storm clouds off in the distance. And I wanted to get back to the road and to Frank's house so dinner would not be held for me. We had talked for a long time by the sun, yet it seemed like a short time. "Grandfather, I should leave soon. I need to join Two Bears and his relative for dinner and might need extra time going back if I get lost. I am very thankful for this time we have had. Mitakuye Oyasin."

"You will never get lost if you remember it is a journey. If you get lost, spend time finding yourself. Your spirit, because that is what will be lost. Take a little longer and we can sit, burn some more sage and pray to Great Spirit together."

"Of course. I would like that."

So we moved into the shade next to two small standing people [trees], sat, pulled out his sage bowl and lit a large handful of sage. He reached into a pocket and brought out another plant – it looked like a root – and added it to the sage.

"This is Osha – Bear root. It is for healing. Healing of all the people and healing of the lost connection between the people and the Mother. Use it often as you walk ahead. It will be good for you."

I inhaled deeply, as did he. Then we took turns sending our prayers to Great Spirit. As we finished these I started to get up. He stopped me with a hand motion.

"I would make one more prayer Grandson: To the Earth Mother; so that she may see us; so that she may see you."

"Aho," I agreed readily.

"Earth Mother, Ina [mother] to all who walk here, I ask you to see us this day – my relative here and myself. Grandson and Grandfather. I ask you to see we sit upon your place in honor and respect. I ask you to see this washicun [white man], who is ska, but is sa, zi, sapa and tozi – all five colors. See this one works with you and wishes to work with you. This one wishes to walk canku luta [red road] so he may do what he is meant to do. I ask you to be with him so he will be who he is. I ask this for all the relatives of all there is. Ho, mitakuye oyasin."

He closed his eyes and sat silently, so I did the same. I leaned back against the tree next to me and let my brain go silent. I sat this way for some time, as my legs got sore crossed beneath me. I shifted my weight to ease them and heard softly, "Leave when you are ready.

I will be praying in this way for some time. Thank you for this. I will see you again."

I wanted to speak more, but honored what he asked – quietly getting up and heading back to my gear around the hill where I had eaten. As I approached my 'stuff' in a few minutes I realized it seemed like I had eaten a very long time ago. Yet I was still full and not thirsty. Just as quickly I realized I had all my water and had not offered to leave any for Grandfather, although I did not see that he carried any of his own. Grandfather? How could I not have asked his name? I thought back to our long talk and remembered when he asked for my name, but had no memory of asking for his. I don't do that. I am not rude in this way. I felt terrible on both counts. Yet he had 'excused' me with his words and manner. He had done so in a good way, but clearly to me I had been excused. After a little more reflection, I decided to quietly walk back. If he were still in prayer or journey state, I would simply leave one of my water bottles near enough to him that he would see it. If he was no longer in prayer, and indicated I could come to him again, I would apologize for my stupidity and ask his name. With this in mind, I picked up a water and headed back through the shrubs and around the little hill that had separated us at first.

As I cleared the shrubs and the hill and neared where we prayed I saw no one. I went a little further, thinking it was the next swell of the hill we sat beyond. No one. I thought he might have left in the direction opposite of the way I had come, so I walked around the hill further until I could see beyond it and onto the plain on the other side. Still no one. And no car nor anything else in sight, and I could see far over the flat expanse. Where could he have gone? I wasn't gone that long and there were not many directions he could go in. I walked towards the next hill – maybe ten minutes off – to see if he had rounded that and gone that way. I picked up speed without even realizing it and was in a slow trot as I got there, breathing hard. As I passed around this hill there was again a flat plain until other hills reached up in the far distance. And, again, nothing in any direction. I supposed he could have climbed a hill for another place to pray, but I didn't feel like starting that process with the half dozen hills nearby. I ran back to our original spot, caught my breath and called out, "Grandfather. Relative. It's Jim. I brought water back for you. Can you hear me?"

I stood and waited, then yelled out once again. Again I waited, but heard nothing. I had no idea where he had gone and no way to find him quickly, so I turned back, went to my gear, packed my backpack and headed to my car. I replayed the elders' words in my head as I walked, realizing how many things I had not questioned. Walking in this thoughtful way allowed me to trip, fall and slide across a rock — cutting open my left leg just below the knee. It bled at once and I wrapped my kerchief around it, muttering curses about my own stupidity. I knew to stay alert whenever you hike, but the talk had flustered me. Well, some ointment and a bandage would take care of this. And I had both in the car.

When I got back to the car I found four large feathers in the windshield. Sitting between the windshield and the hood. I didn't recognize them, but asked permission to take them with me. As I sensed I could take them, I placed them in the back of the Jeep, got in and drove off. I had no trouble retracing my path and was soon back at the shot-up sign and the road just beyond it. I had checked the sun before driving out so my direction would be true and thought it was not as far advanced into the day as I thought. Well, I was still learning to judge these things. The clouds were also gone — they must have blown through while I drove. Just some of the puffy, white clouds were visible meandering slowly across the sky. I headed back to Frank's — a ride of about forty minutes once I had reached the road.

28 | Stepping Up

THE RIDE BACK WAS UNEVENTFUL — AS BEST AS I REMEMBER SINCE I was going over and over in my head what had happened out on the land. And being confused, forgetting to go into my heart around it, not my head. Soon I pulled up to Frank's house and walked over to Two Bears and Frank, who were sitting on the porch on the side of the building.

"Ho," I called out as I walked towards them.

"Ho, Jim," Two Bears answered. "Did you fall?"

"Yes. My head somewhere else as I walked back from some hills. I put ointment on it. It is just a cut."

"So, I thought you would be much longer," Frank spoke up.

"I thought it was getting late and didn't want you to hold dinner for me. Or want you to eat all the elk," I said with a smile. "And the heavy clouds coming in earlier made me think it was a good time to go."

"Dinner is two hours off. You have only been gone about three hours," Frank responded.

I never took any metal or electronic devices with me when I did ceremony, meditated or journeyed. I was taught that way by Yellowhair first, and other teachers later. These things can interfere with your spiritual field and life energy. I found later, when working with alternative healers, the same belief held. So I had no watch with me and the clock on the Jeep's dash had been reading twelve o'clock for over a year now. The three hundred dollars they wanted to fix it made me very comfortable with its twelve reading.

"That can't be right. I drove over an hour to where I stopped for a walk, hiked in thirty minutes, ate and rested, then spent over two hours with an elder I met, then had to go back the same way."

"Still, it has only been three hours," Two Bears confirmed.

I had to have been gone at least five hours, maybe more. Yet it had seemed later, by the sun, when I was in the hills than when I was driving back to the road. This all seemed a perfect fit, as nothing that had happened today made sense to my rational mind. Maybe I was dreaming this and would awake to find we were all still back in Rapid City waiting to go to breakfast.

"Who did you meet?" Two Bears asked solemnly.

"An elder grandfather. We sat and talked and burned sage and prayed for two to three hours."

"His name," Two Bears prompted.

"I am foolish, relatives. I never asked. I don't know how that happened. He asked for mine and he asked about you Grandfather. I felt very good about our time together. It flowed in a good way. But I don't know his name. How stupid."

"No, maybe not so," Two Bears continued. "What did he look like? Where did you meet? How did he get there?"

I began telling the story of my time with the elder, when Two Bears stopped me.

"Start when you left your car and tell me everything you remember. Even if a grass looked small or a rock looked like something else," he instructed.

So I started from the time I left the car and tried to remember all that I could. When I got to the point the elder and I were going to do prayers, he stopped me again.

"What did this elder look like?"

I described the man I had met in all the detail I recalled, then added how good it felt being with him. How I felt he was questioning me, but also teaching me. And how he offered to teach me more at some later time, but I did not know how to find him. Then again, I had met with other elders in Central America by chance in areas different from where we first met. So who knew – maybe.

"Good. Finish your story," Two Bears instructed.

I did as I was told and finished the story to the point I got back into the Jeep and headed down the dirt road towards the paved road.

"Good. When did it seem it was earlier than you thought?" Two Bears asked.

"I don't know, Two Bears. I remember thinking the sun was higher than I thought as I headed down the dirt road. I thought I remembered it being lower when I looked at the big storm clouds to the east of where we sat and prayed."

"Good. Describe the elder once again. All the details you have," Two Bears instructed further.

"I don't think I will remember any more, but I will try." With this, I again described the elder I had met.

When I finished I saw Frank was looking at Two Bears, who was deep in thought. I looked to him also and waited quietly while he sat peering at his hands. After a while he grunted and looked up at me. Then he looked to Frank.

"Frank, you still have all those books you love so much?"

"I do, brother. The back room now has shelves on three walls and they are mostly filled," Frank answered.

"You have *Black Elk Speaks*?"

"Several copies," Frank responded.

"Would you get them for us?" Two Bears asked.

Frank got up and headed for the door. Two Bears watched him go, then turned back to me. "Do you know of Black Elk?"

"I have heard the name. Wallace Black Elk isn't it? A medicine person on one of the Sioux Reservations I think," I answered.

"No. Black Elk. Wallace is his grandson or something who lives up this a way. Black Elk of many visions. Black Elk, of the book *Black Elk Speaks*."

"I have heard of the book – or saw it somewhere, but I never read it. I thought Wallace Black Elk was the full name of Black Elk," I said.

"Um. Let's wait for Frank," Two Bears said and took a long drink from a coffee mug beside him. I had not seen him drink while we were speaking and thought the coffee must be cold.

"Do you want me to get you some hot coffee Grandfather?"

"Yes. This sits cold in me. Thank you, aho," he said as he handed me his mug.

I went inside, passing Frank along the way, and asking if there was more coffee.

"Pot's almost empty, but the coffee is still on the counter. Make a pot for our relative. He takes his black. Bring me one if you will. Black, also. I will keep my brother company until you get back. Oh, mugs are above the sink. Pick one for you, also."

I went in and made coffee, then poured three cups of the hot, black, strong coffee I had brewed in the pot. It was camp coffee, so I strained it through some paper towels I found. Then I carefully carried all three back outside. Two Bears and Frank were sitting talking, the book open between them on a small table. They moved the open book and another, unopened beneath it, to the side so I could put the mugs down. We each took a couple of sips, then Frank spoke up, "Good coffee. I like mine strong. You like yours even more strong."

"I was telling Jim here just a little about Black Elk. He thought Wallace and Black Elk were the same. I told him they were related," Two Bears explained to Frank.

"Ah, yes. Wallace still lives up this way. Here in Pine Ridge, but he travels a lot."

"Frank and I have been looking at *Black Elk Speaks* while you brought coffee. Please tell me of the looks of the elder once more, with all the details," Two Bears bade me to do.

I thought he was testing me, or having fun with me but, as I looked up at him, I could see he was very serious. As was Frank, when I glanced his way. So I swallowed the joke I was about to make and began describing the elder for a third time.

They listened, drinking coffee and Two Bears softly uttering "um" or "ho" on occasion. He smiled a couple of times as he listened. When I was done Two Bears looked at Frank and nodded once...like a question. Frank nodded back.

"Look at this book, Jim. Tell me what is says to you, if it speaks to you," Two Bears said as he handed me the well-read copy of *Black Elk Speaks*; the one that had been sitting open on the table.

I took the book and felt it in my hand. Then I turned it over and looked at the cover art. Tipis clustered on an open plain, if I remember correctly. I leafed through it next and scanned down the chapter titles. I saw, in the beginning of the foreword, it was written by a John Neihardt, as Black Elk told it to him.

"It looks and feels like a book I will read Two Bears. If I ever get the time with all the course books I need to keep up with. I like it's energy – just from the cover and the chapter titles," I told Two Bears.

"Look more. Look more deeply. Take your time," he guided me.

I leafed through the pages, more slowly this time, and saw there were pictures or drawings in the middle. I went to these and looked at them as I flipped the pages. Pictures of Sioux life, drawings of some of Black Elk's visions and pictures of various people. I saw elders in traditional garb, then a white man with two Indian men, then a family, then. . . I went back to the picture of the white man and the two Indian men. The Indian next to the white man – Neihardt in the note under it – was Black Elk – also by the note. It was also the elder I was with today; I was certain of this. Maybe a little younger, but still him.

"This is the elder I spoke with and prayed with today, Two Bears. I met Black Elk? That's amazing. And I never asked his name. Frank, do you know where he lives here on the rez?"

"I know where he lived Jim," Frank offered. "But Black Elk took his walk about forty years ago. I think his grave is about twenty miles north of Wounded Knee."

"I must be wrong then," I said. "But it looks exactly like him. Does Wallace look like him?"

"A little, I think," Frank answered. "But you even talked about his clothes and hair. They are like that in the picture."

"No mistake Jim. Do not worry about how. You met Black Elk," Two Bears said quietly. "You have met your first spirit guide. Usually this is in dreamtime, but you met face-to-face. This is very powerful. I don't know I ever heard a story like this before, this soon on the road. He will be a powerful teacher for you. You can ask him to be so, he has already offered. He may come in dreams or during ceremony, but maybe, some time along, he will come as a two-legged again."

"You mean all this Grandfather?"

He did not speak, but just looked me in the eyes. Yes, he meant all this.

"Black Elk was at the Battle of Little Big Horn and later, wounded at Wounded Knee. As I recall in the books, it was after Wounded Knee that he thought he had failed his reason for being that he had seen in his visions," Frank told me. "Here, this is yours," he said as he handed me the other copy of *Black Elk Speaks*, which he had picked up off the table as he spoke.

"Thanks for this, Frank," I said taking the book from him. "I feel all out of balance, relatives. Too many things coming at me here today. Now, Two Bears, you are telling me Black Elk, dead forty years, is visiting me and will be a guide. I don't know. You've told me stories of things like this. And I've read what you and others have guided me to. But, come on. I'm a few years on this road, but just a beginner. Two Bears, you've walked the spirit road your whole life. You're a teacher and healer. Why are all these things coming my way so quickly? I understand purpose and roles – I get that. And I committed to God to serve when Bonnie and I came here, but I thought that would be my non-profit work and working with young people. I didn't know it meant all these new ways I'm learning. I love them, it seems like I am home, but how can I be worthy of all everyone is sharing with me? I think..."

"Ho. Slow down, you are getting all confused. Going into doubt and fear," Two Bears broke in on me. "Don't question what comes and what happens. Just be with it. Have I not taught you this is the way? Do you question what Great Spirit has for you to do? You are when you speak of not being worthy or doubting what you see and hear. Be still a few minutes and we will all drink our coffee."

I sat, finishing my coffee, with so many ideas and images racing through my head I felt like I would explode. I knew I needed to go into my heart, as Two Bears always taught, but couldn't seem to stop my rational brain from taking over. The man I met certainly looked like the picture of Black Elk they shared with me. But that made no sense to my brain. All the things I was being taught flooded through me, tripping over each other. These were wonderful things when you read about them or heard stories about others, but when you had to believe them and accept them where they centered on you – this was not computing. My heart was racing and I was sweating, so I closed my eyes and focused on calming my mind and going into my heart. In a few minutes I felt a little ease of the tension in my body and reopened my eyes. Two Bears and Frank were softly talking together about dinner.

"May I go sit by your inipi by myself for a while Frank?" I asked.

"Of course. Go in with sage if you like."

"Before you go," Two Bears spoke up, "Let me speak. Being worthy is something all two-leggeds fight with. Worthy of what? Who? If Great Spirit has given us work to do, how can we not be worthy? Do we know more than Wanka Tanka?"

"Thank you, Grandfather. I hear your words and know they are true, but..."

"I am not done Jim. You have always been on the spirit road. Even on this walk, it has been the road of spirit and heart you walk. You have travelled far and met many. And you have worked in your heart. The last three or four years you speak of. Maybe you are now a full time student of the Red Road and the ways of people connected to the Earth. Maybe you needed to be who you were before becoming who you are and who you will be later. When I was a boy my grandfather and father both taught me about the ways. As did my uncle and other teachers. I did not want to hear. I was afraid of much of what I heard. And the white culture was teaching me the Christian ways in the school. It was all confusing, so I let it drop for many years. I went through all I was asked to – lessons from everyone – but no 'chante', no heart, was in it from me. Many go through this way. It is not wrong, it is growth and understanding. Go sit with that now," Two Bears finished.

So I took my shell and sage bag and my Chanunpa and went to Frank's lodge. I started a small fire in the pit, burned sage and smudged myself. Then I realized I did wish to sit in the lodge. I brought the sage, tobacco and pipe in with me and quietly sat along the wall opposite the doorway. The place where male and female lodge participants meet. In the lodge, women enter first, moving around the pit. Then the men enter, so the place I sat was the one place a man and a woman would sit side-by-side. This felt right, so I burned a lot of sage, inhaled deeply and tried not to think. I found some bear root in the bottom of my sage bag, so I added it to the burning sage shell. I also put a small piece under my tongue, as you do for personal healing. I sat for some time just breathing in the sage and osha, calming my mind and letting any pictures that wished to come to me to come. None did, I just experienced a quiet, peaceful darkness. Just what I needed.

At some point I decided to close the lodge door, take out my Chanunpa and sit quietly with it, while the sage and osha continued to burn. I went to the door on hands and knees, in the direction of the sun, closed it and slowly returned to my place. I sat with the Chanunpa cradled in my left arm, bowl in my hand and stem tip resting on my heart and I sent prayers for clarity and understanding up to Great Spirit. When I finished I felt the strong need to load the pipe, which I did with tobacco and sage. This was the strongest I had ever felt the pipes' presence and I wished I could open it and send more prayers that way. I would never do this unless the time came that Two Bears told me it was time. So I lay down with the pipe on my chest, added more sage and osha to the bowl and let my spirit roam. Mental pictures of many animals came to me. First with a large number of wolves looking my way, then birds in huge flocks, then creatures from under the Earths' waters, then wolves again. Then back to quiet blackness – the blackness of the lodge I lay in. Then a high grass plain as far as one could see, dotted with Tatanka – buffalo, in huge numbers. After this the wolves returned and faded back into the dark space. I must have drifted into sleep, because I became aware of achy bones sometime later. I sat up, did a short gratitude prayer, carefully replaced my pipe in its bag, gathered the sage shell and left the lodge. It was almost dark and I was afraid I had held up dinner so I headed to the house. Frank was just bringing the stewpot to the table as I entered, so my timing was perfect. And I was starved.

Two Bears nodded as I entered and, without words, we sat around the table. The fry bread was still hot, sending its aroma into the air. Big potatoes filled another bowl and a salad was next to them. A feast and one I was ready for. Frank said a prayer of thanks and we loaded our plates. The elk stew was wonderful, perfectly spiced and full of tender elk and fresh vegetables. I filled my bowl a second time.

"Many thanks for allowing me to use your lodge that way," I said to Frank.

"Ho. I am glad it helped you."

"How do you feel, Jim?" Two Bears asked.

"A little calmer, but still full of confusion. The time in the lodge was a huge help. I saw and felt a lot."

"Tell us, if you will," Two Bears said.

I told them of what I had done, where I had sat and prayed and what I saw when I journeyed laying down. Two Bears asked several questions about the animals and the settings they were in. I answered these and then told them of the way the pipe felt today, so much stronger than ever before. And how I had wanted to open it and send prayers up in its smoke. And that I had filled it and knew I was to leave it filled when I left the lodge. Two Bears asked where the pipe was while I prayed and journeyed and I told him it lay on my chest.

"What do you feel now, Nephew?" Two Bears then asked.

"Confusion, doubt but also calm and trust in whatever is happening."

"And fear?" from Two Bears.

"Maybe some, but not like before."

"Good. I spoke with Frank here and asked if we could do a lodge tonight. Are you willing?"

"That would be perfect. I would start the fire, if you wish it Frank," I said to Frank. Some like to tend their own fire and others do not ask another to tend theirs until they know them well, but I thought I would ask.

"Yes. That would be good. Go and start the fire and heating the rocks while I clean up here after we finish all this food. There are twenty-eight rocks on the far side of the pit. I was going to use them for the next lodge, so we will use them tonight."

I finished my meal, thanked Frank and went to lay the fire. Usually a meal is not eaten before the lodge, but this had been the most unusual day of my life so far, so why question anything? Frank had a large pile of wood for lodges, so I laid wood on the ground and began working in the rocks. Then I laid the upright logs, making certain all of the grandfather rocks were covered. After a short prayer I lit the pyre. Flames began leaping skyward in just a few minutes. I have always seemed to be able to light and tend a fire in a good way, heating rocks that are hot and red. It seemed it would also be this way tonight. Now I was feeling more comfortable, doing things and preparing for ceremony in a way I knew and understood. Doing ceremony, learning from teachers of different cultures, praying in new ways….then things begin to happen and you need to deal with fear and confusion combined with the wonder and joy of it. Be careful what you ask for I guess. But, it is all good. Things that need to be faced, are faced, or walked away from. It is the decision each of us makes.

I added wood, said prayers and tended the fire for the next two hours. Then Two Bears and Frank walked out and came over to the lodge. I was certain they waited to give me some time alone, which I appreciated. I smudged them both and we went into lodge together. Frank had brought his Chanunpa with him and mine already lay on the side of the altar where Two Bears usually asked me to rest her. Two Bears handed me his Chanunpa and asked me to rest it on the antler that sat on the altar for that purpose. Then Frank asked me to rest his next to it, both held upright by the antler. Two Bears then took my Chanunpa and moved it from the side, also resting it on the antler.

"Frank, Two Bears, I am unsure how you wish to proceed tonight. This is Frank's lodge, so I ask you what you would like?" I said.

"Two Bears and I have spoken and we decided to pour two doors each. It is an honor to have my relative here to pour with me. And I would also be honored if you would carry the rocks, Jim, as Two Bears tells me you do at his lodge," Frank explained.

"Thank you, Frank. I am always honored to work with the rocks and the fire."

With this protocol out of the way, we entered the lodge. After a prayer from Frank, I left the lodge and brought in the first seven rocks. Then I re-entered and took my place to the left of the door. Frank opened with a song of gratitude, then poured water. He spoke of how he found his way to the red road and those who helped him learn the ways and accept what came to him. He spoke of his two-legged teachers among his people and his spirit teachers from the other side. He then spoke of his animal guides and how important they had been to him − guiding, protecting and helping him connect to the Earth Mother. Then he spoke of how far back these traditions and ways went and how far forward they would go. Finally he spoke of how the four colors now needed to come together and practice good ways of walking together and how this was in many of the stories and prophecies of many peoples. A second song and more water followed, then I was asked to open the door.

I left the lodge and brought in seven more, very red, grandfather rocks. Then I again re-entered, closed the flap, and waited for Two Bears to begin the second door. He poured several ladles of water and sat silently for a while, then he beat the drum without a song. Frank and I shook rattles and Frank blew his eagle bone flute several times. The energy of the sounds was strong and cleansing and I allowed my spirit to roam free, with no thoughts, as I participated and listened to the music we made together. Finally Two Bears hit a loud one-two beat and we ended the music.

"This is a powerful lodge we share tonight, brothers," Two Bears began. "The ancestors fill the lodge, as do many spirit animals. This is good as we have things we will speak and do tonight. I see ancestors of all colors here, something I have seen only twice before. I welcome them. As I welcome the animal people."

Frank said 'aho', affirming I assumed, that he too saw many visitors to this lodge. For me, I sensed powerful energy, but saw no one with us.

"I would ask my brother, Frank, that we hold bringing in the Chanunpa until the fourth door. I ask his permission for this, as I see something else will appear to us by then," Two Bears carried on.

"Ho, brother. As you speak it," Frank quietly acquiesced.

"I will sing the lodge song and healing for all the people, then ask Jim to bring in the next seven rocks. I thank him for tending the fire and the rocks. The Grandfathers get very red and hot for him. He has a way. After you bring in the rocks, I ask you to sit the fire for a few minutes so I may speak with Frank. Maybe you would get more water, as we are pouring heavy tonight," Two Bears said.

"Ho, Uncle, as you wish," I answered.

Two Bears poured the remainder of the bucket of water – a ladleful at a time – over the rocks, so they hissed and sang as he began to drum. His song, as always, was strong and spoke to my heart. When he finished, I threw open the door and went for the rocks as requested. He handed the bucket out to me, which I put to the side until I finished bringing in the rocks.

Once the rocks were in the lodge, I set off with the bucket to Frank's house, where I filled it at an outside tap. Then I carried it back to the lodge. I sat near the fire until Two Bears called me – asking me to pass the water back in to him. I handed in the bucket, then re-entered and took my place. Frank began this third door – the healing door – with a song to the Earth Mother. Then he asked if any around the circle wished to speak. Neither Two Bears nor I felt the need at that point, so he poured water as he sang another song. This one to the ancestors – asking their guidance and teaching. He then added the healing herbs to the rocks. He added five different herbs...and he added large amounts, so the lodge filled with their aroma. Bear root – osha – was particularly strong in my nostrils. I breathed it in as I asked for healing and strength to continue to learn the spiritual way.

Then Frank said, "Let us again play the music as we did in the first door. In time to the sound coming from the rocks. Jim, I pass you the drum. Please beat us to where we need to go." He handed me the drum, through the hands of Two Bears so it came in the clockwise direction – like the path of the sun. I was nervous and, yes, again feeling unworthy to lead the drum with these two medicine people in the lodge with me, but I breathed deep, asked for guidance, and began beating what came from my heart. And it worked! I beat out a rhythm I had not played before and whooped when it came to me to do so. Two Bears and Frank also whooped and sang as they played flute and shook rattles. Tears began flooding my face and my voice chocked on several yells, but I laughed at the same time. It was shear pleasure for me. I felt like I was releasing a lot of stress and fear, especially around the things that had happened that day. I went on for a long time – probably twenty minutes or more – then felt it was time to stop, so I yelled three times, hit the drum hard twice and ended. Frank thanked me for connecting to the beauty of the drum and thanked Great Spirit for allowing us this time. Then he spoke.

"I remember the time I was given my Chanunpa and tobacco as we drummed here tonight. And my grandfathers welcoming me to my understanding. And the first inipi I ever poured. These are good things to remember. I also remembered the times I wondered why I had accepted spirit things that have come my way. My doubt and feeling I was less when around them. These are also good things to remember. Jim, please hand me the drum and I will close this door with another song."

I passed him the drum and he started a beautiful, soft, song that was happy and sad at the same time. A song I had never heard before. He poured as he sang and the lodge again filled with steam and the aroma of the herbs. When he finished he asked me to open the door and then wait for Two Bears. I threw open the door and sat watching the steam billow out of the door towards the fire. I was seeing all kinds of shapes and images in the smoke – as you do when looking up at the clouds. I was truly relaxed and in a place of great comfort – and it suddenly came to me this was the first time in a long while that I had felt this way.

"Frank, I would ask you to go out and bring in the rocks for the fourth round. Jim, I ask you to sit and ask Spirit and the ancestors for support and understanding as the rocks enter," Two Bears finally spoke. "When the rocks are in I will also ask Frank to pass in all three Chanunpas and tobacco pouches. Jim, please hold yours to your heart when we close the door. I will speak more then."

I was surprised that all three Chanunpas would be with us for this door and especially surprised that Two Bears was allowing me to bring in my pipe to connect with as we prayed. If a Chanunpa is brought into the lodge, it is the Chanunpa of the one leading the ceremony. Some, like Yellowhair, prefer opening their pipes around the fire after the lodge, others in the lodge like Two Bears. But I had not yet been in a lodge with several Chanunpas present. I felt honored to be included in this way. I began my prayers, silently at first, as Two Bears had instructed me. Soon I felt I needed to speak my words aloud so I did so as Frank brought in the rocks. Two Bears said 'aho' several times as I prayed, so I knew he was connecting with me and felt good about my words. I gave gratitude, asked guidance and prayed for the healing of the hoop wherever it was broken. I finished as Frank came back in and closed the flap so we could begin the fourth round.

Two Bears began pouring water and adding sage to the rocks. This was also not his usual way, as he only added sage at the beginning of the ceremony and in the healing round, but I welcomed the strong smell of the sage as it burned.

"Great Spirit, Earth Mother, ancestors, animal guides, I ask for your guidance as we begin this ceremony of welcoming tonight. I ask you to guide my words and actions and those of my relative here, Frank. And I ask your support and guidance of our relative, Jim here, Redwolf, as he answers what you ask through us," Two Bears spoke with deep sincerity.

Redwolf? What was Redwolf or, more to the point, was I Redwolf? And why a redwolf? My senses were totally alert now, as things were beginning to transpire that were new and yet, I sensed, were to be very powerful for me.

"Now we sing and beat the drum," Two Bears directed. After the song he poured more water and sat inhaling deeply. I could hear him filling his lungs and then exhaling in a huge rush. He did this seven times. Probably to honor the seven directions.

"Jim, I knew we were to take a few journeys and Wounded Knee was to be the first, but I had no thought of what might come out of this. I am surprised to see what has been coming your way here. And glad. I did not expect this piece coming now for some time yet. But these things are not for me to decide, they are Spirit's. So, I ask, are you ready?" Two Bears asked.

"I do not know what it is I am to be ready for, but I have complete faith in you as a teacher, so I am ready."

"Good. And are you ready for the next part of your journey to start, here with me and Frank tonight?" he asked.

"Yes, Uncle. Frank's inipi is a powerful one and I feel at home here. And I see Frank as another with good medicine. I am thankful for him and his place."

"Good. So, tonight, we will ask you the question seven times, in seven ways, and you will seek your answers, which you will give us," Two Bears finished.

I did not answer this at first. I was too stunned. When someone is offered the gift of opening and carrying the Chanunpa he or she is asked seven times whether they are willing to do so. The questions take different forms, as I was told in the past, yet the answer needs to be 'yes' to each before that person moves ahead as a pipe carrier. Two Bears was telling me he felt it was now time for me to step up and carry a Chanunpa, if I was ready. Yet I had been learning and handling a Chanunpa for only a little over four years. How could I be ready for this? I had so much to learn yet.

"Uncle, I am but a small stone on the ground. I did not know if I would ever be able to serve as a Chanunpa carrier, but certainly not this quickly. You, and others, have taught me so much, yet I know so little. I don't feel worthy to be given this gift yet," I spoke.

"Nephew, you have learned much and you will learn much more, and not just of the red ways, but from all the colors of the wheel. Carrying the Chanunpa, and all the responsibilities that gives you, is not something you 'are given'. It is not that you pass a test and it is your time. It does not come from your teachers – it comes from Spirit inside you. And I heard your story today, as did my relative here, Frank, so I hear your Spirit inside is ready for the questions. You are a small stone. That is good, so you do not go into having a big head. Yet, what am I? What is Frank? Yellowhair? Lawrence? Flying Eagle? We are all small stones. That is all any ever is. How can you not be worthy if Great Spirit has guided you to this road? Do you doubt His word? I know you do not. We do not give any gift here tonight, except the questions as we ask them. It is for you to pick up the pipe or walk another way," Two Bears instructed.

"I hear you, Uncle. I bow to your experience," I said.

"Hear me. Hear Frank. But it is you who must decide from the heart," Two Bears responded. "Do you wish to hear the questions?"

"Yes," I said, surprising myself with this answer.

"Of course. As I knew you would answer," Two Bears said. He began pouring water once again and Frank put more sage on the rocks.

"Jim: Take this Bear Root and put it under your tongue. And take this sage and rub it all over your body," Frank told me as he tapped my arm so I would know he held out the herbs to me. "Then put some of this Sweetgrass behind your ears. All of this will cleanse you and open you to all who sit in this inipi."

I did as instructed and waited for the next words from either of my elders here.

"Before we ask the seven questions I have another thing to speak of," Two Bears spoke. "I have listened to you speak several times about the animal spirits guiding you and each time wolf is big. He comes to you and stays your side. As we prayed tonight it came to me your Earth name is to be 'Redwolf'. Do you accept this name I wish to gift you?"

"I am honored to have a name I can be called by my brothers and sisters that has the power of the wolf. But why Redwolf, Uncle? I have never seen a red wolf. Or are they red in the spirit world?"

"There are red wolves. You will see why wolf is your primary totem – at least for now – and why a red wolf when you need to see it and understand it. This is as it always is, even though I know that I have no answer that makes you happy now. I do not know the answer now, but I clearly saw this wolf in the second and third doors."

"It feels good, Uncle. Redwolf. I have black hair, graying beard and a brown mustache on my tanned olive skin, but no red. So maybe it's time for some red in my wolf guide. I like this name and thank the wolf people for travelling with me, guiding me and protecting me as we go," I relied back to Two Bears.

"Good. They will do all these things and much more. You have other strong animal guides and others to be with you later. Stay alert for each and what each is willing to offer you," Two Bears said, completing his thoughts on this. "Now we begin the ceremony of accepting the Chanunpa."

I will share three of the questions asked me that night, but not all seven. There are some things that are not to be shared with all. This is not ego nor trying to be secretive, but simply honoring those who have taught me and my road. Some things need to be learned by each person as he or she has a desire for a particular piece of knowledge. Some of the questions I was asked were specifically around me and my beliefs so my sharing them would not assist anyone else. Just as I would not share all of the prayers, ceremonies and ways of building an inipi. You can google 'sweat lodge' and find a thousand descriptions of how to build a sweat lodge. If you follow many of these you will create a structure that resembles the lodges I have been in and assisted in building. I also gave the general building method of this earlier as I know it. But you would have a structure, not an inipi. The spirit would not be in it. It may well be a good place to sit and meditate, but not a lodge connected to the web of the spirit realm. Knowing too much, without the learning and growth before that knowledge comes, can also be dangerous if misused. As I have seen happen and as we have all read about from time to time. So I ask you to trust me that there are no 'great secrets' I am with holding, but rather honoring the traditions and ways of my spiritual path.

"Redwolf, do you understand the great responsibility of carrying the Chanunpa and, if you do, are you willing to be one who carries the pipe?" Two Bears asked.

"I do Uncle. And I am certain you will guide me well in learning how to honor these responsibilities," I answered. "I am ready to carry the Chanunpa."

"Do you understand you must honor the requests of all who ask you to open your Chanunpa to their aid as long as their way is good?" Frank asked.

"I do, relative," I responded.

"So, are you willing to open and carry this Chanunpa?" he finished his question.

"I am, Frank."

And so the questions continued, some much more difficult than others, so that I spent time being certain that I answered truthfully and with full and open heart. To each of the seven questions I answered that I was ready and willing to carry the pipe. Something I was not sure of before the questions began.

"You have answered in your heart the questions we asked here tonight," Two Bears began after the final question, "So we will now smoke each Chanunpa here, passing them one to the other. Please guide us in a prayer before we do this, Redwolf."

"Great Mystery, Great Spirit, I send gratitude for this ceremony here tonight and for the healing we have asked for wherever it is needed. I humbly ask for your permission to continue to learn the spiritual ways of healing from my elders so I may play whatever role you have for me. I thank my relatives here for their guidance and Two Bears for his continued teaching and patience with me. I open this Chanunpa tonight as the next step on my journey of learning and prayer. I thank White Buffalo Calf Woman for bringing the pipe to the people and for allowing me the honor of carrying one. I ask her for her continued guidance so that I use the abilities I have and the teachings I receive in a good way. I pray again for Two Bears and Frank and all my relatives around the circles in which I sit and in which I do not. I will continue to broaden my commitment I made to serve the common good as I grow and evolve. These things I say not just for myself or my relatives here, but for all the creatures of the Earth Mother so we may help to heal the sacred hoop wherever it is broken. Ho, Mitakuye Oyasin."

"Good," Two Bears responded. "Now we load the pipes as we bring in the seven directions. I ask permission of both of you to pass our pipes around our circle here with each pinch we add so we may fill all of the pipes. And our sacred tobaccos will be joined as one."

"Ho," Frank said in agreement. Then they looked at me and I realized I also now needed to answer this sort of request.

"Ho," I also agreed. We loaded the pipes a pinch of tobacco at a time, burning sage and passing them between us as Two Bears had requested. We also took turns with the short prayer we said to each direction as we did this.

"Redwolf," Two Bears said to me, "Please open your Chanunpa first as you are the one we honor in this way tonight."

I felt like an imposter. I was used to serving Two Bears – tending fires, carrying rocks, bringing water, answering his questions – but not used to being one involved this way in a ceremony. I let that thought go remembering Two Bears words about worthiness. I took my pipe in my hands and raised it to the heavens saying what came into my head, "I am honored to be able to open this pipe and accept all the roles and responsibilities this brings to me for the rest of my walk. I feel ready now. I ask permission of Great Spirit to open this pipe. I ask guidance from White Buffalo Calf Woman. I also ask Black Elk to be here in spirit and guide my hands. I invite in the Wolf People to celebrate with me and keep me safe. And I ask the permission of the Chanunpa to now open it, smoke in a good way and send my prayers and thanks to Great Spirit."

With this said I lowered the pipe and saw my hands were shaking badly. And I was sweating even though we now sat out in the cold air. I took a small twig from the ground and put it into the hot embers of the fire. When it burst into flame I raised it to the Chanunpa and lit the tobacco and herbs in the bowl. As I pulled air through the stem the tobacco caught and billows of pure white smoke began dancing heavenward. I drew in smoke four times and held the pipe for Frank next to me as he had just lit his pipe and was now taking in his four puffs, as was Two Bears next to him around our circle. We passed the pipes, smoking each in turn, until there was only a little tobacco left in each. Then we each took our own pipe back and finished all the tobacco, so that no prayers or intentions would be left in any unburned tobacco in the bowl. We then emptied the ash into the fire.

"How do you feel, Redwolf?" Frank asked.

"Nervous, happy, small, big, tired," I answered him honestly.

"So," he said. "A day that will stay with you your whole journey here on the Earth Mother. You will carry this Chanunpa in a good way. I am certain of that."

"Thank you, Frank. I will do that with whatever skills I can use."

"Remember what we spoke of before," Two Bears spoke up. "Your walk will be different than most. You will walk with all the colors and you will carry many Chanunpas as you go. I do not understand this, but I see it. So be prepared for whatever comes and trust it when it does. What you need will find you when you stay in trust; problems will find you when you do not. Take it all as good things, each with lessons for you to understand. There is much more we can all speak of, but I think our new Chanunpa carrier here needs some rest. We will speak in the morning."

We packed our pipes in their bags and took our tobacco and pipes and headed to Frank's house, where I longed for any place to lay down. I had expected something monumental as I lit the Chanunpa for the first time – and I did feel great energy – but no skies opened, no cows rained down on us and no aliens landed beside us. Then again, with all I had seen and sensed today, what would have seemed monumental? I remember sleeping very soundly and awakening at five in the morning, as was my way back then.

29 | To the Mountain to Meet the Grandmother

I LAID IN MY BED – A FAIRLY NARROW, SHORT ONE FOR MY SIZE – AND LET the day before run through my mind and heart. I felt like I was reading a book, not re-visiting things that had just happened to me. How did this white, Italian kid, raised Catholic, from back East ever end up on this journey? I wondered and marveled at that thought, as I still do today, but did not feel the sense of unworthiness I had so often. Then I began making plans for all the things I needed to do this summer while the University was on break. I had not yet learned the joke of making too many plans. I'm certain I made God laugh many times – probably daily – during this part of my walk. Well, better laughing than crying – and I have done enough of both to attest to that. I smelled coffee about six, so I got up and joined Frank at the table. Two Bears came in just after me and poured his over-sized cup to the top. He took a deep swallow, smacked his lips and looked at us with a big smile.

"You both know how much I love this first coffee," he shared. "How did you sleep, Jim?"

"Like I was dead, Uncle. I slept from the second I lay down until an hour ago. That's a lot for me."

"I would not have been surprised if you slept three days after what came to you," Frank said seriously.

"Yes. I am to call Bonnie this morning, but don't think I will share too much until I can do it in person."

"Does she expect us?" Two Bears asked.

"Not really. She was good with whatever you decided we needed to do. What shall I tell her?"

"Hmmm. Are you ready for more? It is okay if you have had enough for now. You have much to bring into your spirit and make part of you," Two Bears said.

"What did you have in mind?"

"A Hanbleche. I think two nights and three days on the mountain. Frank has agreed to come with us if you wish this. He knows a place that is very sacred, but very far out so no one will disturb you. This is no easy thing. No food or water. The fire burns and we make a small circle around you. You cannot leave this for the whole time. This is as I have told you before, but now you will have your Chanunpa and tobacco and will open it if you think it is so," Two Bears offered.

"I think I want to do this. No, I know I do. Strongly. But let me ask Bonnie if these days are okay with her."

"Good. When can you call her?" Two Bears asked.

"As soon as we finish this coffee. She also gets up early and I know she and Carmen will head to the rocks early. They knew we would not be back until tomorrow at the earliest."

When I called Bonnie, I told her there were many things I would tell her of when we got home. And asked about the days on the mountain. She was happy to hear this plan as she and Carmen had found some fascinating rock structures they wanted to explore. We talked a while longer and then Bonnie said they wanted to get an early start, wished me well and sent her love and we hung up. I went back and told Frank and Two Bears I was ready. We ate, packed some food and water – for them, not me – two sleeping bags – for them – and two blankets for me. Then we headed out.

We took Frank's truck so we could pick up firewood on the way, which we did about forty minutes from his house. Then we headed towards some high ground, following dirt roads and tracks for some time. A dry gulch showed in front of us and Frank pulled down into it, wending his way along the dry bed floor, which was actually a better way to proceed than on the rutted track we had been following. After some twists and turns and a number of miles, he pulled out of the gulch and began driving towards some hills in the distance. I was completely lost – no idea how far we had come and what direction we had taken. I could tell by the sun we were headed west, but that was all I knew. We all sat silent, each in his own thoughts, throughout the trip and I was reluctant to break this silence by asking questions. There would be time when we arrived wherever we going. Besides, you would have to yell any talk because, with the windows open and the lurching truck, you would not be heard otherwise. We finally reached the bottom of some fairly low mountains – at least by my Colorado standards. Frank wormed the truck up the side we were on until he could drive no further without risking damage to the truck – and us. We pulled over next to some large boulders and turned off the engine. I welcomed the silence after the long, dusty, noisy, back challenging ride we just finished. I got out, stretching my back as I held the door open for Two Bears. The three of us had been stuffed in the truck cab – a further affront to our comfort. Frank set the brake, got out and circled the car to the side Two Bears and I stood on. We all stood there stretching, groaning, scratching and rubbing our hands through our hair and scalp. We would have looked like a male dance company getting ready for rehearsal if anyone had been looking. A dance company of middle aged, and older, men who had little of the flexibility of youth still in their bones. But it worked for us and got the kinks out of our bodies.

"Ah, my back aches," Two Bears complained as he stretched. "But we made it here. Where is here, Frank?"

"We are at one of my grandfather's favorite sacred sites here in the Black Hills. He called this mountain the 'Listening Mountain'. He told me it was a good place to listen to the ancestors and a good place for Great Spirit to listen to your prayers. He showed me this place when I was very young, then, after he passed on some time later,

I could not find the spot for fifteen years. One day, when I was out here just connecting to nature, I came upon it again. And the staff my grandfather left up above where we go was still there – leaning against the rock wall, but still standing. Ever since, I come here when I have big things to pray around or I want the teaching of the ancestors. It is why I thought it was good for Jim's vision time," Frank spoke and as he did, I felt very honored that he brought us here, to his place.

"Thank you Frank for bringing us here. I will treat this place of yours with respect. I hope I honor it by spending my time on this mountain well."

"It is a special place for me and you are welcome to it's use because it is the Earth Mother's, not mine."

"Let's have some food and drink some water here before we begin carrying wood and supplies up the mountain," Two Bears suggested. "After we do this, we can make four or five trips and I think we will have enough wood for Jim's circle and our camp, Frank. What do you both think?"

"It will take us about an hour, carrying a load, to climb to the place of my grandfather. I think six trips will do it. The wood will take most of the time and there may be some near the place we go. But I am ready after we eat," Frank told us. "Jim, I ask you to think about how much you eat and drink here. To eat too much now may cause problems while you are up above. The same with too much water."

"Yes, Frank is right," Two Bears took over. "And we will bring water when we visit your place. If you thirst too much and must drink we will give sips, if just washing your mouth does not work. This will be for you to decide."

"Thank you, relatives," I said, abandoning my thoughts of a big 'last' meal and a gallon of water. "I see you are right and I will eat and drink lightly. I hope to make the days without drinking, but will wait for spirit guidance in this. I only have one question."

"You will have many more before we leave you, I think," said Two Bears with a smile and chuckle. "But what for now?"

"You have told me a great deal about the Hanbleche – how I might ask for vision or guidance and how I would certainly face my fears. You told me you saw this day for me – although I thought long from now. But you also told me the way you have sat with those doing their Hanbleche. How the circle is two to three, plus the one to sit alone. Sometimes one plus the one to sit. And you told me all carry what is needed to the place, where the one who will sit is given his fire and the circle he must stay within, then those with him go where he will not see or hear them and set up their camp. That the grandfathers along will visit twice a day, sometimes do ceremony with the one sitting, and bring wood. So am I not to just climb once with my load, which is light, and you uncles will bring wood and water when you come?" I tried not to smile or laugh as I said this and did so pretty well.

"Ho, I have told this as you say," Two Bears said with a bemused look on his face. "Looks like the Redwolf is smarter, or at least slyer, than Jim alone. We will do it so. Frank and I can gather wood after we leave you and set our camp. Frank?"

Frank was really trying hard not to laugh and, suddenly, he lost that fight and let out a long belly laugh. "Yeah. That's fine brother. Are you sure he is Redwolf and not Red Coyote?"

Coyote is the trickster, the one always making mischief, so Frank compared my word trick with the Coyote's gifts. "Okay, I was having fun. I will help carry all you wish, Two Bears," I conceded.

"No. Your words are true. And these days are for you. You are my student and nephew, but also a pipe carrier now looking for teaching from higher than me. So we will carry the wood," Two Bears seriously said.

"I'm sorry Uncle. I was joking. I can carry."

"You think us too old and feeble to do our jobs here?" Two Bears asked me in mock anger.

"No, no. You are not old at all. You are both strong like the buffaloes. I don't mean to insult you, so I will only carry some wood."

We ate and talked a while, then loaded what we could carry to begin the trek up the mountain. When I had my backpack full of what it would hold and a load of wood tied on top I was ready to go. Frank came up to me with more wood, saying, "Could you carry this bit, too? It will get us up there quicker."

"I guess I can make it up the hill with a little more. Tie it on top of the wood already on my back, Frank."

He did as Two Bears came up carrying a satchel with canned food in it. "Jim, these cans need to go, but I am out of hands. Can you carry these? They don't weigh much," he said, without even breaking a smile.

So I now had about fifteen pounds more than I thought I was able to carry and Frank and Two Bears had had their fun – balancing the coyote medicine between us. We started up the mountainside, which was a gradual, but steady, upward climb. I was panting soon, but managed to keep going, even if at a slower pace than I had anticipated. We spoke little as we trekked upwards, saving our breath for the climb. I sipped water as we went as Frank suggested just before we began our climb. It took a little over an hour to reach the area Frank had in mind for my Hanbleche. I happily dumped my load on the ground and then stretched my stiff muscles.

"This is good space Frank," Two Bears said as he reached Frank and I who were a little in front of him. "Redwolf, this feels right I think. I see your place over that a way a little – near that rock wall, but with the view out over the land below."

"Yes Uncle. Whatever spot you think is best. No one place calls to me, so being on the Earth Mother is enough for me."

"So," Two Bears continued. "Frank and I will go back down aways and set our camp if he agrees."

"Of course Two Bears. I come to support you and my new relative here, so you decide what is best here," Frank answered.

"Good, than that is what we shall do and where we each will be," Two Bears decided. "I will 'make the circle' that Jim will remain within now. Frank, please burn some sage as I do this. Jim, sit and pray or connect with the planet or whatever feels good for you. When I have marked the circle we will bring wood for your fire. It will be small, but will bring in fire as my grandfather taught me. Then we will all speak if we need to and speak some prayers before Frank and I go below to set our camp."

"Thank you, Uncle," I began, "But I have a question."

"Ask now if you wish. Or wait until we sit around your fire," said Two Bears as he moved to draw my circle in the dirt and rock.

"I do not want to sound like I am in ego, but I ask if I can ask that I be called 'Redwolf' while we are up here. I am Jim, and I know that name, but my new name you gave me seems like it needs to be used here. I hope to see my animal guides and I hope to connect even stronger than in the past with the Earth, so it seems my Earth name will help. If this is not for me to request, please tell me and I will apologize for asking."

"Why would you begin to apologize now for things you don't know? But no need anyways, because I like your words. They are true to me and carry power. I am glad to see you are listening to your heart and spirit. You shook like an aspen leaf after your walk yesterday, but I see you balancing more now. So, we will speak to you as Redwolf here. If we use Jim, do not answer and we will correct. But I know we will remember that you are Redwolf here now after hearing your words," Two Bears answered my question.

Two Bears finished the circle and Frank carried some wood to the center for my fire. He brought some rocks and made a small fire ring, inside which he placed some wood. The remainder of the wood he laid near the circles' edge. Two Bears carried the two blankets I had brought and set them to the side of the fire ring. Then sage and a shell were added by Frank and a drum by Two Bears. Finally my eagle feather, gifted by Lawrence, was laid next to the shell. I sat and watched from outside the circle, as Frank made clear this was what they wished with a wave of his hand.

When they finished creating my space, Two Bears waved me in. I walked around the circle in the direction of the sun and then entered the circle from the East – the direction of new beginnings. Frank nodded approval and pointed next to my blankets and the sage. Two Bears had left for a minute and returned with my newly opened Chanunpa and my tobacco pouch. He put these on a rock he had placed near the fire. "Is this all good?" he asked me.

"Thank you, Uncles. I feel comfortable here. Safe and at ease, even if I have some doubt with me, also. If I may ask, I would ask for seven rocks to be placed around the circle here. This to honor the seven directions and to bring the energy of Bonnie in, as she is so connected to the rock people."

They nodded and went off to get rocks. In a couple of minutes seven rocks circled me. They were medium sized rocks of several different varieties and colors. Now I felt my space was complete for whatever was to come. "Thank you, Uncles. I am good now."

They both came and sat across the little fire from me, then Two Bears said, "Redwolf, this will be a long time for you here. Or a short time. Two nights and three days I still see is right. You actually began yesterday – you just were not on the mountain yet. What do you wish to know before we leave you?"

"Is there any way I need to do this?"

"Stay within the circle," Frank answered. "Keep a small fire going. Play the drum, sing, pray – do as you see."

"You have two blankets for the cold time of the night. You will need them," Two Bears picked up the talk. "Do not waste your wood or build a large fire. It is not to warm you but to bring fire to your prayers. Ask your guides in as you want. Journey and see where you go. Mostly ask what you will and allow whatever happens to just be. And be ready to face your fears. They will come, probably at night. We will climb back up tonight and sit for a little time."

"Go within when the thirst and hunger begin to sit on your spirit. Use them as tools; as focus. They will help you see what you need to see," Frank took the next turn.

"And know you have strong spirit guides now. Ask them to come. Maybe they will. Ask your wolf people to guard and protect if you feel this is right," Two Bears took over again. "This will be Redwolf with Redwolf and Great Spirit. Use the time well."

"Okay. Can we pray before you leave?" I asked.

"Yes," from Two Bears. "We can smoke together if you wish. Or pray without the Chanunpa."

"I would like to open my pipe and send prayers to Great Spirit before you leave. It will help center me."

So we did a pipe there, within my circle, and then Two Bears and Frank rose and left the circle. They nodded my way, turned and began the trek downhill without a word. Part of me was glad to see them leave so I could get on with this experience and part of me felt fear and doubt. Knowing they would be back sometime this coming night put me a little at ease. But I had a long day and evening yet to come before that occurred.

I sat for about an hour just working on relaxing, praying and getting out of my head and into my heart. I became more relaxed as the time stretched on, but wondered how I would feel three days down the road. When Two Bears first suggested this two-night Hanbleche, I was a little disappointed he had not suggested the traditional three nights and four days. Now, after just a couple of hours here, I was glad the fourth day was not added on. With my time with Black Elk – if it was Black Elk – plus accepting my new name and opening my Chanunpa I now understood what Two Bears had said about yesterday being the first day of my Hanbleche. I had a lot of inner work to do here on this mountain around what had already occurred to me and had no idea if any new pieces of knowledge would come my way. I hoped clarity and understanding around my spirit guides coming to work with me – whether they came 'in the flesh' as my visitor had, or whether they were met in dreamtime or journeying time alone. I felt like I dishonored Two Bears by doubting my visitor with the one he identified as Black Elk, but I had to understand and accept this in my spirit for it to be so. And I knew that was what Two Bears would expect and want – he never looked for blind faith. This, again, demonstrated the difference between church-based religion and people-based spiritual practices. In my past a priest would tell me what 'was' reality and expect me to accept all he said on faith. My teachers now would tell me how they experienced and understood things that happened and then allow me the space to seek my own understanding and answers from within. So I prayed to Great Spirit to make more of the reality of what I was experiencing understandable to me and to provide anything else I needed to move ahead with my walk of service.

A few hours after my relatives departed I lit a bowl of sage and inhaled deeply as I lay back on one of my blankets. It was still quite warm, so I did not need my blankets in that way yet. I slowly beat the drum to the heartbeat of the Earth Mother rhythm – one, two... [pause]...one, two, listening with my heart as I inhaled the sage into my whole body. I continued this until my arms grew weary and my head fogged with the sage and drumbeats, which all put me into a semi-sleep state. I laid the drum down and just let my mind and spirit roam. Images of Black Elk flowed through me, followed by the wolf of many colors and his extended pack and later the opening of my Chanunpa with Two Bears and Frank beside me. Other pictures also came – Bonnie and I climbing some rock formations so she could gather samples; Lawrence and I teaching a group of young children near our lodge; Yellowhair teaching everyone a new lesson around the fire before an inipi; and so on. I just allowed them all to come – even when they started getting jumbled and intermingled.

I went with the flow of these images until, at some point, I must have fallen asleep, because the next thing I remembered I was opening my eyes and it was early dusk. I sat up, crossing my legs under me, and added a few small pieces of wood to the smoldering ashes before me – the remains of my little fire. They flickered into fire beings after a few minutes of being smoke people at which time I took a burning twig and lit the sage in my shell. It was beginning to get chilly so I pulled my second blanket up over my shoulders, wrapping it around me to keep the breeze off. For now I left the first blanket under me so the cold of the ground would not leach up through my body as quickly had I been sitting directly on the ground. I did not know if

Two Bears would bring me any other blankets or robes to keep me warm; so I was experimenting with what I had before it got too cold. The temperature could easily drop forty degrees at night in this part of the world, so I was mentally preparing for a cold night vigil.

My stomach was beginning to speak to me about its long wait for food and the emptiness that was causing. I knew, before this Hanbleche was over, it would be speaking much louder and would be much emptier. More annoying than my stomach was my dry throat — water being much more of a loss than the food. I took a piece of Bear root from my tobacco pouch and stuck it under my lower lip to the front of my mouth. This not only supplied the healing powers of the root to my body, but also helped with saliva manufacture as another grandfather had once taught me. I hoped to be able to last the three days with little sips of water — and a swig to wet the mouth you don't swallow. If I needed more I would not beat myself up, however. My intention was strong and hopefully my body would be just as strong. If not, I would take what was needed when my Uncles offered. Actually, it was not as much the body going with tiny amounts of water for three days, but the games the mind played telling you that death by thirst was an awful thing. Much like being in the inipi for the first time, it's the fear that triggers physical reactions. So I was looking at this as another opportunity to face myself and my fears and not give in to them.

I sat, with eyes closed, and asked my wolf relatives to come and take me on a journey to wherever I needed to be or to see whatever I needed to see. I sensed animal guides all around me, but got no strong presence nor any spirit travelling from me on its journey. I did not try to push it, but rather thanked any animal guides or ancestors there with me for sitting this mountain with me and went back to thinking more about my meeting with Black Elk. I had already tired of thinking about 'Was this Black Elk in physical form or my imaging him? Or just a kind old Grandfather who walked off in a direction I missed?' I would call him Black Elk, in respect of my elder's surety, and see how that surety grew, or didn't grow, in my awareness. Suddenly I left this chain of thought and went back to the lodge where I had journeyed far and wide in place and time. I had forgotten much of this night of journeying, but now it came winging back like Raven on the morning breeze. This night of ceremony and journeying and my meeting with Black Elk were closely connected was what my heart told me, so I explored that idea for a while. One reason we were here in the Black Hills was the visions I had had that night – so that connection certainly existed. Still, I wanted to think more on this. A minute later, before I could follow this line of thought, I heard footfalls a little way down the mountain.

I was glad my relatives were coming to visit so we could do a Chanunpa together then, just as quickly, I thought "What if it's not them, but an animal on the prowl?" So I tried to make my ears 'super ears' and hear every touch of sound. I heard footfalls again, along with some small stones sliding across the ground. Before I could work myself up too much, I saw the outline of two men come into sight. Two Bears and Frank quietly approached me, stopping outside my circle.

"Did you hear us come, Redwolf?" Frank asked.

"I heard someone coming and hoped it was you," I answered sincerely.

"Yes, I thought you might," Two Bears chuckled. "This is the big part of the Hanbleche – the fear part. You must be able to face your fears before you can hope to see or hear anything else. As the night goes deep and animals move and the cold builds – your fears, whatever they are, will visit you. And as you grow hungry and thirsty, they will come some more. Will two more blankets be enough? You look chilled already."

"I am cold and I don't know if two more are enough. Or three, or four or ten. So I leave it up to you," I answered.

"Ah, the mountain makes him wiser already brother," Frank said to Two Bears, laughing as he spoke.

"So, do you need a sip of water Redwolf?" Two Bears asked.

"No. I am thirsty and may regret this answer, but no," I said quietly.

"When we leave, I offer that you let your tiny fire die out for the night. It will make facing what needs to be faced more intense and fast. The small fire gives comfort. It is your choice, but I offer you that choice. Shall we three open our Chanunpas? We have brought ours up," Two Bears finished.

"Yes, please. I had hoped we would do this. A lot of mental pictures have been walking through me, but no visits, visions or journeys. Even my animal guides seem unclear. Doing tobacco will focus me. But I didn't want to do another before you came," I said.

Two Bears and Frank entered my circle and sat across from me placing their Chanunaps and tobacco between themselves and my tiny fire. Two Bears took out his shell, filled it with good white sage and lit it as he began an opening prayer. He prayed for all the creatures of Mother Earth and then for all of his relatives and friends. Finally, he prayed that I would be given whatever I needed at this time here on the mountain. He then nodded to Frank, who began a prayer to the seven directions. As he prayed, we each filled our pipes – adding a little more tobacco each time he ended his prayers to a direction. As he finished, we lifted our pipes to the skies and silently thanked Great Spirit – each in our own way. Then we lit our Chanunpas and blew white bellows of smoke in the seven directions. When we were done, we emptied the ash into the small fire and I ended our ceremony with a short prayer of gratitude.

"So, we would stay for a while if that is good with you, Redwolf," Two Bears said.

"I am happy for the company. I think it will be a long night," I answered him.

"Good. Let's sit quietly and speak to the ancestors in our hearts," Two Bears offered.

And so for about an hour, we sat together silently and connected with whomever or whatever we wished. For my part, I asked my animal guides to be with me during the coming night and I prayed for the strength to face the dark and the night sounds I knew were coming. Then I let my mind take me wherever it wanted me to go.

I remember thinking about the day before and what I was doing here, now, on this mountain and was amazed that these things were happening to me.

"I offer water once more, to drink or wash your mouth out," Two Bears said at the end of the hour or so we sat there.

"I would like to wash my mouth and drink two sips to get me through the night," I responded. He uncapped his water bottle and handed it to me. I took a small amount in and swished it around my mouth, then spit it on the rocks. Then I slowly took a small mouthful, which I swallowed with huge pleasure. Then a second. "Thank you, Uncle. That takes the dust away."

"You will be thirsty tonight, but this will help you in your spirit work. I am leaving these two blankets for you, also. They will break the cold, but not keep you too warm," Two Bears said as he lay the blankets beside me.

"Thank you, Uncle. And thank you both for being here. I guess I will see you next when I do," I said.

They both nodded to me and, without another word, stepped out of my circle, turned and headed back down the mountain trail to their campsite. To a fire, water and food I thought, with jealousy creeping into my heart. I quickly released that with the thought that they could both be warm and comfortable at Frank's house, but they chose to bring me here and be here for me.

I let the small fire burn out and arranged two blankets under me and one over my shoulders. The fourth I put to the side, determined not to use it if possible. It was dark – black dark – except for the wonderful star display above. And that was quite a display. With no lights anywhere within my sight, the stars shone and twinkled in a happy way. I was comforted by this little show of light and hoped the sky would remain clear throughout the night. It was full night now – probably around nine or ten if I read the moon placement correctly – and I should have been tired after the exercise and emotion of the day, but I was not. I was fully awake and rapidly feeling colder by the minute. I pulled my blanket more closely around me to keep out the mild wind now flowing around me. I began some mental exercises several of my teachers had taught me around regulating my body temperature from within. After some minutes I began to feel a little warmer, or at least not as aware of the wind. I felt good about this as I had been practicing this mental body control for some time now and had had only marginal success up to this time. If I could continue to maintain some body warmth this way throughout the night I would not only feel physically more comfortable, but would be gratified that another teaching was becoming a practical tool. So, as per the teaching, as I felt warmer I released my mind from controlling this with the positive belief that my body would hold this extra warmth now without having to focus on doing this. This was the area I had had trouble in the past – slowly losing the warming or cooling effect as I withdrew conscious effort on the temperature regulation. Sometime later in this long night I came to realize that, although I got colder as the time wore on, I did not get as cold as the dropping temperature and rising wind would have led me to expect. So I assumed I had progressed further in this management of my body. A great time for this breakthrough!

I must have sat there on the hard rock beneath me, working on my body comfort and watching the stars above for a couple of hours as my arms and legs began to stiffen since I had not moved them around or repositioned them much at all. In the lodge I can sit for hours cross-legged as I have shared before. But I do re-cross my legs periodically – changing the top and bottom leg positions – and stretching my back so I don't stiffen. I began slowly shifting now so as not to cause muscle spasms. Leg cramps now, with little space to walk in within my rock-lined circle, would not be a pleasant experience. After a few minutes, the stiffening eased up and I began to relax into my space. I felt no need to lie down yet, but I might if and when I started to journey—as I often did with no conscious awareness of this. I filled my shell with sage and red cedar and lit it with a wooden match – one of twenty or thirty Two Bears had left me. I breathed in the wonderful aroma as I again watched the stars dance in the skies. I offered some prayers and then asked for any instruction I might need at this time to come my way. I asked for further 'seeing' of the vision I had had near the beginning of my working with Two Bears those years back if it was time for this. And I asked the ancestors and my animal guides to protect me while I remained here on the mountain and to help guide me in spirit wherever I needed to go. I did not ask for the aide of angels, archangels or any other beings that 'smacked' of organized religion. (It would be many years, and much personal soul work undertaken, before I could disassociate these light beings from religions and churches. In fact, it would be many years before I could begin to understand and accept that organized religion, despite all the fear and bloodshed it had created, played some necessary role in human evolution.) Today, I would add the angels, archangels and prophets to my list of those I would ask for assistance on my journey, but back then, those I asked for assistance were those I needed at that time – as is always the case.

I soon began thinking I could drum to help me get into a meditative mood. No, in truth, it would help distract me from the slow-moving time and the sounds now entering my awareness. For someone used to moving and doing day and night, sitting for hours on end was not easy. As I mused through these and other thoughts the night air was getting progressively cooler. While I thought my attempts at body temperature regulation were still assisting me to stay as warm as possible, I could not kid myself – I was cold and getting colder. I considered getting up and jumping in place, but knew I would feel even colder when I eventually stopped. I pulled the last blanket to me and wrapped it around my waist and legs. Then I began singing some lodge songs quietly. That stopped when I heard some crackling noise from my north – noise like twigs breaking or snapping. I held my breath and listened for more and was rewarded by a couple more series of snapping wood sounds. My mind began creating boogey-men sneaking up on my flank. Lions and tigers and bears – oh my! I listened intently for long minutes, but the snapping twigs no longer fired my imagination. But it had got me started down the road of "what will I do?" What will I do if something attacks? I have no weapons. What will I do if I am bitten by some wild animal? If I get too cold?

And on and on. I slowly got a handle on these thoughts and reeled them in as best I could. I knew coyotes and small animals would roam this mountain, but I had not asked Frank about larger animals. To get off this chain of thought, I revisited all that had happened to me since Two Bears and I arrived at Wounded Knee just a day and a half ago. As I began down this road of remembrance, an owl hooted loudly from somewhere below me, down the face of the mountain. I have always loved owls and so was comforted by this ones' arrival. He hooted on a regular basis for a long while and I found myself anticipating his next vocal offering. Then I remembered the Great Horned owl along the Poudre River next to the lodge of my first inipi and how I had shared this sighting with everyone. You may remember the silence that greeted this, as I was instructed by Yellowhair about the owl being a sign of death to his clan. But tonight I smiled and hoped it would be the death of my fear and confusion and not of my mind and body.

I listened to the owl and looked for my animal guides to appear and listened to the sound of the wind, which had now picked up even more. And, somehow – sometime, I dropped into sleep. At least, I think I was asleep. Probably more like being in that gray time and place between being awake and asleep. I am certain I still heard the owl, who I realized had somewhat hypnotized me with his voice. Suddenly – asleep or awake…or both – I was no longer alone. I felt the wolf people approaching me and circling around my little space even as my brother, the wolf of many colors, came and sat before me, staring me straight in the eyes as he had done in the past. I felt complete comfort as I felt them encircle me. Fear of anything harming me was gone in an instant. I thanked these four-leggeds for their presence and for the guidance I knew they would provide me this night.

As I lay there – for I had lain down at some point—I felt myself as a wolf; as one of the pack. I could feel my four legs and strong chest. And I was aware of my increased sense of smell and sight. I relaxed into this feeling and paid attention to every nuance of it. In a while, my multi-colored guide rose and I found we were walking together – walking in daylight across an open field. At the same time I was looking around my little dirt and rock circle where I lay 'being' a wolf. Or feeling like a wolf. Walking and lying in my circle? I began feeling disoriented and, as I put attention to this, I no longer could feel myself as a wolf, but rather a confused human trying to sort competing images.

I came to accept the reality – years later – of these times when I was seeing and feeling as another being. And/or I was in two or more places or times at once. Usually two places, although on occasion I have inhabited three spots. And not in sleep time, but in a fully awake state. Dreams, reality, temporary dementia, gifts – I don't know or care, I simply accept things occur we can't always explain. Seem confusing? It is until you accept it for what it is. It put me in pure panic many times until I learned to accept. Partly, it is shape shifting as it is practiced by some cultures. My Lakota and Mayan teachers both taught me much about this talent. Europeans in the Americas thought shape shifting meant turning into a bear or an owl or an eagle – or whatever form the medicine person was able to assume. Indigenous people, it is said, gave up trying to explain and found it amusing that Europeans believed they actually changed form.

One Lakota friend of mine had wonderful stories about how his great grandfather made up tales of his turning into animals at night and telling them to Europeans, especially priests and ministers who then wanted to 'save his poor heathen soul'. But physically turning into another creature is not shape shifting at all by my teachings. Rather it is the ability to enter into some other form and 'become' it—but in an energetic and spiritual way, not a physical way. My Australian aborigine teachers taught me many ways to focus yourself in order to achieve this state. They also taught me that, beyond this practice, is the ability to become one with another human at some other place or time – again at an energetic level. This person is often someone in your family line, sometimes even you from an earlier life, but sometimes it is someone with no lifeline connection to you. They believed these were the most powerful 'before times' – providing some insight or vision needed for your present life's work. I have encountered similar beliefs in many cultures I have spent time in and, while not identical, the stories and teachings all have the basic ideas I have shared here with you.

Although I talk here of shape shifting as joining with another creature, or spirit, in an energetic way, that does not mean I believe that makes it 'less' than if you actually turned into another entity. I see, hear, smell and touch as if I were that entity while I experience these events, as I have been told many others also do. And I have met with some medicine people who claim they actually can change form. I do not know if they were being literal or if this distinction between physical and energetic is so fine that it does not matter which state is reality.

As I came back into full awareness of my body and the circle I still occupied I could sense the energy of the Wolf People, but could no longer see them around me. I was fine with that, knowing my animal guides were with me, ready to assist if I asked. And some more time had passed – time I did not feel the cold and wind since I was in that spiritual state with the wolves. But now I could feel that cold and wind slicing through my blankets and knifing into my goose-bumped flesh. Still, I left the two blankets beneath me, having learned how much quicker and more completely you become cold if you sit on cold earth. I sat, teeth now chattering and body shaking, trying to again moderate my body temperature. It wasn't so cold I needed to worry about frostbite, but cold enough that my body shook trying to generate heat. I began some deep breathing as I concentrated on raising my body temperature and, slowly, the chattering and shaking lessened. It did not stop, but became more bearable, allowing me to think about more than my discomfort. I did a prayer of gratitude for this easing of my pain and, as I ended it, the wind suddenly stopped blowing. Without the wind buffeting me, the cold alone was less able to enter my body and my shaking stopped after a while. As it did I began again to relax and go into my heart, asking for any guide I now needed to see or hear. I also, once again, asked Great Spirit to provide me any vision I now needed to continue my spiritual growth and do the work I was here to do.

It seemed as though the sky was getting lighter as I looked around me, although I knew it was sometime in the middle of the night. And I sensed a 'warmth' I could not explain. I tried not to think and 'figure it out', but rather to stay in my heart and see what came to me, if anything. My cold, thirst, hunger and fatigue had been building over the hours and some will say what I saw and heard while on the mountain were simply outcomes of this. I used to get mad by those who disclaimed all they could not understand, but now I allow each their own beliefs and live with what I know to be true for me. In this way I do not squander time in anger or in trying to convince another, but invest my time in my own growth and evolution. This was another hard lesson to learn and one I offer you for consideration.

As the night seemed to lighten further and my cold and thirst were less in my awareness, I felt another presence with me. At first I thought it the wolf people returning, but knew that to be wrong. While they were around me, they were not actively engaged with guiding me at the moment. Then I thought 'wild animal' and fear leaped into my head. Why do we always let our mind go to 'wild' animal? With negative connotations of attack and fear? Why not just animal or natural animal? But, at that moment, wild animal definitely came to mind. Then it just as quickly passed as I stayed heart centered. And, in a few seconds, I heard a female voice speaking to me. It was very soft at first and I had to concentrate to understand the words.

"Redwolf, it is White Buffalo Calf Woman. I greet you and greet your Chanunpa. It was time for you to open the Chanunpa and so time for me to speak with you."

As I listened I began to make out her image – sitting with my eyes closed, heart open and energy focused. I most often experience directions or visions through pictures and symbols. I may have shared this with you before, but is worth repeating. This has always been the case for me since I began walking the spiritual road. When I do hear someone speaking to me I always pay special attention, because it is so rare for me. And here, a day after Black Elk appearing and speaking, I was visited by White Buffalo Calf Woman. She was not present physically, as Black Elk had been, but I could see her clearly with my heart's eyes. And she was speaking in my mind and heart, not in speech my ears could hear. She was of average height, slim and quite beautiful. I cannot define her features, as they seemed to shift as we spoke, but I could see her long, dark black hair framed stunningly by her white deerskins and red cloth ribbons.

"Thank you for your words, White Buffalo Calf Woman. And for your affirming my opening my Chanunpa," I said to her through my heart. "I continue to feel unworthy to carry the Chanunpa and honor what I need to do in that role. Especially being non-native."

"There is no room for unworthiness in the spirit of awakened humans. You have heard this from many of the spirit realm. And you know all humans are native and tribal in their history and their genes. And you also should know that you have walked as all four colors, some many times. You have had many red walks; it is why so many who are red on this walk now 'see' you; and connect with you. If outside color worries you this much, go paint yourself. If not, stop this talk. You do not see color, sex, shape or age when you are with others. So why do you worry so much what they see in you? And the Chanunpa. I brought the Chanunpa to the red humans since they were best able to understand, use and protect it. It was never meant just for them for all time. Just as the sacred objects of all peoples were meant to be shared when the times called for it. And those times to share ways come now. They come quickly. And you are one who needs to be ready. You have walked many, many walks to be what is needed on this walk. Spirit guides, animal guides and the ancestors will guide you, as they do for so many. But we ask that you stop worrying about the thoughts of others and your own value. This wastes time. You know some will attack you – as some always attack those unlike themselves. Some spiritual walkers will also take you on. Some red will not like you being pipe carrier or, later, water pourer. Some brown will not like you being a keeper of medicine. And so on. Many of the ancient ways and sacred ceremonies still exist because medicine people strictly guarded them from extinction. From those who would eliminate these ways of connecting with Great Spirit. While many sacred ways still need to be protected, they must also be shared with those of the four colors who understand their power and uses. Some will have trouble making this change of heart. Do not blame any, but thank them for keeping the old ways safe for so long. Many will not like the way you will combine your teachings and use this to guide others. Yet you must walk this walk. It will be very hard at times. Painful to the point you will wish to leave. Painful to the point you will doubt your sanity. Yet I know you will persevere when these times come. And grow and evolve as you meet others who you will create with."

"Grandmother, I am at a loss about what to say or think," I began, truly overwhelmed by her words. "Why am I on such a road?"

"Why are you here? Or why are you white? Or why male? Or why are so many teachers finding you? Do not worry over the answers to all your questions. They will come if they are needed. Walk and learn and share. Focus there and accept what comes as it comes."

"I will try. But it is so hard. It goes against everything I learned over my first forty years. And how do I not worry about this pain and suffering I have been told about by several? Or about making mistakes with those I try to help?"

"Most of these things you are being told and shown are so that when the time comes you will remember the words. And you will see what must happen next. In between, you will forget much of what you are told and taught. You will re-walk some of your old ways again before you will see they no longer serve you. Sometimes this is important. Yet all the time you will be advancing, learning and seeing more. The Chanunpa will aide you. As will I. As will Black Elk and all the others who will come if you ask. As will all of the Earth realm, as your teachers already do."

"Why all this learning and preparing? Why forget and repeat? Will I be more ready later?"

"I do not know all the answers. You asked me in tonight when you asked for guidance. And I tell you what I know to be so. But I cannot tell you all the whys if the universe has not given me the answers either. Know many are here to help you, not harm or hurt you. In the ways we are able to help. There are many humans now preparing for what comes soon – in the blink of the universe's eye. Know this is so and work to make that enough."

"I will work on this, White Buffalo Calf Woman. And I ask you to come and teach me whenever it is needed. And to come and protect or work with those around me when I ask it, if you are able. And to guide me in the use of the Chanunpa, so I always use it in a good way and honor the way I am to walk with it."

"I will do all of these things as you ask," she answered me. "Know you will carry the Chanunpa in a different way also. Two Bears is wise and has seen this. As have others who teach you. Do not accept any scorn sent to you for this, but be strong in the knowing that this is your path. You will carry many Chanunpas over time, sometimes more than one. You will see this unfold and question it, but I tell you this is right for you. You will forget much of what I tell you now, as I have said, until it is needed. But your heart will remember and this will help you when your dark time of the soul is at hand. Remember your visions when they come to you and you will walk the red road as you were meant to. You still have much to learn and many things to experience. Still other things to remember, but in a new way. Your balance is not good and all these things will help you get the balance you will need later. Now you worry about not being worthy or ready, yet other times you walk in great ego. Ego you do not yet see. These must balance. Sometimes you walk in fear and uneasiness, yet other times you step forth as a strong warrior and lead in courage. These also must balance. Your past walks and present walk must all be balanced and merged so your future work will be complete. This will all make more sense to you after many falls and rises of your journey here now. It is enough, for now, that you hear me. So, now sleep until the sun visits."

And, like a switch being thrown, that is all I remember. This time with White Buffalo Calf Woman was over. Seldom has she spoken to me since, but usually manifests around me or those with me as

I asked – sometimes visibly and sometimes as an energy I can sense. The few times she has spoken to me since that night on the mountain have always occurred at times of great indecision or stress on my walk and, each time, she has reminded me of some of those things she told me that night. Things that had fogged in my mind or been forgotten, as she foretold.

"It's time. If you are to walk the path of heart, then it is time..."

—Nippawanock, ARAPAHOE

30 | Facing Myself on the Mountain

I REMEMBER BEING AWAKE AS THE SUN CAME UP THAT NEXT MORNING — feeling happy I had made it through one day of three. I don't remember waking, but I must have slept at least three hours judging by the stiffness of my back. My mouth was so dry I had trouble parting my lips, especially with no saliva to ease the process of uncementing them. And my throat felt like I had just taken a ten-mile hike in the desert and forgotten my water bottle. I was also very cold, but knowing the sun would bring some warmth made that more bearable. The hunger I could overlook with the discomfort of the thirst and cold. I slowly got up and began moving my body to work on the sore muscles I had everywhere. As I did so, I went back over what White Buffalo Calf Woman had said to me. That whole experience was so new that I could relive it in full detail, but I wondered for how long, given her assurance much of it would be lost to me until later. I wished I had a way to write it all down, but that was not something allowed up here for this ceremony.

After I worked my body into aches and bruises rather than stabbing pain, I sat down and smudged myself with sage. Then I said my morning gratitude prayers and asked for guidance on what to do next. I felt this was a good time to open my Chanunpa on my own, before my two guardians came for their morning visit. I loaded the pipe and prayed to the seven directions, and then I sent thanks to Great Spirit for the visit of White Buffalo Calf Woman and all she had related to me. I opened the pipe and took deep pulls, holding the tobacco and herb mix in my mouth for a few seconds, and then blowing the clean, white smoke heavenward with my prayers. I prayed for all the creatures of the Earth as the time of change was approaching us. I prayed we might all join and work with the Earth Mother in a better way and we humans with each other without hatred and bloodshed. I then thanked my wolf guides for their protection and asked them to stay by my side for the remaining two days of this quest. When I finished, I smudged the Chanunpa before wrapping it and as I lay it aside, I heard Two Bears and Frank climbing up to me. This time I came to that awareness without thinking of what else might be coming my way. Getting comfortable in my mountainside perch, I supposed.

"How is the wolf this morning?" Frank called out as they walked up to my circle.

"Thirsty, cold, hungry and tired," I answered. "Exactly how I expected to be. How are you caretakers of the Redwolf?"

"He is okay. He still jokes with us," Frank said to Two Bears.

Two Bears looked at me carefully as he arrived at the circle's edge. He had nodded to Frank's comment, but had said nothing yet and was looking quite serious. "Are you alright, Redwolf?"

"Yes, Uncle. It has been a long day and night, but I am all right. I do hurt and I would give anything for a long drink of water, but I want to do this in the best way I can. So I would ask for two small mouthfuls of water again."

He nodded at my response. "Endurance is part of this vision quest, but being open to visions or guidance is the more important part. I have seen men leave feeling in their power because they went the full time without food and little water and without fire or many clothes. Yet they had little to say about what they had seen or heard. Or where they had journeyed. Or who came to them. Maybe they did not bring in guidance with their prayers. Many who sit on a mountain are not ready. Or unwilling, even when they think they are. But maybe they were so focused on being strong warriors that they missed the spirit warrior pieces that came. I do not know, but I give you this for thought."

"I think I understand what you are saying Uncle, and I thank you. I was so cold last night I did not think about being a brave man, but rather thought of ways to get through the cold. But, had I been a little warmer, I may well have been focused on being the stoic white guy on the mountain here. I did think of how I wanted to do this in the best way and how I wished to make you proud of what I did here. But I felt my prayers were strong, especially when I opened my Chanunpa alone for the first time. And I did receive a visit and guidance. White Buffalo Calf Woman came in the middle of the night; some time after my wolf pack came and let me run with them. All this I did, and all without leaving my circle." I told Two Bears all of this in a rush, almost like I might forget something if I did not get it out quickly.

"So, your night was strong. Frank, come over and we will listen to our young wolf speak to us," Two Bears said, calling in Frank who had moved to the edge of the trail looking down the mountainside from there.

Frank and Two Bears came into my circle and Two Bears started a small fire, from which he lit a large bowl of sage. I sat and let him do all of this without a word, especially since my throat burned and lips hurt from the talking I had already done. So little water had certainly had its effect on me and I knew this day would be much worse. Two Bears smudged each of us and then my Chanunpa and tobacco pouch. I saw they had not brought their pipes this morning, but had brought water and more blankets. I knew decision time would come soon.

"So, Redwolf," Two Bears began again. "Would you drink? You have done well, especially since you have had no real time to prepare for this time up here."

"Yes, Uncle. I would like to drink a small amount again and wash my mouth. I wish to do this for as long as I am able. Not out of ego, but because I think this will have me more open for what else may come. But this little bit of water will let me speak without croaking like a sick frog."

He smiled and handed me the water bottle from his pouch. I took in a mouthful and swished it around, then spit it out being careful to drink none as I did this. The pleasure of just this wetting brought tears coursing down my cheeks. I waited a minute and then repeated the wetting process once more. I then took a small mouthful and slowly swallowed it – more tears coming with the shear joy this brought to me. I then slowly swallowed another mouthful and passed the bottle back to Two Bears as I did so. "Thank you, Two Bears," I began with a new voice found, "I cannot say how good that felt. I would like to continue with the blankets I have and not add more. But, I thank you for bringing more."

"Ho. I would like us to sing and pray together at your small fire here, then open your pipe if that feels good to you," Two Bears said to me.

"Of course, Uncle. It will be good to do this before I face being alone again."

"Then, if it is your wish, I would like you to tell Frank and me about what happened last night. Only what you wish and if you wish."

"I would like to do so. I feel I should share these things and maybe you will both add to what I heard and what I understand."

Frank got up, and saying Mitakuye Oyasin, left the circle and went to the bundle he had brought and left off to the side. He took out his lodge drum and re-entered the circle with his drum ready for a beat. Frank began with a song I did not know, so I listened and prayed as he played and sang. Two Bears joined in with Frank, so it was a song he knew, even if not one he generally used. After a few more songs, all of which we sang together to the beat of Frank's drum, Frank went to the quiet one-two heartbeat of Mother Earth. We all sat and privately prayed or connected with the Earth Mother or our guides. At least I connected with the Earth Mother, promising, once again, to continue to learn the best ways to work with her and sharing these ways with others. After Frank stopped the drumbeat, I took my Chanunpa and filled it while praying to the seven directions. My intention for this pipe, I spoke, was connecting with the Earth Mother – each in the best way they can so that we humans could again walk this planet with honor. I offered the pipe to Two Bears to open, and he bowed to me and took the pipe. He took a lit twig from the sputtering fire and lit the tobacco. The smoke poured out full and white and went straight up – all signs of a pipe ceremony Great Spirit would be watching carefully.

When we finished, and I rested the Chanunpa against a rock I had put next to the fire for this purpose, we sat quietly for a few minutes. Then Two Bears spoke, "Redwolf, would you speak now of last night here?"

And so I told the stories of everything that had happened the night before, trying to forget nothing and, in so doing, not forget as White Buffalo Calf Woman had told me I would. It took a while, as I started with my discomfort with the cold and wind and worked through every nuance of the night's events. My throat was dry and hurt, but I croaked out the last half of the story.

"You speak of shape shifting. You have much to learn of this Redwolf, but you see the truth of this gift," Two Bears spoke when I went silent. "We will work on this much more over time, as the gift seems to be in you."

"My grandfather was well respected in his ability as a shape shifter," Frank added. "He told me many stories as I grew up. He told me of the four-leggeds he became and of the rock people and others. This medicine did not make him shift into a live being – as we see that – but any thing that is."

"When you saw your vision in my lodge, you spoke of running with the wolves. Was this the same last night, Redwolf?" Two Bears asked.

"No, Uncle. This was more I think. I don't remember 'being' a wolf in your lodge. But I did wonder how I could run like a wolf. Maybe I was just not ready to see I had shifted into a wolf. Or maybe last night was more. Whatever, I felt I was fully wolf last night and I do not remember that from the past. Sorry if I am unclear, but this is new and confusing."

"No, you are clear in your being unclear," Two Bears smiled at me.

"I was with the wolves both times. As I was with the eagle when the vision came. And with the two-leggeds I saw — although apart at the same time. I travelled far that night, and some other nights since, but last night was different. I was wolf and went with the wolves. Yet I would not say this was a vision, but a more a meeting with White Buffalo Calf Woman to hear her words."

"It is good that you see this difference, Redwolf," Frank spoke to me. "Not everything is a vision. I tire of those who tell me of their visions weekly. But, maybe I am jealous," he smiled at me.

"Yes, you travel with the animals and with the ancestors," Two Bears said to me, picking up the virtual talking stick. "That night of your vision you took me on part of the journey with you. I have not spoken of this until now. I did not wish to shake you like a lodge rattle even more. This happens with some. Be prepared for others to tell you this as you go forward. And be aware it can happen, even though you do no intentional medicine to make it so."

"I did not try to do this and did not know of it until now, Two Bears," I spoke with guilt. "I am sorry, I had no idea. I will be careful of this."

"How can you be careful of that which you do not try to do or have any idea is happening? This would make a good spirit question to take into a lodge," he said with a twinkle in his eyes. "More important to the work ahead is White Buffalo Calf Woman's teaching of how you would forget some of what you learn or see until you need it. This has happened to me and to many others. It is nothing to fear. This whole journey we each take is a slow process of gathering information, which will be known and used when it is needed. I suggest you do not fight this, but accept that it is so."

"I will work on this Two Bears, as I see you are right."

"Frank and I will go to our camp now. We may walk the mountain later in the day, but we will be back for a while this night again. You may wish to rejoice in nature today. Share your joy and thanks with the Earth Mother. Or do some day journeying. You will know. The heat will make you hot and thirsty – the balance side of last night. You have spoken much, so I would ask you to drink a little more water now, before we leave. We will bring water again tonight and ask you to drink again. Will you be okay until we return?"

"Yes I will, relatives. I will do the best I am able with what I have inside," I said as I took the bottle and allowed myself one more small swallow.

"Just so," Two Bears nodded as he spoke, accepting the bottle back. Then he and Frank arose, gathered up their things, stepped out of the circle and quickly disappeared down the mountain trail. And I sat watching, very sorry to see them go. It would be a long, hot day and rapidly cooling evening before I saw them again. And they might not even be down below me somewhere during that time, but roaming the mountains where any call from me would not bring them. Well, this would give me plenty to face.

Judging by the sun it was late morning when they left – maybe 11 AM. And it was getting hot already. Yet, knowing I would sweat, I pulled a blanket over my shoulders again. This was as I had been shown by a Mayan friend. First, you don't lose all your moisture to the air, especially when the humidity is low, as it was in South Dakota. And as your towel absorbs some perspiration you can later put it over your head to help save your throat from drying. I hoped these things would help as I was in huge thirst already once again. I tried to create saliva to swallow, but with little result. As I began some silent prayers and as I stretched my body, my mind kept bringing me back to my thirst. It was telling me I would die of thirst and beating me up for being an ego fool and not drinking more of Two Bears water. I worked on going back into my heart, but it was becoming a major mind/heart battle. After an hour or two of this, I could see lakes below me and hear running water behind me in the rocks. I could feel the difference between these things and the visits I had had the night before. These felt very different and I knew them to be my mind playing tricks on me. The hot sun beating down on me only made things worse. I wanted to leave the towel on, but the heat under it felt extreme, so I put it on my head for a while. This did help with the hot air I was breathing in and the pain in my throat, but the trade off was the baking I felt on my now exposed back.

I began saying the same prayer over and over, as Yellowhair had shown me. This allowed for more focus on my heart and less on the fear my head was trying to instill in me. I don't want to paint my mind as the enemy – that is not so. It was, in part, doing what our brains do – protecting us from perceived harm. A trait as old as humans and one that had helped preserve our species. Yet when it becomes too strong, you go out of balance and react through fear rather than understanding and spirit. It was this balance I tried to attain. By mid-afternoon the day was at its hottest and I seriously considered leaving my circle and going to Two Bears' camp for water. Then I knew I could last the final night and day. I calmed this urge by telling myself I could do this at any time and inviting myself to wait another twenty minutes before doing so. Just to be certain I really needed more water that badly. Then twenty minutes after that, and twenty more and so on throughout the day. Water bubbling and fish swimming came to my ears several times, but I laughed and ignored these false images. Finally it seemed it was cooling slightly. I looked up and saw it was late afternoon now. And I breathed relief. I had not left the circle and I was still lucid – I think. But did my throat and lungs hurt! Searing, hot, dry pain from my mouth down throughout my body. I began counting minutes until my relatives would return and I could swallow a tiny amount of water again. Then I worked to put my thirst and discomfort aside and concentrate on my prayers and songs. I was gratified to find it actually began working this time and I could ignore the physical much more effectively.

With this lessening of awareness of my physical unease, I was able to stay in my heart and spend time feeling the things that had occurred in the past couple of days. And then I was able to cast my mind and spirit back and consider things that had occurred since I stepped on this spiritual path and begin to integrate those things with what was happening now. This did not confuse me more nor cause fear to rear up, but rather it began to allow me to see the broader picture again, something that had been missing for some time. I marveled how clear things became, and how connected in a causal chain, when I achieved the state I was in now. I wished this state were something I could access when I felt the need, rather than a state I suddenly, unexpectedly turned up in on occasion. This was something I decided to work as time went on and see if I could call it in when needed. I had been told by several medicine people and visionaries they also had this state appear on its own schedule, without their ability to manifest it at will. This super clarity, super connectivity, super understanding usually seemed to happen at times of high creativity or visions from the universe. Well, I would explore this more through my spirit and see what I might see, with no expectations of outcome.

I spent the remainder of the day and the early evening resting, experiencing periods when I was very uncomfortable, praying and journeying. At times I went off in spirit over the plains of the land around me. At other times I saw great beaches and oceans I felt were just playthings of my mind. Being able to distinguish between the two would be a huge gift I would leave this mountain with. It would allow me, in most instances, to know if I was in a journey state or simply calling up images from the past or from things I had heard about. I sensed spirit animals and ancestors around me many times, but in a light, low-level way. As the darkness came, my hot body began to cool, then chill, then shake with the cold once again. I began repeating the steps I had taken the night before to provide myself whatever comfort I could. Finally, about nine o'clock by the 'sky' clock, I heard Frank and Two Bears coming uphill. This time I heard them much sooner than I had on their previous visits. I think my senses were now sharpened by hunger, thirst, cold and heat—as well as my meditating – that I could see, hear and smell at much higher levels than my norm. I paid attention to this over the next hour and found it to be true. This heightened sensitivity of the senses was a goal of the vision quest I was on. It allowed one to better connect and 'feel' in all ways, so I welcomed it's coming.

"Aho, Redwolf," Frank called before I could see them, but well after I heard them, coming.

"Aho, relatives. It's good to hear you coming up that way," I called back. A few minutes later they came into view and walked up to my circle.

"I called so you would know it would be us coming since it is dark and you have been here a long time," Frank explained.

"I heard you coming long before you called out, Frank, but I thank you all the same," I answered back.

"Aho, you heard us before Frank called out? We were far down the trail. You must be touching the Earth Mother in a strong way now," Two Bears offered.

"My senses are all very strong. I have been exploring this for some time now. It is the longest time they have ever stayed so sharp," I told the two of them.

"Good, Nephew. This is what you seek while you are up here as I have told you in the past. But feeling it makes it something you can better know. This is what you want when you pray or lead ceremony or work with those who need healing. I am happy you have found it here and are able to visit with it," Two Bears said with obvious pleasure.

We spent the next ninety minutes talking about their day and my day in the circle. We did no singing or ceremony, just visiting and sharing time together. Somehow it was just what I needed – a little bit of every day in the middle of this quest of mine. I don't think I made much sense in my talking as hunger; thirst and cold had robbed me of a lot of my ability to think and act clearly. But they did not comment and finally, as they began to gather their bundles, Two Bears handed me the water bottle and I again rinsed my mouth and followed that with two small drinks of this delicious nectar. Then they each clasped me in a brotherly hug, wished me well this night and headed back to their campsite. Once again I sat in the cold, dark air with a long night before me. So far tonight there was no wind blowing, for which I was extremely grateful. I stretched my body as I straightened my legs out in front of me for a while, trying to work out the stiffness and knots that had again found their way in. Then I lay down, with the intention of trying to get a little sleep.

All types of colors and images began flooding my mind's eye as soon as I got comfortable lying down. And my mind began spinning fast, thinking of my hunger and thirst and how vulnerable I was laying here. Then the cold found me—as the blankets beneath me did not protect me as well from the cold rock as they could when I was seated. I went with this rapid-fire thinking and fear for a while, and then slowly worked on calming my mind and again going into my heart. After a short while I sat up, feeling more comfortable that way. If I fell asleep at some point I would naturally roll over and lay on the ground where I could sleep until I awoke. I burned some sage and sang a few lodge songs quietly. Then I closed my eyes and invited whoever was needed to come and bring me knowledge, questions, answers or whatever else was meant to come my way this night. I thanked Great Spirit in advance for the teachings I would receive, then emptied my mind and let my spirit just 'be'. I have no idea how long this went on, but I remember visiting many places and people in the past of this life through my memory of them, not through journeying. Then for a long while I remember just a peaceful, quiet, easy darkness that I was floating through. I may have slept then, but I am unsure. At some later point, as I was thinking about some friends at Colorado State, I felt my wolf family again form around me. Not as if they were ever gone the entire time that I sat on the mountain, but they manifested stronger at some times, as they did then.

"Welcome, wolf relatives. I am happy to see you coming here in a powerful way," I welcomed them. "I see my many colored brother again steps forward. Would you take me somewhere?"

He stood and looked me directly in the eyes, something he had done in the past, yet with more impact this time. As he went into my eyes, I did the same with him. I felt a deep, deep connection with this animal guide and knew, in that instant, he would be with me as primary spirit guide for the remainder of this life's walk. This brought gratitude and relief into my heart and eased my fear of feeling so different and alone – something that I realized had been with me from birth. Then we separated our gazes and this deep soul connection and began moving up the trail above my circle – all, once again, without me physically moving at all.

As we moved along the trail I began seeing creatures of all sorts – bison, bears, eagles, hawks, elk, whales, bees, otters and on down a long list of those I recognized. Sometimes I saw large numbers of each creature, sometimes just a few. They moved in different directions, each in the manner of their sort. I don't know how I saw sea creatures moving on land, but I did. Sometimes these beings swarmed around us and other times I saw them off in the distance. It was like walking through a beautiful, multi-colored collage of all shapes and sizes. I had never tried any drugs that would give you a psychedelic experience, but I imagined these might be the type of colors and images one might see in that state. Except for the fact that the animals were not paired up, I felt like Noah without an ark. More and more creatures swarmed as wolf and I walked. Below us, over us and around us. As I watched I realized there were animals I had never seen before, nor had I remembered from my readings or studies. At the time I just accepted this as being as normal as everything else around me. I felt no fear or worry, just wonder and awe. I was just engrossed by this Technicolor Disney production I felt I was a part of. If Mickey Mouse had suddenly appeared, I suspect I would have thought 'of course. Where have you been?' But I also knew what I was seeing was more amazing and unique than a Disney movie or any other experience I had ever had. I began thinking, "Am I hallucinating because of the lack of water and food? And the long time sitting, burning sage, praying and asking for a vision or guidance?" As I asked myself this I felt the strong inner thought of "If you can ask that question and consider it, then it is not the cause here." So I released those thoughts and went back to trying to stay present and observe and understand what I was seeing.

As I looked more closely I saw that humans were mixed in with some of the flocks, herds and pods of other creatures. Not many at first, but more as I watched over time. Then all the creatures seemed to move 'into' the land around me, melding into the material of the Earth in a way I do not have words for. Soon, wolf and I moved forward alone. But not for long, as again animals began appearing from the four directions — two-leggeds, four-leggeds, winged, gilled, creepy crawlies and others — as earlier. The tapestry of life wove itself again in an intricate way and then again melded into the Earth. As they did so, I felt the elements around me — wind, fire, water and earth come into my awareness slowly at first, then building into a whirlpool of energy. These too, after a while, disappeared into the earth and sky, as if their job was done. I was enjoying every second, yet nothing seemed to fit together for me. Nothing gave me a message or sign. And...I realized my mind was again sneaking in on my heart and creating 'logic burps' that had no place in this realm I walked. Maybe later, when I sat in my circle or with my human guardians, I would question and dissect what I now experienced — trying to wring clear, understandable answers. I hoped I would stay in balance when that time came — not too much brain or heart — so I would understand whatever I needed to at this time in my life's journey.

As wolf and I again walked up the trail alone, he turned and looked me in the eyes once again. And, playing within me, even as I watched the scene of our walk play before me, was the vision I had received in Two Bears' lodge. I was watching this replay and remembering pieces I had already forgotten as they came back to me. Me, as a human of different colors. The shifts in place and time. The animals. All of it. Yet, as I said, also watching the scene of wolf and I climbing unfold before me, with the colors becoming more 'green' in that scene by the moment. Suddenly, as I was getting anxious because of this dual presence of my being, a third cropped up before me — the circle I still sat in, eyes closed, sage burning, blanket around me for some warmth. I felt myself in all three places at once and the anxious feeling began turning to fear — growing fear. I felt the need to run away from all of this, yet

did not know which 'me' in which 'place' felt this. Nor which place
or places I might run from. Fear quickly began to turn to panic and,
as the autonomic fight or flight response of my human spirit began
to wash over me, I was suddenly just with wolf – the other two places
fading. The panic eased and my body calmed quickly. I remembered
the terror caused by this event, but could not fathom why that was
so. Then, even that train of thought left me and I again enjoyed my
movement with wolf.

As the fear left me and I again thought about the amazing display of life I was walking through, I sensed the Wolf People again approaching. My many colored wolf brother beside me simply looked to
the east as if to affirm my thought. I followed his gaze and saw a pack
of wolves flowing our way out of the east – the place of new starts and
beginnings. There were scores of wolves, again in many colors. I saw
gray, white, black, red, yellow, tawny, brown and probably other colors
in their mix. But not the garish painted colors I had seen before, but
rather the colors these various breeds had naturally. The wolves moved
around us and walked with us for some time. Then flowed back into
the east. I brought my attention back to our trail and saw the green I
had noticed earlier was even more pronounced now. There was a great
deal more plant growth than you would find on my quest mountain
and the types of plants were those you would see in more temperate
terrain. As I watched this, I was aware of the sound of water and then
saw a great wall of water coming at us from above. Fear had no time
to plant itself as, before I had time to think or act, the water engulfed
us as we walked. We were still walking our trail, but the water was in
all directions around us. I had no sense of 'wet', yet it was everywhere.
Then it too moved by and we walked through a realm of green plants
and small bodies of water even as we continued up our trail.

After what seemed a long time on this trek, I saw a thin, wispy
tendril of smoke before us. We had been climbing up the mountain
trail since we began and I wondered how we had not reached the top,
as it was not that far above my circle Two Bears had crafted for me.
I accepted that, in this vision place I seemed to be in, distance, time

and space held no definitive dimensions. To do anything else would be to invite the panic back into my being, and I did not wish this to happen. As we drew nearer the smoke I saw it was the sage burning in my circle, which we had approached from below. Impossible in the physical world – a reality here, wherever 'here' was. To push my rational processes even further, I saw 'me' praying and stretching my sore limbs. As we approached I felt the climbing 'me' and the 'me' in the circle shift into one essence – allowing the easing of my nerves that came with this to wash over me. Wolf entered the circle and sat beside me, in the south. The south – the time of creation, physical exertion, energy and growth. A time of 'doing'. He curled up in a loose ball beside me, laid his head on one paw, looked up at me – and then closed his eyes, obviously feeling we were safe. I added more sage to the shell and considered opening my Chanunpa, but quickly felt that I was not to do so, yet.

I was now back in my circle, but still with the strong feeling of wolf beside me – even if I no longer saw him with my eyes. I breathed deeply of the sage and added a little red cedar to help my poor mind – stretched to places it had great trouble going – to heal a little. I began shaking, and it was not from the cold. Once again I went into my mind and tried to empty it as I headed my spirit in the direction of my heart. I knew my heart could accept what was occurring with a lot less turmoil than my mind. As I did this, with some success, I could feel my heartbeat slow and my shaking lessen. I began to feel something more was coming and tried to accept it as a 'motion picture', hoping to remain calm and alert.

I appeared in my dream, or whatever state this was. Dream defines it as well as anything. I was moving through scenes, obviously learning skills from some and teaching others. And I aged as I went about this. Then got younger again. I worked around nature and spiritual practices – often combined. Then I aged once again and I thought I was being clearly shown these things would occur over many years. People I knew appeared, as did others I did not know showed themselves. Circles formed and work was done. Then circles would fall apart and I would feel disconnected – until other circles formed, of which I was also a part. I opened the Chanunpa and led ceremony with people of all colors, ages and races. And I sat, listening as others led their ceremonies, some teaching me their ways. I poured water and danced at Sun Dance. Then I was on a walkabout in the backcountry somewhere. I learned about plants, animals and water. I could see I was learning about many things – the way I had walked my road so far in this life. And I was taking these things and combining them in ways guided by the ancestors as Great Spirit wished.

Suddenly I was standing surrounded by ashes, with no one near by. I felt my own pain at many levels – physical, mental and emotional— and fear again welled up in me. Then darkness came and I sat in my circle engulfed by total darkness – no light, sound or smell entered this dark place. And the 'me' in the circle began to panic. My heart raced, sweat poured out all over me, my muscles spasmed and I wanted to run and hide again. Yet I could not get my body to move. I sat in physical and mental pain, wishing my sight would return and this vision would end. I have no idea how long this lasted, but then remember seeing the circle around me once again and no longer being in panic – as if it had never happened.

Now I watched the 'movie' unfold before me, up against the back of my closed eyes. No sound – my projection booth was lacking in this area – but full color, wrap-around pictures. I saw 'me' once again – an older me, with gray beard, graying hair and more wrinkles and small blotches on my skin. Maybe sixty or sixty five? Again, I am no good at guessing age, but I think that was about right. I was talking to a group, then I turned and that group faded as another appeared. I spoke with them and the process repeated again. It repeated many times and I was then sitting in circles – one after another – listening and inter-acting with everyone present. The circles were very diverse, with age, gender, color and culture very noticeable. As I continued to watch the circles dissipated into the air and people began coming from the four directions to a place, which was wooded, had ponds and streams and held a view of mountains in the background. Animals were visible as

I looked over the land, as were a good assortment of plants and trees. I sensed a plentitude of all sorts of life, each of which occurred naturally here. This gave me comfort and pleasure. People continued to come, setting up small camps as they arrived. Those already present welcoming and directing.

I walked about speaking, welcoming and listening as the human numbers grew. Those present before the arrival of the many were those I had seen in the earlier circles. They were guiding people to good places to camp, instructing which areas were to be unused by the humans – being left for the other creatures and as places to honor and connect with the Earth Mother. Most of the people were coming in from the east, entering through a natural small valley in the land. I headed that way to welcome others and, as I neared the people streaming in, I saw them looking up at the trees to the side of their trail. I looked up and saw a sign hung from one large, arching grandmother tree:

> "All who come in a good way are welcomed here. Gather here to learn and teach and share our ways. Enter with heart open and ego left behind. No chiefs, only circles here. If this offends you, the ancestors will ask you to leave."   The Earth Mother

I knew this was to be a gathering of many people where the sharing of their customs and spiritual ways were to be undertaken. And where we would share our ways to connect with the Earth Mother. That was why so many beings were also present. Without all beings of Earth represented, the circle was incomplete. This was what I had been speaking to so many about. I knew of many gatherings, such as this, which had occurred in the past. Most had run into problems of ego and control as I had been told. And, the couple I had been to, I saw this with my own eyes. Here, by the words on the sign, this would not be condoned. But how could a gathering this large operate without chiefs? Would it not stumble under the weight of competing ideas? These things were running through the mind of my vision self as my present time self sat in my circle realizing there was even more for me to learn than I realized. I watched as the gathering began and all who wished to speak were given the talking stick. And how male and female members shared circles, as well as met with their fellow women and men at times. Young and old sat in circle, passing the stick and listening to each other with respect. As I began to see this was working, the scene left my awareness – like a fade out—and was replaced by an image of another piece of land, also with flowing streams, ponds, trees and plants and a sign near the dirt road entering it:

Sanctuaries of the Earth Mother

Gateways to Understanding

All creatures welcomed. Teach and learn; give and receive. Stay if you will share the ways of spirit and the Earth and practice the five colors in harmony, without ego or control.

Then, as I looked up, I saw many similar scenes play before me, each with the same sign posted. I felt I was on Turtle Island throughout the scenes of seven locations of these 'sanctuaries'. Some were forested, some on open plains; others were in the mountains, while others were near water. Then I felt myself going high, into the realm of Father Sky, and, as I looked down, I saw many more of these places around the globe. And I saw energy lines connecting them like the strands of a huge spider's web. As I came back down to ground level I saw people now on some of these lands. They were people I recognized from the earlier gathering scattered among the seven locations. While I recognized them from the gathering, I did not know any of them from my current walk. Some were building small domiciles; some teaching in larger buildings or out under the sky; and still others were conducting ceremony. This still all seemed like an extension of what I had seen in Two Bears' lodge months ago. It now gave me some further understanding of what I was seeing. A gathering of equals, without disharmony and ego, from which a web of natural places would evolve. These would be places where all could again learn to partner with the Earth Mother in a sustainable way once again, giving spiritual evolution more space to occur. As these thoughts came from what I was seeing, wolf approached me in my vision persona and I knew he would guide me once again. He turned and began to move and as I followed, I was back in my circle, shivering once again – this time from the cold. And wolf was gone, leaving me to sit and ponder.

I spent the remainder of the night trying to stay warm as I dealt with my thirst and hunger. This took much of my attention. As soon as I had some comfort around my stomach growling loudly, my legs would cramp and I would need to shift, bringing a new discomfort. My brain replayed some of what I had seen and began telling me I must be out of my senses from having sat here so long without nourishment. I went into my heart and asked for any further visions or clarification of what I had seen. None came. I sat on a hard, cold, flat rock perch, feeling myself a fool for being here. Yet my heart knew what I had seen had been so. I realized, later down my road, it was my fear around the dark time that I was attempting to disown by mentally 'pooh poohing' the whole experience. But while I sat on the mountain, I did not comprehend this. In fact, my mind, as a safety valve, quickly began forgetting this dark, painful part. Much of this vision would be forgotten for many years, leaving general images and pieces of what I had seen.

I shivered, shook, stretched and scratched until sunrise, when, after stretching my body, I lit a bowl of sage and got out my Chanunpa. I did a pipe of gratitude to Great Spirit for what I had seen, even if I did not fully understand how I was to make use of this vision. Then I sang a song to the sunrise, welcoming this special time of day into existence. My voice is not the best when aided by a drum, so without a drum and no saliva it was not a pretty sound. Yet it helped me focus and get ready for the shift to day and heat.

My discomfort continued as I again changed my ways of dealing with the temperature change to heat once again. I sat, miserable and tired, praying and chattering to myself for many hours. My guardians from the camp below did not show in the morning as I had thought they would. Finally, around noon, they appeared. My eyes felt glued shut and this fogged my vision so, for a moment, I was not sure if I saw them coming up the trail or if another spirit image was about to appear. I was relieved it was Two Bears and Frank, as I felt I had enough to sort through since arriving in Pine Ridge.

We three sat, as I drank two small sips of water again and then Two Bears began beating his drum and singing one of his favorite lodge songs. Then we quietly sat and watched the sage burn in the bowl. I knew they wished to ask if anything had come with the night, but respected my space and the fact my throat now hurt too much for talking. I was thankful for this and would tell them of what I saw later, when this quest was done. I began to wonder when that might be. It was supposed to be today, but I had assumed the morning – now left hours behind. As I thought about this Two Bears said, "Redwolf, would you leave the mountain now with us or would you stay until sundown to finish anything still needing to be done?"

I was so ready to start back to Frank's that I surprised myself by saying, "I would stay another three hours, if that is alright with you both."

"So. We will go back to camp and return in three hours," Two Bears answered. With this they got up and left – with no further words between us.

I sat for the next three hours letting my heart and mind, at whatever speed and way they wished, roll back all that had come to me. This helped me feel connected to the present, but no new insights or occurrences came. I was not as aware of my physical discomfort as most of my attention was focused on my contemplations. The time moved quickly and about three hours later, I heard Frank and Two Bears coming my way. I stood as they neared as I felt my time sitting in this circle was now over. Whatever I needed to hear and see now complete – at least for the time being. Although it was still hot, I did not sweat, I assumed because there was little moisture in my body available for this.

"Redwolf, you look a little ragged," Frank spoke as they neared. "But not too bad for three days on the mountain. You have done well."

"He has," Two Bears chimed in. "But he needs some work before we bring him to his half side. I am certain Bonnie would have harsh words for him and me if she saw him this here way. Here, slowly have some water, nephew. Let it go down slow so you can feel it."

He handed me a water bottle and I took several long, slow drinks. Then I handed the bottle back to Two Bears, knowing that too much water, too quickly, after this long without would cause a lot of pain and could be harmful to my body. Then he gave me some cheese and a piece of corn tortilla to slowly nibble as we began to pack up my things. Actually, they packed up my things, as I felt very weak and light-headed. I stood and slowly ate my food. A peach followed, with another few drinks of water. By then my things were ready to carry off the mountain. I asked to carry my Chanunpa and tobacco pouch, but gladly allowed them to take the blankets in their arms. We slowly made our way down the trail, mostly for my benefit as I felt I had no 'legs' beneath me yet. We got to their camp in about twenty minutes and they picked up their supplies, which they had packed earlier. Frank stuffed the blankets I had been using in the back of his pack and I bowed my thanks to him. He smiled and nodded back. I had no extra energy to speak much yet, but instead concentrated on the trail below my feet. I'm not sure how long the trip back to Frank's truck took, but I know it was much longer than the initial climb up three days before. I began to apologize for slowing us down, but stopped as I realized that was not necessary and played into that 'not worthy' tape always playing in my head.

We threw our things in the back of Frank's truck as I gave a last look up the mountain where I sat for three days. I felt sure I would do a Hanbleche – vision quest—again, maybe more than once more, but this first one with its visit and vision was something I thought I would never forget, especially as I would learn from it for many years to come. I did not know if I would visit this place again, but I knew I would take it with me into ceremonies down the road. I felt complete in what I needed to do here. I got in the truck, wedged between Frank and Two Bears, sipped a little more water and promptly fell sleep. I awoke when we were pulling up to Frank's house, so my wish to watch how we drove from the mountain back to Frank's went unfulfilled. And I was okay with that.

"Redwolf, would you like some stew and bread?" Frank asked me.

"Yes, thank you, that may give me some energy."

"Will you call Bonnie tonight? Or maybe wait until morning," Two Bears spoke up.

"Maybe a quick call to let her know we are back," I answered. "With your permission, Frank," I said, pointing to his phone.

"Of course. I have plenty of minutes."

I dialed Bonnie and she answered on the second ring. "Hi, how are you?" I asked.

"I'm fine. How are you?" she quickly shot back at me.

"I'm good. Tired, thirsty, hungry and sore, but very, very good. Frank is making me some stew and fry bread and I'm sipping water here with Two Bears."

"You really went without food and water? You know you could really hurt your health playing those games," she said, with some anger in her voice.

"Not games, but my spiritual way now. Let's not fight. Everything is fine. I'll get a good night's sleep and I think Two Bears and I will head your way sometime in the morning. Okay?"

"Sure. We had a great time exploring the geology around here. We went further each time we went out. But now I feel like we've seen enough. So we will hang around town until you guys arrive. Shirley has called twice. She really wants to get up to Wyoming and get started on our horse-packing venture. Randy's ready to go and has got lists of the supplies we'll need. I think we may only get a few days home before we head out again," Bonnie filled me in.

"Whew. So much happening. Good thing I didn't take any summer courses to teach this year. Okay, I'll give a call when I wake up in the morning. Love you. Sleep well."

"Now, eat this slowly and then I think you need to crawl into bed. You look ragged," Frank said with a smile.

"I feel ragged. I'll happily eat, then sleep. Is it okay if we talk in the morning over coffee? I'm still not very alert and I'd like dreamtime to give me time to let things settle in my mind and heart."

"Fine," said Two Bears. "I am also tired and want to be fresh when we listen. Frank, okay?"

"Sure. I am glad to listen whenever we talk," Frank made it unanimous.

So I ate my small meal slowly, sharing my thanks and enjoyment with Frank and answering questions about my body pains, if I was warm now, the state of my throat...and the like. When Two Bears was certain I would survive until morning, he rose and said he would now find his bed. Frank and I bid him good night and chatted a few more minutes while I finished my meal. Then Frank took the dirty dishes and told me to get to bed. I thanked him again and gratefully followed his command.

I remember my head spinning all night and awakening many times to dreams that I could not quite remember. I was certain my brain was working on all the things that had been happening to me. All those things my upbringing would have told me were impossible. Delusions or mental breakdown. Things my heart and spirit now accepted. In other words, the rational and emotional parts of me were trying to reconcile everything in a way each could accept. At some point I did fall into a deep sleep from which I did not awake until nine in the morning – about three hours later than my usual wake up time. Two Bears and Frank must also have slept in, as I smelled the coffee just beginning to brew as I awoke. I pulled off my clothes, dragged myself to the bathroom and took a long, hot shower. I might have stood under the purifying water all day if I had not worried about depleting

Frank's hot water supply. Still, I let the hot, sharp water hit me for a long time, and then I got out, dried off and pulled some clean clothes on. Feeling somewhat alive I went out to join my guardians of the mountain – Two Bears and Frank.

"Morning," I said as I entered the kitchen, still with some 'croak' in my voice as sound rose up my sore throat. "Coffee. I would have given a lot for that those days on the mountain." I poured a mug and added extra cream, not wanting anything too hot or too cold going down my throat yet.

"That's good," Frank said watching me fix my coffee. "You'll want to be careful what you eat and drink for a few days. Drink as much water as you can those days too to bring strength back into you body."

"How do you feel otherwise?" Two Bears asked.

"Not bad physically. My back and knees hurt more than usual. The throat, of course. But not too bad. Mentally, I don't know. So much is going through my head that makes no sense to me. Yet when I go into my heart it makes total sense. Feels like the two are fighting – heart versus head."

"Try not to let them fight, but try to get them to speak together. Sit in council if that idea helps you. The more they fight, the harder it will be on you. Fear and other pieces can then appear. You know this, but it is time to say it again. And don't try to 'make sense' of things – especially not this soon. Pray on it, do Chanunpas for understanding; let your spirit fly free to seek wisdom – but not trying to use your mind to make sense. That will make you witko tko ke – crazy. This is not the time for crazy," Two Bears lectured.

"I'll try, but it's hard not to try and make all that happened fit comfortably in me. I hear your words, though and I know you are right."

"Um. Very hard to change the way you have thought for so many moons. Work on it whenever you feel anger or watogla [nervous]."

"I guess you two want to hear what came to me up there?"

"Only if you wish to speak it, Redwolf," Frank said solemnly.

"I would like to tell you both, it may help me. I think, as you allowed me to do before, I would like to speak about all that came, then here your words or questions. Okay?"

"Story telling is always a good way to speak your words," Two Bears agreed. "Let's get some of that food Frank here made and let me pour more coffee. I will hear better with my stomach filling."

We served ourselves some of the eggs and potatoes Frank had made as we were talking. And took some fry bread, honey and more coffee. Then we sat at the table together and I began telling my story, as you have heard it. As I finished telling of the visit from White Buffalo Calf Woman, we took a short break to use the bathroom, and then pour more coffee. I also went out front and called Bonnie. She and Carmen had also gotten up late and were just about to go to breakfast. We made plans to meet at two in the afternoon at a small café we both knew. Then I went back in, told Two Bears of the timing to meet with Bonnie, and resumed my story. When I finished, they both sat there deep in thought. Or, maybe, doubting my sanity or thinking thirst and exposure had addled me temporarily. No, they were deep in thought and it was not thoughts of my mental health. I picked up my mug, filled it with more coffee and went outside to give them some time to think or speak together if they wished.

I stood watching some small birds darting across the grass on the side of the house, sipping my coffee and generally enjoying the morning. When my cup was empty I took that as a sign to go back inside. Two Bears and Frank were chatting and laughing about some gathering they both were at a few years earlier. I was glad to see this as I had had enough serious demeanor to last me a while.

"Ah, Redwolf. We were having some fun as Frank reminded me is so important," Two Bears turned and told me.

"I'm ready for fun," I agreed. "My brain has had enough new, inexplicable information for now."

"Do you want to tell us your story or hold it for another day?" Two Bears asked.

"I'll talk if you wish to listen, but I hope we can do it with the same sense of fun you both were having."

"Good. Let's. We will try not to be serious old Indians and you try not to be a stressed wasicu [white person]."

"I will try not to be stressed, but wasicu I can't do anything about," I said smiling. I began with a quick rehash of what White Buffalo Calf Woman told me, then began telling of the vision of the second night. I spoke at length of the powerful connection between myself and my wolf guide and how I felt we were one at times. I saw Two Bears nodding as I recounted this. Then I began telling the rest of the vision, with special emphasis on the times I was in two or three places at once and the mental turmoil this caused me. When I finished I realized I was shaking slightly and hoped my Uncles here did not notice.

"It seems your vision here on the mountain was more of the one in my lodge before," Two Bears said astutely. "What do you feel now, as you speak?"

"Fear. Anxiety. Doubt. Wonder." I answered. "All jumbled together."

"Be slow. Handle only what you can – some at a time," Two Bears continued. "You are being shown a great deal. I don't say I see all your answers. But they are your answers, not mine, so you must see them when the time is right. I will continue to guide. As I think my brother Frank will also help with. We came here for a reason and Frank being here is part of it. His grandfather and his father both had powerful medicine. They saw many things and Frank had gotten this from them. Would this be okay, Frank?"

"I will do all I can if Redwolf here wishes it."

"It would be an honor. I feel like all the teachers I can get right now would be a good thing."

"So. You are welcomed here, at my home, any time. Or you can call me whenever you wish. I will call you when I am to tell you things," Frank spoke of how we would connect as he thought it through. "You know, I have not visited my brother here in Boulder for a long time. Maybe I will do this and we can also go into his lodge."

"What do you see of this vision, and the earlier one, which you did not see before?" Two Bears asked.

"Oh. Hm. Let me sit a few minutes with that," I stammered. I saw connections; I saw a pattern; I saw how the two connected – yet I did not have real clarity around all of this. I shared this with the two of them, then added, "I see I will need to be doing things with groups of people for many years. That has been clear both times, and at other times I have journeyed. But what that is, where it is and how it will come forth I am totally unsure of."

"That is good. A lot for now. You may remember other things, as they are needed. Or you may suddenly understand some piece of your vision that was cloudy before. As I have told you in the past," Two Bears lectured.

"Your vision is big Jim," Frank chimed in. "I believe it is all one vision and that it is not yet complete. Like all of us you will have your work to do. If you accept it. Two Bears and I will be here if you need us when your testing comes. As I see it will. As it does for many. Do not rush your learning. Or your understanding. Let the teachers find you that you will need. Know then when they come."

Frank's whole demeanor and style changed as he accepted me as student. I have seen this occur many times and believe I have also shifted in this way when one comes to me for instruction and I accept that request. I think it's the awareness that we have committed to a higher level of interaction with another human that causes this. It is helpful to see and understand a shift like this when it comes your way. It will help you trust and accept the help offered at a deeper, more meaningful level.

"I think you are not yet done with this vision. There are other parts or understandings that will still be brought to you," Two Bears spoke.

"Ah, yes," Frank took this thought forward. "Or the added pieces may come from within. I think both."

"What else would you hear from us now?" Two Bears asked me.

"I don't know what else to ask. I need to let everything sit and work through my being."

"Good," Two Bears said, as Frank also nodded. "Then let's get packed and be on our way. Bonnie expects us and probably wants to see you are in one piece." With this, we packed up our things, thanked Frank and headed out of Pine Ridge, heading west to meet Bonnie and Carmen.

I never expected to share any of this part of my story—in Wounded Knee and Pine Ridge—except with my teachers and those closest to me. Certainly not the visits by Black Elk or White Buffalo Calf Woman. Even as I share these things with you now I find it very slow and difficult to bring forth. Yet it was clear to me I was to share these things: Tell this part of the story and not leave out things I might be more comfortable keeping to myself. As I will continue to do as we journey together so that our circle is strong and complete from this side.

> *"Life is like a path...and we all have to walk the path... As we walk... we'll find experiences like little scraps of paper in front of us along the way. We must pick up those pieces of scrap paper and put them in our pocket... Then, one day, we will have enough scraps of papers to put together and see what they say... Read the information and take it to heart."*
>
> —Uncle Frank Davis (quoting his mother), PAWNEE

31 | Cowboy Time

Two Bears and I met Bonnie and Carmen just as they were getting ready to get some lunch, so we loaded their bags in the Jeep and went to a local café for some Mexican food. From there we decided to begin heading south towards Fort Collins, stopping for the night somewhere along the way so we could talk and share experiences. We headed south rather than taking route 90, stopping along the way at places that interested us. I remember we took about a ninety-minute walk through some rock formations about half way. About six hours later we arrived at Casper, Wyoming, where we took rooms for the night. Over dinner we talked about what the two pairs had done during our time apart. I shared some of my experiences, but was not ready to talk about all that had happened yet. Two Bears spoke of his pleasure in spending time with Frank, whom he had not seen in several years. And Bonnie and Carmen talked about the hikes they had taken and the rocks and wildlife they had encountered. It was an enjoyable evening, but we wrapped it up early since we were all tired by our experiences of the past few days.

Bonnie and I went to our room tired, but wanting to talk a little more before hitting the bed. "I know you have a lot more to say about your time with Two Bears, but I'm glad you are okay. You look more tired than I have ever seen and that cut on your leg looks mean, but otherwise you seem intact," Bonnie spoke, categorizing what she saw as she looked me over. This is something she did often, many times in a way that grated on me. But tonight I had to agree with what she saw.

"Yeah, I am really tired. So much happened that tired me physically, mentally and emotionally that I need some time to let my whole system work things through," I answered her. "I want to go out into the Center [Environmental Learning Center] and sit under the trees and let nature surround me."

"Well, you won't have much time for that for a while," Bonnie told me. "Shirley's called three times to see when we would be back so we could all head up to Cody and meet with Randy. The horses are all bought and ready and we would go with Randy to buy whatever supplies we don't have yet, then head up to the camp for a week. Are you ready for this?"

"I guess so. I was hoping we would have a few weeks so I could do some things at the Center and you and I could just chill. We need some time before we go to England with Hank and Linda, too. Well, it will work out, I guess."

"I'll call Shirley and tell her we'll meet the day after tomorrow and leave two days after that. Okay?"

"Sure. I know it will be an amazing experience, but I could use some nice, gentle, familiar quiet time about now."

"When we get back from this horse trip we will have about a month before Europe. Let's try to book nothing, okay? You can work at the Center and I know you must need time to work on your degree."

"Okay. I won't book anything, except local programs, until after Europe. And I do need time on my Master's work as well as some time on the Wetlands Initiative they asked me to be part of."

"I still don't understand why you have to do so much. I know you love it, but it seems to be running you now. Especially all this spiritual stuff, which all seems to be hard on your mind and is certainly a cold and dirty impact on your body. You and your native friends go out and come back covered in mud. What's the point of it? Oh, Shirley needs another thousand from us for our share of the supplies she bought for the horse packing thing."

"Write her a check, but remind her that's all there is for now, as we all agreed. I hope she got the permit worked out with Randy and the Forest Service. Let's ask her again. Her ability to follow through needs some help along the way," I said. "I won't get into this argument again about my spiritual path. I will stay on it and learn more. I don't ask why you get so absorbed by a bunch of rocks. But you are right about how much I am doing. And you are right about the impacts of this excursion with Two Bears. I'll tell you some of it now if you're not too tired."

"Good, I do want to hear about all of it, but maybe the short version for tonight and more when we are home. I'm sorry for the comments, but you seem to come back from these things in a lot of distress."

"Okay. I hear you. Let me tell you the short version and you will see where the stress and confusion come from. And I can see that if you are not on a spiritual road why this seems like something to avoid." I took about an hour and told Bonnie the events of the past few days and my reactions to them. She was always interested in things I had done, even if they had no interest for her, as I was with her passions, so she listened without saying much until I was done.

"It must have been an old Indian man you met. It makes no sense for a dead person to come back as a live person to talk to you. But, whatever way, that was quite a talk," Bonnie said as I finished.

"Most cultures have stories of ancestors returning, either in the flesh or in spirit form, to deliver messages after they have passed on. I admit, as you well know, this is pretty new to me and something I would have ignored or even mocked in the past. Yet it was something more than a man showing up in the middle of nowhere."

"How do you know when you have someone like the Buffalo Woman appear that you are not dreaming? Especially when you have gone without food or water for so long?"

"Boy, again, it's hard for me to explain, but it was not a dream nor was it my mind shaking with lack of nourishment. The same goes for the animal guides now coming my way stronger all the time. And I sense much more will come of this drawn out vision I am having, but not for a long time."

"I'm not even going there with the spirit animals. I know how connected you are to nature, animals and plants. It's amazing to watch, but I can't see this 'animals as teachers' thing at all. It doesn't compute in my Western mind. But I do respect how powerful it obviously is for you."

"Good, that's all I ask. And all we need do is honor each other's road and continue to connect through the realm of nature. We do not need to be the same, just respectful and understanding of each other. I'm glad this talk is going this way and not along the lines of the fights we've had around this before," I said.

"Me, too," Bonnie responded to me. "I do worry about money and health issues, but I am seeing you have to do what you are doing. That doesn't mean I can understand or easily accept it, but I do understand your need."

Although this non-spiritual versus spiritual way and, later, Western medicine versus other healing options, would continue to plague us, it no longer was a call to battle between us when it came up. This was a good thing for our walk together, even though, for the remainder of our time together, it frustrated me that Bonnie could not accept my help as we went forward. And, I am sure, it frustrated her just as much that I could not walk the materialistic road she still did. It was a partnership, I now see, that had meaning and purpose to the growth of each of us for as long as it was meant to.

We soon lay in bed, exhausted from so much, and quickly dropped off to sleep. I awoke at five AM, as usual, got up, went outside and watched the sun come up. Bonnie joined me just as the sun crested the horizon, so we watched together as we drank weak coffee from the motel lobby. Then we showered, dressed and met Two Bears for breakfast. As we got a table, Carmen joined us. We ate, and then hit the road so we would get to Fort Collins by noon.

Two Bears and Carmen both turned down lunch and opted for climbing into their cars and heading home. Bonnie and I went food shopping, then had a big salad for lunch, after which we began laying out what we would need for the horse-packing trek up behind Yellowstone. Bonnie then went off to campus to check on some papers for the geology class she had taken in the previous semester and I gave Lawrence a call. We met out at the ELC and took a walk as we planned a new version of our White Man, Red Man program we did for K-12 schools, where we taught the different approaches and values of nature to our cultures. After this we went to our lodge there and sat and relaxed together for a long time. We spoke little, as we often did – respecting each other's need and way of connecting to the land we sat on. After a while we burned some sage and smudged ourselves, then headed to our respective homes for dinner. It was good time together that day, as it was when I sat with Lawrence, no matter what we did.

Bonnie had spoken with Shirley and we arranged to leave in two days, giving us one more day to scrape the dirt off ourselves and heal our wounds. I was now all fired up by this next project on our agenda, as was Bonnie who had never ridden a horse the distances we would need to now.

We met Shirley early on the morning we were to drive to Cody, Wyoming, where we would meet Randy, buy the gear we still needed and then head to Red Lodge, Montana, where we would begin our journey to the campsite over Yellowstone. It was a good eight-hour drive to Cody, so we booked rooms for the night and agreed to meet Randy at 7 AM for breakfast the next day. We took Shirley's car and ours, as she had already acquired a fair amount of gear in Fort Collins. We arrived in Cody about six PM, stopped at our rooms and then headed out for dinner at the Irma Hotel, built by Buffalo Bill in the early 1900's. It was here we would meet Randy for breakfast, but Shirley remembered the large steaks and plentiful fries they served and wanted to experience them again.

The Irma Hotel was out of the Old West, both in décor and in the look of some of the patrons. There was a large contingent of tourists—cameras swinging, bright-colored shirts blazing and brand new 'cowboy' hats cocked atop heads. But there were also a good number of locals there to order big steaks and, probably, to enjoy watching the tourists as much as the tourists watched them. Some of the locals were dressed in genuine 'just off the back forty' garb and others were not so genuinely dressed with spurs, leather leggings and deer hide vests. But we enjoyed watching the scene unfold as we ate, wondering what niche we might fall into for those looking at us.

"This place is a trip, Shirley," I said around a mouthful of steak.

"I told you it would be fun," she answered with a smile.

"What look does Randy generally have, Shirley?" Bonnie asked. "Does he come on like a cowboy, ranch hand or nondescript local?"

"You know, I can't say. I guess we'll all be surprised."

After dinner, Shirley was tired and headed back to her room. Bonnie and I began a walk around town, going up the main street and coming back on the more residential streets a couple of blocks below Main Street. We always enjoyed walking through towns we found interesting, seeing much more than you ever did driving. Cody is quite a little tourist mecca, being the gateway town to one of the Yellowstone entrances, but we liked it's look and feel and decided to return another day to explore more. We had been in Cody in the past, but just driving through to get to the park. Now we realized we had missed a place to explore and were glad we had some time here now. After walking for a couple of hours we decided to head back to our room, since the next day promised to be a long one.

I was up at five and after a refreshing, hot shower, I went out for a walk. I walked lazily down the street in the pre-dawn dark, just enjoying the lack of people or noise. My mind wandered over the assortment of varied stimuli I had been getting over the past month and was reeling with random thoughts. After a bit I calmed it and walked back to the room about six, just as Bonnie was beginning to stir.

"Morning," I said as she sat up, still half asleep. "I am going to get some coffee in the lobby if any is made yet while you shower. Want some?"

"Yeah, thanks. I feel really groggy. A cup of black coffee will help. No rush is there?"

"None," I answered. "It's just after six and I don't think we'll see Shirley until eight. She doesn't move fast, especially in the morning."

"Maybe I'll lie down another thirty minutes then. No...maybe not. I'll just feel more tired when I get up. But that coffee, as soon as you can, would be a help," Bonnie smilingly said.

I went to the lobby where the coffee was brewing and filled two cups, sipping mine as I did so. I carried the cups back to our room, spilling some of the hot morning elixir down my hand as I juggled cups while opening the door. Bonnie was drying her hair, which she stopped doing as she came out for her coffee.

"I wish they would use better coffee in motels, but at least it's hot," she said as she sipped from her cup.

"I know, and I wish they would find a way for people to open the always heavy motel room doors without spilling the coffee," I responded smiling.

"Shirley rang while you were getting coffee. We are going to meet her in half an hour at the Irma hotel and have breakfast with Randy."

"Good. I'll load the bags so we will be ready."

Forty minutes later Shirley, Bonnie and I were entering the Irma hotel and taking a table for four. Shirley said Randy was on the way and would arrive soon. After breakfast we could pick up the additional supplies he listed and then head for Red Lodge. About fifteen minutes later, as we sat drinking coffee, Randy entered. Bonnie and I both knew it was him, both by Shirley's description and his garb. He wore jeans covered by leather riding breeches, a big, red bandana, a huge cowboy hat with a silver band and fancy leather boots. He had gotten all 'cowboyed up' to meet his new partners.

"Howdy," Randy said, reaching out a hand to shake. We shook hands, with his clasp being strong and then he shook with Bonnie, followed by a hug for Shirley. "Glad you are all here," he continued. "I'd like to go over some things then get started. Okay?"

We talked for about an hour as we ate – mostly about the campsite and the visitors we hoped to attract. Randy had the horses ready, the six he had bought with our money so far. He seemed all right, even if over the top with the cowboy getup.

"We need some more dishes and supplies for the cook tent," Randy resumed near the end of the meal. "We'll drive on out to a small town along the way. There's a place with the best prices there. Then we can head to Red Lodge and get ready to go up to the camp."

"Sounds good," I said. "We'll follow you. What are you driving?"

"A blue and white Ford pickup. I'm parked around back."

We followed Randy to the general store and picked up the additional supplies he had requested, then we headed for Red Lodge, about two hours away. We took the Highway to the Sun Road, which was a glorious western highway wending high up from which beautiful views abounded. It got colder as we approached Red Lodge and I saw some snow flurries up ahead. It could snow any time of the year in this part of the country and the snow showers were proving this out. By the time we got to Red Lodge a fairly heavy snow was falling and the whole sky was slate gray.

"I thought we might head up this afternoon, but we better stay the night here. This weather will get worse as we climb and none of you are seasoned riders," Randy decided, without discussion. We were okay with this because we were novice riders, but I made a mental note of his unilateral decision, so we could talk later.

We took rooms at a local motel and split up, each on their own way. Bonnie and I decided to walk around this scenic town, braving the snow and wind. We lasted at this for about two hours, and then headed to our room to read and talk. The four of us met for dinner and then all went to our rooms early, so we could get an early start.

We were up and dressed before dawn the next morning and headed sleepily into the lobby to meet the others.

"Let's get some quick breakfast and hit the road to the kickoff point for the campsite," Randy said as we arrived. Shirley was already there, eating an egg and drinking hot, steaming tea.

"Sounds okay to me," I answered Randy. "But I do need some food in me before riding the horses that far." We gathered our things and walked next door to a restaurant, where we all ordered a full breakfast and shared a pot of hot, black coffee. Then we piled into our car and Randy fired up the truck. We drove up the road that connected Red Lodge to the northeast entrance to Yellowstone Park. There was a pull-off where we could leave the cars about twenty-five miles up the road. From there it was horseback in and up – always up.

As we climbed the road snow began falling once again. It got heavier as we continued to gain altitude and was a thick, wet fall when we reached the parking area. We climbed out of our car and Shirley and Randy out of the truck and gathered by the horse trailer Randy had pulled behind him. A young cowboy came over to us. This was Mark, a young man Randy had hired for the summer to help with the horses and camp. Mark tipped his hat our way and shook hands with Randy. Mark had been there all night with the five horses we would ride in to camp. He had slept in his pickup, but was ready for some food and coffee. Randy had brought big portions of both for him. He sat on the fender of the horse trailer and began to eat as we began to discuss the weather.

"I'd like to try and go up this morning. This time of year we might find this weather for a week, so it's go or have a real long wait," Randy explained.

"Is it safe bringing us greenhorns up the mountain in the snow?" I asked.

"Yep. We can always turn back and we might ride out of it. It's often snowing down here, but clear when we get to the high country. But it's up to you all," Randy said.

I had ridden some in the past and could sit a horse fairly well. Shirley had also ridden and was a fair rider, although she was a much larger person now and I didn't know how the cold and altitude might affect her. Bonnie had only ridden a few times when we had taken trail rides – tame compared to this.

"Well, what do you both think?" I asked the ladies.

"I'm ready to go," Bonnie spoke up. "And I have the least experience. But I feel good with the mild manner horse you helped me pick, Randy."

"I'm set also," Shirley said. "Randy is an expert with horses and won't lead us where it's not safe. And we have Mark to help as needed."

"Good. Let Mark and I get the horses loaded and then we will help you all saddle up," Randy said, obviously happy we were game for this.

It took them over an hour to saddle the horses and then load each with what they were to carry. It is an art setting the weight and balance for each horse. I watched Randy and Mark shift things, move packs between horses, test straps and, finally, seem satisfied. They then came over to us and watched as we saddled our horses and pulled ourselves up. It was long past daybreak now, but the heavy snows kept the visibility like twilight. Finally, Randy threaded a line between all the horses. He wanted to keep track of everyone until, and if, the snows eased and visibility improved. We moved out – Randy in the lead, followed by Bonnie, Shirley, me and Mark. We started slowly across the snow swept road and up the barely visible trail on the other side. Soon we were all very cold and very wet, with heavy, wet snow clinging to our clothes and faces. After about an hour I thought the snow was lightening somewhat. Randy stopped our equine train and asked if anyone needed to get rid of their morning coffee. I spoke up, dismounted and went behind a rock outcropping to pee. When I went back to the horses I saw Bonnie and Shirley were both off. A few minutes later, they returned from the backs of other rock outcroppings in the area.

"Does anyone need a rest? I think the snow is lettin' up a hank and I'd like to keep goin'," Randy put forth.

"Let's keep going," Bonnie answered him. "I'd like to get out of this wetness. It's getting into my bones."

"Okay. Saddle up folks," Randy ordered.

After about another forty-five minutes we were riding through snow squalls, broken by long stretches of no snow.

"Whew, that feels good," Shirley said with a big sigh.

"Yeah," I agreed. "Can we lose the lead rope?"

"Sure, if you want to," Randy agreed. "You all want to try some ridin' on your own, huh?"

"I'd sure like to," Bonnie said. She still looked unsure on a horse, but was gung ho to improve her skills.

Mark removed the line joining us and we set off free of the guiding rope. Bonnie's horse, Poncho, immediately began pulling away from the rest. Mark went over and gave her some riding advice and soon she was able to have Poncho go where she wished. She looked very serious for a while, then she turned into all smiles as she felt Poncho working with her.

We stopped to drink some water and enjoy the scenery a while later. We were at about 15,000 feet and our breathing was labored. We still had about another thousand feet to go up and Randy gave us some time to get used to the thin air. The snow had now stopped and we were quickly leaving the clouds below us. It was an awesome, eerie sight to look down on clouds from a sunny place above. It was like being in a plane without the plane. After about four hours of riding, stopping to rest and be awed by views and checking loads and straps, we reached our camp.

There are not many permits in these mountains and Randy had owned this one for years. I'm not sure what I expected, but it was not the cook tent, small log cabin and array of five other tents we came upon. Nor the four other horses corralled to the north of the camp. Even more surprising was the smoke coming out of the cook tent.

"That's Rosalie. She came up three days ago with me and the other horses and supplies. She'll cook and tend the horses when I'm gone. Been a mountain cowgirl her whole life. Need to know anything, just ask her," Randy said, explaining the smoke.

Rosalie came out as Randy spoke, hearing us and wanting to welcome us to camp. She was of average height, with dark hair and sun darkened skin. She was big, without being overweight, with strong hands and a huge smile. "Howdy. Been waiting' for ya all. Wondered if you'd try it. Glad you made it. It's been great weather up here, if mighty cold at night. I cooked up some hot vittles. Thought you might all be cold and hungry."

Immediately I liked Rosalie. She was genuine. Not the practice 'cowboys' we experienced often. I could tell from Bonnie's expression she was also taken by Rosalie. We followed her into the tent as Randy and Mark went to tend to the horses and off load the supplies.

"Take yer time walkin' and don't even try running for a while," Rosalie advised. "You are up mighty high and the air is real thin. It's easy to get sick if you're not careful at first. And if you brought any drinkin' alcohol, I wouldn't have more than one drink − if any. The alcohol goes straight to the blood and yer drunk as the hills in a minute."

"No, no alcohol," Bonnie answered her. "Only for rubbing on our backs."

"That's the good kind up here," Rosalie laughed. "You might need that every day."

We had some beef stew and noodles, along with big slabs of cornbread. Hot coffee and tea were on the table, as were two big pitchers of water. Rosalie had already advised us to drink all the water we could as our bodies adjusted to the altitude. We chatted as we ate, then each went to claim our tents and put our gear inside. Randy came walking over to Bonnie and I as we were choosing a tent.

"I thought you might like the cabin. It's cozy and you're the only couple here this time."

"Sure, if that's okay," Bonnie quickly agreed, as tent camping was not her idea of fun. So we carried our gear into the cabin and set up our bags on two cots ready for us along the wall across from the door. "This is great," Bonnie beamed. "I've been dreading nights in a drafty tent. Now we can sleep in some comfort."

"Yeah, works for me," I agreed.

About an hour later Randy said he thought we should wait for the next day to take a ride to the edge of the mountain, where we could look down into Wyoming far below. We agreed and all decided to just take some walks near the camp and then help Rosalie unpack and store what we had brought up. We spent the rest of the day doing just that, in addition to enjoying a beautiful, multi-colored sunset. We had another great meal of pork chops, beans, bread and cake, followed by steaming cups of tea around the bonfire Mark had built and lit. We sat for hours, telling stories and sharing ideas for the backpacking business we were in together. Finally, we broke up around eleven and headed to our shelters. Bonnie and I were exhausted; by the trek up the mountain and our nervousness on horseback, the thin air and the physical labor of unpacking and stowing supplies. We pulled extra blankets from our supplies, zipped into our bags and tried to sleep. After about thirty minutes of sharing our impressions of the day, we quieted and soon were asleep. I expected to awaken by five as usual. Boy, was I wrong.

I awoke about three AM and lay listening to the quiet for ten or fifteen minutes – thinking I would drop back to sleep. Soon I realized I was not going to go back to sleep easily, so I grabbed a flashlight, quietly crawled out of my bag so as not to awaken Bonnie, felt around until I found my coat and slipped out of the cabin. Starlight and moon glow made for plenty of light to see where I was going. The only question for me was 'where was I going'? I didn't want to go near the horses, as I might spook them and wake the others, but I did want to take a walk, so I headed towards the rock face to the north of the camp. I had pulled a heavy blanket out of the cabin and took this with me also, in case I got cold by the rocks. I found a good place to sit amongst the rocks, where any wind that came up would be blocked by some huge boulders jutting out from the face of the wall. I put the blanket underneath me for warmth, as I had on the mountain in Pine Ridge, and pulled the excess up and over my shoulders. I crossed my legs under me and relaxed into my makeshift 'igloo' of rock and blanket. I was quite comfortable and warm and proceeded to lean back against the rock wall and look up at the sky. I thanked Great Spirit for the blessing and wonder of this trip and place and then began to quietly invite in the seven directions. I had not brought my Chanunpa, tobacco or sage, as I did not know what this journey would entail and, truthfully, none of this group were on a spiritual road and I did not want to explain my ceremonies. Now I realized my mistake, but, as Two Bears had trained me, I began my ceremonies without the need for my 'tools'. I functioned as if my Chanunpa, tobacco and sage were all with me and used them in a virtual way. I even drummed, although I had not brought a drum either.

I allowed my awareness to flow into my heart as I worked to calm my mind. Soon I was floating along in a beautiful way, thinking about the ride up here to camp, the things we could use this camp for and the very different plants, here at 16,000 feet, I could connect with around their healing ways. I could hear the horses milling about, dragging the fetters tied to a leg behind them, neighing at times as they grazed and thought nighttime horse thoughts. I heard a large raptor screeching up above somewhere and believed it to be a hawk. I could also hear an owl hooting somewhere down below where we were camped – as if the sound were rising up the side on the escarp-ment we were on, as I suspect it was. And I could hear the wind softly whishing along the rocks around me. The smell of night blooming flowers was moving along with these soft breezes. I thought I would sit here until dawn, quietly sensing all around me, as I was in such a state of pleasure. Although I knew there were bears up here I did not fear their presence as long as I was close to camp and the fire. Randy had shared this comforting thought, while also balancing that with the reminder that they could come into camp, especially if we were sloppy with food storage. I sent a silent prayer of gratitude to all the creatures who lived here on this mountaintop and assured them I meant no harm and would do no harm to their home here. Then I silenced my chattering thoughts and again checked in with all around me through all my senses.

As I lay there relaxing and connecting in with the energies of the land around me I began to feel some creature approaching. I did not feel any fear, but I did sharpen my concentration on my hearing as I tried to hear from where it came. But I could hear nothing – nor were any of my other senses helping me pinpoint this visitor, if there even was one. After several more minutes of this sensory watchfulness I heard, smelled or saw nothing, so I assumed I had just imagined a visitor. I relaxed once again, quieted my mind and re-entered my heart's realm. As I did this I realized I was again sensing an animal guest and, in an instant, sensed my wolf guide beside me – ever watchful and patient. As I welcomed him I remember my brain thinking 'Why would my guides come now? Why here where there are no others on a spiritual road? This is not a logical time for this'. And of course it was not a 'logical' time for my spirit guide to appear as, in fact, no time for a spiritual event was based on logic. If I had to wait for logic to dictate when the time was correct for another spiritual enlightenment, I would still be that nervous, unsure white guy waiting to go in his first lodge. So I simply welcomed my four-legged guide and waited to see what, if anything, he wished me to do.

I sat there in the presence of my wolf guide for some time just waiting for what might come next, realizing nothing may come, especially as I was not journeying nor had I asked for any guidance. I had yet to learn that sometimes things just came, unbidden and unrequested, when the time was right or the need present. I began to see wolf with my heart's eyes as we sat here – flesh and spirit – side by side in the rocks. I again wondered at his coat of so many colors and the way they seemed to flow and shift as I watched. I had thought about these colors on wolf often, wondering what they represented, as colors had so much meaning in the cultures I was working with. I wondered if they were the colors of people; the colors of the seasons of the medicine wheel; the colors of the wolf clans or the colors of the direction. And I had given up this game as nonproductive, as no answer presented itself, and decided they may represent any of these things at different times – or none of them.

As these thoughts went through my head I heard a spirit voice calling from my heart and again calmed my mind, relaxed and invited what might come. The voice simply said, "there is more". And with this, I saw Black Elk standing next to me circled by several other ancestors I did not recognize. He was here in spirit, but looked very much as he did that day he came to me on the rez. He may have been somewhat older, but I was unsure of this, as he was not in clear 'focus' as he appeared to me. He looked at me with a serious expression and held up his right hand in the direction of the sky. As he did a swirl of people and images I had seen before in Two Bears' lodge and on the mountain went across my field of vision. After a short time these pictures in my head ceased and I could only see Black Elk before me – and the other elders behind him. These elders were very fuzzy – more a vague impression of people seated around what seemed to be a fire.

Then pictures again came – pictures of people gathering and the Sanctuaries that would later evolve. And I was again moving among the people in various locations where these groups formed on the Earth Mother. People were working together and gathered around fires or tables or in rooms or out on the land. The workings of various groups, no matter how geographically separated, seemed in harmony between them, and yet each had elements that were their own. I was seeing what I had seen before and wondering why it was brought to me again. As this thought passed through me the pictures vanished and Black Elk stood shaking his head. I did not understand and mentally sent this to both he and wolf. He nodded and the pictures began again, yet I still saw little difference from what I had seen before. I was a little frustrated, my minimal patience again getting in my way. The pictures again ceased and I was in circle with Black Elk and the others. I then got the message I was to bring these things together. I began thinking, "I can't do that. There are others with the connections to do this" and watched Black Elk frown. From the collective circle I was getting the impression I was to pull people to this – those who were needed there. I was to be a catalyst; a role I already played often in other areas. I was to bring the teachings of the Earth Mother to the group – some of which would be reminders of what many had taught through time, some new ways to interact with her. I would help bring the 'green' in with the four colors of the wheel. Then I would be one of the circle, helping explore new ways to create as a group, without one or a few controlling. I was 'hearing' all of this through all of my senses. I don't know how to explain or describe this other than that statement. Then I was shown I had a great deal more to learn and that I was to continue to learn 'portions' of many things – not all of one or two things. Finally, I was shown that the humans and the other creatures in this recurring vision were connected in ways we did not possess at this time. Some of these ways we were capable of in the past, others were new skills we would need to develop as we evolved and again connected with the Earth Mother. And when humans again became truly aware that our minds, bodies and spirits were truly one. When we really trusted and understood that we would be able to use them collectively in ways no one element of this group could provide. This is how and why the various Sanctuaries were connected without obvious electronic infrastructure.

I sat thinking how much crazier this seemed to get all the time and that I would continue to honor my promise to Great Spirit by serving through non-profits and my teaching. But this huge gathering and creating of natural spaces and working with others to evolve new skills was way beyond me. As I thought these things the ancestors around me, who had almost faded from my perception as my head again took over, came back into a little more focus. Their collective teaching was that I had free will, but this pulling together of the people around this work was why I walked this time. I would decide later, when more came to me, what I could and would do. And then all were gone, including wolf, and I sat looking up at the stars and the moon. Wondering again why this had come now and, to be honest, again questioning if I should check my mental health with the CSU medical staff. Well, for now, I would put all this away. I was, after all, working on our horse-packing endeavor, which would also serve many people and help provide new ways to connect to nature. I did not realize that these repeated 'visions' were actually one vision I was being given as I was able to handle it and that I would not be given more for many years. Nor did I realize I would forget much of this, as I have shared, until much later down the road. True to my pledge to myself, I put all of this out of my mind and enjoyed the approaching sun-up.

"I think I have told you, but if I have not, you must have understood, that a man who has a vision is not able to use the power of it until after he has performed the vision on earth for the people to see."

—Black Elk

I went to the cook tent shortly after sunup, being led by the smell of coffee growing stronger by the moment. When I entered the tent I found Rosalie pouring herself a large cup of the freshly brewed camp coffee.

"How'd you sleep, Jim? Seems I heard you moving about mighty early."

"Fine, Rosalie. Yeah, that was me. I am always up by five and moving into my day, but I awoke in the middle of the night and couldn't get back to sleep. I went outside and just sat listening to the night until the dawn came."

"Doesn't rate as good sleepin' to me, but each to their own. Feel like helpin' by cutting up some fruit while I make some pancake batter?"

"Sure. No problem. As long as I can have some coffee," I answered.

While we began making breakfast, Randy walked in with his empty mug in his hand.

"Morning all," he said as he filled his mug from the coffee pot. "Jim, I reckon we all can take a ride to the back side of this mesa and take a look down into the park. It's about a two-hour ride. What do you think?"

"Sounds good. My butt hurts, but I'll get used to the horse moving under me again soon. Let's ask the others."

"They're comin' this way. Be here in a minute. Later we can ride to the east and look down on the ranch I throw my sleeping bag in for the winter. It's down far, but visible. The riding will give you all an idea of the land up here and what it has to offer."

We all agreed this was a good idea for our first full day up here. So after a good, hearty breakfast we saddled up and headed west. We followed trails that were hardly visible into landscape that gave no real unique markers along the way, so I was glad Randy knew this land so well. We went at a slow pace, allowing us as novice riders the opportunity to better move with our horses. We crossed many streams – sometimes jumping them and sometimes letting the horses feel their way across, wetting our shoes and pants in the process. A couple of the streams were fairly deep and wide, so we followed upstream until better places to cross appeared. It was a magical ride, with majestic, snow-covered mountaintops around us, trees of all shapes and sizes appearing around each bend. Often wonderland trees, bent and twisted into imagination tweaking shapes by the winds and weather where we rode. We often heard birds before we saw them, their voices and songs carried far in the thin air. I was surprised to see magpies, not expecting them at this altitude. Most of the birds were small and fast, but we saw a good number of hawks along the way as well. Lichens and mosses of stunning colors showed themselves often, especially when we passed hillsides or rock outcroppings.

Bonnie and I chatted as we rode, commenting about how we felt we were in an old Western. Finally we reached the overlook Randy wanted us to see and we stood looking out over the vast vista before us. It was a breath taking sight, with sweeping land going down deep, deep below us with hills and mountains rising at spots out of the lowlands to soar at our level or higher. I wondered where the faeries were and was certain the ogres walked the valleys below. We separated and sat and enjoyed the scene and sounds for some time, then came together in a group and talked about the land, animals and plants all around us. Each of us noted just how small and insignificant we felt standing here, but also how blessed we felt to be given the chance to see and experience this land that so few actually visited. After eating bag lunches Rosalie had sent with us, we remounted and began heading back to camp. I would visit this spot many times that summer, but this first time was one of the 'extraordinary nature' pictures imprinted in my brain and heart with others from the Earth Mother's special places.

When we got back to camp we were tired from the altitude and the riding, but we still wanted to go west and see that view. We agreed to rest for an hour and then meet by the cook tent. Randy wanted to swap out two horses and check on some meat he had hung, making sure any bears would not be drawn in by it. Bonnie and I went to our cabin and lay down to rest. About forty-five minutes later, I heard one of the horses whinnying and snorting and quickly went out to see what was wrong. Randy had the lead to one of the horses – a big Roan – in one hand and a whip in the other. He was yelling at the horse and flicking the whip against his neck, attempting to pull him down on his side. I went over to them as fast as I could, not really knowing what was going on, but pained by the horse's distress.

"Randy, what's wrong?" I yelled so he could hear over the noise.

"Horse won't work with me to get ready for the ride. I'm reminding him who the lead is here."

Bonnie had followed me out and was standing behind me. "He may be the cowboy, but those are our horses," she said to me. Then she raised her voice, "Randy, that is not what I will ever accept with any animal. And certainly not our horses!"

Randy was furious at the 'horse who would not obey him', but obviously equally confused with how to answer Bonnie's words.

"This is the only way horses learn who is in charge. And up here we need our horses. I'm not hurting him physically, but I am putting fear into him. I'll have everything in control in a few minutes," he panted out.

"Let that horse up now!" I yelled in a fury. My anger overcame me, once again, and I let it fly. I would have been much better served to let Bonnie continue talking, but I still had many anger issues. And seeing an animal in pain – physical or not – was sure to trigger me every time.

"I'm the leader when we are up here and I'll work with the horses the way I always have," Randy yelled back, as angry as me.

"Let the horse up, Randy," Bonnie said somewhat more rationally than we two males were screaming at each other. "If you don't I'll pull my share of the funding and the work from this business and you won't be able to be up here without money."

Somehow I managed to keep my mouth shut and just wait. In a few seconds Randy let the horse up and came over to us. I hoped there would be no fistfight between us, since he was younger and stronger than I was. But my anger was so red hot; part of me hoped he would come at me.

"I told you I ain't hurting' the horses, just getting them to obey," he yelled at both of us.

"Not with me here and not with our horses," Bonnie quietly said.

"Look, I been doin' this for a lot of years. I know what I'm doing."

"Not with our horses," Bonnie repeated. "What if we had paying guests along? What do you think they would say or feel watching you mistreat the horses?"

"Ain't no one ever complained about the trip or how I take care of the horses."

"Maybe too afraid of you or too shocked by your behavior to say anything," I said.

"You people come up here, think you know it all and can just tell everyone what to do. Bullshit to that. I lead the trips and I give the orders up here!"

"I don't know anything about horse packing, except what I've learned since we teamed up. But I do know what I won't allow. And

I will take my share of the funds out of this with her. That means you can't even get up here where you want to be. And you lose your permit. You want to tell us how to ride, or pack a saddle, or cut wood or any other thing we are novices and I will happily listen and do it. But when it comes to the horses you will need to find another way. I've watched my sister get her horses to do all she wishes with strong words and guidance. No reason these horses can't be treated with the same respect."

"I'll try to go easier, but don't point at me if a horse doesn't behave and someone gets hurt. But, up here, I'm the boss. We don't want no one getting hurt."

"No one's arguing about you being boss, Randy," Bonnie said with a pleasant smile, "Only with how you were treating a horse. So, we got this over with. Randy's the camp boss, but he will find a new way to work with our horses. I'm going to get my gear so I'm ready for a ride. That ride this morning was almost unreal, Randy. Can you match it going the other way?"

"Sure. The views are pretty wonderful anyway we might go. I'll show you some rocks that might interest you," Randy answered Bonnie, seemingly forgetting how angry he was a few minutes ago.

I wished I had learned more lasting lessons as I watched others, like Bonnie did here, work with someone like Randy. But when you threatened me or mine or attacked things I held dear, I attacked back just as fiercely. Yet other times I could get people to come together and work in unison. Maybe there is a time for both – or was. I don't think we now have the time or energy to fight with all who may disagree with us.

Shirley and Rosalie had stood outside the cook tent and watched the scene between Randy, Bonnie and I. As I approached them, Shirley pulled me aside. "Jim, without Randy we don't have the unique opportunity to get students and others up here. He knows what he's doing. He would never really hurt one of the horses..."

"Shirley, I have no intention to argue with you defending him. It's simple, Bonnie and I are out if he does anything like that again."

"Okay, I'll talk with him."

"Leave it alone. Maybe it will pass and we can all move forward."
But I knew Randy would probably never forgive me for 'showing
him up', as he would see it. And probably not forgive Bonnie for dar-
ing, as a woman, to argue with how he did his job. I just hoped we
could move forward with this business because the natural world up
here was so valuable as a teacher.

We stayed on the mountain for nine days, enjoying every moment
seeing something new almost everywhere we turned. And learning
about horses and camping in remote and extreme environments. By
the third day, Bonnie and I felt comfortable enough to ride off on
short sojourns by ourselves. We would pack our bags, take some food
and head to a new place each time. A compass and paying new attention to landmarks got us back to camp each time.

In camp we all took turns helping with cooking and clean up.
I enjoyed these chores and chatting with Rosalie, who always had
a funny story to share. At night we could hear snuffling around the
cabin and growls coming not too far from camp. Coyotes serenaded us
often, as did night birds. It reminded me of the jungle in Belize, even
if the environment was completely different. Finally the day came to
leave and we packed and left early. The ride back to the car and truck
was much easier than the ride up had been. There was no snow and
we were much more comfortable in the saddle. We hated going, but
knew we would be back in a month with a group from our department at Colorado State.

During the month between trips to the camp above Yellowstone,
I spent a great deal of time out in nature. Often Bonnie would come
along, but sometimes she sensed I needed time alone with the trees,
birds, wind and sun. I kept trying to rationally 'figure out' the escalat-
ing spiritual encounters and occurrences of the past year. I had yet to
learn that using the head in spiritual matters was a sure-fire way to just
add to my doubt and confusion. I tried to stay in my heart as so many
had suggested, but had a great deal of difficulty mastering this skill. I
find most people brought up in the Western culture have a difficult

time staying in their heart. I still struggle with this today, but am at least able to recognize when the head holds too much sway in my experience of the moment and am able to shift to heart lead.

The plan Shirley, Bonnie and I had developed for the horse packing business was to bring in six groups of eight people for a trip to the camp. This was what Randy had done in the past, but he lacked the knowledge and time to promote the trips so business had dried up. We thought to promote this special adventure in both the East and West Coast regions, charging a premium price for an experience few people would ever have. When these were booked we would have paid for our time and the salaries Randy and the other help needed. The remainder of the income would go to providing trips for groups of students, so they might learn about this fragile environment first-hand. This was the real reason we had agreed to Randys' request to become the business partners of the venture. In order to get university credit for the students we had booked a trip taking Ron, Hank, Linda, Sam, Shirley and myself. This would give half of our department faculty time to see what we had developed. Bonnie was not included since we were short a horse and it was considered a department retreat. Usually she didn't care when things came up I needed to be at, as I did not when she went off on geology field treks. But this time not including her turned out to be a bad idea, especially for me. We got into a fierce argument and didn't speak for days. Then, when we had both cooled off, we talked about it more and her point that she was one of the owners of the business and therefore entitled to a place, made sense to me. Shirley was not happy with this, but Bonnie and I out-voted her on this. So we called Randy and had him secure another horse – something we would have to do the following spring regardless.

And so we headed back to Red Lodge a month later to meet up with Randy and the crew. We drove up separately and all arrived by late afternoon, late in the summer, to another snowstorm with strong, biting wind. Happily we had intended to spend the night in Red Lodge and ride up in the morning, so, after cleaning up, we all met for a steak dinner and drinks. Randy met us and we introduced him around after which he began talking about the trip coming in the morning. After dinner, we ordered some more drinks and partied until eleven, when Randy reminded us we would be up by dawn. Hank and Linda had more than a few drinks and Bonnie reminded me someone needed to discuss the effects of alcohol on people at the altitude we would be at. I decided to ask Rosalie, who was again cook, to talk about this as she had with us on the first trip. I did not want to rock the boat with Hank and Linda since they were both on my academic committee.

We got up in the morning to find it snowing once again, this time in the middle of summer. Summer up here often means 'less chance of snow' rather than 'break out the beachwear'. It was not too heavy a snow, however, and Randy decided it was okay to head towards camp. We got to the parking area just as dawn broke and the snow slowed. Once again, Randy and Mark got the horses all packed and saddled, instructing our guests about their mounts and the need to be careful given the deep snow we would be in for at least part of the trip. Ron, always the 'rah-rah' type of guy, was pushing to begin the ride.

"Got it, Randy. We'll be careful where we ride and stay close together," he said loudly as Randy was helping Sam get on his horse. "Come on Sam, get your butt in the saddle so we can get on up this mountain!" With this, Ron crossed the road and began moving up the trail. He looked back, saw the rest of us still waiting on Randy and reined his horse in—waiting impatiently.

I looked around and observed the nervousness of Hank and Linda, the false bravado of Sam, the slightly more comfortable Bonnie and the 'let's race ahead' demeanor of Ron as I waited for Randy to lead us out. Shirley just sat her horse, waiting patiently for the ride. She was obviously enjoying just being here and being around Randy, whom she still had feelings for. Finally, Sam said he was ready and Randy turned towards the trail and led us out. I saw him wave Ron over to him, chat a moment and then move out again. This time Ron followed behind him, big grin on his face and a wink in my direction. I really like Ron. We had become friends before I arrived at CSU, when he accepted me as one of his graduate students, but he was prone to being a ham at times, which could be both fun and annoying at the same time. I assumed Randy had told him to follow, not lead, on this trek.

We slowly wended our way up the mountain with the horses working their way through the two feet of snow on the ground. It was a beautiful sight – snow everywhere, decorating the trees and rocks we rode past. After a while Ron again began testing Randys' patience, riding out a couple hundred feet from the group. Randy just looked and said nothing.

"This is like riding through a dream!" Ron bellowed as he beamed. "I'm feeling more comfortable all the time. Look at that stream rushing over there. Boy, this is a thrill!"

Ron rushed towards the stream he mentioned, obviously with the intention of jumping his horse over it.

"Ron," I called out. "You can't really see what's beneath this snow. You might want to take it slow and..."

At that point Ron reached one side of the stream and urged his horse to jump it. The stream was much wider and deeper than you could see through the snow, so the next thing we all saw was Ron's horse going through the snow and up to his nose in the water below the snowy surface. The icy, fast moving, biting cold water. Ron was almost submerged as he fell to the side of his horse, hanging on with shock in his face. Somehow he pulled himself erect again and let his horse ride through the water and out. Ron was soaked and shaken as we watched him rein in to a stop. Randy started over to him with a big – BIG – grin on his face. The rest of us, all shocked at first, then began to laugh. Ron was okay, just soaking wet and cold, so our laughter grew as Ron joined in.

"God damn it, that was something. Guess I didn't do that too well. And I hate it when people don't listen to me when I'm in the lead. Sorry, Randy. Won't happen again. I'll remember this. Bet on it!"

"I know you will," Randy began. "You are going to be mighty cold the rest of the way, at least another ninety minutes. Take one of those blankets off Sam's horse and put it around you. Might help a little."

Mark had taken our clothes and other supplies up the day before, so there were no dry clothes for Ron until we reached camp. Ron laughed again as he realized this and wrapped a large, woolen blanket around himself. "Hell, I look like one of your friends at the sweat lodge now Jim."

"You're a poor excuse for an Indian, Ron," I kidded him. "You wouldn't be soaking wet and miserable if you were an Indian on this ride."

With that we all started off again and reached camp without any other problems and with a Ron riding carefully and following directions.

When we arrived, Rosalie once again had lots of good hot coffee and some buns for us. Ron went and changed in his tent and came back looking dryer, but still chilled. Rosalie talked about camp life and the reality of being this high up. She spoke of alcohol and some prescription drugs as I asked here as soon as we arrived. She told of how she had seen some people, used to a few drinks down below, wasted on two beers up here. She also spoke about eating and not over-filling your stomach until you adjusted to the altitude – stomach gas being a really painful possibility if you did. Some of the new folks asked questions and she answered by telling stories from camps of the past. Often she had us all laughing and shaking our heads. After a while the snow quit and we all went for a short ride so everyone could get a feel for where we were. When we got back, we all broke up to unpack, hike, read or visit the cook tent. This time Bonnie and I had agreed to take a tent, leaving the small cabin for Hank and Linda. We all just relaxed for the rest of the day, agreeing to meet at six for dinner. When we got to dinner, Ron had laid out a nice wood fire for afterwards.

"Figured we could have a good, old campfire and tell stories or jokes after dinner," Ron said. "Least I could do after my little boy pranks today."

"Great," Hank said, Linda nodding her head in agreement. They had come to dinner with a bottle of Scotch, their favorite drink, and a bottle of club soda. "We want to be careful and not drink much," Hank continued. "Don't need any high altitude hangovers."

Rosalie looked over to me and shrugged her shoulders, as much as to say, 'Hey, they're big kids and can take care of themselves'.

Dinner was great, with bison stew, corn, dark bread, salad and several vegetables spread out family style. We all laughed and talked as we ate. I saw Hank and Linda pour a good-sized drink, which they sipped as we all enjoyed our meal. I hoped, for their sake that was all they had had.

After dinner, Ron went to light the fire and Sam went to get his guitar. Hank and Linda came over to Bonnie and I.

"Hey, guys, this is just great," Hank beamed, red faced.

"Yes, we never would have been in a place like this without you two and Shirley. I can't wait to bring some graduate students up here," Linda said. She was also very animated.

"Hey, it will take old Ron a while to get the fire lit. Let's go run down the hill!" Hank said, making little sense.

With that he got up and began running, full speed, downhill. He started singing "The Hills Are Alive" from "The Sound of Music" as he swished his hair out from his head. Bonnie and I looked at each other. "Well, they were warned. Can't stop adults from being children. He won't get hurt and he is really funny when he's had a lot to drink," Bonnie noted.

Linda began laughing much more than the sight was worth and fell off the log she was sitting on. Then Hank came running back and took Linda's hand, pulling her up and into a run also. In a moment they both fell – right into and through the roaring fire Ron had made. Luckily Ron and I were close to them and helped them get clear before they really got burned. They sat down and just continued to laugh and we all laughed with them. Ron fixed the fire and we all drew up logs. Sam played a few tunes and we all started telling stories – mostly ghost stories. It turned into a great night, but a night Hank and Linda left early, saying they were tired and had headaches.

Sam started telling a lot of stories about the past few years at CSU in our College. Each story told to make Sam seem the hero or the problem solver. Bonnie looked at me, slightly shaking her head and we just listened, saying nothing. I asked Ron about his wilderness camping and how this compared. As he was answering, Sam began to interrupt with stories of his camping prowess. And his knowledge of the plants and animals and their behaviors. Shirley finally nudged him and said we wanted to hear from our Chair about his time in wilderness with groups. Sam was not amused, but did stay quiet for a while.

A few hours of ghost stories and songs and we were all ready to turn in.

"We need to hang the food higher so the bears don't get it," Sam started in as we doused the fire. "Make sure you check your tent for any gaps the flies can get in," he continued. From there he began to lecture all of us, mostly on taking precautions so the wild animals didn't give us a problem.

"Long day, let's call it quits," I broke in so we could leave this unnecessary lecture.

"Yeah, I'm pooped," Ron agreed. So we all went to our tents.

Ron snored like a polar bear half the night, as I had experienced when we camped together before, I had carefully chosen a tent for Bonnie and I on the other side of the compound from his. Others had more chance for a Ron nighttime serenade.

In the morning I was up just before dawn, enjoying some coffee with Rosalie. "Boy, that Sam sure has an ego," she said as we sipped super hot brew.

"Yeah, it can be a real pain at times," I agreed.

"Needs someone to loosen his necktie a bit," she said with a smile. I wasn't sure what this meant, but got the gist of it.

"You might be right," I answered with a wise guy grin. I got out and went towards Sam's tent. When I got there I stepped carefully to the side of the door and listened to his soft snoring for a moment. Then I grabbed the top support pole, shaking it wildly as I let out a surprisingly real sounding bear roar. In a second I repeated it, as Bonnie and Ron poked their heads out of their tents. In a second, Sam came rolling out of his tent, moved to a low crouch with his fists in front of him, with a look of fear in his white face. Then Ron, Bonnie and I all started laughing and I watched Sam's anger build. In a few seconds I saw him swallow that and begin loudly saying he knew it was a joke all along, that no bear would behave that way. It was a childish trick on my part and I'm sure bought me some more of Sam's dislike.

A few minutes later Hank and Linda, drawn by the noise, came towards the cook tent. They looked like walking death. They sat with cups of coffee and told us of how sick they were all night and of the terrible headaches they had now. They said they should have listened to Rosalie and not had their usual four drinks. We did not see them until mid-day.

After we got some of this silliness and childishness out of the way we had a wonderful five days on the mountain. I didn't know Bonnie and I would only make one other trip up there and that our plans for this business would end in conflict and anger. Shirley never did her job of promoting the trips and Randy became more petulant over time. He never filed the permit under our name and Shirley did not follow-up as was her job. So, after a year and a half, we could take Randy to court or just walk away. We opted to walk away and sold the horses and supplies that belonged to us. Bonnie, Shirley and I kept our horses and continued to ride in Colorado until we moved east some years later.

Even though this venture did not work as we had hoped, we received an incredible number of lessons and experiences while it lasted. And I had received another part of my vision to help me continue down my spiritual road.

32 | Sanctuaries of the Earth Mother

I THINK IT'S TIME TO SPEND SOME TIME IN NATURE AND TALK A LITTLE about where my visions are taking me now. I keep asking for guidance on what parts of my road I need to share in this book and continued to be surprised by the inclusions and omissions coming to me as I do so. I seem to be just touching on many things I thought would require more detail and going into more detail on other pieces I thought – hoped – I might leave out. While I worked and learned steadily from Native American, Mayan, African, Australian aborigine and Celtic teachers over my years on this road, it seems the red road is getting much of the focus. Perhaps I will need to bring more of the other teachings to you at a later time, but for now just being aware of this is adequate. Likewise, I could write many, many chapters on my work in Central America, South America, and the Western United States. But again it seems selected samples are good for now. Certainly my learnings around nature, something I share happily with any who ask, could fill their own book. Maybe it will be you, and any others who decide to journey with us, who will instruct me on what books I need to manifest later. I am feeling like this journey together is beginning to draw to a close. How close to ending I'm not sure, but it is clearly approaching. There are still some things I am being guided to say; things we must look at together, then I will gratefully take a rest from this writing. At least I think I will be given a rest. Already actions I must take are becoming clear as I document my walk, but I will share a little of this just before we close.

Let me start with a piece I saw by Lelanie Anderson on her website. I have heard this story, or versions of it, many times in many of the cultures with which I spent time. This version seemed clear and concise and yet spoke to me as I read it. Enjoy.

Warriors of the Rainbow
Native American Lore
　　There was an old lady, from the Cree tribe, named Eyes of Fire, who prophesied that one day, because of the white man's or Yo-ne-gi's greed, there would come a time, when the fish would die in the streams, the birds would fall from the air, the waters would be blackened, and the trees would no longer be, mankind as we would know it, would all but cease to exist.

　　There would come a time when the "keepers of the legend, stories, culture rituals, and myths, and all the Ancient Tribal Customs" would be needed to restore us to health. They would be mankinds' key to survival, they were the "Warriors of the Rainbow".

　　There would come a day of awakening when all the peoples of all the tribes would form a New World of Justice, Peace, Freedom and recognition of the Great Spirit. The "Warriors of the Rainbow" would spread these messages and teach all peoples of the Earth or "Elohi". They would teach them how to live the "Way of the Great Spirit".

　　They would tell them of how the world today has turned away from the Great Spirit and that is why our Earth is "Sick". The "Warriors of the Rainbow" would show the peoples that this "Ancient Being" (the Great Spirit), is full of love and understanding, and teach them how to make the Earth or "Elohi" beautiful again.

　　These Warriors would give the people principles or rules to follow to make their path right with the world. These principles would be those of the Ancient Tribes. The Warriors of the Rainbow would

teach the people of the ancient practices of Unity, Love and Understanding. They would teach of Harmony among people in all four
corners of the Earth. Like the Ancient Tribes, they would teach the
people how to pray to the Great Spirit with love that flows like the
beautiful mountain stream, and flows along the path to the ocean
of life. Once again, they would be able to feel joy in solitude and
in councils. They would be free of petty jealousies and love all
mankind as their brothers, regardless of color, race or religion. They
would feel happiness enter their hearts, and become as one with the
entire human race. Their hearts would be pure and radiate warmth,
understanding and respect for all mankind, Nature, and the Great
Spirit.

They would once again fill their minds, hearts, souls, and deeds
with the purest of thoughts. They would seek the beauty of the Master of Life—the Great Spirit! They would find strength and beauty in
prayer and the solitudes of life. Their children would once again be
able to run free and enjoy the treasures of Nature and Mother Earth.

Free from the fears of toxins and destruction, wrought by the Yo-
ne-gi and his practices of greed. The rivers would again run clear, the
forests be abundant and beautiful, the animals and birds would be
replenished. The powers of the plants and animals would again be
respected and conservation of all that is beautiful would become a
way of life.

The poor, sick and needy would be cared for by their brothers
and sisters of the Earth. These practices would again become a part
of their daily lives. The leaders of the people would be chosen in the
old way—not by their political party, or who could speak the loudest, boast the most, or by name calling or mud slinging, but by those
whose actions spoke the loudest. Those who demonstrated their
love, wisdom, and courage and those who showed that they could
and did work for the good of all, would be chosen as the leaders or
Chiefs.

They would be chosen by their "quality" and not the amount of
money they had obtained. Like the thoughtful and devoted "Ancient

Chiefs", they would understand the people with love, and see that their young were educated with the love and wisdom of their surroundings.

They would show them that miracles can be accomplished to heal this world of its ills, and restore it to health and beauty. The tasks of these "Warriors of the Rainbow" are many and great.

There will be terrifying mountains of ignorance to conquer and they shall find prejudice and hatred. They must be dedicated, unwavering in their strength, and strong of heart. They will find willing hearts and minds that will follow them on this road of returning "Mother Earth" to beauty and plenty—once more.

The day will come, it is not far away. The day that we shall see how we owe our very existence to the people of all tribes that have maintained their culture and heritage. Those that have kept the rituals, stories, legends, and myths alive. It will be with this knowledge, the knowledge that they have preserved, that we shall once again return to "harmony" with Nature, Mother Earth, and mankind. It will be with this knowledge that we shall find our "Key to our Survival".

Lelanie Fuller Anderson, 1990
From her website, www.angelfire.com

When the Earth is sick, the animals will begin to disappear, when that happens, The Warriors of the Rainbow will come to save them.

—Chief Seattle, SUQUAMIS

There are so many indigenous teachings and prophecies around relearning how to exist in harmony with the Earth Mother once again. And I know that is a big part of what we humans must do if we are to survive and prosper. I have seen it many times in many ways – through teachings, in dreams and in the lives of people still closely connected to our planet and all the creatures on it. This is also a large part of the vision I have had over the years and part of what I will be spending my time helping create for the remainder of my walk here.

I have heard many stories of the people of all colors coming together and sharing their knowledge so that we may heal ourselves by
addressing the wrongs we have perpetrated on our planet and each
other. The Warriors of the Rainbow writing, for example, I just shared
with you. I see this sharing as something that will happen only after
we forgive each other all past wrongs done to us or by us. Red forgiving White; Jew forgiving Muslim; Muslim/Christian; Black/White;
Catholic/Protestant; and on and on. This is not an easy task, but a
necessary, at least for those who wish to awaken and become part of
the solution. As we do this we must also ask forgiveness of the Earth
for the wrongs we have done there. And ask to be allowed to re-learn
how she wishes us to work with her. This will not only open the door
to proceeding with working in a sustainable, harmonious way with
our planet, but will also allow us to complete our own healings as
humans. The Earth Mother and our physical bodies are connected as
one. When we do something to harm the Earth, we harm ourselves. If
we poison the Earth's waters – we poison our own blood. Poison the
air and poison our lungs. Think about this and follow the thread further. You will see as many examples of this connection as you care to
make. This is a good thing, since we can become healthier as we assist
the Earth in becoming healthier. Let me share some of Chief Seattle's
words on this. There have been many writings by many people capturing Chief's words and ideas, but the thoughts are all Chief Seattle's.

CHIEF SEATTLE'S LETTER

"The President in Washington sends word that he wishes to buy
our land. But how can you buy or sell the sky? the land? The idea
is strange to us. If we do not own the freshness of the air and the
sparkle of the water, how can you buy them?

Every part of the earth is sacred to my people. Every shining pine
needle, every sandy shore, every mist in the dark woods, every
meadow, every humming insect. All are holy in the memory and experience of my people.

We know the sap which courses through the trees as we know the blood that courses through our veins. We are part of the earth and it is part of us. The perfumed flowers are our sisters. The bear, the deer, the great eagle, these are our brothers. The rocky crests, the dew in the meadow, the body heat of the pony, and man all belong to the same family.

The shining water that moves in the streams and rivers is not just water, but the blood of our ancestors. If we sell you our land, you must remember that it is sacred. Each glossy reflection in the clear waters of the lakes tells of events and memories in the life of my people. The waters' murmur is the voice of my fathers' father.

The rivers are our brothers. They quench our thirst. They carry our canoes and feed our children. So you must give the rivers the kindness that you would give any brother.

If we sell you our land, remember that the air is precious to us, that the air shares its spirit with all the life that it supports. The wind that gave our grandfather his first breath also received his last sigh. The wind also gives our children the spirit of life. So if we sell our land, you must keep it apart and sacred, as a place where man can go to taste the wind that is sweetened by the meadow flowers.

Will you teach your children what we have taught our children? That the earth is our mother? What befalls the earth befalls all the sons of the earth.

This we know: the earth does not belong to man, man belongs to the earth. All things are connected like the blood that unites us all. Man did not weave the web of life, he is merely a strand in it. Whatever he does to the web, he does to himself.

One thing we know: our God is also your God. The earth is precious to him and to harm the earth is to heap contempt on its creator.

So the parts in my vision where I see people working together to create sustainable communities where they share wisdom and ways is just that. Nothing new or novel in this part, but it is now a critical need. There are other pieces to this part of my vision. It is not just about living in harmony with the Earth and each other and teaching each other and those who are to follow, but it is new knowledge to be explored and mastered. It will be learning how to evolve as humans to the next level of our existence, as we are meant to do if we are to flourish. We will be finding ways to connect to each other and other groups around Turtle Island and around the globe without all the technology we now require. We will learn how to use additional portions of our brains, which have been waiting for the proper time to open, just as my vision waited for the proper time to come back into my awareness. And just as it is happening to so many who are awakening now.

I am not speaking Rainbow Warriors such as some of the groups in existence already. Groups that I have seen working in ego or fantasy. I am not judging these, but I am saying that is not what this is about. Not what the Sanctuaries are about. I will write more, much more, at a later time about the Sanctuaries, but felt some needed to be present here, now, so that those who know they are needed in this work will appear.

What I have seen in further pieces of my vision becoming clear to me are Sanctuaries around the world, connected by the spider web of existence upon which they sit. These are the places which will help prepare our children and children's children – the seven generations – with what they need to know so that we leave a legacy of light, not dark; joy, not gloom; evolvement, not doom. If it for those to follow that these things must come to pass and why I have committed myself to the work – as much as I would like to go sit on a mountain, write, read and just enjoy my later years. The creation of these Sanctuaries will provide all involved with joy and understanding which will dwarf any other possible way they might spend the remainder of their time. This I have seen and surely believe.

I have seen much of this work to be done in and through the Sanctuaries of the Earth Mother over time, with many gaps now being filled in. The parts of my vision I have already shared have shown you some of these pieces. The last part of this vision, which I will relate at the end of this book, told me even more of my personal role in the work. Once this vision began to become clear, remembering parts as I was able, I was able to actually begin to start writing and creating what was needed for the vision to begin to manifest in my heart. I thought the piece of the vision I just promised to open to you at the end of this book was 'the whole picture', but, as I began writing this for you, more about the Sanctuaries began to be revealed to me.

We will create this web of Sanctuaries as have been shown to me. We will honor the five colors in these places and teach others how this is done. While the four colors of man are critical – white, black, red and yellow – the fifth color, green, is the 'glue' holding all others together. The green of the Earth Mother – the green in each of us. I smiled the other day when I awoke from a dream with my old joke about being of the Olive Skinned Nation in my mind. The small joke I made when I wanted to detract from any who attacked me for being white. I was being shown in this dream that, as an olive skinned person, I truly carried some of the fifth color myself. I did not realize the teaching inherent in my joke, but will appreciate it more fully from here onward. The green is the wisest and truest teacher, if we but be silent and listen, as we will in the Sanctuaries.

"The basis of knowledge is the fire, rock, water, and green. But when that power was given to man, he used it to twist his own mind. Tunkashila gave man just one drop of that wisdom."

—Wallace Black Elk, LAKOTA

In these Sanctuaries all creatures will be welcomed and accepted as teachers in their own right. This is also as the Old Ones knew, but

we have long since forgotten. We will work to remedy the words of
our relative below –

*"Someone must speak for them. I do not see a delegation for the
four footed. I see no seat for eagles. We forget and we consider ourselves superior, but we are after all a mere part of the Creation."*
—Oren R. Lyons, Spokesman Traditional Circle of Elders

Again, there will be much, much more on the Sanctuaries later –
this I am clearly feeling. I hope many of you will also walk this journey with me, hearing more about what I have seen in my vision and
considering your role, if any, in it. I wish to be clear here that I have
been referring to 'my vision' and the parts of my vision as I've shared
them. That is correct—they are the vision I have received over so
many years—yet my vision only in the sense that I am the one they
were sent to, to hold and now transcribe. In the broader, more important sense, they are 'the' vision, because it is the circle that will manifest
and build the vision into reality. It is the 'we', not 'I', who will nurture
this work.

We have rested nicely as this small piece of the Sanctuaries of the
Earth Mother have been uncovered for us, but now let's get up and
continue our journey. I know you must be ready to move on again.

33 | Across the Big Pond

As I have told you, I have not shared many things I've experienced on this journey we take together. Not intentionally, but simply because they did not surface at this time. But I now see I need to at least tell a couple of short stories so you see where and when some of my teachers appeared.

Bonnie and I took many trips to Europe, Great Britain, Eastern Bloc countries as well as Caribbean island nations before we moved to Colorado and I began my walk in a spiritual and nature-based existence. While I was not learning these ways at a conscious level, I feel certain I was already beginning my lessons as a sub-conscious, energetic level. We immersed ourselves in hikes, walks, climbs and river walking throughout these journeys, learning much about the land and the people as we did so. We met fascinating people in strange, out-of-the-way places and listened to them tell their stories. In looking back I see that I was meeting people and learning in some of the parts of the globe where 'civilization' was said to have evolved before it did here in the Americas before we began our treks around Turtle Island. All of this travel taught me, at the big picture level, how cultures flourished around the world at the same time civilization was said to been born. The evidence of these cultures were just different, therefore they were judged by the viewers or, centuries later, by those who studied them.

I know, as we move ahead as a race, we will once again learn to hear what each culture or group has to contribute to the whole.

I remember many of the people we met and the stories they told, but there are some that I did not recognize as stories to be remembered and so I only dimly remember them—their teachings lost. Believe me, there are no wasted stories, no insignificant stories, only listeners who sometimes miss the subtle nuances of the tales others tell. When someone sits with you and shares a story—listen. There is a reason. And don't just listen, but hear and remember what is said. It will move you along the road of spirit at a faster, smoother pace.

I also see, in looking back, that doors to future teachers and teachings were opened by these chance encounters across the Big Pond. In Wales, walking through an abandoned slate mine I came upon two black men looking carefully at the rocks around them. They were small and thin and carried themselves very straight. I waved and one of the men waved back. A short while later, as I crested a ridge within the old quarry, I found myself just above the men.

"Hello," I called out.

"Day," one of the men said quietly.

I approached them as I scampered down the rock-debris covered slope. "Warm out here today, but I find this place fascinating," I said, making conversation.

"Yes, very fine stone here in this place," the second, slightly taller man said. "You are from Europe or America?"

"I am from the States—Pennsylvania."

"Ah. On the east side," the man said as he nodded. "I knew you were not of this land."

"And where are you from? I know you are also not of this land."

"We are from Australia. From the outback country in the north. We are aborigines. Our people have walked that land from the beginning. We are here to play our music and tell our stories."

"What do you play?"

"Nose flutes and the didgeridoo."

"Why here in Great Britain?"

"We are citizens as people of Australia. Not many of our people travel out of the ancestral lands, but Tom and I were brought up by settlers until our late teens, so we have had a different way. These are some of the stories we tell."

"I'm Jim. You said your friend is Tom. And you?"

"Alex."

"Well, I am about to eat my lunch. I still have a few hours before I meet my wife who's at a geology lecture. Would you like to share with me?" I asked.

"Sure," Tom said with a big grin.

We sat and I took out the cheese, bread, fruit and cold cuts I had with me and my new friends broke out some raw vegetables and fruit they were carrying. We all had water, so thirst was no issue. As we ate, they asked what I did and I told them of my businesses. They wanted to know what Pennsylvania was like, as they had only been to California in the States. I told them of the Eastern states and how they differed from the West Coast.

"It is good to hear of other places from people who live there," Tom said. "We hope to bring our music and words to other places later, then we can see for ourselves."

"Tell me about your part of Australia," I requested.

They spoke at length about their land, the plants and animals of it, the extreme weather they sometimes had and, lastly, the different people who lived there.

"We are lucky in our land in the north. Not many non-aborigines live there, or even come there. It's a harsh, hard land and you must be ready for it," Alex continued. "Our people have been treated badly since the settlers came. Much like your own Indian people in the States. We were both taken from our families and sent to live with whites and be educated and taught the white religion. I did not even know of this until I turned sixteen since I was so young when they took me. Tom was a little older and so he remembered. It's hard for some of us because we don't look as aboriginal as others. Look at us. Tom's features make him easier to identify as aboriginal, mine could be a mix of many bloods. For us, the important thing is we found our people and returned to learn from them. Now we take these stories with us so that these things will not happen in other places. And we bring our strong healing music to any who wish to listen."

"Wow. My childhood has no interest compared to that!" I exclaimed.

"All stories are interesting," Tom said to that.

Tom and Alex told me they had done programs around Wales for the past two weeks and were going to London the next day. They had a program in three nights if I was near London. It happened Bonnie and I were going back to London in two days, so I told them to look for us. We caught two of their musical performances in the next week and spent an evening at a house in London where they told their stories to an invited audience.

Years later while we were in Fort Collins, Bonnie and I took a trip to California. Along the way we stopped to hear three Australians playing their didges for an evening In Los Angeles. It was of course, Tom and Alex and a third friend. We reunited and had dinner together the following night. This Australian connection continued with the didge player we heard speak in Colorado Springs whom I believe I mentioned earlier. This same man showed up about six years ago doing some teaching and healing in Pennsylvania while we were there.

Many times I met with Australian aborigines—no coincidence. So when I met Lou Tomba, another aboriginal man from the north of Australia, I was not surprised. Lou was an amazing storyteller, healer with plants and spiritual guide. We met in Denver, while I was attending a conference around indigenous cultures, and immediately became friends. This began a ten-year stretch where Lou taught me many new ways. Ways his people had followed for millennia. Coincidence? I hope you no longer use or believe that word.

On this same trip I met Tom and Alex I also met Thom, in Glastonbury, England. We met at Stonehenge in the evening, waiting to go through the fences and on the grounds in the evening. Thom and

I hit it off and he began telling me of his work in understanding the ancient Celtic ways and the power places, like Stonehenge.

Six months after meeting Thom, he called to say he would be in the States and would love to visit. He came and stayed three weeks with us. Bonnie was thrilled, as his other interest was geology. Thom and I stayed connected for years, each teaching the other—he teaching me Celtic lore and healing ways and me teaching him what I learned from my Lakota friends. Today, here in Sedona, one of my best friends, Stephen, also hails from Glastonbury and is a pursuer of spiritual growth. More coincidence?

I could list many more of these places and people, but I believe you see the thread—the web. And so I will not overburden you with sample stories, just the awareness of the multi-colored, multi-cultural teachers I was blessed to work with. And the knowledge that if you want to walk this spiritual road you only need to strongly put that intention out there, begin doing some learning on your own and the teachers will find you.

In this universe, all activities, events, and entities are related. Indians believe that everything in the universe has value and instructs us in some aspect of life. Everything is alive and is making choices that determine the future, so the world is constantly creating itself... With the wisdom and time for reflection that old age provides, we may discover unsuspected relationships.

—Vine Deloria, Jr, STANDING ROCK SIOUX

34 | Lodge Attack

OVER MY YEARS IN FORT COLLINS, LAWRENCE AND I STAYED CLOSE friends. Even now, although we lost touch for some time, we occasionally connect. This also is part of the way the circle works. Once again people connecting and disconnecting as needed. Sometimes to re-connect again later if needed, sometimes to move in their own direction. With Lawrence I always knew we would remain connected no matter where we were or what we were doing. And so it has been. We spent many afternoons providing natural and culture classes in the field to students from around our region. For some of the kids, it was the first time they had walked an unpaved trail. I found it fascinating that in a place like Colorado and a city like Denver—so close to glorious parks and mountains—that many young people were never taken to these natural gems. This is another indicator of why we are in the ecological and spiritual mess we now wallow in. Hopefully this will begin to change rapidly, allowing the young ones not only opportunities to experience nature, but to learn how to survive and prosper within it. I know other places like the Sanctuaries of the Earth Mother will appear to help with this work. For Lawrence and I this work began twenty years ago when we met. And others—of all colors—also then appeared with whom I worked to design programs in nature, centered on different cultures, to teach the lessons to the

Earth and the ways of the ancestors. This is a good place to begin to understand the place of humans in nature.

Lawrence also continued to be a central figure in the inipis being run at the Environmental Learning Center, always working on the site or inviting medicine people to pour the water. As the Student President of the Native American Student Association, he was also the contact for many of the Native American students on campus. The programs and excursions we began taking with the CSU students after a few years also allowed us to share together with another student level. All these things we did on a regular basis, as time and the needs of those we worked with required. Although I worked with many different and committed people, my connection with Lawrence allowed for teaching rarely available to most people—a red man and a white man working together and talking from their experiences and cultural background.

We had our issues as we did this work, sometimes with Lawrence's temper, sometimes with my impatience. But we always managed to provide what was asked of us. Of course, not everyone liked the ceremonies we did at the Center, as I have mentioned before. Not all of the Native American people we came in contact with liked the lodges when non-Native people were invited. And not all the Christians liked this 'pagan' religion being practiced on the University's land. We somehow always managed to address these issues when they arose or, when possible, just ignore them and move on. For years none of the cross-cultural work so many of us were involved in was seriously challenged.

This changed in my eighth year at CSU, when a new Director of Native American Services came to CSU. I do not remember her name and so will call her Sandra Deer. Carolyn Fiscus, who had been so pivotal to the Native American connection at the Center and in my life, had left CSU for Nebraska and Sandra had come to fill the void. Sandra was of the Blackfoot Nation and had a PhD to bring to the position. Lawrence and I invited her to lunch shortly after she arrived. It was not a good lunch, with Sandra obviously not wishing to be with us. But we ate and told her of some of the projects we were working on, especially those that served the Native American students.

When we paused she asked, "Who built that inipi out at your Center, Jim?"

"That was a joint effort of many people, Sandra. But Lyman Yellowhair led the actual building."

She nodded somberly, with no smile. "I don't think it's built the way our traditional leaders would want it. And I don't see why the two lodges need to be so close to each other."

"Lyman is a medicine man; well known and respected here," Lawrence said, heating up quickly.

"Well, I don't know him," Sandra countered. "And I don't think all the non-Native people I've been told attend the ceremonies is a good thing."

"You don't know what you are speaking of," Lawrence was now angry and confused. "This is a Lakota lodge, led by a Lakota medicine person. And other medicine people at times. We invite other people so we can all share together. Other times, just us Indians go in. Why don't you call Carolyn and talk to her. She helped us all meet and build this."

"I don't need to talk to Carolyn. I'm the director here now. And I will need to look into this more. Thank you for lunch," she finished as she rose and left.

"I don't think she will be a help. What an ego. One who does not wish to share between people. I don't like any of it," Lawrence said.

"Yeah, it sure wasn't a good meeting. I'll let Ron know what's going on. My department will back us if trouble comes—I think."

About a week later I was told Sandra had invited her 'medicine person' to visit the lodge at the Center and tell her what he thought. This was done with no one notifying my department or me. Ron was told this medicine person, Robert Flying Eagle, reported to Sandra that the lodge was not built correctly; built in the wrong place; and built without the proper ceremony. He also, like Sandra, did not like non-Native people invited to the lodges. I was furious—my temper taking over as I shouted "Bullshit, Ron! He's another 'Indian only' sort who's trying to cause trouble and give Sandra a reason to attack Lawrence and the lodge. I'll be happy to take this to the media and let them have fun with it!"

"Relax, Jim. Of course he's a plant. Maybe a phony, I don't know. But you ranting at me won't help anything. I'm the messenger," Ron said quietly.

"Sorry, boss. I'm just livid. She came off as against anything we all were doing together at the Center at that first lunch and has given Lawrence and the Native American Student Association grief since. Where did they find this woman? She seems to want to undo everything Carolyn got started and we all have created."

"I don't know, but I suspect her PhD helped a lot. You don't find many Native people with PhD's willing to take this type of job on."

"Great. She's smart, but with no common sense and no concern for the Native students we're trying to serve."

"Calm down or you'll fry yourself before we start working on this!" Ron said, getting heated by my anger. "She also said you and Lawrence were drinking when she saw you having lunch together the week after she went to lunch with you. At Chicago Pizza in town, during the day."

"Who the hell cares? Lawrence just earned his degree. You know what that means. The hard work and his past problems he had to overcome. So we had a drink to celebrate. He's thirty-three and I'm over forty. What's that got to do with anything?"

"She's saying it sets a bad example, especially when you are both working as University employees. On the clock."

"More bullshit. First, neither of us are employees of the University. Lawrence is a funded undergrad and I'm a funded graduate student and an independent contractor paid to teach. Even if that were not the case, I'd say we had a good cause for a harassment complaint. She's attacking our integrity. Has Lawrence been told of her nonsense?"

"No. I wanted to talk to you. But I hoped you'd be more rational so we could plan our course of action."

"Okay. Okay. You're right. Why don't I ask for a meeting with Sandra and this George the medicine man and ask some questions. What do you think?"

"Maybe it's best to just let it sit for a while. It might just blow over. Just be low profile out there for now and ask Lawrence to stay cool."

I sat with this advice for a few days, then called Sandra and asked for a meeting with she and Robert Flying Eagle. Two days later I met with Sandra and Robert in the Service Learning offices.

"Hi, thanks for the meeting," I said with a lot of energy and a full-face smile as I reached out to shake hands with Sandra.

"It's my job," Sandra said, with no smile or emotion.

"Well, mine too, but we all put time aside quickly for this meeting. If there's an issue with the work we are doing with our Lakota friends at the Center, I want to get it resolved right away if we can, so we can continue to serve all the Native undergrads we have been. So, Robert, don't think I know you. Live here in Colorado?" I asked.

"No, I live in the Northwest, last few years up near Seattle. Sandra asked me to come and take a look at the programs and ceremonies here. I am called a medicine person by my people. I am Blackfoot and Crow."

"Ah, I see. Well, welcome," I said as I shook hands with Robert. "Well, I've heard several things about the ceremonies and the sweat lodge out at the Center, but I'd like to hear from Robert directly what he thinks. I wish I had known you were going out there. I could have come along. Must have forgotten to notify my department that you were going out there on University business."

"I asked Robert to go and look at the lodge, since I am no expert," Sandra explained. "So I never thought to let your department know. I considered it an Indian issue."

"Well, it's nice being in the loop when an issue comes up."

"Well, anyway, what do you have to tell us, Robert?" I asked.

"I can tell you the lodge is not built correctly and does not face the right way. I also sensed the prayers said were not strong enough or not said with the right intention. And it is not our way to have non-Indian people in ceremonies like the inipi."

"I was there when the lodges were built," I said, trying my very best to swallow my anger and the words I really wanted to sling at Sandra and Robert. "Well, first, the inipis were built some time ago after meetings with the Director of Native American Services at the time and Native American leaders in the region and on campus. Two were built at the request of the women so they could do a woman's lodge when they wished. Lyman Yellowhair and other medicine people led the building, but Lyman was the primary leader and he led the prayers and ceremonies done around it. Lyman is a Lakota medicine man. And the lodge is Lakota and so was built in the Lakota fashion as directed by Lyman. I remember Lyman teaching how the door could face east or west—rising or sinking sun—depending on how the medicine person felt, so he faced this door to the west. Robert, I respect that you are a medicine person for your people, but you are not Lakota. Not even Sioux. So I am confused why a non-Sioux has been called in as an expert on a Lakota tradition and ceremony. Would it not have been better to invite a Lakota medicine person, Sandra? And I have a problem accepting your words about the prayers and ceremony that went into building the lodges. You were not there and, again, you are not Lakota. Forgive my ignorance here, but do the Blackfoot even do sweat ceremonies? And where is your tribe located? In Seattle?"

"The Blackfoot do sweat lodges. The Lakota have done great work preserving the sweat lodges and other ceremonies for all the people, but my people also do lodges now. My tribe is in Canada, in Alberta. I am working in Seattle now."

"Okay. So the Lakota were the keepers of many ceremonies, including lodges, when Native Americans could not do them. And the lodges at the Center are Lakota, as are the medicine people who pour the water in them. Your people are even from another country, certainly nowhere near the Lakota nation in South Dakota. Are non-Indians never allowed to attend your sweat ceremonies?" I asked.

"I have said this. We do not allow women in the lodges either. The ceremony was created for men by the wishes of Great Spirit."

"Wait now. Let me get this right. Not even Indian women can go in a sweat lodge by your opinion?"

"Yes. They have their own ways and traditions they follow," Robert said with a stern face.

"I guess I'd like to hear from Sandra about why she asked someone whose practices seem so different from those native people who built and use the sweat lodges here to come and give an opinion on this."

"Robert is a friend and a well-respected spiritual leader among his people. He has written many books and lectures many places. He has been a friend for many years and he was coming to Colorado, so I asked him to do this. It is expensive to bring people here from South Dakota and I had no budget, so Robert, with his credentials, was here at the right time."

"I'm having trouble with this," I said. "A number of respected Native American spiritual leaders and medicine people have been involved with my department through people in your organization Sandra, through Lawrence and through me. None has questioned the programs or ceremonies and several have thanked me, personally, for what we are providing the students."

"There is no more to talk about. Lawrence is trouble and not helping the students he is supposed to lead. And our customs should not be abused this way. I thought we could explain these things and you would remove the lodges from the University's land. Goodbye," Sandra said, as she turned and headed out the door. George turned and followed her without a word.

Sandra was really angry, so I just watched her go. I said no more. Maybe I had said too much. I could have been more 'political' about it, but that just wasn't my way. Well, we would see what happened next, if anything. I figured I had probably made things worse and would have been better served to have taken Ron's advice and let it all lay. But, spilt milk—wasn't going back in the bottle. I didn't tell Ron anything about this meeting, keeping him out of the fray. If I had made a stronger enemy, I would deal with it. Funny thing was that, as this whole affair unfolded, Ron never mentioned my meeting with Sandra or George, nor did our Dean. I assume Sandra felt her actions were not something she wanted to speak about either.

We continued all programs at the Center as the weeks went on, having scheduled them long before the issue with the lodges had arisen. And we went in the inipi for ceremony twice. I wanted to keep my head low as Ron had suggested, but I didn't want to just stop what was being done. After about a month, Ron called me in to his office. I thought it might be about my meeting with Sandra, but it was not.

"Jim, the Dean wants us to meet with Sandra and him this afternoon at two. Clear your schedule. Okay?"

"Sure. What's the meeting about?"

"The sweat lodges you all have at the Center. Same issues, I guess, but he'll tell us."

At two we met in a conference room in the Natural Resource Administrative building. It was the Dean, Ron, Sandra and I. We sat and made small talk for a couple of minutes, then the Dean opened the talk.

"Thanks for coming everyone. Sandra here has some problems with the sweat lodges out at the ELC. I thought it best if we all just meet and talk this through. I have some knowledge of the lodges since I went to a ceremony when Lawrence and Jim invited me. It was a very powerful ceremony for me. But, I want to be certain we are not distressing our Native American Association people with the work out there. Sandra, why don't you start?" the Dean asked her.

"Many thanks, Dean," Sandra began. "Those lodges at the Center have been looked at by a medicine person who is a good friend of mine. He has many issues with them, including their use by non-Indian people. I don't think we are giving the right messages to our Native students by teaching that our ceremonies are open to all. And Lawrence Little Thunder is involved. He is a troubled man and a troublemaker. He should have no..."

"Whoa. Wait," I interrupted. "I thought we were here to talk about the lodges and their place at the Center, not talk about Lawrence. If we are going to talk about him, let's call him and invite him over. If not, I need to leave." I was angry again and began to rise as I spoke.

"No. No. We are not here to talk about Lawrence," the Dean said. "Sandra, please speak with Lawrence about your concerns with him. He is in your organization, not our college."

"Of course," she said, also obviously angry herself. She glared at me as she repeated some of the same comments she and Robert had made when we met. When she finished, the Dean asked me to comment.

"Yes, sir. I wish Robert was still in town so we could question him directly," I started. "I have many problems with his comments. He is not Lakota, or Sioux of any tribe. He lives in Canada, where they may well do very different ceremonies—I'm not sure. And I've heard they do not even allow women in their lodges—including their own tribal women. If it had been a Lakota medicine person I might be more inclined to think about his words. And even then, I know there are some Lakota who would agree with Robert and Sandra. Just as there are some white Christians who don't like the sharing of spiritual ways out there. What I do know is that we have the good words and often the participation of many Lakota medicine people and teachers here. And we non-Indian folks always ask before doing or saying anything around the lodges or the educational programs we provide. We started this work at the request of the people of Native American Services, since so many Native students leave the University. The hope was this work would help them feel more at home and it seems to do that for many. There are churches and places of worship in many places on campus, this is just another opportunity for our diverse population to worship in this way if they wish."

"Well, we have a difference of opinion here for sure," the Dean said. "Sandra, is there anything we can do to make you more comfortable with the programs and ceremonies happening at the Center Jim runs?"

"Take down the lodges and let us Indians work with our students. They need Native American people to work with and learn from, so their ways remain their ways."

"Jim, thoughts?" the Dean then asked me.

"Dean, there would be all kinds of problems if we did what Sandra just asked. Many Native and non-Native people on campus and in the community are involved with the work out there. And many come to various ceremonies together—to share; including inipi ceremonies. Taking this all apart to placate one person makes no sense to me. Even Sandra's words seem to indicate the Native American population on campus should just keep to themselves. That was one of the problems we were asked to help with. It seems contrary to the reason for coming to a place of learning."

"Let me think on this everyone," the Dean continued. "It's a tricky issue. Thank you all for being here. I'll get back to you." And the meeting was over. Sandra glared at me, as I did at her, as we left.

I met briefly with Ron and the Dean back at our building and asked what they thought about all of this.

"Jim, let it play out," Ron said.

"It's difficult, Jim. Sandra was brought in to head the Native American organization and, being Native and a woman, it will be hard to go against her wishes," the Dean followed with.

"Well, it's nuts. She is an 'Indian only' proponent. I've run into that many places, but it doesn't belong here. And she wants her word to be the word. Robert, her 'expert' has no background in Lakota ways or what was built here. If she comes at us, I will take it to the media and the other groups involved," I said, getting angrier as I spoke.

"Jim, don't get angry with us," Ron said with a smile. "You just need to let us play the politics. Sandra may well hang herself if she keeps this sort of behavior up. But I'm telling you to keep a lower profile around the cultural things at the Center for now. Do you agree, Dean?"

"Absolutely. Give us some help here, Jim. And give me a chance to work through this."

"Okay. I'll do as you ask, as best we can. But I do not want to just cancel things already booked or tell Lyman or anyone else we can't do lodges. I'll try to keep it to two a month, inviting those already a part. Okay?"

"Good, thanks," the Dean responded.

For the next six months, I hated Sandra and all she stood for. I cursed her backward ways and Red only attitude. I made everything her organization asked for as difficult as possible, except when the students came and asked themselves. And I'm certain I shared my anger with others. Lawrence, even less politically correct than me, badmouthed her whenever he had the opportunity. We continued delivering programs and doing some lodges in the way I had committed to the Dean. And no more issues about the lodges or the programs came my way, but I kept waiting for the other shoe to fall. Waiting and eating myself up with my anger and dislike. Then, after nine months, I heard Sandra had stepped down and would be leaving in a week. I was amazed. I thought she was politically untouchable. What had I missed? I met with the Dean and was told she had repeatedly enacted processes that would disconnect the Native American students from other parts of the University community. And he also told me that Native students had complained about her and her rules and restrictions. Some of this I was certain was due to Lawrence, as the Native American students looked to him as a leader. So, she had been asked to resign and told, if she did not, she would be fired.

For nine months I made myself sick with anger and hatred. Physically and emotionally sick, even losing sleep wondering how I would deal with this loss of programs and ceremonies. Worrying about what their loss would mean to Native and non-Native students alike. And then she was gone. Fired. Canned. What we were doing vindicated, I thought. I hoped. I had invested all that time, energy and karma in negative space. Just letting go, trusting and waiting would have handled this issue in a good way. I wish I could tell you this lesson, taught me once or twice, was well learned. It was not.

I realize now that my patience was wearing ever more thin at this time and my anger much closer to the surface, waiting opportunities to erupt. After last years' remembrances I see the reason for this as well. But that to follow in a little while. For now, sharing these stories, which demonstrate the value in waiting calmly before you act—no matter the wrong you feel was done you or others—is something we need in our circle here. And waiting is not just a day or two, but may be months or even years. Your spirit, your inner essence, will guide you in this if you practice asking your core what to do—and then carefully listening for the answers.

About a year and a half before Bonnie and I left Colorado, Ron announced he was separating from Laura, his wife of many years. A couple of months later he announced he was engaged to a former graduate student of his, Alice. This was no surprise to me, or many others, as suspicion of a relationship between them had been circulating for years. Just before Ron announced this, he met over some beers with me.

"Jim, I couldn't take living the lie with Laura any longer. Her problems with drinking and dependence on people were something I couldn't take any longer. I hope you and Bonnie remain her friend if that's possible. She'll continue to need people."

"Ron, we will, but not to the extent of being her constant support."

"Good. Thanks. Listen, this is probably a surprise, but I'm going to tell everyone Alice and I are engaged soon. What do you think of that?"

"No surprise. It's an 'unsecret' secret that you two were more than teacher and student. I think those who want the department to go more into research and less teaching hands-on and applied skills are going to use this. You may have some strong attacks coming your way."

"Nah. I can handle that. I've been chair a long time and the Dean likes the way our department functions."

"Okay, but I'm telling you, the undercurrents around your relationship with Alice are strong with some."

"Okay. Thanks. I'm going to make Alice the lead at the ELC and have her teach the classroom sections of Interpretation. You still are Assistant Director and teach the applied parts and, when you get your degree finished, we'll see how we bring you in, too. For now, it's the place I can get her more permanent faculty status."

Wham—up came my anger immediately. "Ron, what is this nonsense? I am director there—as you have said so often. What's happened to, "nothing would ever have come of the Center without you"? Alice may be good in academic teaching, but she has no performance understanding of interpretation nor any idea how to run a center or organization. And, although I see she's been 'touting' her service-learning credentials, it's me with the understanding, positions and awards in that."

"Relax. You'll run the things as you always have. And there are plenty of classes for you to teach."

"Sure, and Alice is to get the rewards of my knowledge and skills, just like you have for eight years? You know, what really makes me angry is you're not asking or discussing, you're just telling me. Nice friend."

"Sorry, but that's the need for now. Haven't I taken care of your needs since you've been here?"

"Sure. You have. But because what I do has made you look good. That's fine. No problem with that. But this is different. You are putting someone with no skills in a position that may affect my work. And in a place where even more attacks may be leveled at you."

"Well, we need to do this. Let's talk more tomorrow."

I went home and told Bonnie what Ron was planning. She listened carefully, asking a few questions as I talked at length. She knew I was mad—really mad. When I finished she asked, "What is this about? You or Ron?"

"What do you mean? I've built that place, my courses and the partnerships for eight years. Now he wants to use it as a means to reward someone who got a weak doctorate degree with Ron as her committee chair and no skill in the things I've created."

"So, it is about you. And your dislike of Alice."

"Some of it. I feel stabbed in the back. Ron has always said that place was mine to create and I would be the Interpretation and Environmental Education person for the department once I finished my PhD. Now, who knows what will happen. And I know Hank, Linda and Warren will really go after Ron and Alice. They don't think she belongs in the department, even as associate faculty."

"Sounds like you agree with them. And it also sounds like you are afraid that if Ron tumbles, so do you. He's been your friend and supporter since we got here. What's really going on? The fact he didn't confide in you sooner? Or ask your thoughts on this whole thing?"

"He could have if we are such good friends. But, instead, he denied everything. And I don't agree with those three, even though I see Alice as weak in many areas. She's good in teaching ideas and concepts. She's good in the classroom with academic instruction. And that matches some students preferred learning styles, so they love her. Others like more hands on and they resonate to me. But to make her director in name and lead on the interpretation classes, assuming I would still do all the heavy lifting, is bullshit!"

"Whoa. I'm just asking questions. Don't get furious with me or we can stop talking now! You asked me the questions and asked me to listen to what's happening. I'm your biggest supporter. You know that. I've watched you do impossible things many times. But I also know your lack of patience and temper. And right now my temper is matching yours. So let's chill."

"Okay, sorry. Yes, I'm asking for your thoughts, but I really just want you to affirm my own. Let's try again. Okay? I need some calming down here."

"Okay, fine. Now, do you really know you want to stay with CSU forever? I know you like the limelight and recognition. And you love to teach and lead projects. But what if we want to do something later? Maybe everything will work for the best. Alice will succeed or fail over time and you will take over, or not, based on what you and we want then."

"Okay, I'll try to hold that thought. Thanks. Let's go for a walk. Okay?"

"Great. Let's hike up Horsetooth. Shouldn't be anyone there today."

The next day I went in and talked to Ron. I apologized for my outburst and he apologized for not having said something sooner. Then I left and went to my teaching preparation.

Not long after this, Ron announced his engagement and Hank, Linda and Warren attacked with guns blazing. They each scheduled meetings with the Dean and voiced their concerns and issues. I heard some of this, but managed to stay out of the main fray. Yet I knew, as Bonnie so aptly put it, that my fortunes were tied to Ron's in our department. Hank, Linda and Warren had their own graduate students they would rather fund doing their research than see me funded for the teaching and community and hands-on work I did. The fight began in earnest when Ron announced Alice's expanded teaching role and role at the ELC. Being a University—an institution more political than politics—nothing happened quickly. Fear of repercussions causes everyone to move slowly in this environment. As it did with the sweat lodge issue at the Center. Yet I was more and more frustrated and angry with what was evolving.

I began concentrating on my studies and teaching and doing less at the Center. When I had spare time, I would hole up in my office in the department. I would spend hours on the computer, enjoying fun sites and searching for jobs, which might be of interest. Some months later a memo came from the Dean's office announcing Alice as the College lead on the ELC, with Ron becoming an advisory person. I again went into a rage and went to see the Dean. I remember exploding about the work I had done, the recognition the College had received and the funding I had brought in. I also ranted about all the partners I had attracted and all the projects I engaged in for the University. This was not rational or well thought out, yet I felt I was being driven to 'protect my turf'.

Ron and Alice got married at a center up in the mountains. Bonnie and I were invited and I tried to enjoy myself, but I really just stewed over his stupidity and the wrongs being done me. Not long afterwards, Ron stepped down as department chair and a search for a replacement was begun. Seeing this as a real problem for my role in the department

I began checking for positions more regularly. I applied for several positions in Colorado and elsewhere, but none seemed quite right. While the College sought a new department chair, Warren served as interim chair. More handwriting on the wall for me, I thought.

About this time I realized I did not want to be primarily a researcher. I wanted to do research and study, but then apply what I had discovered. This was an early understanding that I wished to work on the causes of things I felt were not being done in a good way, rather than just document their existence or work solely on the symptoms. It's when I told my committee I would not be finishing my dissertation and completing my PhD work. I am not sure if this was a viable decision, given I was so close and so much of the work complete, but it allowed me the freedom to pursue over non-profit work without the burden of work still on me.

In preparing for leaving CSU, I visited several environmental non-profits, three of which wanted me to come aboard as executive director, Bonnie and I decided we needed to be back east for a while, closer to our mothers and family. A position opened near Lookout Mountain, Georgia and we decided to give it a go. More 'reasons' to leave the west and my spiritual training and work—we needed to be near our families; we were tired of the isolation of Fort Collins; the winters were getting hard; my position with the University would change—and on. All of these may have played a small role in the decision to go elsewhere, but the last lodge with Two Bears, although temporarily forgotten, was the driving force. And that, in retrospect, is perfectly okay. I had more to learn on other levels and some teaching to do not related to my spiritual path. And, although I would have given anything to avoid it, I had my 'losing' to walk through and my near-death road to travel. Why, I am still unsure, but I see it was so. And, maybe most importantly, I had the remainder of my time with Bonnie to experience and all the learning and understanding that came to both of us when her time to transition out of this reality came. Nor how much pain and suffering her passing would cause me, with the doubt and guilt that comes with that.

Two months before we left Colorado State vandals went to the Center one night and burned the lodges and destroyed the site. This broke my heart then—now I see the work of that place was done for the time being. Six months after I left, vandals again attacked the Center and burned down the old farmstead we had been working to preserve. I had my suspicions about both incidents, especially since no one would want the responsibility for these aspects of the Center if I were not there to facilitate them and take the heat if needed. I again laid the blame on those I thought responsible, triggering more anger and disgust in myself. Leaving the issues lie, as no one really knew who had committed these offenses, would have been easier and more in tune with the universe.

A year after I left Fort Collins, I heard that Ron was in another department at CSU, Warren was named Chair after two others declined the job and Alice was no longer at CSU, but doing consulting work on her own. Another case where patience and silence could possibly altered things in my favor had I practiced them. Then again, who is to say—it may well have been my time to move on and, since I was not heeding Spirit's guidance in this directive, the 'motivations' to do so kept getting stronger. I've long ago stopped trying to analyze and understand these things, but have gone to listening to my inner voice and heeding what I hear, accepting wherever it takes me.

I had no idea where the road would take us when we left Fort Collins. No crystal ball to show me the new times we would start criss-crossing Turtle Island, living and serving in different capacities in different parts of the States. Looking back I see the beautiful natural places I have been allowed to live as I learned and did my work. This continues to this day and, I am certain, will continue until my work is done here.

35 | Remembrance and Vision

S<small>TARTING WITH THE</small> 'NOTE TO READERS' <small>BELOW IS THE WRITING I DID</small> in 2010, which began to bring some of my vision back into my awareness. It also brought a better understanding of some of the joys and pains I had walked through. The biggest plus to me in receiving this remembrance was simply the ability to write it down. I have known I needed to write and share some of my path and my vision for ten years, but have not been able to. I may have told you this. I was able to read and write less and less during that time and, for the three years prior to this remembrance I could hardly do either at all. Each time I tried to write I was in immediate physical pain, went in to fight or flight mode and felt my brain feel as if it would melt down. So I would stop and go lie in bed, writhing in pain, until it passed. Hard for me to imagine now, but it is so. Even today, as I write, I have some pain and emotional distress to deal with afterwards. I am still energetically and physically clearing what I have gone through over the past seven years and refilling my psyche with the energy I now need. As so many are at this time. Seven years—hard to believe. But seven years of pain and loss—officially occurring in seventeen days from now. How many times have I heard of healers and spiritual people who have suffered for seven years? Many, from many places. And after a year of my pain I remember thinking—'boy, another year of this and I would be ready to check out. How could anyone stand this level of pain for a long period of time?' Well, I didn't check out and I endured the most intense pain—hovering near death—for three of the seven years. I believe I will document this seven years and all that happened to me and around me at some other time. It may well assist others who are still to walk their dark time of the soul to the edge of death, as hearing and reading about others who went through these things helped me. Somewhat, at least. No one could ever fully understand the pain of this walk without going through it, but at least the fact others have trod that ground helps with acceptance.

I am changing nothing that I wrote a year ago, so the context or wording may seem odd, but I think it important to leave it as written. This especially since it was the first writing of any depth for so long. As always, accept it for what it is. For me, I began to see where all the anger—and fear I did not recognize at the time—was coming from the last two years at Colorado State. I was seeking reasons I could accept for leaving Colorado and my educational, cultural and spiritual work there. So, by burying and forgetting this remembrance, I was able to believe I left because of the attacks on the lodge and those involved with it and Ron's backstabbing and the change in our department. You will see, as I did, after reading this part, the real reason for my leaving. We will pick up this thread after you read about my last lodge alone with Two Bears.

NOTE TO READERS

I am capturing the remembering and the vision that came to me on the night of July 8, 2010. It came as I slept on the first night of the Star Nations Conference in Farmington, New Mexico. And again, at three the following morning as I awoke and the same rememberings and vision came in conscious time. I am re-visiting and adding to this on top of a mountain just north of Santa Fe, New Mexico, on July 13, while at my friend Jacks' home. I am visiting Jack with my partner Sue and my four-legged brother, Onyx. I wanted to run from this again this morning – seeking something to 'do' today. So that action and motion would stop me writing this. Sue said no, let's relax and just 'be' today. I got the message at the conference and so I wrote and write more five days later. I won't share this—I don't want adulation, attacks, ridicule or followers. Yet I know it's not up to me. I will have Sue read it and hear her words, then ask Spirit what I am to do. For now it is written and that is enough.

MITAKUYE OYASIN – All My Relations
Jim Graywolf Petruzzi

◇ ◇ ◇

I awoke, as usual, at 3 on the morning of July 9. But this time from a deep sleep whose dream is still before me. Vision is a word grossly over-used these days, but this was both a remembering and a vision. They are the only words that define it to me, so I use them. It came directly from Spirit. Great Spirit, God, Allah…whatever name you give the universal being. I lay there awake and could replay the dreamtime pictures and words perfectly – as many times as needed. As I can now. And I do as I write this five days later. This is new for me—this level of clarity I achieved during this vision. Or am I simply remembering how to achieve clarity as I have in past visions or portions of this vision?

This writing may jump around. Later I will put some 'time' order to it – if needed. No apologies for form or structure. It is what comes through me that I now write.

As has happened to me often when I journey, this vision began with pictures and colors and me. Me as an infant in the crib: banging my head on the headboard by rocking on my hands and knees. I am remembering the rocking and banging that went on for hours at a time. Then the image of a doctor speaking to my mother, "It's okay. He will outgrow it." This image I had seen for many years and confirmed the content with my mother, Rita. But I never understood why I did it – why the head banging. Now I could go back into the young me and ask why. "Fear of the road ahead. Remembering some of what I had committed to and was to do in this life. Fear of the pain to come." I knew as an infant – or remembered – what I was and what I was to be and do. Then, after months of head banging, Jim the infant pushed down what he knew, denied it...and the head banging stopped. Pushing it down where it stayed until now. Always knowing I was different and taking great pains to hide it from everyone as I have shared in other writings and story telling circles. Especially hiding from myself.

Then I was older in my dream, now a boy hiding his intelligence and his gifts and tools. Hiding the fact I sometimes knew what others would say before they said it and do before they did it. Having them constantly ask, "What did you say?" when I had said nothing. Denying it. Fearing it. Certainly not understanding it nor wanting to bring it to the surface so I could look at it.

Then the awareness came to me of the fifty-four years I had spent of not allowing it to come – of forcing it down as deeply as I could. Pushing down any knowledge of what I could do or could learn to do. In fact, the knowledge of what I had agreed to do before coming here for this walk on the Earth Mother. I watched 'flash' scenes of myself not facing these things by running and 'doing' to block it. Scenes of doing what I could so I could not hear my inner voice or the directions of Spirit. Even as projects that should have been impossible manifested around me I continued to avoid asking myself how that could be time after time. I watched myself become aware of projects and things that happened or appeared that I saw well in advance and then watched myself deny I had actually seen anything. And on and on.....

Then the Lodge with Two Bears I had totally forgotten for thirteen years. A Sweat Lodge I did with Two Bears in 1997. Now, in the vision, I am 47 and readying for the Lodge – heating the rocks; bringing water; saying my gratitude prayers and going into my heart. Now I can watch, remember and hear that inipi just the two of us shared.

Two Bears was a Lakota teacher of mine, whom I worked closely with while I lived in Colorado. I next see Two Bears in Fort Collins, Colorado, working with me on creating an educational program. Suddenly he stops dead in what he is saying and just looks at me—with no words. I wait and ask if he is okay and still I only get a silent stare back at me. This has happened a couple of times when we were doing powerful lodges, but it is far from his usual demeanor. I can see and sense his confusion and then an 'awareness' of something. A smile then crosses his face, followed by a frown and then his asking me to come into Lodge with him four nights forward. "I have more things I must share now", he simply tells me. I am remembering earlier lodges when Two Bears saw some of the walk before me and shared some of what he saw causing me confusion and fear. I did not remember these times too completely, but did remember their existence and how I had felt then.

For months before Two Bears invited me to this Lodge several of my teachers had been telling me that we were brothers now. Not just teachers, with me as their student any longer. They told me that what I was and what I carried was beyond their ability to help me as a teacher in the traditional way. We would learn from each other as knowledge needed to be shared and that would be how it must be. They also said my power was broad and strong and unique in many ways, if I was willing to accept and use it. Each of these teachers, four in all, said similar things or parts of this same thought. [I can hardly write this. Seems like pure ego to me. It is not. It is as I heard it – and am seeing and hearing it again now. I've let denial block it for too long. No more time for that now. Or for worry about what others might think.] The truth was I liked them all being 'teachers', as it took responsibility and accountability off of me. If I was a student I could be expected to make mistakes or miss things. Yet we all make mistakes – they are powerful learning tools. I didn't need the tag of 'student' to be able to err – the tag of human was enough. I wish I had realized that back then.

The next images I saw were around the night of the inipi and Two Bears and I sitting at the fire heating the rocks. We did not speak too much, mostly silently sitting watching the rocks heat for a couple of hours after I arrived.

Finally Two Bears said, "The rocks are ready. I hope we are. Please pour the first three doors and allow me the last. I will share in the fourth door what has come to me this past week, as we did years back in an early lodge together and as we did in Pine Ridge as well. Know I will share because Spirit wants it so and because I love you as student, brother, teacher and friend. Four directions of love. And I respect what you are and what you will do. I will be there when I am needed, if I am needed down the way. Let's go in."

I am confused and unsure. Not afraid, but overwhelmed by his words. He has seldom spoken this way. From Sanchez or Walking Stick – other teachers of mine – I might expect words like this. But not from Two Bears. I watch as we go in the lodge after I bring in the first seven rocks.

As always, we pray, chant and sing together. I call in the directions, the ancestors and Spirit and I give thanks and ask for guidance. Two Bears gives thanks and commits this Lodge to the healing of all people – two-legged, four-legged, winged, finned, creepy crawlers and others. And he asks that we may both better understand our roles in the changing times ahead. Then we sing another Lakota gratitude song and I open the door. Two Bears wishes to carry the rocks for the second door and he goes out and brings in seven more grandfathers. We complete the second door and then the third, with me pouring a lot of water.

Two Bears takes over the fourth door and also pours heavy as he adds many sacred herbs to the rocks, especially a lot of white sage. He again asks for the healing of all creatures and the Earth Mother we all exist on or around. Then he speaks of her strong connection to me and my many levels of connection to her. With this he asks her to give me the power and strength 'to be' as I move forward.

I am feeling more confused and a little fearful, with some anger beginning to build. I am unclear what I am angry about, and this fuels my emotions even further. I think, "What is this? Why all the 'talk around'?" I am not a patient person at this time, with most of my teachers working with me on this lacking trait. We sit silently for a long time and then he brings in his Chanupa and we open it. He opens and smokes and we pass it to and fro. He asks for guidance and I hear him chocking up. I feel that fear of the unknown again building in me. That fear I had in the earlier vision lodge, when I did my first vision quest on the mountain and when I went into the jungle alone. I wish I could leave, like in my first lodge with Yellowhair, but know I cannot.

Again, I can hardly write this. I am there and here. Seeing every motion, hearing every word and sound, tasting the pipe, smelling the sage. I have strong stabbing pain through my right shoulder as I write. I could write much more – every nuance. Yet this is enough. And it is time.

Two Bears asks me to leave my head and go totally into my heart once again. He knows I still tend to go too much into my head and so feed fear and doubt. He wants me to truly hear him as he will not speak, but will be the hollow bone through which Spirit shares tonight. This is as he has taught me for so long, yet it puts me off tonight, even as I suddenly know he speaks for my spirit teacher and guide, Black Elk, as well.

He adds even more sage to the rocks. "Jim – Redwolf. You have many teachers in the Old Ways and the Spirit Ways. Even though I told you this early on it has always fascinated me. It is as if you are being taught the spirit ways of many people at once. Why? I had a clear vision the other day as we sat and I have done three pipes since then around it. Your teachers have told you of your power and gifts. You push us, and these words, away. You joke, fearing ego if you listen. Or you just fear. It does not matter why..."

I interrupt, "Two Bears, I still say I am a middle aged white guy on the road only ten years or so. You all have walked this road your entire lives. I support and learn, but....."

Two Bears, "NO! Not this time! I ask you to listen, not speak. All know you speak well. But not now. Hear with your heart and spirit. Then do as you wish."

Embarrassed, I respond, "Sorry, uncle."

Two Bears, "No to you again. Not uncle now – brother now. As we have told you. I have seen much and cry for what you will have to go through if you accept your gifts and role. And I laugh and rejoice for you – and others – if you can walk through the storm ahead. The storm to come—in you and around you. And the storm around all of us when we each play our role as the time of the Earth shift approaches. We have each been chosen for our role and accepted before we came here this time. You have walked many, many times to be in this place and role now, as many of us have. You know this – have heard me many times – but now you really need to know this."

He pauses and pours more water. Adding more sage he asks Spirit to send through clearly what he wishes he, Two Bears – to speak.

"Jim, remember Mitakuye Oyasin – all my relations. It is not just here on Mother. It is all the universe. We are but a tiny blot. This I remind you of as I share that the universe is truly one. We are here now because the next Earth approaches – the fifth as in so many prophecies. The Earth of more love, harmony and balance. But first we face the changes, which will be painful, intense and tearing. This will happen in many places across creation as I see now, but especially strong here on the Earth Mother." And he pauses and sighs deeply, with some tears rolling down his face, as I am sure as they are also rolling down my cheeks.

Two Bears, "You know the Star Nations are working with us, even though I know you have doubts of this. You will know more about the star people when you need to. Star Children will appear in larger numbers as we move ahead. Some will be silent until it is their time. Many will call this autism or mental disorder. They will be wrong. Words like Crystal and Indigo will be applied even more than now. These words are all two-leggeds trying to understand and make sense. The new ones will simply understand and wait."

He stopped and we breathed in the healing sage smoke. Then he began again, "You have made many walks, Jim, in many forms and colors. You are connected to Mother like few others. You are sensitive at levels I can only guess at and assume. You see things before they can be seen. Feel things as they occur anywhere. And manifest with your words and actions backed by your spirit. I have felt you ask me to come or call in my head and heart many times. And seen these things in you many times. As have others. It is why so many have taught you and why others have feared and attacked you. You joke these things away – yet inside you know it is so. Some of this I have said to you before, but you need to hear it until you see it is so or at least consider it as so."

I wanted to stop him in any way, gag him if I have to. Then we could go hike together, or teach a group or drink coffee or…anything to stop his words and allow us to function as we had for this past decade.

Yet he continues, "A small number were asked to accept a role as trail blazers on whom the changes about to occur in the near future would be put on first. Those asked have had many walks and needed much courage. You are one of these people and the road will get harder and much more painful for your group soon. Most will cross over to the spirit realm but a small number will walk through this storm of pain and change and be there to guide and teach the larger numbers when the shift to the fifth Earth occurs. Those who stay will work directly with Mother as She shifts. If you decide to stay you will be one of these – possibly one of the first. I believe you will choose to stay. If you survive [he begins to choke up again as he speaks and I want to run from the lodge – fear has my whole being] you will lose all you think is yours. What you think is yours is an illusion, as it is for everyone. We own nothing, not even this skin we wear while we work here on the Mother. Yet the pain of these loses for you will be enormous. Still, I see you surviving this storm and that is why so many teachers for you and so many lessons. Lessons coming as quickly as you can absorb them, as I know this type of teaching time is not wasted on those who will not use the words. You will be allowed by Spirit to decide whether you will stay and work or leave at some point. If you stay, you will walk to deaths' edge, where you will grow through your agony. From that place you will find those you need to walk with from there and you will later find the others like you when it is time. There is more, but not now. I can love and support you, but not take away any of your coming pain. That is for you and I accept whatever is and whatever you do from here. I offer this for you also."

I sit, scared to death. And let the anger well up. What gibberish. What crap to put on me. I thought he was a teacher and a brother. He says he loves me as a brother then tells me I am about to enter the storm—a storm that sounds like hell to me where I will lose everything. My fear keeps fueling my anger this way, so each builds by the moment. And I am out of heart and totally into head. Thinking how "woo-woo" this nonsense is. Give me a break! My most balanced teacher sounding like a New Ager. Damn him.

After a few minutes I blow up. I call Two Bears—my brother—a lunatic. A liar. A fool. A bastard. I rant and rave – making little sense even to me. But fear and anger rule my actions and words. I curse the first day I stepped on the Red Road and all those I have met and walked with and learned from. As I erupt, Two Bears remains silent. This makes me even angrier so I ask for the door to be opened. As he opens it, I leave the Lodge as quickly as I can – proper form be damned. I'm in a pure fury now, which is actually total fear. We were to share food after the Lodge as always, but I gather my sacred things and leave, without another word to Two Bears.

I went back to my work at the Environmental Center, my teaching, my degree and my projects. I put everything said behind me and slowly, methodically, buried it deep in my subconscious. A few months later the attacks began. The attacks were on our Lodges; on some of us; on Lawrence; on Ron as department chair and other parts of my life at CSU. These attacks came at many levels, but were brutal and painful. A couple of years later, after having gone through many battles, I left Colorado State, put my sacred things away and walked away from the Red Road. I thought it was because I was sickened by the constant attacks and changes around me, so I would take my skills to non-profits elsewhere, escaping the politics of the University system. Later

I thought it was because my teachers were speaking of my power, which I did not want to face, as I was afraid. But Two Bears' words, more than anything, were what really made me run, even though I had no conscious memory of these words. I ran across country as far as I could going into other non-profit work and never remembered anything of this Lodge and his words until now—totally blanked out and gone until last week. All the things that Two Bears foresaw occurred to me, as those who know me personally know. Everything I 'owned' was gone from me – people, things, health, money and energy. I will speak more of this another time—as it will help others to hear this story then—but not yet. And, as Two Bears also predicted, I was given three chances by Spirit to stay or leave this life. I stayed after much tortured thought on the matter.

The first night of the Star Nations Conference at three AM Great Spirit spoke to me. "Remember this. Accept this. Be this." Then it all came as I have recorded here, with some more of the vision of the road ahead. With my new partner, Sue, who is part of me and me of her, my four-legged brother, Onyx, who connects me to the animal people and myself, and other humans I have yet to meet.

◇ ◇ ◇

Three months after I remembered this lodge and Two Bears' words I called a few friends and got Two Bears' current phone number and address. I gave him a call four days later, once I got up my nerve to again face this friend who had taught me so much and whom I had attacked for only speaking what he saw. Someone I now needed to call who I cherished as a friend and elder, yet one whom I had not spoken to for years.

I called and hoped I would get a message machine, but instead I heard "Hello" in Two Bears' voice. "Hello, Two Bears. It is Jim from Colorado State days," I pushed out.

"Ah, Redwolf. It is good to hear you. So, do you remember now?"

I might have been surprised that he knew I had forgotten everything of that lodge we had done together, but I was not. Actually, for him to never have asked or brought it up again, he had to know I either had no memory or would not speak of it.

"Yes, I remember a lot of the inipi when you told me what you saw ahead. The last inipi you and I did together, without others present. And I remember the way I attacked you and accused you of so many things. I want to say I am sorry, but don't know how to begin."

"No need," Two Bears interrupted my words. "You were afraid and so attacked the one saying those things that gave you fear. Killing the messenger, eh? I knew you would return some day. How is your walk?"

"I am taking it and know I must stay on it for some time yet. I have agreed to this, even though I did not know why I did when I had the choice. All you spoke of has come to me and the pain was even more than my fear guessed at. Yet now many things have changed and, when I remembered your words, I knew we had to speak. Thank you for everything and I hope you will forgive me and chose to walk part of the road together again."

"Of course we will walk together more, as we were meant to. You have more work to do before you can come to the mountains here and rest a while, but we will be in touch. Where are you?"

"I am in Sedona, down in Arizona here. Still working on my healing and working with my new half side, Sue. Bonnie passed over three years ago now and that was the hardest of the things I lost."

"I am sorry to hear this, yet it must have been her time. I remember the story you both told about asking for twenty years to walk together when she learned of her cancer, so I am not surprised now to hear that that time was honored and then called in."

"Yes. There is a lot to speak about this and many other things, but I sense you are correct and the time for this is later. For now I have changed my name from Red Wolf to Gray Wolf. Are you comfortable with this?"

"So. Gray Wolf is not as threatened as Redwolf and is bigger and stronger. It is fitting that your name shifted that way," Two Bears agreed.

36 | On the Road Again

For me, as I write, things once again are beginning to shift. For the past two years I have dwelled in Sedona, Arizona, working on my own healing as I guide others who seek me on their healing path. And I have done a great deal of non-profit work, as you heard earlier. I now see it is time to take the vision I have received out into the land and let the Sanctuaries of the Earth Mother manifest around me and those who will connect with me as I roam. Sue and Onyx will be part of this journey with me, each fulfilling their roles, as I will mine. Sue and I acquired an RV a few weeks ago and we will head off, with Onyx, in four weeks. The plan is vague, yet it is what Great Spirit wants of us at this time. I feel we will be back in Sedona before the end of the year, but we shall see. Friends are already involved. Stephen here in Sedona will anchor the land trust while we are gone and begin nurturing the lands we are working to preserve as one of the Sanctuaries. My good friends, Jack and Jim, are committed to serving this vision and other good works as we three are creating Grandfathers for the 7 Generations— a business to generate funds to support the Sanctuaries vision and other, similar non-profits. Sue, Onyx and I will travel Turtle Island as we are guided immersing ourselves in nature, providing healings with the community drum we are caretakers of, preparing plant and flower essences to make the shift easier for others, providing teachings and stories and, most importantly, allowing the Sanctuary vision to manifest just by our 'being' where we are directed to be. Sound vague? It is. Does it sound like a lot of trust based on little data? It is. Yet how can I have walked the last twenty-five years learning that surrender and trust are of paramount importance at this time—that nothing else can truly occur before these skills are mastered—and not surrender to that trust in Spirit now? And so, I work on complete surrender and trust each day. Sue and I will be following the road in trust together, doing the work asked of us. Join us out here—it will be fun!

I thought writing this book something Spirit wished me to do. And I thought other books would follow, as I felt the energy of their coming birth as I wrote this book. I am certain I am correct on both counts, but failed to see what else would be created around me as I wrote. This is another great reminder that it's all about the journey, not the destination.

As Jack finished reading an early draft of the book we began talking about the visions I had shared and the work needing to be done in order to provide a better legacy for our children and their children than the one we have crafted to date. Into these talks came Jim, our friend from Connecticut. And so we three grandfathers, sitting around Jack's table in his home atop a mountain just north of Santa Fe, New Mexico, created Grandfathers for the 7 Generations (GF7G). This was with Jack's expertise and vision guiding us. GF7G is a for-profit business designed to create cash flow, which can, in part, be gifted to non-profits that exist to work with and for future generations. We three grandfathers expect more grandfathers to show at our doorsteps and be welcomed into the work. It is, after all, time for more grandfathers to step up as peaceful warriors and assist the groups of grandmothers who have been working towards a better future for some time.

As we talked more and Jack and Jim quizzed me further on the meaning of my visions, I expanded on what I knew. I knew I was to work with circles of people to find and provide safe havens on the land where teaching and ceremony around nature and old, more sustainable ways of living could be taught to the young. I had seen the seven 'sanctuaries' on Turtle Island (the U.S.) to begin this process. Sue and I had spoken of this often and wondered how we were to proceed with this mission. At Jack's table, as we played more with names, the Sanctuaries of the Earth Mother (SOTEM) name evolved. This organization would be formed as a non-profit to help enact the mission of my vision. And so it began.

About three months after we three 'gray hairs' met, I finished the book and we all made plans to create SOTEM. Then Sue and I were clearly shown we needed to leave Sedona for a time and begin travelling the country on the work of the Sanctuaries. Nothing came to us that was clearer than that—but that came very clearly. So we bought an old RV, gave up our lease, and hit the road. We planned on stopping in Santa Fe, with Jack, for a week to sign papers and finish creating GF7G and SOTEM. As I write this, five weeks later, we are still there. Working on a property for a Sanctuary, near Santa Fe, and two others for a Sanctuary near Sedona. We now expect to continue on the road, welcoming other potential SOTEM sites and groups, as we roll across the country. Meanwhile, GF7G has become a publisher, with this book its first work. Ah, how the circles turn and mesh.

More will be shared about the Grandfathers and the Sanctuaries as the stories are written by Spirit and we all follow the script. As I have invited all to join me in the journey of this book, so too I invite any who wish to join in the work of the Grandfathers and the Sanctuaries. Websites are being created and virtual coverage of the journey Sue and I are about to undertake will be sent to all in the Universe—through email, Facebook, Youtube and websites. We will be looking for your feedback and suggestions as we begin this trek and provide communication. After all, we do not know how this is all to evolve and so we seek the input of ever expanding circles.

Find more as our website grows—www.SOTEM.org. Or check out our group on Facebook at Sanctuaries of the Earth Mother. I can also be emailed at jim.petruzzi@grandfathersforsevengenerations. com. I will listen and I will respond.

Be well friends.

Special Thanks

I HAVE MENTIONED MY GOOD FRIEND BEARCLOUD AND THE SPECIAL gift of the artwork for the book cover, but I feel I need to add a little more to the story of our connection. Bearcloud, his artwork and his vision are a primary reason I moved to Sedona, which set in motion many other connections. His vision of preserving the glyphs, the crop circles, of the Star Nations in living form in gardens captivated me. These gardens are to be housed in a huge pyramid, in the tradition of the Egyptian pyramids. The work he has done around uncovering the secrets of these huge structures further enthralled me. This vision is being pursued by his non-profit, the Chameleon Project. And his work with both the pyramids and the gardens is beautifully presented in his book, 7 Fires. I have worked on this project with him and been honored to be asked to be on his board of directors, so I see the connections of his vision and the Sanctuaries coming towards us. I suggest anyone wishing to learn more to order his book at http://7fires.net or visit his on line gallery at www.bearcloudgallery. com. Thank you, relative, for your gift to this book and your work for the Seven Generations.

Afterword

I HAD NO INTENTIONS OR GOALS WHEN I BEGAN WRITING THIS BOOK — starting this journey with each of you. It seems to have evolved into a trip that is part bio, part presentation of indigenous ways, part teaching, part spiritual, part nature writing and, I hope, part fun and humor. An interesting mix — or a confusing one? I don't know, that is not my job. But I see the parts are the parts of the life I have walked — sometimes running and skipping, sometimes struggling through quicksand. As have many before me and will many more after me. I don't even know what a publisher will think of this tome — find it fascinating and want to be involved, or full of too many elements and send it back with a form letter. Again, this is not my job. My job was to listen to the God within and the one above and capture what I was to capture here. If I have done that, I have honored this part of my contract with the universe and all my fellow creatures.

Our journey, for now, ends here. You have seen my travels, felt my joys and pain, seen me make mistakes, have successes and, most importantly, hopefully learned some things along the way. There is much more to share, much more road to walk together, for and with any of you who have enjoyed this first walk and gotten something you can take away and use. For this group, I invite you into the circle this first book has begun creating — in whatever ways that evolves. It is you I will be honored to be in circle with and create new ways together. For those who did not find this journey enlightening, useful or, at least, interesting – I send you love and blessings. I wish you well in whatever way you walk forward from here. I hope, from my spirit's core, that you find or create other ways that we humans, together, can recreate a better way to walk the Earth Mother and move into a positive connection with all that exists.

With that I say to each one of you – all my relations – be well.

"Even the seasons form a great circle in their changing, and always come back again to where they were. The life of a man is a circle from childhood to childhood and so it is everything where power moves."

—Black Elk (Hehaka sapa), OGLALA SIOUX